Wireless Networks

Series Editor
Xuemin Sherman Shen, University of Waterloo, Waterloo, Canada

The purpose of Springer's Wireless Networks book series is to establish the state of the art and set the course for future research and development in wireless communication networks. The scope of this series includes not only all aspects of wireless networks (including cellular networks, WiFi, sensor networks, and vehicular networks), but related areas such as cloud computing and big data. The series serves as a central source of references for wireless networks research and development. It aims to publish thorough and cohesive overviews on specific topics in wireless networks, as well as works that are larger in scope than survey articles and that contain more detailed background information. The series also provides coverage of advanced and timely topics worthy of monographs, contributed volumes, textbooks and handbooks.

Wanming Hao • Fuhui Zhou • Zihan Gao • Nana Li

Intelligent Mobile Edge Computing and Sensing

Springer

Wanming Hao
School of Electrical and Information Engineering
Zhengzhou University
Zhengzhou, Henan, China

Fuhui Zhou
College of Electronic and Information Engineering
Nanjing University of Astro. and Aero.
Nanjing, Jiangsu, China

Zihan Gao
School of Computer and Information Engineering
Henan University of Economics and Law
Zhengzhou, Henan, China

Nana Li
School of Electrical and Information Engineering
Zhengzhou University
Zhengzhou, Henan, China

ISSN 2366-1186 ISSN 2366-1445 (electronic)
Wireless Networks
ISBN 978-981-96-9399-3 ISBN 978-981-96-9400-6 (eBook)
https://doi.org/10.1007/978-981-96-9400-6

This Springer imprint is published by the registered company Springer Nature Singapore Pte Ltd.
The registered company address is: 152 Beach Road, #21-01/04 Gateway East, Singapore 189721, Singapore

Foreword

The field of edge computing is advancing quickly, with new algorithms, architectures, and use cases emerging regularly. Intelligent mobile edge computing (MEC) includes various domains—such as IoT, AI, and telecommunications—making it essential to provide a holistic view that bridges these areas for researchers and practitioners. There is a growing need for practical insights and case studies that illustrate how edge computing can be effectively implemented in industries like healthcare, smart cities, and manufacturing. This book explores the potential of MEC in wireless intelligent and sensing environments. This comprehensive guide delves into cutting-edge technologies that enable computing resource optimization and decision-making at the edge or cloud, reducing latency and bandwidth consumption. It provides a comprehensive and accessible resource that addresses the rapid MEC-related technologies. As the demand for real-time data processing and low-latency applications grows for future 6G wireless communications, this book can help readers to understand the implications, challenges, and opportunities presented by these innovations.

The contents of this book are organized as follows. Chapter 1 briefly introduces the intelligent MEC and sensing as well as the overall structure. Chapter 2 gives the fundamentals of intelligent MEC and sensing, including the MEC, integrated MEC and sensing, and reconfigurable intelligent surface (RIS) techniques. Chapters 3, 4, and 5 focus on how to optimize resources under different systems, namely, RIS-aided MEC, cooperative cloud and MEC, and integrated communication, computing and sensing, respectively. Specifically, Chap. 3 presents a general framework for RIS-aided MEC systems, where the practical phase shift and reflection models are considered. Chapter 4 studies the multilevel resource design for the cooperative cloud and MEC systems. Chapter 5 presents the integrated communication, computing and sensing techniques, including perfect and imperfect channel state information. Finally, in Chap. 5, we conclude this book and give some related merging topics.

Zhengzhou, China Wanming Hao
Nanjing, China Fuhui Zhou
Zhengzhou, China Zihan Gao
Zhengzhou, China Nana Li
May 2025

Declarations

Competing Interests

Please declare any competing interests in the context of your chapter. The following sentences can be regarded as examples.

This study was funded by [X] [grant number X].

[Author A] has a received research grant from [Company W].

[Author B] has received a speaker honorarium from [Company X] and owns stock in [Company Y].

[Author C] is a member of [committee Z].

The authors have no conflicts of interest to declare that are relevant to the content of this chapter.

Ethics Approval

If your chapter includes primary studies with humans please declare the adherence of ethical standards. Example text: This study was performed in line with the principles of the Declaration of Helsinki. Approval was granted by the Ethics Committee of University B (Date . . . /No. . . .).

In addition, for human participants, authors are required to include a statement that informed consent (to participate and/or to publish) was obtained from individual participants or parents/guardians if the participant is minor or incapable.

If animals are studied, authors should make sure that the legal requirements or guidelines in the country and/or state or province for the care and use of animals have been followed or specify that no ethics approval was required.

Contents

Acronyms

2D	two-dimensional
ADMM	alternating direction method of multipliers
AETC	application energy-time cost
AL	augmented Lagrangian
AO	alternative optimization
AOA	angle of arrival
AOD	angle of departure
AR	augmented reality
AWGN	additive white Gaussian noise
BCA	block coordinate ascent
BCD	block coordinate descent
BPS	basic phase shift
BSs	base stations
CC	cloud computing
CCC	collaborative cloud computing
CCI	co-channel interference
CD	coordinate descent
CM-UEs	communication users
CP-UEs	computing users
CPU	central processing unit
CSI	channel state information
DAG	directed acyclic graph
DVFS	dynamic voltage and frequency scaling
EH	energy harvesting
EM	electromagnetic
EVD	eigenvalue decomposition
FD	full duplex
FET	field-effect transistors
FNO	fixed number offloading
FPGA	field programmable gate array
GS-MEMA	Gale-Shapley based mobile-edge matching algorithm

GS-MOA	Gale-Shapley based minimum offloading algorithm
GS-SOA	Gale-Shapley based sequential offloading algorithm
GTS	genetic-based task scheduling
HAPs	hybrid access points
HD	half duplex
HIF	heuristic information function
ICCS	integrated communication, computing and sensing
ICI	inter-cell interference
IIoT	industrial IoT
IoT	Internet of Things
ISAC	integrated sensing and communication
JSSP	job shop scheduling problem
KKT	Karush-Kuhn Tucker
LDR	Lagrangian dual reformulation
LOS	line-of-sight
MCQT	multidimensional complex quadratic transform
MDP	Markov decision process
MEC	mobile edge computing
MEMS	micro-electro-mechanical systems
MIMO	multiple-input multiple-output
MINLP	mixed-integer nonlinear programming
MLSO	maximum local searching offloading
MM	majorization-minimization
MMSE	minimum mean square error
MRC	maximum ratio combining
MSE	mean square error
MUD	multi-user detection
MU-OFDM	multi-user orthogonal frequency division multiplexing
NLoS	non-line-of-sight
OEO	optimal enumerate offloading
PIN	positive intrinsic negative
POX	precedence operation crossover
QLOF	Q-Learning based offloading
QoE	quality of experience
QoS	quality of service
REs	reflecting elements
RF	radio frequency
RIS	reconfigurable intelligent surface
RX	receive antennas
SCA	successive convex approximation
SDP	semidefinite programming
SDR	semidefinite relaxation
SEs	sensing elements
SETC	system energy-time cost
SI	self-interference

SIC	successive interference cancellation
SINR	signal-to-interference plus noise-ratio
SOCP	second-order cone programming
SSO	sequential searching offloading
STLF	state loss function
SVD	singular value decomposition
SWIPT	simultaneous wireless information and power transfer
SYLF	system loss function
TETC	task energy-time cost
TX	transmit antennas
ULA	uniform linear array
VMs	virtual machines
WDs	wireless devices
WET	wireless energy transmission
WMMSE	weighted minimum mean square error
WP	wireless powered
WSR	weighted sum rate

Chapter 1
Introduction to Intelligent Mobile Edge Computing and Sensing

1.1 Background for Intelligent MEC and Sensing

In recent years, the Internet of Things (IoT) technology has achieved rapid development, and various IoT devices with communication, computing and sensing capabilities have been widely deployed around the world [1]. From smart appliances and security cameras in smart homes, to sensors and smart meters in the industrial field, to wearable devices in the healthcare industry and internet of vehicles terminals in transportation, the number of IoT devices is growing exponentially [2]. The massive data transmission and computing requirements generated by such a large number of IoT devices pose severe challenges to traditional cloud computing architecture. In this case, if all tasks rely on the cloud computing center for processing, it will inevitably lead to serious congestion in the cloud computing core network, significantly increase data transmission delays, and seriously affect user experience [3].

However, due to strict limitations of factors such as device size and production cost, wireless devices (WDs) are usually equipped with limited-capacity batteries and low-performance processors. This means that WDs are often unable to cope with computationally intensive tasks with strict latency requirements. Therefore, how to improve the computing power of mobile devices to handle computationally intensive tasks with strict latency requirements becomes a key challenge for future wireless communication networks [4, 5]. Based on this, mobile edge computing (MEC) came into being [6]. MEC is defined as "providing IoT service environment and cloud computing capabilities at the edge of mobile networks". Its core idea is to sink the traditional cloud computing center to the edge of the network, thereby greatly shortening the distance between users and services [7, 8]. It reduces end-to-end communication latency while alleviating core network congestion. However, with the continuous expansion and deepening of intelligent application scenarios, simple MEC technology has gradually revealed some shortcomings, especially in terms of sensing capabilities and intelligent decision-making, which makes it

W. Hao et al., *Intelligent Mobile Edge Computing and Sensing*, Wireless Networks,
https://doi.org/10.1007/978-981-96-9400-6_1

difficult to meet complex and changing environments and user needs. This has prompted the combination of intelligent MEC and sensing technology, aiming to further enhance the system's intelligence level and ability to cope with complex tasks, and provide more solid technical support for future intelligent applications [9].

1.2 Introduction for Intelligent MEC and Sensing

Intelligent MEC and sensing are an innovative system that integrates cutting-edge communication, computing and sensing technologies. It aims to break the limitations of data processing and sensing in traditional network architecture, and sink powerful computing power and keen sensing capabilities to the edge of the network, adjacent to the data source and user end, thereby building a real-time, efficient and intelligent information processing and interaction environment [10]. In this system, MEC, as a core component, implements nearby data processing by deploying servers or computing resources at network edge nodes such as base stations (BSs) and wireless access points. Unlike traditional cloud computing that relies on remote data centers, MEC greatly shortens the data transmission path, effectively reduces transmission delays, and significantly improves the response speed and real-time performance of the system. Sensing technology is an important part of the intelligent MEC system. As the front end of data collection, various sensors are responsible for real-time sensing of information about the surrounding environment, and converting it into digital signals for further processing and analysis by edge computing devices. The close integration of sensing technology and intelligent MEC enables the system to obtain detailed information about the surrounding environment in real time, and make intelligent decisions as well as controls based on this information.

With the rapid development of information technology and the acceleration of digital transformation, intelligent MEC and sensing technology will develop in a more intelligent, efficient and collaborative direction. With the in-depth application of artificial intelligence and machine learning technologies in edge computing, edge devices will have stronger autonomous decision-making capabilities and intelligence levels, and will be able to make more accurate analysis and decisions based on real-time perceived data. At the same time, edge computing will further integrate and collaborate with cloud computing, fog computing and other computing modes to form a multi-level, distributed computing architecture, providing more flexible and efficient computing services for different types of applications [11].

1.3 Structure of This Book

The content framework of this book is shown in Fig. 1.1: This book is divided into 6 chapters, with the following structure.

Chapter 1 mainly explains the relevant background and introduction of intelligent MEC and sensing, and describes the overall framework structure of the book.

Chapter 2 introduces the relevant theoretical basis of intelligent MEC and sensing, and presents the relevant concepts of MEC, integrated MEC and sensing, and reconfigurable intelligent surface (RIS).

Chapter 3 conducts research on resource optimization of RIS-assisted MEC system. First, an RIS-assisted cell-free MEC system is constructed to minimize the maximum WD delay through joint optimization; second, a multi-RIS-assisted wireless powered (WP)-MEC system based on an actual reflection model is considered, and multiple variables are jointly optimized to maximize the total computing rate under energy consumption constraints, and a solution is given and the effect is verified; third, for broadband multi-carrier frequency selective channels, based on the amplitude-phase shift-frequency three-dimensional reflection model, the resource optimization problem of the RIS-assisted broadband MEC system is considered, an algorithm is proposed, and its performance gain and related necessity are verified by simulation.

Chapter 4 conducts research on computing offloading based on user and task dependencies in cloud-edge collaborative systems. First, for the single-user computing offloading problem, a Q-Learning based offloading (QLOF) algorithm is

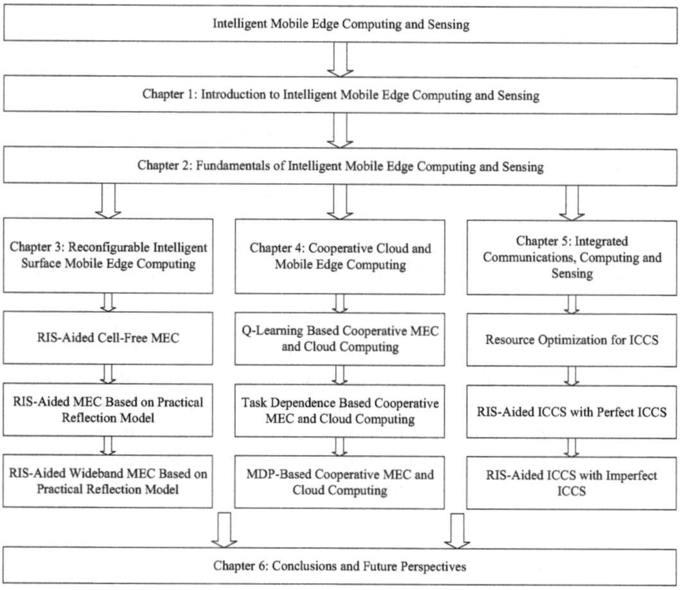

Fig. 1.1 The structure of this book

proposed, and the application energy-time cost (AETC) minimization problem is constructed by comprehensively considering the delay and energy consumption; second, for the multi-user multi-edge cloud computing offloading problem based on bilateral matching, Gale-Shapley based minimum offloading algorithm (GS-MOA) and Gale-Shapley based sequential offloading algorithm (GS-SOA) algorithms are proposed, which comprehensively consider the delay and energy consumption, and use the dichotomy method, polynomial analysis method and bilateral matching to solve the coupling problem; third, for the multi-user multi-edge cloud computing offloading problem based on task dependency scheduling, maximum local searching offloading (MLSO), sequential searching offloading (SSO) and genetic-based task scheduling (GTS) algorithms are proposed. The system energy-time cost (SETC) minimization problem is constructed by comprehensively considering the delay and energy consumption, subtask dependency and the coupling of the combined offloading decision and edge computing resources.

Chapter 5 conducts research on integrated communication, computing and sensing (ICCS) resource optimization. First, for ICCS networks with multi-functional BS that perform multiple functions, multiple variables are jointly optimized to maximize the weighted sum rate; second, the RIS-assisted ICCS system is studied, caching strategies are designed, and algorithms are developed to solve optimization problems; third, the system resource allocation design of RIS-assisted ICCS with imperfect channels in actual situations is considered, multiple variables are jointly optimized to maximize the sum rate, and a solution is given and the effect is verified.

Chapter 6 is the summary and outlook of this book. It systematically summarizes the research work of this book and looks forward to future research work.

References

1. M. Liu, S. Fang, H. Dong et al., Review of digital twin about concepts, technologies, and industrial applications. J. Manuf. Syst. **58**, 346–361 (2021)
2. Q. Wu, X. Guan, R. Zhang, Intelligent reflecting surface-aided wireless energy and information transmission: an overview. Proc. IEEE **110**(1), 150–170 (2022)
3. J. Zhao, Q. Li, Y. Gong et al., Computation offloading and resource allocation for cloud assisted mobile edge computing in vehicular networks. IEEE Trans. Veh. Technol. **68**(8), 7944–7956 (2019)
4. B. Liu, C. Liu, M. Peng, Resource allocation for energy-efficient MEC in NOMA-enabled massive IoT networks. IEEE J. Selected Areas Commun. **39**(4), 1015–1027 (2021)
5. N. Li, W. Hao, F. Zhou et al., Min–max latency optimization for IRS-aided cell-free mobile edge computing systems. IEEE Internet Things J. **11**(5), 8757–8770 (2023)
6. M. Patel, B. Naughton, C. Chan et al., Mobile-edge computing introductory technical white paper. White Paper, Mobile-edge Computing (MEC) Industry Initiative **29**, 854–864 (2014)
7. Y. Chen, Z. Chang, G. Min et al., Joint optimization of sensing and computation for status update in mobile edge computing systems. IEEE Trans. Wirel. Commun. **22**(11), 8230–8243 (2023)
8. D.S. Lakew, A.T. Tran, N.N. Dao et al., Intelligent offloading and resource allocation in heterogeneous aerial access IoT networks. IEEE Internet Things J. **10**(7), 5704–5718 (2022)

9. R. Xu, Z. Chang, Z. Han et al., Energy-efficient joint optimization of sensing and computation in MEC-assisted IoT using mean-field game. IEEE Internet of Things J. **11**(23), 37857–37871 (2024)
10. X. Chen, Z. Feng, J.A. Zhang et al., Integrated communication, sensing, and computation framework for 6G networks. Sensors **24**(10), 2968 (2024)
11. X. Li, C. Zhang, B. Gu et al., Optimal pricing and service selection in the mobile cloud architectures. IEEE Access **7**, 43564–43572 (2019)

Chapter 2
Fundamentals of Intelligent Mobile Edge Computing and Sensing

2.1 Introduction

This chapter introduces the fundamentals of RIS-aided intelligent MEC and sensing as well as their integration in next-generation communication system. The first section discusses MEC, where it decentralizes computational resources to the network edge, minimizing latency and enabling real-time data processing. The second section introduces the background and definition of integrated MEC and sensing, the benefits of integration, use cases and challenges. The final section introduces the RIS hardware structure and reflection model, including narrowband two-dimension reflection model and wideband three-dimension reflection model.

2.2 Mobile Edge Computing

MEC has emerged as a transformative technology in modern communication networks. By bringing computation and storage capabilities closer to users, MEC enables low-latency, large-bandwidth services that cater to the needs of compute-intensive and delay-sensitive applications such as augmented reality, autonomous vehicles, and smart manufacturing. The overall architecture of MEC is structured into three layers from top to bottom: the cloud layer, the edge layer, and the device layer, with the edge layer serving as the core component of the system [1]. Positioned between the cloud layer and device layer, the edge layer connects to various terminal devices below and interfaces with cloud computing centers above. The device layer includes sensors, mobile devices, actuators and other nodes, which can also be called the user layer. Terminal devices can establish connections with edge servers through various type of networks, such as 4G, 5G, Wi-Fi, etc., to realize the interconnection between terminals and edges. Data and control information can be transferred between the device layer and edge layer. The edge layer is

W. Hao et al., *Intelligent Mobile Edge Computing and Sensing*, Wireless Networks,
https://doi.org/10.1007/978-981-96-9400-6_2

also known as the edge node, including access points, wireless base stations, edge servers and other devices with storage and computing power. In addition to having certain computational capabilities, the edge layer can also receive and forward information from terminals, offering users computational services such as data analysis, knowledge reasoning, and model training. In addition, edge nodes and cloud computing centers can also act as controllers and schedulers for network flow control, task scheduling and so on. Compared to traditional cloud computing, edge computing offers advantages such as low latency, low cost, low core network congestion, and high system security. Moreover, with the explosive growth of mobile devices, the computational capacity of cloud data centers is insufficient to support such massive workloads. Therefore, shifting computation from the cloud to the edge is necessary.

Due to the limited computing resources, battery capacity and storage space, WDs cannot independently complete some computationally intensive applications, thus affecting the quality of service. The computation offloading technique in MEC systems transfer computational tasks from WD devices to edge servers, thereby addressing the conflict between resource-constrained devices and computation-intensive tasks. Task offloading decisions are influenced by a variety of factors, such as user demand, channel state information, mobile device battery and central processing unit (CPU) performance, edge node computing power, and current availability. In addition, the task model is also an important factor affecting the offloading strategy, determining whether the overall/partial offloading is suitable [2].

- Full Offloading: Also referred to as binary offloading, the computational task is indivisible, meaning that it can either be fully offloaded or entirely processed locally. In this mode, the key aspect of the task offloading strategy lies in determining whether to offload the task or not.
- Partial Offloading: The computational tasks can be divided into arbitrary-size subtasks or fixed-size subtasks. In partial offloading model, the key aspect of the offloading strategy is determining the amount of tasks to be offloaded.

2.3 Integrated MEC and Sensing

The 6G scenarios are an extension of the 5G framework, expanding three directions into six dimensions [3], as shown in Fig. 2.1, which consolidates the current global consensus on 6G, outlining its objectives and trends. Artificial intelligence and integrated communication-sensing are two key components that will play a significant role in 6G. For example, in transportation scenarios, autonomous vehicles and drones not only require precise positioning services but also need accurate perception of their surrounding environment, with the data being transmitted and processed with ultra-low latency. Deploying dedicated radar infrastructure may lead to low efficiency and high hardware cost. Therefore, leveraging existing

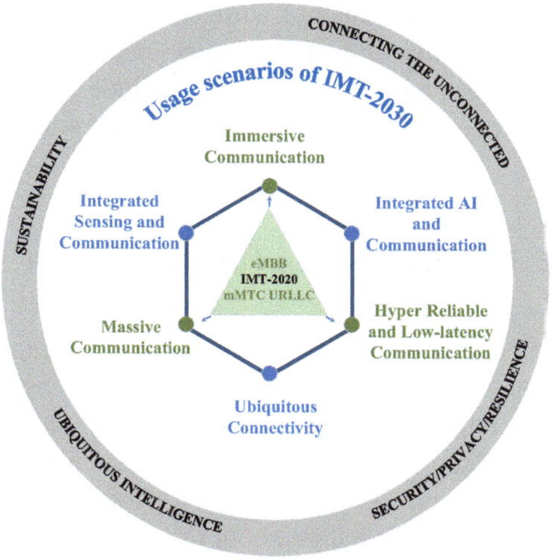

Fig. 2.1 Six key scenarios and four core principles of IMT-2030

communication infrastructure and deploying radar sensing systems, while utilizing cloud computing servers deployed at the edge, can effectively reduce hardware costs and improve resources utilization efficiency.

As an indispensable part of 6G, sensing can be used to the human sensory system, which detects the environment and obtains information through electromagnetic waves, and then analyzes and makes decisions through the computing system to achieve accurate control of the system. In addition, network devices acquire rich environmental information through sensing, including climate, obstructions, and multipath effects, and complete the process of environment reconstruction and channel estimation with the help of network computing, so that the network owns a certain prior understanding of the mobile communication environment, providing important support for global optimization and improving the overall communication performance.

2.3.1 Sensing Technologies

Sensing technologies refer to systems that enable the network to "perceive" its environment. These systems use sensors (e.g., radar, LiDAR, cameras, environmental sensors) to collect real-time data, including physical surroundings, user behaviors, traffic patterns, or environmental conditions. The sensing technologies include following

- Environmental Sensing: Includes temperature, humidity, pollution, and other atmospheric parameters sensing, often used for smart city applications.
- Radar and LiDAR Sensing: Used in advanced automotive and industrial systems for object detection, tracking, and environment mapping.

- RF-based Sensing: Utilizes radio frequency signals to sense movement, detect obstacles, or even determine location (e.g., indoor positioning systems).
- Image and Video Sensing: Includes visual sensors (cameras) for facial recognition, object tracking, and security applications.

2.3.2 Background and Definition

Integrated MEC and sensing is an emerging paradigm that combines edge computing capabilities with environmental sensing to enable more efficient, context-aware, and intelligent systems. MEC, by offloading and processing computation tasks at the edge of the network, reduces latency and energy consumption, while sensing technologies, such as radio-based sensing and environmental monitoring, provide real-time information about the physical environment and user behavior.

The integration of MEC and sensing leverages the strengths of both technologies to enhance the system performance. Furthermore, the integration of MEC and sensing bridges the gap between computational resources and real-world information. By embedding sensing functionalities into the MEC infrastructure, this approach not only enhances the performance of traditional MEC services but also provides new possibilities for edge intelligence, real-time decision-making, and adaptive system designs. This synergy enables a range of new capabilities and use cases, especially in 5G and 6G networks, where ultra-low latency, high reliability, and real-time intelligence are required. The integration benefits includes:

- **Real-Time Data Processing and Analysis:** Sensing systems collect massive amounts of environmental or contextual data, which are processed locally by MEC infrastructure. This reduces the dependency on cloud-based processing and minimizes the communication overhead, enabling real-time decision-making. For example, in autonomous driving, sensors collect data on the surrounding environment (traffic, pedestrians, road conditions), and then these data are processed real time by edge servers to make immediate driving decisions.
- **Enhanced Context-Awareness:** The integration allows the network to become context-aware by combining sensory inputs (e.g., environmental data, movement detection) with the computational capabilities at the edge. This enables services such as smart city applications, intelligent transportation systems, and predictive maintenance. For instance, in smart cities, edge-based sensing can be used to monitor traffic flows, air quality, and energy consumption, allowing local authorities to make intelligent, data-driven decisions.
- **Effective Network Optimization:** By sensing, MEC network can optimize resources dynamically based on the sensed data. For example, sensors can collect factory data, and MEC system can quickly analyze the data and optimize factory operations real time.
- **Privacy and Security:** Since both sensing and computing take place at the network edge, sensitive data do not need to be transmitted to a centralized cloud

server. This reduces potential vulnerabilities in data transmission and enhances information privacy.
- **Scalability and Adaptability:** The integrated MEC and sensing architecture is highly scalable. As more sensors are deployed across the network (e.g., in a smart city or industrial IoT system), MEC can provide the necessary computational power at the edge to process the data. This approach enables networks to handle an increasing number of devices and sensors without overwhelming centralized infrastructure.

2.3.3 Use Cases

The integration of MEC and sensing enables a variety of advanced applications, especially for low latency, high reliability, and real-time processing scenarios.

- Autonomous Vehicles: Edge computing at traffic intersections and road-side units combined with sensing (radar, cameras, LiDAR) allows vehicles to process environmental data instantly and make real-time driving decisions.
- Smart Cities: Sensors deployed across cities collect data on traffic, energy usage, and environmental conditions, while MEC processes this data at the edge to optimize traffic management, resource distribution, and urban planning.
- Industrial IoT: In factories, sensors can detect machinery performance and environmental factors, while MEC processes these data to provide predictive maintenance, safety monitoring, and operational optimization.
- Healthcare: Wearable sensors can monitor patient vitals and transmit these data to nearby MEC infrastructure for real time analysis, enabling timely intervention and personalized healthcare delivery.

2.3.4 Challenges

The 6G framework of Integrated MEC and sensing is shown in Fig. 2.2. To build a integrated network, a series of technical challenges must be addressed. The development and application of these technologies will provide strong support for future digital transformation.

- **Interoperability:** Ensuring seamless communication and compatibility between various sensing devices (such as radar, cameras, and environmental sensors) and edge computing infrastructure remains a significant challenge. Different manufacturers may use different standards, protocols, and data formats, making it difficult to integrate them into a unified system.
- **Data Fusion and Analysis:** Integrating and processing data from heterogeneous sensors (e.g., radar, LiDAR, temperature sensors, cameras) is complex. Effective data fusion algorithms must be developed to ensure that the data is accurately

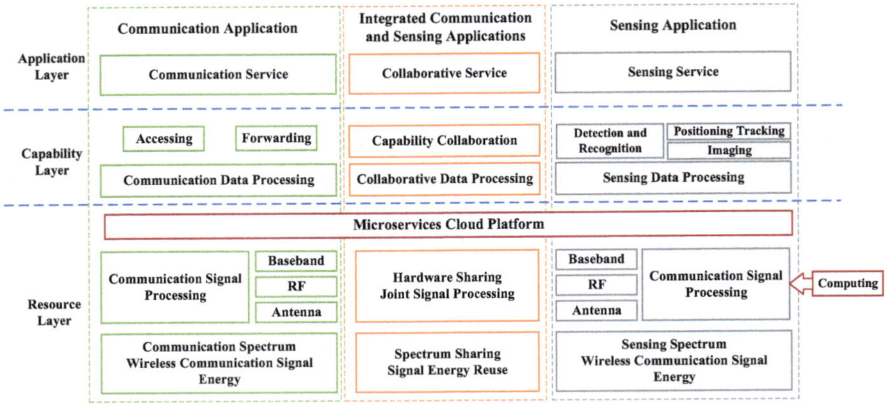

Fig. 2.2 6G framework for integrated MEC and sensing

combined to provide reliable insights. Additionally, real-time processing requirements add another layer of complexity.

- **Resource Management:** Efficiently managing computational resources at the edge is crucial. With increasing numbers of devices and sensors, MEC platforms must allocate computational and storage resources dynamically to handle diverse tasks without overloading the system. Balancing these resources while ensuring low latency and high performance is a significant challenge.
- **Latency and Reliability:** MEC and sensing systems must meet ultra-low latency and high reliability standards, particularly in time-sensitive applications such as autonomous driving and industrial automation. Any delay or loss of data in the system can result in critical failures or inefficiencies.
- **Security and Privacy:** As sensing devices collect sensitive data, such as personal health information or security surveillance data, ensuring the privacy and security of the collected data is vital. MEC can help address some of these concerns by processing data locally, but robust security measures are needed to prevent potential vulnerabilities in the system.

2.4 Reconfigurable Intelligent Surface

RIS is a two-dimensional planar array composed of numerous reflective elements, implemented using reconfigurable electromagnetic devices, which operate with extremely low power consumption. Each reflective element independently adjusts the phase shift and amplitude of the incident electromagnetic wave in a programmable manner, enabling cooperative beamforming of the reflected waves. Deploying RIS in existing communication networks can create a favorable propagation environment and provide additional degrees of freedom for network optimization. Moreover, these lightweight, hardware-efficient, and cost-effective reflective elements offer portability and mobility for various practical applications of RIS, enabling large-scale RIS deployment in real-world scenarios and achieving higher passive beamforming gain, thereby significantly improving transmission Quality of Service. This section introduces the hardware structure of RIS, the amplitude-phase shift reflection model of RIS for narrowband systems, and the amplitude-phase shift-frequency reflection model of RIS for wideband systems.

2.4.1 Hardware Structure

Figure 2.3 illustrates the typical architecture of an RIS, consisting of a surface with a three-layer structure and a controller. The first layer of the surface is composed of numerous metallic patches, which are printed on a dielectric substrate and directly interact with the incident signal [4]. The middle layer is typically made of copper to reduce energy leakage during the signal reflection process. The final layer is the control panel, which is responsible for exciting and controlling the reflective elements, dynamically adjusting the signal reflection coefficients[5]. The controller is generally implemented using a Field Programmable Gate Array, which coordinates the control panels across the RIS surface. Additionally, the controller can serve as a gateway, facilitating communication with other network components (such as the Base Station/Access Point and user terminals) through a dedicated control link, either wired or wireless.

To achieve highly controllable reflection on the RIS surface, there are generally three typical implementation methods: (1) mechanical drive, such as translation and rotation; (2) functional materials, such as liquid crystals and graphene; (3) electronic devices [6], such as Photodiodes (Positive Intrinsic Negative, PIN), Field-Effect Transistors, or Micro-Electro-Mechanical Systems switches. Among these methods, the third one is widely adopted due to its advantages of fast response, low reflection loss, and low energy consumption and hardware cost. By applying different bias voltages to the PIN photodiode through a DC feed line, it can switch between "ON" and "OFF" states, causing the reflective element to introduce a phase shift of π to the incident signal. Regarding switching frequency, PIN photodiodes can operate at

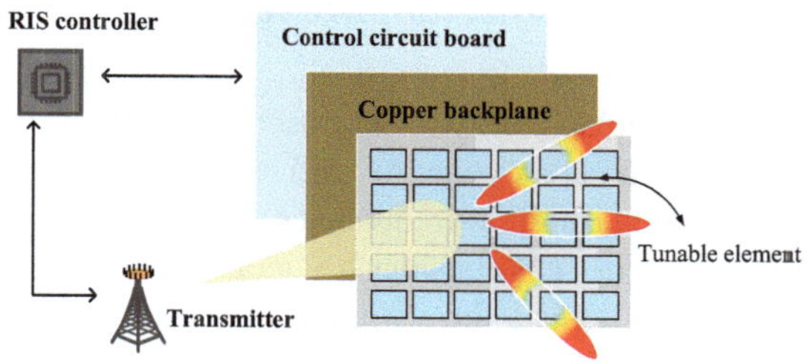

Fig. 2.3 Typical RIS architecture

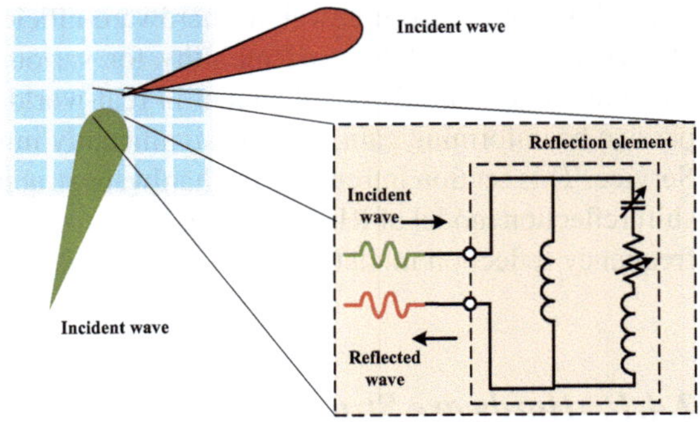

Fig. 2.4 The equivalent circuit of an RIS reflective element

up to 5 MHz, corresponding to a switching time of 0.2 microseconds, which is much smaller than the typical channel coherence time on the millisecond scale [7].

Figure 2.4 shows the equivalent circuit of a PIN photodiode. For an incident signal with frequency f, the impedance of the RIS element can be expressed as [8]:

$$Z_n(C_n, f_n, R_n) = \frac{j2\pi f_n L_1 \left(j2\pi f_n L_2 + \frac{1}{j2\pi f_n C_n} + R_n\right)}{j2\pi f_n L_1 + j2\pi f_n L_2 + \frac{1}{j2\pi f_n C_n} + R_n} \tag{2.1}$$

where L_1, L_2, C_n and R_n represent the inductance of the metal plates, outer inductance, effective capacitance, and loss resistance, respectively [9]. The reflection coefficient of each RIS element can be modeled as the ratio of the reflected signal power to the incident signal power, which is mathematically expressed as [10, 11]

$$\phi_n = \frac{Z_n(C_n, f_n, R_n) - Z_0}{Z_n(C_n, f_n, R_n) + Z_0} \tag{2.2}$$

where Z_0 represents the impedance of free space. From the above equation, it can be seen that the reflection coefficient ϕ_n is a function of C_n and f_n. When the capacitance of the RIS reflection element C_n is fixed, its response coefficient is dependent on the frequency of the incident signal.

2.4.2 *RIS Reflection Model*

From formula (2.2), we can observe that the same RIS elements with determined circuit parameters generate different responses (i.e., reflection coefficients) to the signals with different frequencies. To illustrate the importance of this phenomenon, the author in [12] consider a wideband system with center frequency at 2.4 GHz. Figure 2.5 depicts the variation of phase shift and amplitude with respect to the frequency of incident signal. It can be observed that when the RIS element is configured to provide a 0° phase shift for a 2.4 GHz signal, it generates significantly

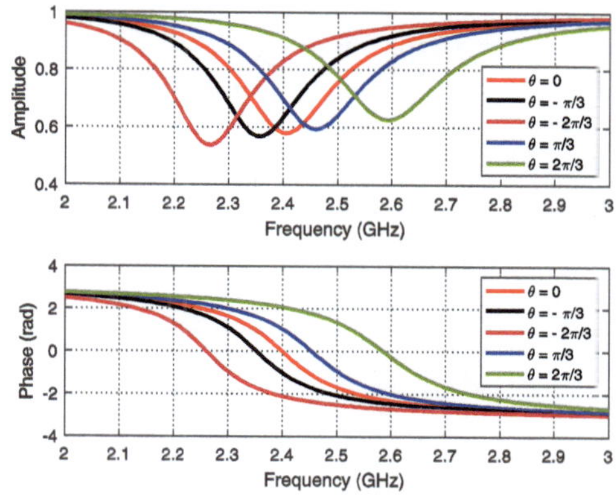

Fig. 2.5 The illustration of the dual phase- and amplitude-squint [1]

different phase shifts for signals at other frequencies. Similarly, Fig. 2.7 also depicts the function relationship between amplitude and frequency, with different curves representing different phase shift at the center frequency. It can be observed that the amplitudes of the reflected signals heavily depend on the frequency. The minimum amplitude occurs when the frequency of the incident signal matches the resonant frequency of the reflection circuit. This happens because, in this scenario, the reflective current aligns in phase with the element voltage, resulting in the maximum dielectric, metallic, and ohmic losses.

In order to characterize the fundamental relationship between amplitude/phase shift and frequency, the authors in [12] propose an analytical model to describe the amplitude and phase shift for the signals with different frequencies. The reflection coefficient of the n-th element of RIS can be defined as

$$\phi_n = A_n e^{j\theta_n}, \forall n, \tag{2.3}$$

where $A_n \in [0, 1]$ and $\theta_n \in [-\pi, \pi)$ denote the amplitude and phase of ϕ_n, respectively. Consequently, the amplitude $A_n(\angle\phi_c, f)$ and phase shift $\theta_n(\angle\phi_c, f)$ can be modeled as [12]

$$\begin{aligned} A_n(\angle\phi_c, f) &= -\frac{\alpha_4\angle\phi_c + \beta_3}{\left(\left(f - \mathcal{F}_1(\angle\phi_c)\right)/0.05\right)^2 + 4} + 1, \forall n, \\ \theta_n(\angle\phi_c, f) &= -2\tan^{-1}\left[\mathcal{F}_2(\angle\phi_c)\left(f/10^9 - \mathcal{F}_1(\angle\phi_c)\right)\right], \forall n, \\ \mathcal{F}_1(\angle\phi_c) &= \alpha_1\tan(\angle\phi_c/3) + \alpha_2\sin(\angle\phi_c) + \beta_1, \\ \mathcal{F}_2(\angle\phi_c) &= \alpha_3\angle\phi_c + \beta_2, \end{aligned} \tag{2.4}$$

where $\alpha_1, \alpha_2, \alpha_3, \alpha_4, \beta_1, \beta_2, \beta_3$ are parameters related to a specific circuit implementation and can be easily obtained using standard curve-fitting tools.

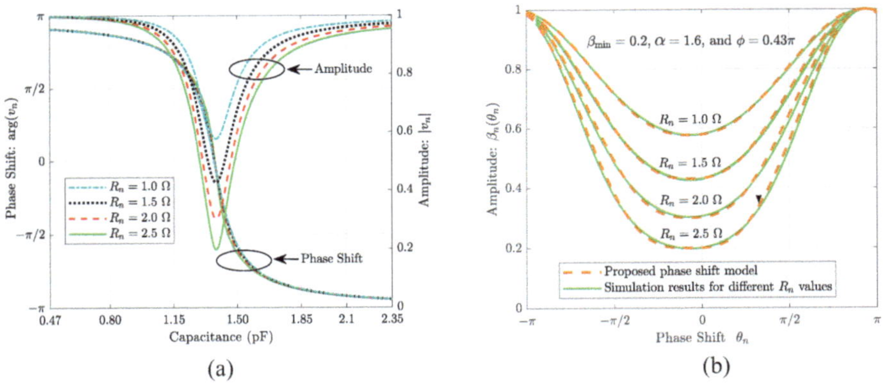

Fig. 2.6 Two-dimensional RIS reflection coefficient. (**a**) The phase shift and magnitude vary with the parameters C_n and R_n. (**b**) Amplitude variation with phase shift

2.4.2.1 Two-Dimensional RIS Reflection Model

The variation of the reflection coefficient with respect to various parameters in a single-carrier/narrowband system is shown in Fig. 2.6. It can be observed that, although the reflective elements are capable of achieving a full 2π phase shift, both its phase shift and reflection amplitude vary with C_n and R_n. The minimum amplitude occurs near zero phase shift, while the maximum amplitude, close to 1, occurs at phase shifts of π and $-\pi$ [13]. This is because when the phase shift is near π and $-\pi$, the reflected current is out of phase with the element current, causing both the electric field and the current inside the element decrease, resulting in the minimal energy loss and maximal reflection amplitude. In contrast, when the phase shift is near zero, the reflected current is in phase with the element current, resulting in an enhancement of both the electric field and the current inside the element. This leads to a sharp increase in dielectric loss, metal loss, and ohmic loss, resulting in maximum energy loss and minimum reflection amplitude.

In Fig. 2.6b, the red dashed line and the green solid line represent the simulation results of the phase shift model and the non-ideal reflection model proposed in [14], respectively. The single-carrier two-dimensional phase shift model provided in [14] is expressed as

$$\beta_n(\theta_n) = (1-\beta_{\min})\left(\frac{\sin(\theta_n-\phi)+1}{2}\right)^{\alpha} + \beta_{\min}, \tag{2.5}$$

Here, β_n represents the reflection amplitude, which is a function of the phase shift θ_n. $\beta_{\min}$, ϕ, and α are non-negative constants related to the specific circuit implementation. Specifically, in the amplitude-phase shift curve, $\beta_{\min}$ denotes the minimum amplitude, ϕ represents the horizontal distance between -2π and $\beta_{\min}$, and α controls the steepness of the curve. It is important to note that when $\beta_{\min} = 1$

or $\alpha = 0$, the practical non-ideal narrowband RIS reflection model reduces to the ideal reflection model. In this case, the reflection amplitude is independent of the phase shift for incident signals at different frequencies, and the reflection amplitude is constant 1. Additionally, in practical scenarios, once the RIS circuit is fabricated, these parameters become fixed. As a result, these parameters can be easily obtained through standard curve fitting tools.

2.4.2.2 Three-Dimensional RIS Reflection Model

When considering more general broadband/multiband systems, the narrowband RIS reflection model described above no longer applies. As can be seen from Eqs. (2.1) and (2.2), the phase shift and amplitude of the reflected signal are also dependent on the frequency of the incident signal. In other words, altering the basic phase shift θ of the central carrier results in significant changes in both the reflection phase shift and amplitude of incident signals at other frequencies. This dual dependence on phase shift and amplitude can result in severe beam misalignment. Figure 2.7 illustrates this dual dependence effect. It is important to note that this is an inherent phenomenon that depends on the specific circuit implementation and cannot be simply ignored in RIS broadband systems. Therefore, using an accurate RIS reflection model is crucial for the design of reflection beamforming. Reference [15] provides an accurate three-dimensional amplitude-phase-frequency reflection model. However, this model is very complex, significantly increasing the difficulty and complexity of RIS phase shift optimization. Furthermore, in practical broadband systems, the relative bandwidth, i.e., the ratio of bandwidth to the central carrier frequency, is generally less than 5%. For example, in the case of a 100 MHz bandwidth, the amplitude-phase shift curves at different frequencies do not show significant differences. Under these conditions, the relationship between the reflected amplitude and phase shift for signals at different frequencies can be

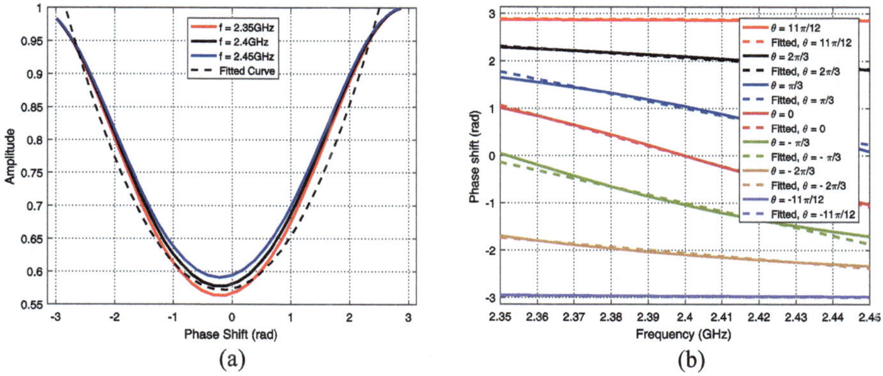

Fig. 2.7 RIS reflection coefficient. (**a**) The variation of amplitude with phase shift at a specific carrier frequency. (**b**) The variation of phase shift with frequency

approximated by a quadratic function. Additionally, as shown in Fig. 2.7b, the phase shift as a function of frequency can be approximately fitted as a straight line.

When the basic phase shift θ of the RIS element changes, both the slope and intercept of the phase-frequency line will vary accordingly. For an incident signal frequency f, the reflection amplitude F(θ, f) and phase shift G(θ, f) for a specific reflective element can be modeled as [16]

$$\begin{aligned} \mathrm{F}(\theta, f) &= a_1 \mathrm{G}^2(\theta, f) + b_1 \mathrm{G}(\theta, f) + c_1, \\ \mathrm{G}(\theta, f) &= \mathrm{K}(\theta) f + \mathrm{B}(\theta), \\ \mathrm{K}(\theta) &= a_2 \sin(b_2\theta + c_2) + a_3 \sin(b_3\theta + c_3), \\ \mathrm{B}(\theta) &= a_4 \sin(b_4\theta + c_4) + a_5 \sin(b_5\theta + c_5) \end{aligned} \tag{2.6}$$

Here, K(θ) and B represent the slope and intercept of the phase-frequency line, respectively. $\{a_i, b_i, c_i\}_i^5$ are parameters that are related to the specific circuit implementation.

References

1. N. Abbas et al., Mobile edge computing: a survey. IEEE Internet of Things J. **5**(1), 450–465 (2018)
2. T. Bai, C. Pan, Y. Deng, M. Elkashlan, A. Nallanathan, L. Hanzo, Latency minimization for intelligent reflecting surface aided mobile edge computing. IEEE J. Sel. Areas Commun. **38**(11), 2666–2682 (2020)
3. ITU-R, Framework and overall objectives of the future development of IMT for 2030 and beyond. ITU-R Recommendation M.2160-0 (2023)
4. Q. Wu, R. Zhang, Towards smart and reconfigurable environment: intelligent reflecting surface aided wireless network. IEEE Commun. Mag. **58**(1), 106–112 (2020)
5. M. Tavana, M. Masoudi, E. Björnson, Amplitude-based sequential optimization of energy harvesting with reconfigurable intelligent surfaces, in *Proceedings of the 57th Asilomar Conference on Signals, Systems, and Computers, Pacific Grove, CA, USA* (2023), pp. 480–485
6. R. Xiong, J. Zhang, F. Wang, Z. Wang, X. Ren, J. Liu, J. Lu, K. Wan, T. Mi, R.C. Qiu, Design of reconfigurable intelligent surfaces for wireless communication: a review (2023). arXiv:2304.14232
7. L. Zhang, X.Q. Chen, S. Liu et al., Space-time-coding digital metasurfaces. Nat. Commun. **9**(1), 4334 (2018)
8. A.S. de Sena, M. Rasti, N.H. Mahmood, M. Latva-aho, Beyond diagonal RIS for multi-band multi-cell MIMO networks: a practical frequency-dependent model and performance analysis (2024). arXiv:2401.06475
9. D. Fei, C. Chen, P. Zheng, M. You, J. Ding, W. Wang, J. Zhang, B. Ai, S. Jin, T. Cui, Research and experimental verification of reconfigurable intelligent surface in indoor coverage enhancement. J. Electron. Inf. Technol. **44**(7), 2374–2381 (2022)
10. W. Cai, R. Liu, M. Li, Y. Liu, Q. Wu, Q. Liu, IRS-assisted multicell multiband systems: practical reflection model and joint beamforming design. IEEE Trans. Commun. **70**(6), 3897–3911 (2022)
11. D.M. Pozar, *Microwave Engineering*, 3rd edn. (John Wiley & Sons, New York, 2005)

12. W. Cai, H. Li, M. Li, Q. Liu, Practical modeling and beamforming for intelligent reflecting surface aided wideband systems. IEEE Commun. Lett. **24**(7), 1568–1571 (2020)
13. S. Hashemi, M. Ardakani, H. Jiang, RIS with coupled phase shift and amplitude: capacity maximization and configuration set selection (2024). arXiv:2411.15696
14. S. Abeywickrama et al., Intelligent reflecting surface: practical phase shift model and beamforming optimization. IEEE Trans. Commun. **68**(9), 5849–5863 (2020)
15. W. Cai et al., Practical modeling and beamforming for intelligent reflecting surface aided wideband systems. IEEE Commun. Lett. **24**(7), 1568–1571 (2020)
16. H. Li, W. Cai, Y. Liu, M. Li, Q. Liu, Q. Wu, Intelligent reflecting surface enhanced wideband MIMO-OFDM communications: from practical model to reflection optimization. IEEE Trans. Commun. **69**(7), 4807–4820 (2021)

Chapter 3
Reconfigurable Intelligent Surface Mobile Edge Computing

3.1 Introduction

The performance of MEC may be affected by wireless offloading links, the offloading delay is large specifically when the links are week. In this case, the RIS with low cost and hardware complexity can be deployed to build virtual links as so to improve the strength of offloading signal at receiver by adjusting RIS reflection coefficients. However, current studies on RIS-assisted MEC have the following limitations. First, the latency fairness among multiple WDs is not considered; Second, current studies on IRS-assisted MEC systems assume the ideal phase shift model, i.e., each RIS element owns constant magnitude, variable phase shift, and the same response for wideband signals, which will inevitably suffer from serious performance loss in the practical system. Due to the introduction of RIS reflection constraints, the existing RIS reflecting coefficients optimization schemes are no longer suitable for practical IRS-based MEC systems. Third, the communication and computation resources affect each other, so the joint optimization is still difficult.

This chapter thoroughly studies the above issues, which is organized as follows. Section 3.2 investigates the minimization of the maximum latency in RIS-assisted cell-free MEC systems. Section 3.3 focuses on maximizing the sum computation rate in IRS-assisted wireless powered MEC systems under a practical reflection model. Section 3.4 explores the weighted sum delay minimization in IRS-assisted wideband MEC systems under practical RIS three-dimensional reflection model.

W. Hao et al., *Intelligent Mobile Edge Computing and Sensing*, Wireless Networks,
https://doi.org/10.1007/978-981-96-9400-6_3

3.2 RIS-Aided Cell-Free MEC

3.2.1 System Model and Problem Formulation

As shown in Fig. 3.1, we consider an RIS-aided cell-free MEC system, where multiple distributed BSs cooperatively serve WDs with the help of RISs. All RISs and BSs are connected to a central processing unit by high-throughput optical cables. The considered system consists of K single-antenna WDs, I RISs, and B BSs. The number of elements at the i-th RIS and number of antennas at the b-th BS are denoted by N_i and M_b, respectively. For simplicity, we set $N_i = N$ and $M_b = M$ for any i and b, and let $\mathcal{N} \in \{1, \ldots, N\}$, $\mathcal{B} \in \{1, \ldots, B\}$, $\mathcal{I} \in \{1, \ldots, I\}$, and $\mathcal{K} \in \{1, \ldots, K\}$ denote the index sets of RIS elements, BSs, RISs, and WDs, respectively. We consider a block-fading channel model, where the wireless channels remain constant during the current time block but change over different time blocks, and assume that the CSIs of all involved channels are available by using existing advanced channel estimation methods [1, 2].

3.2.1.1 Communication Model

Figure 3.2 shows the channel model of the RIS-aided cell-free MEC system. The direct channel vector from the k-th WD to the b-th BS is denoted by $\mathbf{h}_{d,b,k} \in \mathbb{C}^{M\times 1}$, and the reflect channel vectors from the k-th WD to the i-th RIS and the i-th RIS to the b-th BS are denoted by $\mathbf{h}_{r,i,k} \in \mathbb{C}^{N\times 1}$ and $\mathbf{G}_{b,i} \in \mathbb{C}^{M\times N}$, respectively. The phase shift coefficient vector of the i-th RIS is denoted by $\boldsymbol{\theta}_i = \left[\theta_{i,1}, \theta_{i,2}, \ldots, \theta_{i,N}\right]^T$, where $\theta_{i,n} \in [0, 2\pi)$ for all $i \in \mathcal{I}$ and $n \in \mathcal{N}$. Then, the diagonal reflecting matrix of the i-th RIS is given by

$$\boldsymbol{\Theta}_i \triangleq \text{diag}\left(\beta_{i,1}e^{j\theta_{i,1}}, \ldots, \beta_{i,N}e^{j\theta_{i,N}}\right), \forall i \in \mathcal{I}, \tag{3.1}$$

where $\beta_{i,n} \in [0, 1]$ stands for the reflection amplitudes of RIS elements and each of them is fixed to one for maximizing the reflected signal power. It is worth

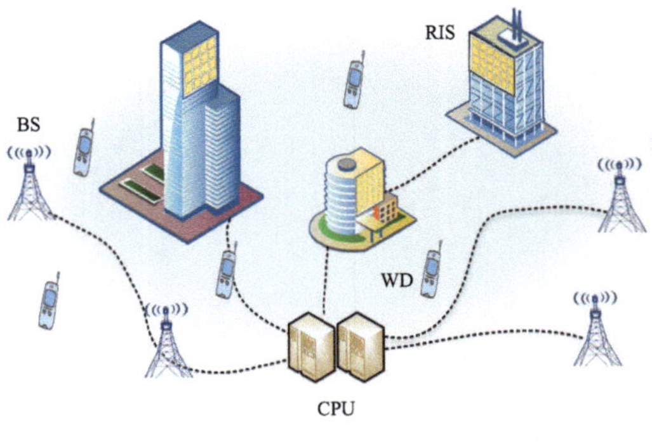

Fig. 3.1 The proposed RIS-aided cell-free MEC system

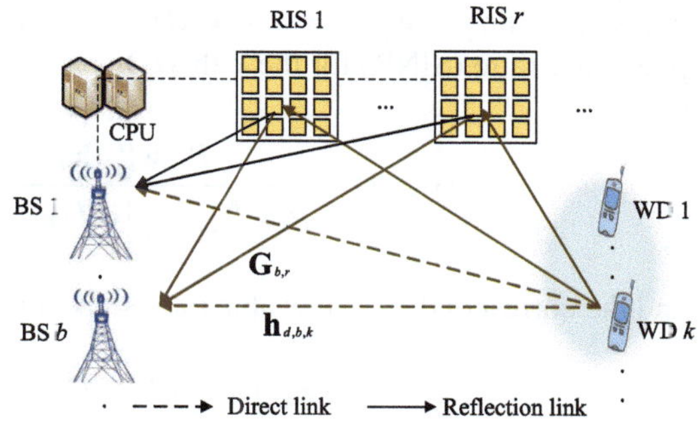

Fig. 3.2 The channels model of the RIS-aided cell-free MEC system

noting that double/multi-hop reflections between RISs also occur in the multi-RIS communication environment. However, due to the severe multiplicative path loss in multi-hop reflection, we only consider the one-way reflection as in [3–5]. Thus, the combined effective channel from the k-th WD to the b-th BS can be defined as

$$\mathbf{h}_{b,k} = \mathbf{h}_{d,b,k} + \sum\nolimits_{i=1}^{I} \mathbf{G}_{b,i}\boldsymbol{\Theta}_i \mathbf{h}_{r,i,k}. \tag{3.2}$$

Let P_t and $\mathbf{s} = [s_1, s_2, \ldots, s_K]^T$ denote the offloading power and signal of K WDs, respectively. Here, we assume that all WDs transmit the same power for simplicity as in [6]. Let $\mathbf{w}_{b,k} \in \mathbb{C}^{M\times 1}$ denote the multi-user detection (MUD) vector of the b-th BS for the k-th WD. Hence, the detected signal at BSs for the k-th WD can be formulated as

$$\begin{aligned}
\hat{s}_k &= \sum_{b=1}^{B} \mathbf{w}_{b,k}^H \left[\sqrt{P_t} \sum_{j=1}^{K} \left(\mathbf{h}_{d,b,j} + \sum_{i=1}^{I} \mathbf{G}_{b,i}\boldsymbol{\Theta}_i \mathbf{h}_{r,i,j} \right) s_j + \mathbf{n}_b \right] \\
&\overset{(a)}{=} \mathbf{w}_k^H \left[\sqrt{P_t} \sum_{j=1}^{K} \left(\mathbf{h}_{d,j} + \sum_{i=1}^{I} \mathbf{G}_i\boldsymbol{\Theta}_i \mathbf{h}_{r,i,j} \right) s_j + \mathbf{n} \right] \\
&\overset{(b)}{=} \mathbf{w}_k^H \left[\sqrt{P_t} \sum_{j=1}^{K} \left(\mathbf{h}_{d,j} + \mathbf{G}\boldsymbol{\Theta}\mathbf{h}_{r,j} \right) s_j + \mathbf{n} \right] \\
&\overset{(c)}{=} \mathbf{w}_k^H \left[\sqrt{P_t} \sum_{j=1}^{K} \mathbf{h}_j s_j + \mathbf{n} \right],
\end{aligned} \tag{3.3}$$

where $\mathbf{n}_b \in \mathbb{C}^{M\times 1}$ denotes the received noise vector of the b-th BS, $\mathbf{w}_k \in \mathbb{C}^{MB\times 1}$ is the k-th column of the MUD matrix $\mathbf{W} \in \mathbb{C}^{MB\times K}$, where $\mathbf{W} = \left[\mathbf{w}_1^T, \ldots, \mathbf{w}_K^T\right]^T$, (a) holds by defining $\mathbf{w}_k = \left[\mathbf{w}_{1,k}^T, \ldots, \mathbf{w}_{B,k}^T\right]^T$, $\mathbf{h}_{d,k} = \left[\mathbf{h}_{d,1,k}^T, \ldots, \mathbf{h}_{d,B,k}^T\right]^T$, $\mathbf{G}_i = \left[\mathbf{G}_{1,i}^T, \ldots, \mathbf{G}_{B,i}^T\right]^T$, and $\mathbf{n} = \left[\mathbf{n}_1^T, \ldots, \mathbf{n}_B^T\right]^T$, (b) holds by defining $\mathbf{G} = \left[\mathbf{G}_1^T, \ldots, \mathbf{G}_I^T\right]^T$, $\boldsymbol{\Theta} = \mathrm{diag}\left(\boldsymbol{\Theta}_1, \ldots, \boldsymbol{\Theta}_I\right)$, and $\mathbf{h}_{r,k} = \left[\mathbf{h}_{r,1,k}^T, \ldots, \mathbf{h}_{r,I,k}^T\right]^T$, and (c)

holds according to $\mathbf{h}_k = \mathbf{h}_{d,k} + \mathbf{G}\boldsymbol{\Theta}\mathbf{h}_{r,k}$. Thus, the received signal-to-interference plus noise ratio (SINR) for the k-th WD is

$$\gamma_k(\mathbf{w}_k, \boldsymbol{\theta}) = \frac{P_t \left|\mathbf{w}_k^H \left(\mathbf{h}_{d,k} + \mathbf{G}\boldsymbol{\Theta}\mathbf{h}_{r,k}\right)\right|^2}{P_t \sum_{j=1, j\neq k}^{K} \left|\mathbf{w}_k^H \left(\mathbf{h}_{d,j} + \mathbf{G}\boldsymbol{\Theta}\mathbf{h}_{r,j}\right)\right|^2 + \sigma^2}, \tag{3.4}$$

and the corresponding achievable rate is given by

$$R_k(\mathbf{w}_k, \theta) = \eta \log_2 \left(1 + \gamma_k(\mathbf{w}_k, \boldsymbol{\theta})\right), \tag{3.5}$$

where η is the system bandwidth.

3.2.1.2 Computing Model

Here, the partial offloading scheme is considered, and the computing models for both local and edge processing are presented, respectively.

- *Local computing:* Let f_k^l, L_k, ℓ_k and c_k denote the local CPU-cycle frequency (cycles/s), total input data size to be processed, offloading data size, and the number of CPU cycles required to compute a single bit for the k-th WD, respectively. Thus, the latency imposed by local computing is formulated as $D_k^l(\ell_k) = (L_k - \ell_k)\, c_k / f_k^l$.
- *Edge computing:* The latency for edge computing usually includes three parts: a) offloading latency for transmitting computing data to BSs; b) processing latency for executing offloaded data at MEC server; c) return latency for transmitting computing results to WDs. Let f_{total}^e and f_k^e denote the total computing resource of MEC server and the computing resource allocated to the k-th WD, respectively, satisfying $\sum_{k=1}^{K} f_k^e \le f_{total}^e$. Here, we ignore the return latency since the returning results are usually small size [7, 8]. Therefore, the total latency for edge processing can be written as $D_k^e\left(\mathbf{w}_k, \boldsymbol{\theta}, \ell_k, f_k^e\right) = \ell_k / R_k(\mathbf{w}_k, \boldsymbol{\theta}) + \ell_k c_k / f_k^e$.

On this basis, the overall latency for the k-th WD can be formulated as:

$$\begin{aligned} D_k\left(\mathbf{w}_k, \boldsymbol{\theta}, \ell_k, f_k^e\right) &= \max\left\{D_k^l(\ell_k),\, D_k^e\left(\mathbf{w}_k, \boldsymbol{\theta}, \ell_k, f_k^e\right)\right\} \\ &= \max\left\{\frac{(L_k - \ell_k)\, c_k}{f_k^l},\, \frac{\ell_k}{R_k(\mathbf{w}_k, \boldsymbol{\theta})} + \frac{\ell_k c_k}{f_k^e}\right\}. \end{aligned} \tag{3.6}$$

3.2.1.3 Problem Formulation

Considering fairness among WDs, we minimize the maximum WD latency by jointly optimizing offloading data size $\boldsymbol{\ell} = [\ell_1, \ell_2, \ldots, \ell_K]^T$, edge computing resource $\mathbf{f}^e = \left[f_1^e, f_2^e, \ldots, f_K^e\right]^T$, MUD matrix $\mathbf{W}$, and reflecting beamforming vector $\boldsymbol{\theta}$, which can be formulated as

$$\min_{\boldsymbol{\ell},\mathbf{f}^e,\mathbf{W},\boldsymbol{\theta}} \max_{k\in\mathcal{K}} D_k\left(\mathbf{w}_k, \boldsymbol{\theta}, \ell_k, f_k^e\right) \tag{3.7a}$$

$$\text{s.t. } 0 \le \theta_{i,n} < 2\pi, \quad \forall i \in \mathcal{I}, \forall n \in \mathcal{N}, \tag{3.7b}$$

$$\ell_k \in \{0, 1, \ldots, L_k\}, \forall k \in \mathcal{K}, \tag{3.7c}$$

$$\sum\nolimits_{k=1}^{K} f_k^e \le f_{\text{total}}^e, \tag{3.7d}$$

$$f_k^e \ge 0, \quad \forall k \in \mathcal{K}, \tag{3.7e}$$

$$\|\mathbf{w}_k\|^2 \le 1, \quad \forall k \in \mathcal{K}, \tag{3.7f}$$

where (3.7b) is RIS reflection coefficients constrains, (3.7c) implies that the k-th WD offloaded data size should be an integer between zero and the total input data L_k. Equation (3.7d) denotes the computing resource allocated to all WDs should not exceed the total edge computing resource. Equation (3.7f) represents unit-norm detection vector constrains for the k-th WD.

It is clear that problem (3.7) is difficult to be directly solved. Next, we first introduce an auxiliary variable t to transform (3.7) into the following problem, given by

$$\min_{\boldsymbol{\ell},\mathbf{f}^e,\mathbf{W},\boldsymbol{\theta}} \ t \tag{3.8a}$$

$$\text{s.t. } D_k\left(\mathbf{w}_k, \boldsymbol{\theta}, \ell_k, f_k^e\right) \le t, \forall k \in \mathcal{K}, \tag{3.8b}$$

$$(3.7\text{b}), (3.7\text{c}), (3.7\text{d}), (3.7\text{e}), (3.7\text{f}). \tag{3.8c}$$

Although the objective function (OF) of (3.8) and constraints in (3.8c) are linear, it is still challenging to directly solve problem (3.8) due to the following three aspects: (a) the segmented form of (3.8b), (b) MUD matrix $\mathbf{W}$ and reflecting beamforming vector $\boldsymbol{\theta}$ are coupled together, (c) (3.8b) is non-convex with respect to $\boldsymbol{\theta}$. In general, there is no standard method to find a globally optimal solution of such a non-convex optimization problem. To proceed, we develop an iterative framework to obtain a locally optimal solution. Specifically, the segmented form of (3.8b) is reformulated as a linear form relying on the block coordinate descent (BCD) technique. Then, fixing the computing setting, we optimize the MUD matrix and reflecting beamforming vector alternately. Finally, we develop two efficient algorithms based on semi-definite relaxation (SDR) and successive convex approximation (SCA) techniques to obtain a locally optimal solution of $\boldsymbol{\theta}$, respectively.

3.2.2 Proposed Solutions for RIS-Aided Cell-Free MEC

In this section, we first divide problem (3.8) into two independent subproblems relying on the BCD technique. Specifically, given $\mathbf{W}$ and $\boldsymbol{\theta}$, the offloading data size $\boldsymbol{\ell}$ and edge computing resource $\mathbf{f}^e$ are optimized. Then, based on the obtained $\boldsymbol{\ell}$ and $\mathbf{f}^e$, the MUD matrix $\mathbf{W}$ and reflecting beamforming vector $\boldsymbol{\theta}$ are optimized. The above procedure is repeated until convergence.

3.2.2.1 Jointly Optimizing $\boldsymbol{\ell}$ and $\mathbf{f}^e$ for Given $\mathbf{W}$ and $\boldsymbol{\theta}$

For given $\mathbf{W}$ and $\boldsymbol{\theta}$, problem (3.8) can be reformulated as follows

$$\min_{\boldsymbol{\ell},\mathbf{f}^e,t} t \tag{3.9a}$$

$$\text{s.t. } D_k\left(\ell_k, f_k^e\right) \leq t, \forall k \in \mathcal{K}, \tag{3.9b}$$

$$\ell_k \in \{0, 1, \ldots, L_k\}, \forall k \in \mathcal{K}, \tag{3.9c}$$

$$\sum\nolimits_{k=1}^{K} f_k^e \leq f_{\text{total}}^e, \tag{3.9d}$$

$$f_k^e \geq 0, \quad \forall k \in \mathcal{K}. \tag{3.9e}$$

Based on the following Proposition 3.1, we optimize the offloading data size $\boldsymbol{\ell}$.

Proposition 3.1 *For given $\mathbf{f}^e$, the optimal offloading data size is given by*

$$\ell_k^* = \mathop{\arg\min}_{\hat{\ell}_k \in \left\{\left\lfloor \hat{\ell}_k^* \right\rfloor, \left\lceil \hat{\ell}_k^* \right\rceil\right\}} D_k\left(\hat{\ell}_k\right), \tag{3.10}$$

where $\lfloor . \rfloor$ and $\lceil . \rceil$ denote the floor and ceiling operations, respectively. Thus, the value of $\hat{\ell}_k^*$ is selected for ensuring that $D_k^l(\hat{\ell}_k) = D_k^e(\hat{\ell}_k)$, i.e.,

$$\hat{\ell}_k^* = \frac{L_k c_k R_k f_k^e}{f_k^e f_k^l + c_k R_k \left(f_k^e + f_k^l\right)}. \tag{3.11}$$

Proof For notational convenience, let $\hat{\ell}_k \in [0, L_k]$ denote the relaxation of integer value $\ell_k \in \{0, 1, \ldots, L_k\}$. In addition, fixing $\mathbf{f}^e$, we denote the overall latency of the k-th WD by $\hat{D}_k\left(\hat{\ell}_k\right) \triangleq \max\left\{D_k^l\left(\hat{\ell}_k\right), D_k^e\left(\hat{\ell}_k\right)\right\}$. Based on (3.6), $\hat{D}_k\left(\hat{\ell}_k\right)$ can be re-expressed as

$$\hat{D}_k\left(\hat{\ell}_k\right) = \begin{cases} \frac{\left(L_k - \hat{\ell}_k\right) c_k}{f_k^l}, & 0 \leq \hat{\ell}_k \leq \frac{L_k c_k R_k f_k^e}{f_k^e f_k^l + c_k R_k \left(f_k^l + f_k^e\right)}, \\ \frac{\hat{\ell}_k}{R_k} + \frac{\hat{\ell}_k c_k}{f_k^e}, & \frac{L_k c_k R_k f_k^e}{f_k^e f_k^l + c_k R_k \left(f_k^l + f_k^e\right)} < \hat{\ell}_k \leq L_k. \end{cases} \tag{3.12}$$

It is obvious that, when $\hat{\ell}_k$ increases from 0 to $\frac{L_k c_k R_k f_k^e}{f_k^e f_k^l + c_k R_k (f_k^l + f_k^e)}$, latency $\hat{D}_k\left(\hat{\ell}_k\right)$ reduces, whereas, when $\hat{\ell}_k$ increases from $\frac{L_k c_k R_k f_k^e}{f_k^e f_k^l + c_k R_k (f_k^l + f_k^e)}$ to L_k, latency $\hat{D}_k\left(\hat{\ell}_k\right)$ increases. Thus, when we set $\hat{\ell}_k = \hat{\ell}_k^* = \frac{L_k c_k R_k f_k^e}{f_k^e f_k^l + c_k R_k (f_k^l + f_k^e)}$, the minimum latency of the k-th WD is achieved. Note that the value of offloading data size has to be a non-negative integer, and thus, we can obtain the optimal ℓ_k after carrying out the operation $\ell_k^* = \underset{\hat{\ell} \in \left\{\left\lfloor \hat{\ell}_k^* \right\rfloor, \left\lceil \hat{\ell}_k^* \right\rceil\right\}}{\arg\min}\ D_k\left(\hat{\ell}_k\right)$. □

After obtaining the relation between offloading data size and edge computing resource, we substitute (3.11) into (3.9b), then problem (3.9) can be written as:

$$\min_{\mathbf{f}^e, t} t \tag{3.13a}$$

$$\text{s.t.}\ \frac{\left(L_k c_k^2 R_k + L_k c_k f_k^e\right)}{f_k^e f_k^l + c_k R_k \left(f_k^e + f_k^l\right)} \le t, \forall k \in \mathcal{K}, \tag{3.13b}$$

$$\sum\nolimits_{k=1}^{K} f_k^e \le f_{\text{total}}^e, \tag{3.13c}$$

$$f_k^e \ge 0, \quad \forall k \in \mathcal{K}. \tag{3.13d}$$

Note that (3.13) is a non-convex problem. To proceed it, we first reformulate (3.13b) as $\left(L_k c_k^2 R_k + L_k c_k f_k^e\right) - t\left(f_k^e f_k^l + c_k R_k \left(f_k^e + f_k^l\right)\right) \le 0$. Then, with the help of a bisection search over t, problem (3.13) can be equivalently transformed into the following feasibility problem, given as

$$\text{Find} : \mathbf{f}^e \tag{3.14a}$$

$$\text{s.t.}\ \left(L_k c_k^2 R_k + L_k c_k f_k^e\right) - t^{l_1}\left(f_k^e f_k^l + c_k R_k \left(f_k^e + f_k^l\right)\right) \le 0, \forall k \in \mathcal{K}, \tag{3.14b}$$

$$\sum\nolimits_{k=1}^{K} f_k^e \le f_{\text{total}}^e, \tag{3.14c}$$

$$f_k^e \ge 0, \quad \forall k \in \mathcal{K}, \tag{3.14d}$$

where t^{l_1} is the value of t at the l_1-th iteration. For a given latency target t^{l_1}, the above optimization problem is convex, and thus the global optimal solution of problem (3.14) can be found via existing convex optimization techniques, e.g., CVX solver.

Note that if problem (3.14) is feasible, the given latency t can be achieved. Assuming that the optimal solution of problem (3.13) is $\hat{t}$, we can infer that, for any given t, if problem (3.14) is feasible, we have $t \ge \hat{t}$, while if problem (3.14) is infeasible, we have $t \le \hat{t}$. Therefore, with the aid of a bisection search

Algorithm 1 Joint optimization scheme for solving problem (3.9)

Input: $\mathbf{h}_k$, B, p_t, σ^2, L_k, c_k, K, f^e_{total}, ϵ_1, $\mathbf{W}$, and $\boldsymbol{\theta}$
Output: Optimal $\boldsymbol{\ell}$ and $\mathbf{f}^e$
1. Initialization
Initialize $l_1 = 0$, calculate R_k according to (3.5), $\forall k \in \mathcal{K}$
2. Joint optimization of t and $\mathbf{f}^e$
repeat:
Calculate $t^{(l_1)}$ using the bisection search method
Solving problem (3.14) to obtain optimal $\mathbf{f}^{e(l_1)}$
Update $l_1 \leftarrow l_1 + 1$
until Convergence
3. Calculate $\{\ell_k\}$ using (3.11), $\forall k \in \mathcal{K}$

over t, problem (3.13) can be equivalently solved by checking the feasibility of problem (3.14) for a given $t \geq 0$.

The procedure for solving problem (3.9) is presented as Algorithm 1.

3.2.2.2 Jointly Optimizing W and $\boldsymbol{\theta}$ for Given $\boldsymbol{\ell}$ and $\mathbf{f}^e$

Given a set of offloading data size $\boldsymbol{\ell}$ and edge computing resource allocation $\mathbf{f}^e$, problem (3.8) can be simplified as

$$\min_{\mathbf{W},\boldsymbol{\theta},t} t \tag{3.15a}$$

$$\text{s.t. } D_k(\mathbf{w}_k, \boldsymbol{\theta}) \leq t, \quad \forall k \in \mathcal{K} \tag{3.15b}$$

$$0 \leq \theta_{i,n} < 2\pi, \quad \forall i \in \mathcal{I}, \forall n \in \mathcal{N}, \tag{3.15c}$$

$$\|\mathbf{w}_k\|^2 \leq 1, \quad \forall k \in \mathcal{K}. \tag{3.15d}$$

The segmented form of $D_k(\mathbf{w}_k, \boldsymbol{\theta})$ makes problem (3.15) difficult to be solved directly. Bearing in mind that the optimal solution of problem (3.7) results in $D_k = D_k^l = D_k^e$ as proved in Proposition 3.1. Hence upon replacing D_k by D_k^e, problem (3.15) can be rewritten as

$$\min_{\mathbf{W},\boldsymbol{\theta},t} t \tag{3.16a}$$

$$\text{s.t. } \frac{\ell_k}{R_k(\mathbf{w}_k, \boldsymbol{\theta})} + \frac{\ell_k c_k}{f_k^e} \leq t, \quad \forall k \in \mathcal{K} \tag{3.16b}$$

$$0 \leq \theta_{i,n} < 2\pi, \quad \forall i \in \mathcal{I}, \forall n \in \mathcal{N}, \tag{3.16c}$$

$$\|\mathbf{w}_k\|^2 \leq 1, \quad \forall k \in \mathcal{K}. \tag{3.16d}$$

Remark 3.1 Solving problem (3.16) involves a joint optimization of MUD matrix $\mathbf{W}$, reflecting beamforming vector $\boldsymbol{\theta}$ and latency t, which is challenging. Next, we develop an alternately iterative optimization algorithm to solve problem (3.16).

Optimization of MUD Matrix W For given reflecting beamforming vector $\boldsymbol{\theta}$, the original problem can be rewritten as

$$\min_{\mathbf{W},t} t \tag{3.17a}$$

$$\text{s.t.} \ \frac{\ell_k}{R_k\left(\mathbf{w}_k, \boldsymbol{\theta}\right)} + \frac{\ell_k c_k}{f_k^e} \leq t, \forall k \in \mathcal{K}, \tag{3.17b}$$

$$\|\mathbf{w}_k\|^2 \leq 1, \quad \forall k \in \mathcal{K}. \tag{3.17c}$$

Since problem (3.17) is still non-convex, we introduce the following feasibility-check problem by fixing t like problem (3.14).

$$\text{Find} \ \{\mathbf{w}_k\} \tag{3.18a}$$

$$\text{s.t.} \ (3.17\text{b}), \ (3.17\text{c}). \tag{3.18b}$$

Assuming that the optimal solution of problem (3.17) is t^*, similar to the analysis in Sect. 3.2.2.1, for any given $t \geq t^*$, t is a feasible solution to problem (3.18). Whereas, if $t \leq t^*$, problem (3.18) is infeasible. Thus, with the aid of a bisection search over $t \geq 0$, problem (3.17) can be solved equivalently by checking the feasibility of problem (3.18).

Next, we investigate how to solve problem (3.18). The inequality in (3.17b) can be rewritten as

$$\begin{aligned} &\left(1+\frac{1}{2^{\frac{\ell_k}{\eta\left(t-t_{c,k}\right)}}-1}\right) P_t \left|\mathbf{w}_k^H \left(\mathbf{h}_{d,k}+\mathbf{G}\boldsymbol{\Theta}\mathbf{h}_{r,k}\right)\right|^2 \\ &\geq P_t \textstyle\sum_{j=1}^K \left|\mathbf{w}_k^H \left(\mathbf{h}_{d,j}+\mathbf{G}\boldsymbol{\Theta}\mathbf{h}_{r,j}\right)\right|^2+\sigma^2, \\ &\qquad \forall k \in \mathcal{K}, \end{aligned} \tag{3.19}$$

where $t_{c,k} = \ell_k c_k / f_k^e$. According to (3.19), it is clear that for any feasible solution $\{\mathbf{w}_k\}$, problem (3.18) is still feasible after any phase rotation. Without loss of optimality, we select a set of $\{\mathbf{w}_k\}$ so that $\mathbf{w}_k^H \left(\mathbf{h}_{d,k} + \mathbf{G}\boldsymbol{\Theta}\mathbf{h}_{r,k}\right)$ is non-negative value for any WDs $k \in \mathcal{K}$. Hence, we have the following constraints:

$$\mathbf{w}_k^H \left(\mathbf{h}_{d,k} + \mathbf{G}\boldsymbol{\Theta}\mathbf{h}_{r,k}\right) \geq 0, \forall k \in \mathcal{K}. \tag{3.20}$$

Let $\text{Re}\,(x)$ and $\text{Im}\,(x)$ denote the real and imaginary parts operation. The real part and imaginary part of $\mathbf{w}_k^H \left(\mathbf{h}_{d,k} + \mathbf{G}\boldsymbol{\Theta}\mathbf{h}_{r,k}\right)$ are non-negative and zero, respectively, i.e., $\text{Re}\left(\mathbf{w}_k^H \left(\mathbf{h}_{d,k} + \mathbf{G}\boldsymbol{\Theta}\mathbf{h}_{r,k}\right)\right) \geq 0$ and $\text{Im}\left(\mathbf{w}_k^H \left(\mathbf{h}_{d,k}+ \ \mathbf{G}\boldsymbol{\Theta}\mathbf{h}_{r,k}\right)\right) = 0$. Then, we define a matrix $\mathbf{A}$, in which the (j,k)-th element is $\sqrt{P_t}\mathbf{w}_k^H\left(\mathbf{h}_{d,j}+\mathbf{G}\boldsymbol{\Theta}\mathbf{h}_{r,j}\right)$. Let $\|.\|_2$ denote the 2-norm of a vector, and thus (3.19) can be reformulated as

$$\sqrt{1+\frac{1}{2^{\frac{\ell_k}{\eta\left(t-t_{c,k}\right)}}-1}}\,\mathbf{w}_k^H\left(\mathbf{h}_{d,k}+\mathbf{G}\boldsymbol{\Theta}\mathbf{h}_{r,k}\right)\geq\left\|\frac{\mathbf{A}^H\mathbf{e}_k}{\sigma_k}\right\|_2,\ \forall k\in\mathcal{K},\tag{3.21}$$

where $\mathbf{e}_k\in\mathbb{C}^{K\times 1}$ represents a vector, in which the k-th element is one and other elements are zero. Hence, for a given t at the l-th iteration, problem (3.18) can be equivalently expressed as

$$\text{Find}:\{\mathbf{w}_k\}\tag{3.22a}$$

$$\text{s.t.}\ \ (3.17\text{c}),\ (3.20),\tag{3.22b}$$

$$\sqrt{1+\frac{1}{2^{\frac{\ell_k}{\eta\left(t^l-t_{c,k}\right)}}-1}}\,\mathbf{w}_k^H\left(\mathbf{h}_{d,k}+\mathbf{G}\boldsymbol{\Theta}\mathbf{h}_{r,k}\right)\geq\left\|\frac{\mathbf{A}^H\mathbf{e}_k}{\sigma_k}\right\|_2,\ \forall k\in\mathcal{K}.\tag{3.22c}$$

It is not difficult to observe that problem (3.22) is an second-order cone programming (SOCP) problem and can be solved using the existing standard convex optimization techniques (i.e., CVX solver) [9].

Optimization of Reflecting Beamforming Vector $\boldsymbol{\theta}$ Different from solving $\mathbf{W}$, the SOCP technique cannot be used to find the optimal $\boldsymbol{\theta}$ since $\boldsymbol{\Theta}$ is common, resulting in $\mathbf{w}_k^H\left(\mathbf{h}_{d,k}+\mathbf{G}\boldsymbol{\Theta}\mathbf{h}_{r,k}\right)$ cannot be ensured to be real numbers for all $k\in\mathcal{K}$.

To proceed, we first define $\mathbf{v}=\left[\beta_1 e^{j\theta_1},\ldots,\beta_{RN}e^{j\theta_{IN}}\right]^T$, $\mathbf{a}_{k,j}=\sqrt{P_t}\,\mathrm{diag}(\mathbf{h}_{r,k}^H)\mathbf{G}^H\mathbf{w}_k$ and $d_{k,j}=\sqrt{P_t}\mathbf{w}_k^H\mathbf{h}_{d,j}$, $\forall k,j\in\mathcal{K}$. Consequently, we have

$$P_t\left|\mathbf{w}_k^H\left(\mathbf{h}_{d,j}+\mathbf{G}\boldsymbol{\Theta}\mathbf{h}_{r,j}\right)\right|^2=\mathbf{v}^H\mathbf{C}_{k,j}\mathbf{v}+2\mathrm{Re}\left\{\mathbf{v}^H\mathbf{u}_{k,j}\right\}+\left|d_{k,j}\right|^2,\tag{3.23}$$

where $\mathbf{C}_{k,j}=\mathbf{a}_{k,j}\mathbf{a}_{k,j}^H$ and $\mathbf{u}_{k,j}=\sqrt{P_t}\mathbf{w}_k^H\mathbf{h}_{d,j}\,\mathrm{diag}\left(\mathbf{h}_{r,j}^H\right)\mathbf{G}^H\mathbf{w}_k$. After obtaining $\mathbf{W}$, problem (3.16) can be reformulated as

$$\min_{\mathbf{v},t}\ t\tag{3.24a}$$

$$\text{s.t.}\ \frac{\mathbf{v}^H\mathbf{C}_{k,k}\mathbf{v}+2\,\mathrm{Re}\left\{\mathbf{v}^H\mathbf{u}_{k,k}\right\}+\left|d_{k,k}\right|^2}{\sum_{j=1,j\neq k}^{K}\left(\mathbf{v}^H\mathbf{C}_{k,j}\mathbf{v}+2\,\mathrm{Re}\left\{\mathbf{v}^H\mathbf{u}_{k,j}\right\}+\left|d_{k,j}\right|^2\right)+\sigma^2}\geq 2^{\frac{\ell_k}{\eta\left(t-\frac{\ell_k c_k}{f_k^e}\right)}}-1,\ \forall k\in\mathcal{K},\tag{3.24b}$$

$$\left|v_n\right|^2=1,\ n=1,2,\ldots,IN.\tag{3.24c}$$

problem (3.24) is still difficult to be solved directly due to non-convex constraints (3.24b) and (3.24c). Next, we develop two effective schemes based on SDR and SCA techniques to solve it.

To solve problem (3.24), we first reformulate it as

$$\min_{\overline{\mathbf{v}},t} t \tag{3.25a}$$

$$\text{s.t.} \ \frac{\overline{\mathbf{v}}^H \mathbf{R}_{k,k} \overline{\mathbf{v}} + \left|d_{k,k}\right|^2}{\sum_{j=1,j\neq k}^{K} \left(\overline{\mathbf{v}}^H \mathbf{R}_{k,j} \overline{\mathbf{v}} + \left|d_{k,j}\right|^2\right) + \sigma^2} \geq \alpha_k\left(t\right), \forall k \in \mathcal{K}, \tag{3.25b}$$

$$|\bar{v}_n| = 1, n = 1, 2, \ldots, IN + 1, \tag{3.25c}$$

where $\alpha_k\left(t\right) = 2^{\frac{\ell_k}{\eta\left(t - \frac{\ell_k c_k}{f_k^e}\right)}} - 1$, $\mathbf{R}_{k,j}$ and $\overline{\mathbf{v}}$ are defined as

$$\mathbf{R}_{k,j} = \begin{bmatrix} \mathbf{C}_{k,j} & \mathbf{u}_{k,j} \\ \mathbf{u}_{k,j}^H & 0 \end{bmatrix} \text{ and } \overline{\mathbf{v}} = \begin{bmatrix} \mathbf{v} \\ 1 \end{bmatrix}, \tag{3.25}$$

respectively. Define $\mathbf{V} = \overline{\mathbf{v}}\overline{\mathbf{v}}^H$, which needs to satisfy $\mathbf{V} \succeq 0$ and $\text{rank}(\mathbf{V}) = 1$. Accordingly, problem (3.25) can be re-expressed as

$$\min_{\mathbf{V},t} t \tag{3.27a}$$

$$\text{s.t.} \ \frac{\text{Tr}\left(\mathbf{R}_{k,k}\mathbf{V}\right) + \left|d_{k,k}\right|^2}{\sum_{j=1,j\neq k}^{K} \left(\text{Tr}\left(\mathbf{R}_{k,j}\mathbf{V}\right) + \left|d_{k,j}\right|^2\right) + \sigma_k^2} \geq \alpha_k\left(t\right), \forall k \in \mathcal{K}, \tag{3.27b}$$

$$\mathbf{V}_{n,n} = 1, \quad n = 1, \ldots, IN + 1, \tag{3.27c}$$

$$\mathbf{V} \succeq 0, \tag{3.27d}$$

$$\text{rank}(\mathbf{V}) = 1, \tag{3.27e}$$

where $\text{Tr}(\cdot)$ represents the trace operation. Problem (3.27) is non-convex due to the rank-one constraint. To proceed it, we relax this rank-one constraint and solve problem (3.27) by solving the following feasibility problem based on the above analysis, with a bisection search over t, which is formulated as

$$\text{Find: } \mathbf{V} \tag{3.28a}$$

$$\text{s.t. } \text{Tr}\left(\mathbf{R}_{k,k}\mathbf{V}\right) + \left|d_{k,k}\right|^2 \geq \alpha_k\left(t^{l_2}\right)$$

$$\times\left(\sum_{j\neq k, j\in\mathcal{K}}\left(\mathrm{Tr}\left(\mathbf{R}_{k,j}\mathbf{V}\right)+\left|d_{k,j}\right|^2\right)+\sigma_k^2\right), \forall k\in\mathcal{K} \tag{3.28b}$$

$$\mathbf{V}_{n,n}=1, n=1,\ldots,IN+1 \tag{3.28c}$$

$$\mathbf{V}\succeq 0, \tag{3.28d}$$

where t^{l_2} is the value of t at the l_2-th iteration. It is obvious that problem (3.28) is a classical SDR problem, and the optimal solution can be found by CVX solver. However, the SDR may not be tight for problem (3.27). In this case, we can use the Gaussian randomization technique [10] to obtain a feasible solution to problem (3.27).

In summary, we solve problem (3.16) by alternately solving problem (3.22) and (3.28), and the detailed procedure is presented in Algorithm 2. For each iteration, problem (3.22) is first solved based on obtained $\boldsymbol{\theta}$ at the previous iteration, and then problem (3.28) is solved based on obtained $\mathbf{W}$ in step 3. We start from solving problem (3.22) instead of solving problem (3.28) because problem (3.22) is always feasible under any given $\boldsymbol{\theta}$, but the reverse may not be true. Furthermore, the rigorous proof of convergence is provided in Proposition 3.2.

Proposition 3.2 *The OF of problem (3.16) is monotonically non-increasing based on the proposed Algorithm 2.*

Proof We define the value of OF in $\mathcal{P}3.1$ based on a set of solutions $(\mathbf{W},\boldsymbol{\theta})$ as $t=g(\mathbf{W},\boldsymbol{\theta})=\max_{k\in\mathcal{K}}D_k^e(\mathbf{W},\boldsymbol{\theta})$. At the (l_2)-th iteration, if $\mathcal{P}3.8$ is feasible, the solution $\left(\mathbf{W}^{(l_2)},\boldsymbol{\theta}^{(l_2+1)}\right)$ is also a feasible solution to problem $\mathcal{P}3.4$. Denote $\left(\mathbf{W}^{(l_2)},\boldsymbol{\theta}^{(l_2)}\right)$ and $\left(\mathbf{W}^{(l_2+1)},\boldsymbol{\theta}^{(l_2+1)}\right)$ as the optimal solutions to $\mathcal{P}3.4$ at the (l_2)-th and (l_2+1)-th iteration, respectively. Since $\mathbf{W}^{(l_2+1)}$ is the optimal solution of $\mathcal{P}3.4$, then, we have $g\left(\mathbf{W}^{(l_2+1)},\boldsymbol{\theta}^{(l_2+1)}\right)\le g\left(\mathbf{W}^{l_2},\boldsymbol{\theta}^{(l_2+1)}\right)$. As a result, we have the following inequality $g\left(\mathbf{W}^{(l_2+1)},\boldsymbol{\theta}^{(l_2+1)}\right)\le g\left(\mathbf{W}^{l_2},\boldsymbol{\theta}^{(l_2+1)}\right)\le g\left(\mathbf{W}^{l_2},\boldsymbol{\theta}^{l_2}\right)$. □

Remark 3.2 When the solution of problem (3.28) is not rank-one, we need to reconstruct a rank-one solution by leveraging the Gaussian randomization procedure. Therefore, the performance of the reconstructed solution critically depends on the generated Gaussian randomization number. For example, due to the uncertainty in randomizations, we may find a highly suboptimal solution to problem (3.24), which will lead to a compromised performance. In addition, to find a better solution, we need to generate a large number of Gaussian randomizations. Besides, solving the SDR problem is time-consuming, especially when the matrix dimension is large. Therefore, in order to reduce the computational complexity and guarantee performance, we need to further develop an efficient algorithm.

Algorithm 2 Joint optimization of t, $\mathbf{W}$, and $\boldsymbol{\theta}$ with SDR

Input: $l_2 = 0$, $\boldsymbol{\theta}^{(0)}$ and accuracy threshold $\epsilon_2 > 0$.
1: **repeat**:
2: Under given $\left(t^{(l_2)}, \boldsymbol{\theta}^{(l_2)}\right)$, solving problem (3.22) to obtain $t^\star$ and $\mathbf{W}^\star$, and set $t^{*(l_2)} = t^\star$, $\mathbf{W}^{(l_2)} = \mathbf{W}^\star$
3: Under given $\left(t^{*(l_2)}, \mathbf{W}^{(l_2)}\right)$, solving problem (3.28) to obtain $t^\star$ and $\boldsymbol{\theta}^\star$, and set $t^{(l_2+1)} = t^\star$, $\boldsymbol{\theta}^{(l_2+1)} = \boldsymbol{\theta}^\star$
4: Update $l_2 \leftarrow l_2 + 1$
5: **until** Convergence

To overcome the drawbacks of the SDR technique, we propose an efficient scheme to update the reflecting beamforming vector $\mathbf{v}$ based on the SCA technique. Instead of solving problem (3.24) directly, we try to find a feasible solution $\mathbf{v}$ to reduce the maximum edge computing latency. Particularly, for a specific iteration $l \geq 1$, we first define $\mathbf{v}^{(l-1)}$ as the value of $\mathbf{v}$ obtained at the previous iteration. Then, for given $\left(\left\{\mathbf{w}_k^l\right\}, \mathbf{v}^{(l-1)}\right)$, the achieved maximum WD edge computing latency is denoted by $t^{(l)} = \max_{k\in\mathcal{K}} D_k^e\left(\left\{\mathbf{w}_k^l\right\}, \mathbf{v}^{(l-1)}\right)$.

Firstly, according to (3.24b), we introduce an auxiliary function $\mathcal{F}_k$, which is defined as

$$\mathcal{F}_k\left(\mathbf{v}, \{\mathbf{w}_k\}, t\right) = \alpha_k(t)\left[\sum_{j\neq k, j\in\mathcal{K}}\left(\mathbf{v}^H\mathbf{C}_{k,j}\mathbf{v} + 2\operatorname{Re}\left\{\mathbf{v}^H\mathbf{u}_{k,j}\right\} + \left|d_{k,j}\right|^2\right) + \sigma_k^2\right] - \left(\mathbf{v}^H\mathbf{C}_{k,k}\mathbf{v} + 2\operatorname{Re}\left\{\mathbf{v}^H\mathbf{u}_{k,k}\right\} + \left|d_{k,k}\right|^2\right), \forall k \in \mathcal{K}. \tag{3.29}$$

If $(\mathbf{v}, \{\mathbf{w}_k\}, t)$ is a set of feasible solutions to problem (3.24), we have $\mathcal{F}_k \leq 0$, $\forall k \in \mathcal{K}$. After solving problem (3.17) at each iteration, the maximum $\mathcal{F}_k$ at WDs is equal to 0, i.e., $\max_{k\in\mathcal{K}}\mathcal{F}_k\left(\mathbf{v}^{(l-1)}, \left\{\mathbf{w}_k^{(l)}\right\}, t^{(l)}\right) = 0$. Consequently, the reflecting beamforming vector can be updated by equivalently solving the following optimization problem

$$\min_{\mathbf{v}} \max_{k\in\mathcal{K}} \mathcal{F}_k\left(\mathbf{v}, \left\{\mathbf{w}_k^{(l)}\right\}, t^{(l)}\right) \quad \text{s.t. (3.24c)}. \tag{3.30}$$

When $\max_{k\in\mathcal{K}}\mathcal{F}\left(\mathbf{v}^{(l)}, \left\{\mathbf{w}_k^{(l)}\right\}, t^{(l)}\right) < 0$, it can be easily proved that $\max_{k\in\mathcal{K}} D_k^e\left(\mathbf{v}^{(l)}, \left\{\mathbf{w}_k^{(l)}\right\}\right) < \max_{k\in\mathcal{K}} D_k^e\left(\mathbf{v}^{(l-1)}, \left\{\mathbf{w}_k^{(l)}\right\}\right)$, i.e., the maximum edge computing latency is reduced. Thus, problem (3.24) can be equivalently solved by solving problem (3.30). Next, we investigate how to solve problem (3.30).

Since the OF of problem (3.30) is non-convex, it is difficult to solve problem (3.30) directly. Inspired by the SCA technique, we first obtain a convex upper bound on $\mathcal{F}_k$ by approximating the second convex term based on its first-order Taylor expansion. Therefore, under given $t^{(l)}$, $\left\{\mathbf{w}_k^{(l)}\right\}$, and local point $\mathbf{v}^{(l-1)}$, the lower bounded of $\mathcal{F}_k$ is

$$\begin{aligned}
&\mathcal{F}_k\left(\mathbf{v},\left\{\mathbf{w}_k^{(l)}\right\},t^{(l)}\right)\\
&\quad\le \alpha_k\left(t^{(l)}\right)\left[\sum_{j\neq k,j\in\mathcal{K}}\left(\mathbf{v}^H\mathbf{C}_{k,j}\mathbf{v}+2\,\mathrm{Re}\left\{\mathbf{v}^H\mathbf{u}_{k,j}\right\}+\left|d_{k,j}\right|^2\right)+\sigma_k^2\right]\\
&\quad-\left(\mathbf{v}^{(l-1)^H}\mathbf{C}_{k,k}\mathbf{v}^{(l-1)}+2\,\mathrm{Re}\left\{\mathbf{v}^{(l-1)^H}\mathbf{u}_{k,k}\right\}+\left|d_{k,k}\right|^2\right)\\
&\quad-2\left(\mathbf{C}_{k,k}^H\mathbf{v}^{(l-1)}+\mathbf{u}_{k,k}\right)^H\left(\mathbf{v}-\mathbf{v}^{(l-1)}\right)\\
&\triangleq \mathcal{F}_k^{\mathrm{up}}\left(\mathbf{v},\left\{\mathbf{w}_k^{(l)}\right\},t^{(l)},\mathbf{v}^{(l-1)}\right).
\end{aligned}\tag{3.31}$$

Next, we replace $\mathcal{F}_k\left(\mathbf{v},\left\{\mathbf{w}_k^{(l)}\right\},t^{(l)}\right)$ by $\mathcal{F}_k^{\mathrm{up}}\left(\mathbf{v},\left\{\mathbf{w}_k^{(l)}\right\},t^{(l)},\mathbf{v}^{(l-1)}\right)$ and introduce another auxiliary variable z, problem (3.30) can be approximated as

$$\min_{\mathbf{v},z}\ z \tag{3.32a}$$

$$\text{s.t. } \mathcal{F}_k^{\mathrm{up}}\left(\mathbf{v},\left\{\mathbf{w}_k^{(l)}\right\},t^{(l)},\mathbf{v}^{(l-1)}\right)\le z,\ \forall k\in\mathcal{K}, \tag{3.32b}$$

$$(3.24\text{c}). \tag{3.32c}$$

So far, we have transformed problem (3.30) into a convex form, which can be solved by existing convex optimization solvers such as CVX [9]. Suppose that $\mathbf{v}^*$ is the optimal solution to problem (3.32). By substituting ($\mathbf{v}^*$, $\left\{\mathbf{w}_k^{(l)}\right\}$, $t^{(l)}$) into problem (3.30), it is observed that the feasible solution of problem (3.32) is still feasible to problem (3.30), and thus solving problem (3.32) can achieve a smaller value than solving problem (3.30). The details of the SCA-based algorithm are presented in Algorithm 3.

Algorithm 3 Joint optimization of t, $\mathbf{W}$ and $\boldsymbol{\theta}$ with SCA

Input: Initialize the phase shift vector $\mathbf{v}^{(0)}$, set $l_3 = 1$ and accuracy threshold $\epsilon_3 > 0$.
1: **repeat**:
2: Under given $\left(t^{(l_3-1)},\mathbf{v}^{(l_3-1)}\right)$, solve $\mathcal{P}3.4$ to obtain $t^\star$ and $\mathbf{W}^\star$, and set $t^{(l_3)} = t^\star$, $\mathbf{W}^{(l_3)} = \mathbf{W}^\star$
3: Under given $\left(t^{(l_3)},\mathbf{W}^{(l_3)}\right)$, solve $\mathcal{P}3.10$ to update $\mathbf{v}$, and set $\mathbf{v}^{l_3} = \mathbf{v}^\star$
4: Update $l_3 \leftarrow l_3 + 1$
5: **until** Convergence

Algorithm 4 Joint Optimization of $\boldsymbol{\ell}$, $\mathbf{f}^e$, $\mathbf{W}$ and $\boldsymbol{\theta}$

Input: $\mathbf{h}_k$, B, p_t, σ^2, L_k, c_k, K, f^e_{total}, ϵ_4, and maximum number of iterations $l_4^{\max}$.
Output: Optimal $\boldsymbol{\ell}$, $\mathbf{f}^e$, $\mathbf{W}$ and $\boldsymbol{\theta}$
1. Initialization
Initialize $l_4 = 1$, $\epsilon_4^{(0)} \geq 0$
Initialize $\mathbf{W}^{(0)}$ satisfying (3.7f), $\boldsymbol{\theta}^{(0)}$ satisfying (3.7b), and calculate R_k according to (3.5), $\forall k \in \mathcal{K}$
2. Joint optimization of t, $\boldsymbol{\ell}$ and $\mathbf{f}^e$, given $\mathbf{R}^{(l_4-1)}$
Calculate $\mathbf{f}^{e(l_4)}$ and $\boldsymbol{\ell}^{(l_4)}$ and update t relying on Algorithm 1
3. Joint optimization of t, $\mathbf{W}$ and $\boldsymbol{\theta}$, given $\boldsymbol{\ell}^{(l_4)}$ and $\mathbf{f}^{e(l_4)}$
Calculate $\mathbf{W}^{(l_4)}$ and $\boldsymbol{\theta}^{(l_4)}$ and update t relying on the Algorithm 2 or Algorithm 3
4. Convergence checking
$$\epsilon_4^{(l_4)} = \frac{\left|\text{obj}\left(\boldsymbol{\ell}^{(l_4)}, \mathbf{f}^{e(l_4)}, \mathbf{w}^{(l_4)}, \boldsymbol{\theta}^{(l_4)}\right) - \text{obj}\left(\boldsymbol{\ell}^{(l_4-1)}, \mathbf{f}^{e(l_4-1)}, \mathbf{w}^{(l_4-1)}, \boldsymbol{\theta}^{(l_4-1)}\right)\right|}{\text{obj}\left(\boldsymbol{\ell}^{(l_4)}, \mathbf{f}^{e(l_4)}, \mathbf{w}^{(l_4)}, \boldsymbol{\theta}^{(l_4)}\right)}$$
if $\epsilon_4^{(l_4)} > \epsilon_4$ && $l_4 < l_4^{\max}$ hold **then**
  Calculate $\mathbf{R}^{(l_4)}$ using (3.5)
  $l_4 \leftarrow l_4 + 1$
  Go to Step 2
else
  Output $\boldsymbol{\ell}$, $\mathbf{f}^e$, $\mathbf{W}$ and $\boldsymbol{\theta}$
end if

3.2.2.3 Overall Algorithm to Solve Problem (3.8)

In Algorithm 4, we provide the details of the BCD-based algorithm for solving problem (3.8). It is worth noting that the auxiliary variable t, which is also the OF of problem (3.8), is constantly updated with the implementation of steps 2 and 3. Let $g\left(\boldsymbol{\ell}^{(l_4-1)}, \mathbf{f}^{e(l_4-1)}, \mathbf{W}^{(l_4-1)}, \boldsymbol{\theta}^{(l_4-1)}\right)$ and $g\left(\boldsymbol{\ell}^{(l_4)}, \mathbf{f}^{e(l_4)}, \mathbf{W}^{(l_4-1)}, \boldsymbol{\theta}^{(l_4-1)}\right)$ denote the value of t after implementing step 3 at the (l_4-1)-th iteration, and the value of t after implementing step 2 at the l_4-th iteration, respectively. It follows that $g\left(\boldsymbol{\ell}^{(l_4-1)}, \mathbf{f}^{e(l_4-1)}, \mathbf{W}^{(l_4-1)}, \boldsymbol{\theta}^{(l_4-1)}\right) \leq g\left(\boldsymbol{\ell}^{(l_4)}, \mathbf{f}^{e(l_4)}, \mathbf{W}^{(l_4-1)}, \boldsymbol{\theta}^{(l_4-1)}\right)$, this is due to that in step 2, $t = g\left(\boldsymbol{\ell}^{(l_4)}, \mathbf{f}^{e(l_4)}, \mathbf{W}^{(l_4-1)}, \boldsymbol{\theta}^{(l_4-1)}\right)$ can be regarded as the overall maximum WD latency, while in step 3, $t = g\left(\boldsymbol{\ell}^{(l_4)}, \mathbf{f}^{e(l_4)}, \mathbf{W}^{(l_4)}, \boldsymbol{\theta}^{(l_4)}\right)$ refers to the maximum WD latency for edge computing. However, the convergence of Algorithm 4 can be guaranteed due to the WD overall latency and WD edge processing latency are both reduced at different iterations. Hence, we have $g\left(\boldsymbol{\ell}^{(l_4)}, \mathbf{f}^{e(l_4)}, \mathbf{W}^{(l_4)}, \boldsymbol{\theta}^{(l_4)}\right) \leq g\left(\boldsymbol{\ell}^{(l_4-1)}, \mathbf{f}^{e(l_4-1)}, \mathbf{W}^{(l_4-1)}, \boldsymbol{\theta}^{(l_4-1)}\right) \leq g\left(\boldsymbol{\ell}^{(l_4)}, \mathbf{f}^{e(l_4)}, \mathbf{W}^{(l_4-1)}, \boldsymbol{\theta}^{(l_4-1)}\right)$. The termination condition is given by $\epsilon_4^{(l_4)} < \epsilon_4$ or $l_4 > l_4^{\max}$.

To further describe the proposed algorithm, a flowchart is provided in Fig. 3.3. As the flowchart shows, we first introduce auxiliary variable t to transform problem (7) into problem (8), which is difficult to be directly solved. To proceed, we decouple problem (8) into two subproblems relying on the BCD technique. Specifically, in the

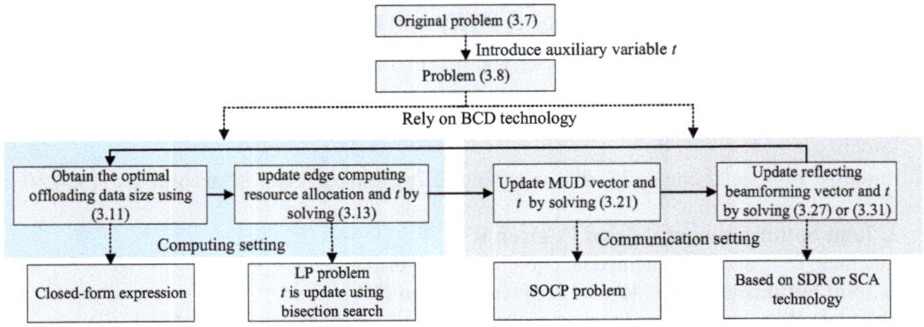

Fig. 3.3 The flowchart of the proposed iterative optimization algorithm

first subproblem, we optimize the offloading data size and edge computing resource with fixed communication setting, while in the second subproblem, we optimize the MUD vector based on SOCP technology and the reflecting beamforming vector based on BCD and SCA technology with fixed computing setting. Note that auxiliary variable t is constantly updated at each step using the bisection search method.

3.2.3 The Single WD Scenario

To further investigate the beneficial role of RIS in the cell-free MEC system, we consider a single WD scenario in this section. Compared with the multi-WD scenario, the single-WD scenario is more tractable. This is because a) the min-max latency optimization problem (3.7) becomes a simple latency minimization problem, which is more tractable, b) there is no involved computing resource allocation, c) there is no multi-WD interference. Thus, the overall latency is reformulated as

$$D(\mathbf{w}, \boldsymbol{\theta}, \ell) = \max \left\{ \frac{(L-\ell)c}{f^l}, \frac{\ell}{R(\mathbf{w}, \boldsymbol{\theta})} + \frac{\ell c}{f^e_{\text{total}}} \right\}. \tag{3.33}$$

On this basis, problem (3.7) is simplified to

$$\min_{\ell, \mathbf{w}, \boldsymbol{\theta}} D(\mathbf{w}, \boldsymbol{\theta}, \ell) \tag{3.34a}$$

$$\text{s.t. } 0 \le \theta_n < 2\pi, \quad n = 1, 2, \ldots, IN, \tag{3.34b}$$

$$\ell \in \{0, 1, \ldots, L\}, \tag{3.34c}$$

$$\|\mathbf{w}\|^2 \le 1. \tag{3.34d}$$

Like Proposition 3.1, fixing $\mathbf{w}$ and $\boldsymbol{\theta}$, $D(\mathbf{w}, \boldsymbol{\theta}, \ell)$ reaches its minimum threshold when ℓ is chosen to ensure that local computing latency is equivalent to edge computing latency, i.e., $\frac{(L-\ell)c}{f^l} = \frac{\ell}{R(\mathbf{w},\boldsymbol{\theta})} + \frac{\ell c}{f^e_{\text{total}}}$. Thus, the optimal offloading data size is given by

$$\hat{\ell}^* = \frac{LcRf^e_{\text{total}}}{f^e_{\text{total}} f^l + cR\left(f^e_{\text{total}} + f^l\right)}. \tag{3.35}$$

Based on obtaining ℓ, problem (3.34) can be equivalently transformed into

$$\min_{\mathbf{w},\boldsymbol{\theta}} \frac{\ell}{R(\mathbf{w}, \boldsymbol{\theta})} + \frac{\ell c}{f^e_{\text{total}}} \tag{3.36a}$$

$$\text{s.t. } 0 \leq \theta_n < 2\pi, \quad n = 1, 2, \ldots, IN, \tag{3.36b}$$

$$\|\mathbf{w}\|^2 \leq 1. \tag{3.36c}$$

Based on (3.4) and (3.5), problem (3.36) can be simplified to

$$\max_{\mathbf{w},\boldsymbol{\theta}} \frac{P_t \left|\mathbf{w}^H \left(\mathbf{h}_d + \mathbf{G}\boldsymbol{\Theta}\mathbf{h}_r\right)\right|^2}{\sigma^2 \left\|\mathbf{w}^H\right\|^2} \tag{3.37a}$$

$$\text{s.t. } 0 \leq \theta_n < 2\pi, \quad n = 1, 2, \ldots, IN. \tag{3.37b}$$

$$\|\mathbf{w}\|^2 \leq 1. \tag{3.37c}$$

Next, we jointly optimize $\mathbf{w}$ and $\boldsymbol{\theta}$ by using the BCD technique. Specifically, fixing $\boldsymbol{\theta}$, the maximum ratio combining technique can be applied to find optimal $\mathbf{w}$, which is formulated as

$$\mathbf{w} = \sqrt{P_t}\left(\mathbf{h}_d + \mathbf{G}\boldsymbol{\Theta}\mathbf{h}_r\right)/\sigma. \tag{3.38}$$

Then, after obtaining $\mathbf{w}$, we optimize the reflecting beamforming vector $\boldsymbol{\theta}$. The SINR is upper bounded by

$$\frac{P_t \left|\mathbf{w}^H \left(\mathbf{h}_d + \mathbf{G}\boldsymbol{\Theta}\mathbf{h}_r\right)\right|^2}{\sigma^2 \left\|\mathbf{w}^H\right\|^2} \leq \frac{P_t \left|\mathbf{w}^H \mathbf{h}_d\right|^2}{\sigma^2 \left\|\mathbf{w}^H\right\|^2} + \frac{P_t \left|\mathbf{w}^H \mathbf{G}\boldsymbol{\Theta}\mathbf{h}_r\right|^2}{\sigma^2 \left\|\mathbf{w}^H\right\|^2}, \tag{3.39}$$

The equality in (3.39) is achieved when $\boldsymbol{\theta}$ satisfies $\arg\left\{\mathbf{w}^H\mathbf{h}_d\right\} = \arg\left\{\mathbf{w}^H\mathbf{G}\boldsymbol{\Theta}\mathbf{h}_r\right\}$. Thus, the optimal $\boldsymbol{\theta}$ is given by

$$\boldsymbol{\theta} = \arg\left\{\mathbf{w}^H\mathbf{h}_d\right\} - \arg\left\{\text{diag}\left\{\mathbf{w}^H G\right\}\mathbf{h}_r\right\}. \tag{3.40}$$

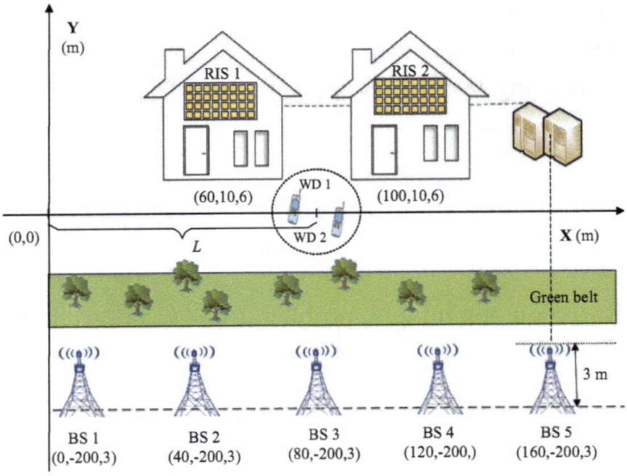

Fig. 3.4 The simulation scenario where two WDs offload data to five BSs with the assistance of two RISs

Table 3.1 Default simulation parameter setting

Description	Parameter and value
Location model	BS: (40(i − 1) m, −200 m, 3 m), RIS: (60 m, 10 m, 6 m), (100 m, 10 m, 6 m)
Communication model	Bandwidth=1 MHz, $\kappa_{UB} = 4.6$, $\kappa_{UI} = 2.2$, $\kappa_{IB} = 2.8$, $K = 2R = 2$, $B = 5$, $M = 2$, $N = 10$, $P_t = 1$ mW, $\sigma^2 = 3.98 \times 10^{-12}$ mW
Computing model	$L_k = [250, 350]$ Kb, $c_k = [700, 800]$ cycle/bit $f_k^l = [4, 6] \times 10^8$ cycle/s, $f_{total}^e = 50 \times 10^9$ cycle/s

3.2.4 Performance Evaluation

In this section, we evaluate the performance of the proposed algorithms by simulation [11]. Similar to [12], we consider a three-dimensional system model, which is presented in Fig. 3.4. Five BSs simultaneously serve two WDs, and WDs can choose to offload a portion of the computing data to MEC nodes for remote execution with the help of two RISs. It is worth noting that the RISs are usually installed on the transmitter and receiver side to fully exploited the benefit of RIS. The detailed location settings for BSs and RISs are given by [13] and provided in the "Location model" block of Table 3.1.

The distance-dependent path loss model is given by [14]

$$L(d) = C_0 \left(\frac{d}{d_0} \right)^{-\kappa}, \tag{3.41}$$

where $C_0 = -30$ dB refers to the path loss at a reference distance $d_0 = 1$m, d stands for the individual channel distance, κ denotes the path loss exponent. The specific setting of "Communication model" is given by [6] and presented in Table 3.1. Then, for the small-scale fading, we consider a Rician fading channel model for all involved channels. Thus, the channel model **H** is given by

$$\mathbf{H} = \sqrt{\frac{\beta_{\text{UB}}}{1+\beta_{\text{UB}}}}\mathbf{H}^{\text{LoS}} + \sqrt{\frac{1}{1+\beta_{\text{UB}}}}\mathbf{H}^{\text{NLoS}}, \tag{3.42}$$

where β_{UB} refers to the Rician factor, $\mathbf{H}^{\text{LoS}}$ and $\mathbf{H}^{\text{NLoS}}$ denote the line of sight (LoS) deterministic components and the non-LOS Rayleigh fading components, respectively. **H** is equivalent to a Rayleigh fading channel when $\beta_{\text{UB}} = 0$ and a LoS channel when $\beta_{\text{UB}} \to \infty$. Note that for the WD-BS channel model, we need to multiply the square root of the large-scale fading coefficient by the elements of the small scale fading coefficient. Similarly, the WD-RIS and RIS-BS channels can also be generated by following the above procedure with β_{UI} and β_{IB} denoting the Rician factors of them. Furthermore, we set $\beta_{IB} \to \infty$, $\beta_{UI} \to \infty$, and $\beta_{UB} = 0$ as [14]. The default settings of these parameters are specified in the "Communications model" block of Table 3.1. Besides, the computing settings follow [6], and are specified in the "Computing model" block of Table 3.1.

In the following, we provide simulation results to evaluate the maximum WD's latency achieved by our proposed BCD-based algorithm in various simulation environments, and compare them with the following baseline algorithms:

- *Without RIS:* The reflection matrix $\boldsymbol{\Theta}$ is set to a zero matrix, while the other optimization variables are optimized using Algorithm 4.
- *Without direct link:* Assume that all direct links between WDs and BSs are completely blocked by some moving or static object, i.e., $\mathbf{H} = 0$, then, we optimize all variables using Algorithm 4.
- *Random phase shift:* The RIS phase shift is set as a uniformly distributed random value in the range of $[0, 2\pi)$, while other optimization variables are optimized as Algorithm 4.

Figures 3.5, 3.6, 3.7, 3.8, and 3.9 show the latency under different parameter settings.

1. Impact of WDs Locations Figure 3.5 shows the latency achieved under different algorithms/schemes versus WDs' locations. It is observed that, compared to baseline algorithms, our proposed two algorithms can achieve a lower latency, especially when WDs are close to RISs. Besides, for all considered schemes with RIS, there are two obvious valleys at $L = 60$ m and $L = 100$ m. This is because RISs can receive stronger signals transmitted from WDs when WDs approach either of two RISs. Additionally, we observe that the latency increases when WDs are far away from BSs under the "Without RIS" scheme. Compared to "Without RIS" scheme, the reduced latency by the "Random phase shift" scheme is very limited. Furthermore, it is observed that "Without direct link" scheme achieves the highest latency, and the latency gap is larger than that of the proposed schemes when WDs approach one of two RISs. Therefore, we conclude that deploying RISs with optimized phase shift

Fig. 3.5 Maximum latency against the distance

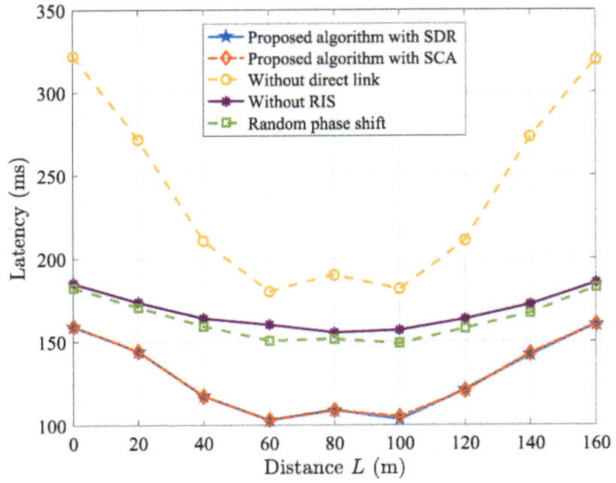

Fig. 3.6 Maximum latency against the edge computing capability

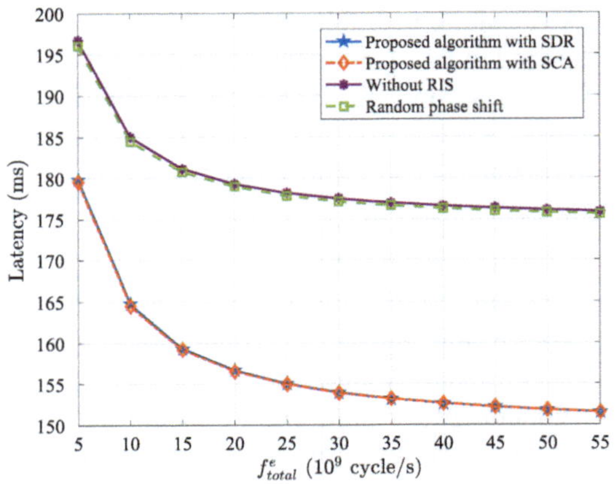

Fig. 3.7 Maximum latency against the number of iterations

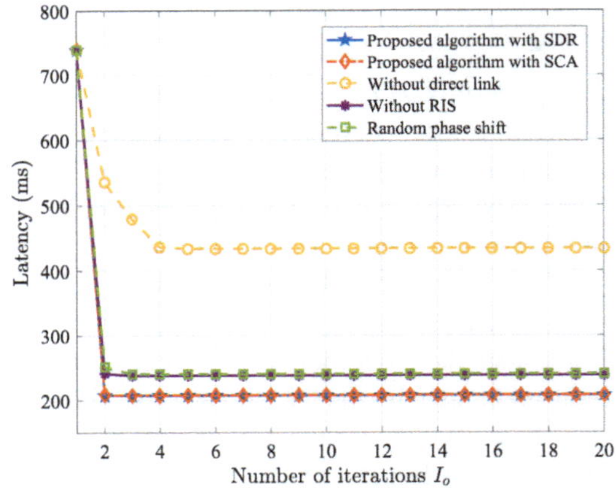

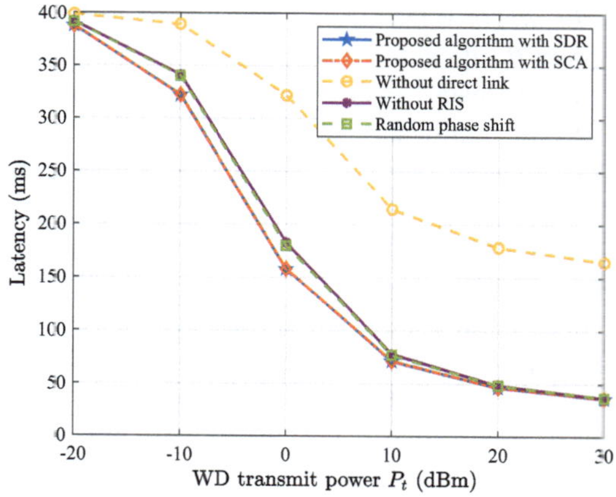

Fig. 3.8 Maximum latency against the WD transmit power

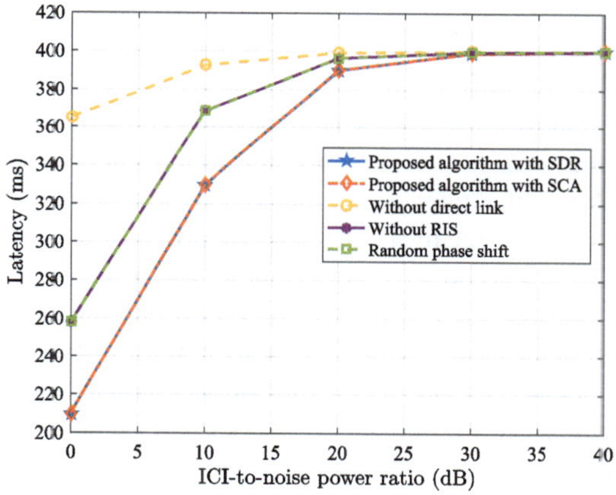

Fig. 3.9 Maximum latency against the ICI-to-noise ratio

design can extend the signal coverage, improve signal transmission environment, and reduce latency.

2. Impact of Edge Computing Capability Figure 3.6 shows the latency versus the edge computing capability f_{total}^{e} under different schemes. It is observed that, for all schemes, when f_{total}^{e} is small, the latency reduces drastically with the increase of f_{total}^{e}, while the latency reduces slowly when f_{total}^{e} reaches a certain value, i.e., 30×10^9 cycle/s. This is because when f_{total}^{e} is small, the edge processing latency plays a dominant role, while when f_{total}^{e} becomes large, the offloading latency dominates. This indicates that, to minimize latency, adding appropriate computing capability at edge server is cost-effective.

3. Convergence To show the convergency of the proposed algorithms, we present the latency against the number of iterations I_o in Fig. 3.7. It is observed that all the considered algorithms enjoy a fast convergence, which verifies its practical implementation.

4. Impact of WD Transmit Power Figure 3.8 shows the latency versus WD transmit power P_t. It can be readily observed that, for all schemes, the increase of transmit power P_t leads to a decrease in latency. Moreover, the reduced latency by employing RISs is significant when WD transmit power is moderate. To elaborate, when WD transmit power is low (i.e. -20 dBm), the signals reflected by RISs are so weak that the contribution of employing RISs is limited. In addition, the reduced latency by employing RISs is also negligible when the transmit power is high (i.e., 20 dBm), and this is because the WD-BS link is dominant for high transmit power. Additionally, it can be observed that as the transmit power increases, the latency gap between "Without direct link" scheme and "Without RIS" scheme becomes large. Here, "Without direct link" scheme means that BSs only receive signal transmitted from the WD-RIS-BS links, while "Without RIS" means that BSs only receive signals transmitted from the WD-BS links [14]. This implies that, compared to "Without direct link" scheme, the "Without RIS" scheme can achieve a lower latency. In this case, the BSs will tend to design sophisticated MUD matrix to receive more power from the WD-BS links, which weakens the role of RISs.

5. Impact of Inter-Cell Interference It is worth pointing out that the inter-cell interference (ICI) also affects computing offloading in realistic scenarios. Figure 3.9 shows the latency versus ICI-to-noise power ratio, where the BS is assumed to know the received interference power but not the specific signal transmitted from other cells. It is observed that, when the ICI-to-noise power ratio is small, upon increasing ICI-to-noise power ratio, the latency increases. Whereas, when the ICI-to-noise power ratio reaches a certain threshold, (i.e., 30 dB), the latency remains unchanged. This is because that, increasing the ICI-to-noise power ratio, WDs will choose to offload less data for edge computing, and when the ICI-to-noise power ratio reaches a certain threshold, all data computing will be performed locally. Therefore, to fully exploite the potential of RISs and improve the network capacity, the inter-cell interference need to be eliminated. Thus, this also demonstrates the necessity of BSs collaboration.

3.3 RIS-Aided MEC with Practical Phase Shift Model

3.3.1 System Model and Problem Formulation

In this section, we first introduce the system model, including phase shift model, uplink task offloading model, downlink energy transfer model, and computing model. Then, we formulate the computing rate maximization problem under several practical constraints.

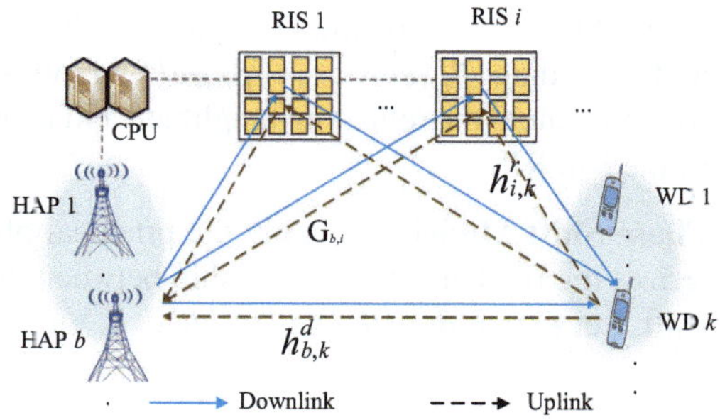

Fig. 3.10 RIS-aided WP-MEC networks

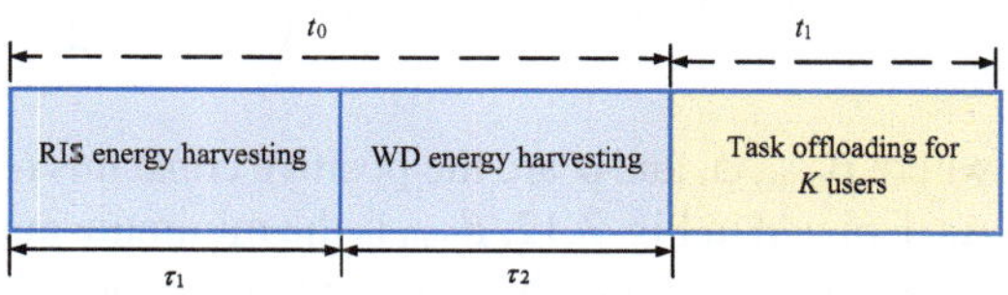

Fig. 3.11 An illustration of the harvest-then-computing protocol

3.3.1.1 System Model

As illustrated in Fig. 3.10, we consider an RIS-assisted wireless powered mobile edge computing (WP-MEC) network, which comprises of B distributed hybrid access point (HAP) indexed by $\mathcal{B} \in \{1, \ldots, B\}$, I RISs indexed by $\mathcal{I} \in \{1, \ldots, I\}$, and K energy-constrained WDs indexed by $\mathcal{K} \in \{1, \ldots, K\}$. Each HAP is equipped with an edge server and all HAPs are interconnected to CPU through reliable backhaul links. Similar to [15–17], we assume that RISs and WDs do not have any embedded energy supply available, and they need to collect the energy from the HAPs. After harvesting energy, RISs can assist the downlink energy transfer and uplink task offloading, and WDs can process its computing task by local computing and task offloading. As shown in Fig. 3.11, we adopt the "harvest-then-computing" mechanism [16, 18], and the system operates in a two-phase manner in each time block T, which is assumed to be no larger than the tolerant latency of computing task. The number of antennas at the b-th HAP, and the number of reflecting elements at the i-th RIS are M_b and N_i, respectively. For convenience, we set M_b and N_i equal to M and N for all $b \in \mathcal{B}$ and $i \in \mathcal{I}$, respectively.

The channel coefficients from the b-th HAP to the k-th WD, from the b-th HAP to the i-th RIS, and from the i-th RIS to the k-th WD are denoted by $\mathbf{h}_{b,k}^{d} \in \mathbb{C}^{M\times 1}$, $\mathbf{G}_{b,i} \in \mathbb{C}^{M\times N}$ and $\mathbf{h}_{i,k}^{r} \in \mathbb{C}^{N\times 1}$, respectively. Without loss of generality, we assume that all channels remain constant over each time block, and the CSI can be perfectly obtained by HAPs via the advanced channel estimation technique proposed in [19]. The results with perfect CSI as a theoretical performance upper bound for the practical system. The equivalent channel $\mathbf{h}_{b,k} \in \mathbb{C}^{M\times 1}$ from the b-th HAP to the k-th WD can be expressed as

$$\mathbf{h}_{b,k} = \mathbf{h}_{b,k}^{d} + \sum_{i=1}^{I} \mathbf{G}_{b,i}\boldsymbol{\Theta}_i\mathbf{h}_{i,k}^{r}, \tag{3.43}$$

where $\boldsymbol{\Theta}_i \in \mathbb{C}^{N\times N}$ denotes the phase shift matrix at the i-th RIS, which is defined as $\boldsymbol{\Theta}_i \triangleq \text{diag}\left(\beta_{i,1}e^{j\theta_{i,1}}, \ldots, \beta_{i,N}e^{j\theta_{i,N}}\right), \forall i \in \mathcal{I}$, where $\beta_{i,n} \in [0, 1]$ and $\theta_{i,n} \in [0, 2\pi)$ denote the reflecting amplitude and phase shift at the n-th reflecting element of the i-th RIS.

Phase Shift Model We apply the practical phase shift model here, and it characterizes the fundamental relationship between the reflecting amplitude and the phase shift. Let $v_{i,n} = \beta_{i,n}\left(\theta_{i,n}\right)e^{j\theta_{i,n}}, \forall i \in \mathcal{I}, \forall n \in \mathcal{N}$, $\beta_{i,n}\left(\theta_{i,n}\right)$ is given by [20]

$$\beta_{i,n}\left(\theta_{i,n}\right) = (1-\beta_{\min})\left(\frac{\sin\left(\theta_{i,n}-\phi\right)+1}{2}\right)^{\alpha} + \beta_{\min}, \tag{3.44}$$

where $\beta_{\min}$, ϕ, and α are the positive constants related to the circuit implementation. As depicted in Fig. 3.12, $\beta_{\min}$ is the minimum amplitude, ϕ is the horizontal distance between $-\pi/2$ and the minimum amplitude $\beta_{\min}$, and α controls the steepness of the function curve. Note that $\beta_{\min} = 1$ corresponds to the ideal phase shift model with unit amplitude.

Uplink Task Offloading Model Let $\mathbf{s} = [s_1, s_2, \ldots, s_K]^T$, where s_k denotes the transmit signal of the k-th WD and $\mathbb{E}\left\{\mathbf{s}\mathbf{s}^H\right\} = \mathbf{I}_K$. Thus, the received signal at the b-th HAP for the k-th WD can be expressed as

$$\hat{s}_{b,k} = \mathbf{u}_{b,k}^H\left[\sqrt{P_k}\sum_{j=1}^{K}\mathbf{h}_{b,j}s_j + \mathbf{n}_b\right], \tag{3.45}$$

where $\mathbf{u}_{b,k}$ denotes the MUD vector for the k-th WD, P_k is the transmit power of the k-th WD, and $\mathbf{n}_b = \left[n_{b,1}, n_{b,2}, \ldots, n_{b,M}\right]^T$ is the received noise vector of the b-th HAP where we assume $n_{b,m} \sim \mathcal{CN}\left(0, \sigma^2\right)$ for all $b \in \mathcal{B}$, and $m \in \mathcal{M}$. Since there are B HAPs serving K WDs simultaneously, the overall recovered signal $\hat{s}_k$

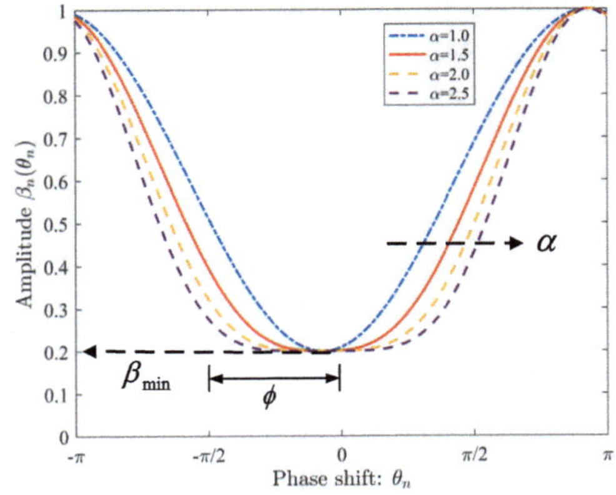

Fig. 3.12 The practical phase shift model with different parameters

for the k-th WD can be formulated as

$$\begin{aligned}\hat{s}_k &= \sum_{b=1}^{B} \mathbf{u}_{b,k}^H \left[\sum_{j=1}^{K} \sqrt{P_k} \left(\mathbf{h}_{b,j}^d + \sum_{i=1}^{I} \mathbf{G}_{b,i} \boldsymbol{\Theta}_i \mathbf{h}_{i,j}^r \right) s_j + \mathbf{n}_b \right] \\ &\overset{(a)}{=} \mathbf{u}_k^H \left[\sum_{j=1}^{K} \sqrt{P_k} \left(\mathbf{h}_j^d + \sum_{i=1}^{I} \mathbf{G}_i \boldsymbol{\Theta}_i \mathbf{h}_{i,j}^r \right) s_j + \mathbf{n} \right] \\ &\overset{(b)}{=} \mathbf{u}_k^H \left[\sum_{j=1}^{K} \sqrt{P_k} \left(\mathbf{h}_j^d + \mathbf{G} \boldsymbol{\Theta} \mathbf{h}_j^r \right) s_j + \mathbf{n} \right] \\ &\overset{(c)}{=} \mathbf{u}_k^H \left[\sum_{j=1}^{K} \sqrt{P_k} \mathbf{h}_j s_j + \mathbf{n} \right],\end{aligned} \tag{3.46}$$

(a) holds by defining $\mathbf{u}_k = \left[\mathbf{u}_{1,k}^T, \ldots, \mathbf{u}_{B,k}^T\right]^T$, $\mathbf{h}_k^d = \left[\mathbf{h}_{1,k}^{d\ T}, \ldots, \mathbf{h}_{B,k}^{d\ T}\right]^T$, $\mathbf{G}_i = \left[\mathbf{G}_{1,i}^T, \ldots, \mathbf{G}_{B,i}^T\right]^T$, and $\mathbf{n} = \left[\mathbf{n}_1^T, \ldots, \mathbf{n}_B^T\right]^T$, (b) holds by defining $\mathbf{G} = \left[\mathbf{G}_1^T, \ldots, \mathbf{G}_I^T\right]^T$, $\boldsymbol{\Theta} = \mathrm{diag}\left(\boldsymbol{\Theta}_1, \ldots, \boldsymbol{\Theta}_I\right)$, and $\mathbf{h}_k^r = \left[\mathbf{h}_{1,k}^{r\ T}, \ldots, \mathbf{h}_{I,k}^{r\ T}\right]^T$, and (c) holds according to $\mathbf{h}_k = \mathbf{h}_k^d + \mathbf{G}\boldsymbol{\Theta}\mathbf{h}_k^r$. Thus, the SINR of the k-th WD can be expressed as

$$\gamma_k(\mathbf{P}, \mathbf{U}, \boldsymbol{\Theta}) = \frac{P_k \left|\mathbf{u}_k^H \left(\mathbf{h}_k^d + \mathbf{G}\boldsymbol{\Theta}\mathbf{h}_k^r\right)\right|^2}{\sum_{j=1, j\neq k}^{K} P_j \left|\mathbf{u}_k^H \left(\mathbf{h}_j^d + \mathbf{G}\boldsymbol{\Theta}\mathbf{h}_j^r\right)\right|^2 + \sigma^2}, \tag{3.47}$$

where $\mathbf{P} = [P_1, \ldots, P_K]$, $\mathbf{U} = \left[\mathbf{u}_1^T, \ldots, \mathbf{u}_K^T\right]^T$. Thereby, the offloading rate of the k-th WD is given by

$$R_k\left(\mathbf{P}, \mathbf{U}, \boldsymbol{\Theta}\right) = \omega \log_2\left(1 + \gamma_k\left(\mathbf{P}, \mathbf{U}, \boldsymbol{\Theta}\right)\right), \tag{3.48}$$

where ω is the bandwidth.

Downlink Energy Transfer Model At the beginning of each time block as shown in Fig. 3.11, HAPs first generate energy beamforming to charge RISs or WDs. We further divide the energy transfer duration t_0 into two sub-slots τ_1 and τ_2, which satisfies $t_0 = \tau_1 + \tau_2$.

In the first sub-slot τ_1, RISs operate in the energy harvesting mode for collecting the radio-frequency energy from HAPs. Note that the harvested direct current power is generally nonlinear with respect to the received radio frequency power. The nonlinear conversion largely depends on the input power level and the transmit waveform and there have been a plethora of recent works on analytic nonlinear energy harvesting (EH) model. However, there is still a lack of a generic EH model that captures all practical issues [21]. Therefore, we consider a linear EH model here, which has been commonly adopted in the WPT literature [22–25]. Let $\mathbf{e} \in \mathbb{C}^{BM\times 1}$ denote the downlink energy-bearing transmit signal, which is assumed as a random signal with its power spectral density satisfying certain regulations on radio-frequency radiation [26]. Let $\mathbf{W} \triangleq \mathbb{E}\left[\mathbf{e}\mathbf{e}^{\boldsymbol{H}}\right] \succeq \mathbf{0}$ denote the energy transmit covariance matrix and the transmit power is given by $\mathbb{E}\left[\|\mathbf{e}\|^2\right] = \text{tr}(\mathbf{W})$. In general, HAPs can apply multiple beams to deliver wireless energy, i.e., $\mathbf{W}$ can be of any rank. Assuming $r = \text{rank}(\mathbf{W}) \leq BM$, then a total of r energy beams can be obtained via the eigenvalue decomposition (EVD) of $\mathbf{W}$ [26]. Since the noise power is much lower than the received power transmitted from HAPs, the energy harvested from the noise can be ignored. Hence, the harvested energy of the i-th RIS can be expressed as

$$E_{RIS}\left(i, \tau_1, \mathbf{W}\right) = \tau_1 \eta \,\text{tr}\left(\mathbf{G}_i' \mathbf{W}\right), \tag{3.49}$$

where η denotes the linear energy conversion efficiency, and $\mathbf{G}_i' \triangleq \mathbf{G}_i \mathbf{G}_i^H$.

In the second sub-slot τ_2, HAPs charge WDs with the help of RISs. Let $\mathbf{x} \in \mathbb{C}^{BM\times 1}$ denote the energy-bearing transmit signal. $\mathbf{Q} \triangleq \mathbb{E}\left[\mathbf{x}\mathbf{x}^{\boldsymbol{H}}\right] \succeq \mathbf{0}$ denotes the energy transmit covariance matrix and the transmit power is given by $\mathbb{E}\left[\|\mathbf{x}\|^2\right] = \text{tr}(\mathbf{Q})$. The energy harvested by the k-th device is given by

$$E_k\left(\tau_2, \mathbf{Q}, \mathbf{v}^E\right) = \tau_2 \eta \,\text{tr}\left(\mathbf{Q}\mathbf{H}_k\right), \tag{3.50}$$

where $\mathbf{H}_k \triangleq \mathbf{h}_k \mathbf{h}_k^H$, and $\mathbf{v}^E = \boldsymbol{\Theta}\mathbf{1}_{IN}$ denotes the RIS passive beamforming at the second energy harvesting sub-slot. Additionally, WDs can also collect the wireless energy at the first sub-slot, but the energy is very weak since HAPs mainly formulate the high gain energy beamforming towards to RISs, thus can be omitted.

Computing Model In the second phase, WDs utilize the harvested energy to perform local computing and task offloading with the duration of t_1, which satisfies $t_1 = T - t_0$.

- Local Computing: Upon denoting the CPU cycles required to process a single bit input data and the computing speed of the k-th WD by c_k and f_k, respectively, we formulate the local computing data size and energy consumption of the k-th WD as [27]

$$D_{k,loc} = \frac{f_k t_1}{c_k}, \tag{3.51a}$$

$$E_{k,loc} = \kappa f_k^2 t_1, \tag{3.51b}$$

where κ is computation energy efficiency coefficient, which depends on the hardware architecture [28, 29].

- Task Offloading: Apart from local computing, WDs can also choose to offload a part of its computing task to the edge server. Combining formula (3.48), the offloading data size can be expressed as

$$D_{k,off} = t_1 R_k \left(\mathbf{P}, \mathbf{U}, \mathbf{v}^I\right), \tag{3.52}$$

where $\mathbf{v}^I = \mathbf{\Theta 1}_{IN}$ is the RIS passive beamforming at the data computing phase. Since the edge server has powerful computing capability compared with WDs and the size of computing result is usually small, thus we ignore the delay of edge computing and result reture as in [30–32].

3.3.1.2 Problem Formulation

We aim to maximize the total computation bits of all WDs by jointly optimizing the downlink/uplink passive beamforming $\left\{\mathbf{v}^E, \mathbf{v}^I\right\}$, downlink energy beamforming $\{\mathbf{W}, \mathbf{Q}\}$, uplink MUD vector $\mathbf{U}$, offloading power $\mathbf{P}$ and local CPU-cycle frequency $\mathbf{f} = [f_1, \ldots, f_K]$ at WDs, and the time slot allocation $\mathbf{t} = [\tau_1, \tau_2, t_1]$, and the joint optimization problem is formulated as

$$\underset{\{\mathbf{x}_0\}}{\text{maximize}} \quad t_1 \sum_{k=1}^{K} \omega \log_2 (1 + \gamma_k) + \sum_{k=1}^{K} \frac{f_k t_1}{C_k} \tag{3.53a}$$

$$\text{s.t. } \tau_1 + \tau_2 + t_1 \le T, \tag{3.53b}$$

$$0 \le f_k \le f_{k,\max}, \forall k \in \mathcal{K}, \tag{3.53c}$$

$$v_{i,n} = \beta_{i,n}\left(\theta_{i,n}\right) e^{J\theta_{i,n}}, \forall i \in \mathcal{I}, \forall n \in \mathcal{N}, \tag{3.53d}$$

$$-\pi \le \theta_{i,n} \le \pi, \forall i \in \mathcal{I}, \forall n \in \mathcal{N}, \tag{3.53e}$$

$$\operatorname{tr}\left(\mathbf{W}\mathbf{D}_b\right) \le P_{\max}, \forall b \in \mathcal{B}, \tag{3.53f}$$

$$\operatorname{tr}\left(\mathbf{Q}\mathbf{D}_b\right) \le P_{\max}, \forall b \in \mathcal{B}, \tag{3.53g}$$

$$\left\|\mathbf{u}_{b,k}\right\|^2 \le 1, \forall b \in \mathcal{B}, \forall k \in \mathcal{K}, \tag{3.53h}$$

$$(T - \tau_1) N\mu \le E_{RIS}\left(i, \tau_1, \mathbf{W}\right), \forall i \in \mathcal{I}, \tag{3.53i}$$

$$t_1 \left[\kappa f_k^2 + (P_k + P_c)\right] \le E_k \left(\tau_2, \mathbf{Q}, \mathbf{v}^E\right), \forall k \in \mathcal{K}, \tag{3.53j}$$

where $\mathbf{D}_b = \mathbf{C}_b \otimes \mathbf{I}_M$, $\mathbf{C}_b \in \mathbb{C}^{B \times B}$ is a matrix with the element at the b-th row and the b-th column being 1, and the other elements being 0s. μ is the power consumption of each RIS reflecting element [33, 34]. $P_{\max}$ and P_c denote the maximum transmit power of each HAP and the constant circuit power. The optimization variables $\{\mathbf{x}_0\} = \left\{\mathbf{W}, \mathbf{Q}, \mathbf{v}^E, \left\{\theta_{i,n}^E\right\}, \mathbf{U}, \mathbf{v}^I, \left\{\theta_{i,n}^I\right\}, \mathbf{P}, \mathbf{f}, \mathbf{t}\right\}$. (3.53b) indicates the time constraint, (3.53c) is the local computing capability constraint, (3.53d) gives the reflecting coefficient constraint of RISs, (3.53e) restricts the range of the phase shift, (3.53f) and (3.53g) represent the downlink transmit power constraints, (3.53h) is the unit-norm detection vector constraint, and (3.53i) and (3.53j) imply that the energy consumption of RISs and WDs should not exceed their harvested energy. It is obvious that problem (3.53) is a nonconvex optimization problem and thus intractable. Next, we propose an effective scheme to deal with it.

3.3.2 *Proposed Algorithm for Optimization Problem*

In the first sub-slot τ_1, HAPs transmit energy beamforming to charge RISs, and then RISs assist the downlink energy transfer in the second sub-slot τ_2 and uplink task offloading in the second phase t_1. From problem (3.53), one can observe that the computing data size increases with t_1, and thus we can decrease τ_1 and increase τ_2/t_1 to enhance the harvested energy by WDs or offloading time so as to increase computation bits. By combining with (3.53i), we can directly obtain the optimal τ_1 for the i-th RIS as

$$\tau_{1,i}^{\star} = \frac{N\mu T}{N\mu + \eta \operatorname{tr}\left(\mathbf{G}_i'\mathbf{W}\right)}, \forall i \in \mathcal{I}. \tag{3.54}$$

To satisfy the energy requirement for each RIS and simultaneously minimize the sub-slot τ_1, we formulate the following optimization problem.

$$\min_{\mathbf{W},\tau_1} \quad \tau_1 \tag{3.55a}$$

$$\text{s.t.} \ \frac{N\mu T}{N\mu + \eta \operatorname{tr}\left(\mathbf{G}_i'\mathbf{W}\right)} \le \tau_1, \forall i \in \mathcal{I}, \tag{3.55b}$$

$$\operatorname{tr}\left(\mathbf{W}\mathbf{D}_b\right) \le P_{\max}, \forall b \in \mathcal{B}, \tag{3.55c}$$

$$\mathbf{W} \succeq \mathbf{0}. \tag{3.55d}$$

It is obvious that problem (3.55) is a non-convex optimization problem, and we reformulate (3.55b) as $N\mu T \le \tau_1 \left(N\mu + \eta \operatorname{tr}\left(\mathbf{G}_i'\mathbf{W}\right)\right)$. Then, with the help of a bisection search over τ_1, problem (3.55) can be equivalently transformed into the following convex optimization problem, given as

$$\text{Find} \quad \mathbf{W} \tag{3.56a}$$

$$\text{s.t.} \ N\mu T \le \tau_1^l \left(N\mu + \eta \operatorname{tr}\left(\mathbf{G}_i'\mathbf{W}\right)\right), \forall i \in \mathcal{I} \tag{3.56b}$$

$$\operatorname{tr}(\mathbf{W}\mathbf{D}_b) \le P_{\max}, \forall b \in \mathcal{B}, \tag{3.56c}$$

$$\mathbf{W} \succeq \mathbf{0}, \tag{3.56d}$$

where τ_1^l is the value of τ_1 at the l-th iteration.

After obtaining the optimal τ_1 and $\mathbf{W}$, the original problem (3.53) can be equivalently transformed into the following problem

$$\underset{\{\mathbf{x}_1\}}{\text{maximize}} \quad t_1 \sum_{k=1}^{K} \omega \log_2(1+\gamma_k) + \sum_{k=1}^{K} \frac{f_k t_1}{C_k} \tag{3.57a}$$

$$\text{s.t. } \tau_2 + t_1 \le T - \tau_1 \tag{3.57b}$$

$$(3.53c)\text{–}(3.53e), (3.53g), (3.53h), (3.53j), \tag{3.57c}$$

where $\{\mathbf{x}_1\} = \left\{\mathbf{Q}, \mathbf{v}^E, \left\{\theta_{i,n}^E\right\}, \mathbf{U}, \mathbf{v}^I, \left\{\theta_{i,n}^I\right\}, \mathbf{P}, \mathbf{f}, \tau_2\right\}$. One can observe that it is still difficult to directly solve problem (3.57). In the rest of this section, we will propose an effective algorithm to solve it.

Note that $\left\{\mathbf{Q}, \mathbf{v}^E, \left\{\theta_{i,n}^E\right\}\right\}$ are related to the WPT setting of the second sub-slot, and $\left\{\mathbf{U}, \mathbf{v}^I, \left\{\theta_{i,n}^I\right\}, \mathbf{P}, \mathbf{f}\right\}$ are related to the computing setting of the second phase. Therefore, if we fix τ_2, problem (3.57) can be divided into the following two independent sub-problems, i.e., problem (3.58) and (3.59).

$$\text{Find} \left\{\mathbf{Q}, \mathbf{v}^E, \left\{\theta_{i,n}^E\right\}\right\} \tag{3.58a}$$

$$\text{s.t. } (3.53d), (3.53e), (3.53g), \tag{3.58b}$$

$$t_1\left[\kappa f_k^2 + (P_k + P_c)\right] \le \tau_2 \eta \operatorname{tr}(\mathbf{Q}\mathbf{H}_k), \forall k \in \mathcal{K}, \tag{3.58c}$$

where $t_1 = T - \tau_1 - \tau_2$.

$$\max_{\{\mathbf{x}_2\}} \quad \sum_{k=1}^{K} \omega \log_2(1+\gamma_k) + \sum_{k=1}^{K} \frac{f_k}{C_k} \tag{3.59a}$$

$$\text{s.t. } (3.53c) - (3.53e), (3.53h), \tag{3.59b}$$

$$t_1\left[\kappa f_k^2 + (P_k + P_c)\right] \le \tau_2 \eta \operatorname{tr}(\mathbf{Q}\mathbf{H}_k), \forall k \in \mathcal{K}, \tag{3.59c}$$

where $\{\mathbf{x}_2\} = \left\{\mathbf{U}, \mathbf{v}^I, \left\{\theta_{i,n}^I\right\}, \mathbf{P}, \mathbf{f}\right\}$.

Here, we need to solve problem (3.58) first and then solve problem (3.59) according to the obtained $\left\{\mathbf{Q}, \mathbf{v}^E, \left\{\theta_{i,n}^E\right\}\right\}$ based on problem (3.58). Meanwhile, we can apply one dimensional search method to obtain the optimal τ_2. Next, we only need to solve problem (3.58) and (3.59) in sequence.

3.3.2.1 Solution of Problem (3.58)

In fact, there may be many feasible solutions for problem (3.58), and it seems difficult to decide which one is the optimal. However, from (3.59c) of problem (3.59), one can observe that a larger $\operatorname{tr}(\mathbf{QH}_k)$ can obtain a larger objective function for problem (3.59). Since $\operatorname{tr}(\mathbf{QH}_k)$ is related to problem (3.58), we can select one of feasible solutions of problem (3.59) that owns the maximum $\operatorname{tr}(\mathbf{QH}_k)$. Based on the above analysis, we can transform problem (3.58) into the following optimization problem as

$$\max_{\mathbf{Q},\mathbf{v}^E,\left\{\theta_{i,n}^E\right\}} \sum_{k=1}^{K} \operatorname{tr}(\mathbf{QH_k}) \tag{3.60a}$$

$$\text{s.t. } (3.53\text{d}), (3.53\text{e}), (3.53\text{g}), \tag{3.60b}$$

$$\mathbf{Q} \succeq \mathbf{0}, \tag{3.60c}$$

$$\operatorname{rank}(\mathbf{Q}) = 1. \tag{3.60d}$$

To facilitate the solution, we transform problem (3.60) to its equivalent problem, by introducing auxiliary variable $\{\zeta_k\}$ as

$$\max_{\mathbf{Q},\mathbf{v}^E,\left\{\theta_{i,n}^E\right\},\{\zeta_k\}} \sum_{k=1}^{K} \zeta_k \tag{3.61a}$$

$$\text{s.t. } (3.53\text{d}), (3.53\text{e}), (3.53\text{g}), (3.60\text{c}), (3.60\text{d}), \tag{3.61b}$$

$$\operatorname{tr}(\mathbf{QH_k}) \geq \zeta_k, \forall k \in \mathcal{K}. \tag{3.61c}$$

Due to the non-convex constraint (3.53d), it is difficult to solve problem (3.61). To proceed it, we propose a penalty-based method by adding a penalty term to the OF, which can be reformulated as

$$\min_{\mathbf{Q},\mathbf{v}^E,\left\{\theta_{i,n}^E\right\},\{\zeta_k\}} -\sum_{k=1}^{K} \zeta_k + \iota_1 \sum_{n=1}^{N} \left| v_{i,n} - \beta_{i,n}\left(\theta_{i,n}\right) e^{J\theta_{i,n}} \right|^2 \tag{3.62a}$$

$$\text{s.t.} (3.53\text{e}), (3.53\text{g}), (3.60\text{c}), (3.60\text{d}), (3.61\text{c}), \tag{3.62b}$$

where $\iota_1 > 0$ is the penalty parameter that imposes a cost for the constraint violation of (3.53d). We propose a two-layer iterative algorithm, where the inner layer solves the penalized optimization problem (3.62) by adopting the BCD method while the outer layer updates ι_1, until the convergence is achieved. Specifically, the optimization variables in problem (3.62) can be partitioned into three blocks, i.e., $\mathbf{Q}$, $\mathbf{v}^E$ and $\left\{\theta_{i,n}^E\right\}$, and each of them is alternately optimized in one iteration with the other two blocks fixed, until the convergence is reached.

Note that the initial value of ι_1 should be set to a sufficiently small number, even though this point may be infeasible for (3.61). We can maximize the OF, i.e., $\sum_{k=1}^K \zeta_k$, by gradually increasing ι_1 by a factor of $\varrho > 1$. When ι_1 is sufficiently large, we can obtain a solution that satisfies all the constraints in (3.61) within a predefined accuracy.

Next, we provide the details for solving problem (3.62).

Optimizing energy transmit covariance matrix $\mathbf{Q}$ while fixing the passive beamforming $\mathbf{v}^E$ and RIS phase shift $\left\{\theta_{i,n}^E\right\}$ For given $\left\{\mathbf{v}^E, \left\{\theta_{i,n}^E\right\}\right\}$, problem (3.61) can be simplified as

$$\max_{\mathbf{Q},\{\zeta_k\}} \sum_{k=1}^K \zeta_k \tag{3.63a}$$

$$\text{s.t. (3.53g), (3.60c), (3.60d), (3.61c).} \tag{3.63b}$$

For the rank-one constraint (3.60d), it is equivalent to $\operatorname{tr}(\mathbf{Q}) - \|\mathbf{Q}\|_2 = 0$ [33], where $\|\mathbf{Q}\|_2$ denotes the spectral norm. For a positive semidefinite matrix $\mathbf{Q}$, there always exists $\operatorname{tr}(\mathbf{Q}) - \|\mathbf{Q}\|_2 \geq 0$, since $\|\mathbf{Q}\|_2$ is the largest singular value while $\operatorname{tr}(\mathbf{Q})$ equals to the sum of all singular value. Thus, $\operatorname{tr}(\mathbf{Q}) - \|\mathbf{Q}\|_2 = 0$ can be transformed into the difference of convex functions as

$$\operatorname{Tr}(\mathbf{Q}) - \|\mathbf{Q}\|_2 \leq 0. \tag{3.64}$$

Then, problem (3.14) can be transformed into

$$\max_{\mathbf{Q},\{\zeta_k\}} \sum_{k=1}^K \zeta_k \tag{3.65a}$$

$$\text{s.t. (3.53g), (3.60c), (3.61c), (3.64).} \tag{3.65b}$$

It is obvious that problem (3.65) is a convex optimization problem, and thus it can be solved by using the standard convex optimization tool.

Optimizing passive beamforming $\mathbf{v}^E$ while fixing energy transmit covariance matrix $\mathbf{Q}$ and RIS phase shift $\left\{\theta_{i,n}^E\right\}$ Firstly, we obtain the energy beamforming vector $\mathbf{x}$ by singular value decomposition (SVD). Then, for convenience, we define $\mathbf{G}\boldsymbol{\Theta}\mathbf{h}_{r,k} = \boldsymbol{\Phi}_k^H \boldsymbol{v}$, $\mathbf{c}_k = \boldsymbol{\Phi}_k\mathbf{x}$, $d_k = \mathbf{h}_{d,k}^H\mathbf{x}$, $\forall k \in \mathcal{K}$, and the left side of constraint

(3.61c) can be rewritten as

$$\operatorname{tr}(\mathbf{QH_k}) = \mathcal{F}_k\left(\mathbf{v}^E\right) = \left(\mathbf{v}^E\right)^H C_k \mathbf{v}^E + 2\operatorname{Re}\left\{\left(\mathbf{v}^E\right)^H \mathbf{u}_k\right\} + |d_k|^2, \tag{3.66a}$$

where $\mathbf{C}_k = \mathbf{c}_k \mathbf{c}_k^H$ and $\mathbf{u}_k = \mathbf{c}_k d_k^H$. Thus, problem (3.62) can be simplified as

$$\min_{\mathbf{v}^E, \{\zeta_k\}} -\sum_{k=1}^{K} \zeta_k + \iota_1 \left\|\mathbf{v}^E - \mathbf{a}^E\right\|^2 \tag{3.67a}$$

$$\text{s.t. } \mathcal{F}_k\left(\mathbf{v}^E\right) \geq \zeta_k, \forall k \in \mathcal{K}, \tag{3.67b}$$

where $\mathbf{a}^E = \left[\beta_{1,1}\left(\theta_{1,1}^E\right) e^{J\theta_{1,1}^E}, \ldots, \beta_{IN}\left(\theta_{IN}^E\right) e^{J\theta_{IN}^E}\right]^T$. For the non-convex constraint (3.67b), we apply the SCA technique to deal with it. The left hand side of (3.67b) is lower bounded by its first-order Taylor expansion at any given point. Thus, at the local point of $\left(\mathbf{v}^E\right)^{(l-1)}$, we have

$$\begin{aligned}
\mathcal{F}_k\left(\mathbf{v}^E\right) \geq & \left(\mathbf{v}^E\right)^{(l-1)^H} \mathbf{C}_k \left(\mathbf{v}^E\right)^{(l-1)} + 2\operatorname{Re}\left\{\left(\mathbf{v}^E\right)^{(l-1)^H} \mathbf{u}_k\right\} + |d_k|^2 \\
& + 2\left(\mathbf{C}_k^H \left(\mathbf{v}^E\right)^{(l-1)} + \mathbf{u}_k\right)^H \left(\left(\mathbf{v}^E\right) - \left(\mathbf{v}^E\right)^{(l-1)}\right) \\
& \triangleq \mathcal{F}_k^{\text{low}}\left(\mathbf{v}^E, \left(\mathbf{v}^E\right)^{(l-1)}\right).
\end{aligned} \tag{3.68}$$

Problem (3.67) can be transformed into

$$\min_{\mathbf{v}^E, \{\zeta_k\}} -\sum_{k=1}^{K} \zeta_k + \iota_1 \left\|\mathbf{v}^E - \mathbf{a}^E\right\|^2 \tag{3.69a}$$

$$\text{s.t. } \left|v_{i,n}^E\right| \leq 1, \forall i \in \mathcal{I}, \forall n \in \mathcal{N}, \tag{3.69b}$$

$$\mathcal{F}_k^{\text{low}}\left(\mathbf{v}^E, \left(\mathbf{v}^E\right)^{(l-1)}\right) \geq \zeta_k, \forall k \in \mathcal{K}. \tag{3.69c}$$

A locally optimal solution can be approached by successively updating $\left(\mathbf{v}^E\right)^{(l-1)}$ based on the solution obtained from the previous iteration, until the objective value converges.

Optimizing RIS phase shift $\left\{\theta_{i,n}^{E}\right\}$ while fixing energy transmit covariance matrix $\mathbf{Q}$ and passive beamforming $\mathbf{v}^{E}$ For given $\mathbf{v}^{E}$, problem (3.62) can be simplified as

$$\min_{\left\{\theta_{i,n}^{E}\right\}} \sum_{i=1}^{I}\sum_{n=1}^{N} \left|v_{i,n}^{E} - \beta_{i,n}\left(\theta_{i,n}^{E}\right) e^{\jmath\theta_{i,n}^{E}}\right|^{2} \tag{3.70a}$$

$$\text{s.t.} \; -\pi \leq \theta_{i,n} \leq \pi, \forall i \in \mathcal{I}, \forall n \in \mathcal{N}. \tag{3.70b}$$

Due to the fact that $\left\{\theta_{i,n}\right\}$ are fully separable in the OF, the solutions of $\left\{\theta_{i,n}\right\}$ can be obtained by independently solving IN subproblems. By expanding $\left|v_{i,n} - \beta_{i,n}\left(\theta_{i,n}\right) e^{\jmath\theta_{i,n}}\right|^{2}$ and omitting the constant terms, each subproblem can be formulated as

$$\max_{\theta_{i,n}} 2\beta_{i,n}\left(\theta_{i,n}\right)\left|v_{i,n}\right| \cos\left(\psi_{i,n} - \theta_{i,n}\right) - \beta_{i,n}^{2}\left(\theta_{i,n}\right) \tag{3.71a}$$

$$\text{s.t.(3.70b)}, \tag{3.71b}$$

where $\psi_{i,n} = \arg\left(v_{i,n}\right)$. As described in [20], the whole function is maximized when $\theta_{i,n}$ slightly deviates away from ψ_{n}. The trust region that encloses the optimal value of $\theta_{i,n}$ is given by [20]

$$\theta_{i,n}^{*} \in \begin{cases} \left[\psi_{i,n}, \psi_{i,n} + (-1)^{\lambda}\Delta\right] & \text{if } \frac{\beta_{i,n}(\psi_{i,n}) + \beta_{i,n}(\psi_{i,n}+\Delta)}{2} < \left|v_{i,n}\right|, \\ \left[\psi_{i,n}, \psi_{i,n} - (-1)^{\lambda}\Delta\right] & \text{if } \frac{\beta_{i,n}(\psi_{i,n}) + \beta_{i,n}(\psi_{i,n}-\Delta)}{2} > \left|v_{i,n}\right|, \end{cases} \tag{3.72}$$

where $\Delta \geq 0$, and $\lambda = 0$ when $\psi_{i,n} \geq 0$ and $\lambda = 1$ otherwise.

An accurate approximate solution can be obtained via the one-dimensional search over the trust region, but it is computationally unaffordable. To address this issue, a closed-form approximate solution to (3.71) can be similarly obtained by fitting a quadratic function through three points over the trust region, i.e., $\theta_{A} = \varphi_{n}, \theta_{B} = \frac{2\varphi_{n} \pm (-1)^{\lambda}\Delta}{2}$, and $\theta_{C} = \varphi_{n} \pm (-1)^{\lambda}\Delta$. Let $f_{1} = f\left(\theta_{A}\right), f_{2} = f\left(\theta_{B}\right)$, and $f_{3} = f\left(\theta_{C}\right)$. Then, we have

$$\hat{\theta}_{n}^{*} = \frac{\theta_{A}\left(f_{1} - 4f_{2} + 3f_{3}\right) + \theta_{C}\left(3f_{1} - 4f_{2} + f_{3}\right)}{4\left(f_{1} - 2f_{2} + f_{3}\right)}. \tag{3.73}$$

Up to now, we finish the solution of problem (3.58) by the proposed AO.

3.3.2.2 Solution of Problem (3.59)

In this subsection, we aim to solve problem (3.59) based on the obtained $\mathbf{Q}$ and $\mathbf{v}^E$ at the above subsection.

To deal with the non-convex sum-logarithms in (3.59a), we propose a method to decouple the logarithms based on the Lagrangian dual reformulation (LDR) technique [35]. Following this, problem (3.59) can be transformed to its equivalent problem, by introducing an auxiliary variable $\boldsymbol{\rho} = [\rho_1, \rho_2, \cdots, \rho_K]^T$ as follows

$$\max_{\mathbf{U},\mathbf{v}^I,\mathbf{P},\mathbf{f},\boldsymbol{\rho}} \; g\left(\mathbf{U}, \mathbf{v}^I, \mathbf{P}, \mathbf{f}, \boldsymbol{\rho}\right) \tag{3.74a}$$

$$\text{s.t. } (3.53\text{c})\text{–}(3.53\text{e}), (3.53\text{h}), (3.53\text{j}), \tag{3.74b}$$

where $g\left(\mathbf{U}, \mathbf{v}^I, \mathbf{P}, \mathbf{f}, \boldsymbol{\rho}\right)$ is given by

$$\begin{aligned} g(\mathbf{U}, \mathbf{v}^I, \mathbf{P}, \mathbf{f}, \boldsymbol{\rho}) = &\sum_{k=1}^{K} \omega \ln(1+\rho_k) - \sum_{k=1}^{K} \omega \rho_k \\ &+ \sum_{k=1}^{K} (1+\rho_k)\, \omega g_k(\mathbf{U}, \mathbf{v}^I, \mathbf{P}) + \sum_{k=1}^{K} \frac{f_k}{C_k}, \end{aligned} \tag{3.75}$$

$g_k(\mathbf{U}, \mathbf{v}^I, \mathbf{P})$ is defined as

$$g_k(\mathbf{U}, \mathbf{v}^I, \mathbf{P}) = P_k \mathbf{h}_k^H \mathbf{u}_k \left(\sum_{j=1}^{K} P_j \mathbf{u}_k^H \mathbf{h}_j \left(\mathbf{u}_k^H \mathbf{h}_j\right)^H + \Xi_{k,p} \right)^{-1} \mathbf{u}_k^H \mathbf{h}_k. \tag{3.76}$$

Similar to problem (3.62), by introducing equality constraint (3.53d) as a penalty term to the OF, problem (3.74) can be converted to the corresponding augmented Lagrangian (AL) problem, which is given by

$$\max_{\mathbf{U},\mathbf{v}^I,\mathbf{P},\mathbf{f},\boldsymbol{\rho}} \; g\left(\mathbf{U}, \mathbf{v}^I, \mathbf{P}, \mathbf{f}, \boldsymbol{\rho}\right) - \iota_2 \left\| \mathbf{v}^I - \mathbf{a}^I \right\|^2 \tag{3.77a}$$

$$\text{s.t.} (3.53\text{c}), (3.53\text{e}), (3.53\text{h}), (3.53\text{j}), \tag{3.77b}$$

where $\mathbf{a}^I = \left[\beta_{1,1}\left(\theta_{1,1}\right) e^{J\theta_{1,1}}, \ldots, \beta_{I,N}\left(\theta_{I,N}\right) e^{J\theta_{I,N}}\right]^T$. We propose a two-layer iterative algorithm to solve problem (3.77), where the inner layer solves the penalized optimization problem (3.77) by the BCD method while the outer layer updates ι_2 by a factor of $\varrho > 1$, until the convergence is achieved. Next, the AO scheme is still applied to solve problem (3.77).

Optimizing $\boldsymbol{\rho}$ with Fixed $\left(\mathbf{U}, \mathbf{v}^I, \mathbf{P}, \mathbf{f}\right)$ Given a feasible solution of $\left(\mathbf{U}^\star, \mathbf{v}^{I\star}, \mathbf{P}^\star, \mathbf{f}^\star\right)$, the optimal $\boldsymbol{\rho}$ can be obtained by setting $\partial g/\partial \rho_k = 0$ for $\forall k \in \mathcal{K}$ and given by

$$\rho_k^{\text{opt}} = \gamma_k^\star, \quad \forall k \in \mathcal{K}. \tag{3.78}$$

Note that once $\boldsymbol{\rho}$ is decided, the objective value in (3.77) is only related to the last two terms of g and the penalty term, i.e., $\sum_{k=1}^{K}(1+\rho_k)\,\omega g_k(\mathbf{U}, \mathbf{v}^I, \mathbf{P}) + \sum_{k=1}^{K}\frac{f_k}{C_k} - \iota_2\left\|\mathbf{v}^I - \mathbf{a}^I\right\|^2$. For the MUD vector and passive beamforming design, the objective value is only related to the third term of g and the penalty term, i.e., $\sum_{k=1}^{K}(1+\rho_k)\,g_k(\mathbf{U}, \mathbf{v}^I, \mathbf{P}) - \iota_2\left\|\mathbf{v}^I - \mathbf{a}^I\right\|^2$.

Optimizing U with Fixed $\left(\mathbf{v}^I, \mathbf{P}, \mathbf{f}, \boldsymbol{\rho}\right)$ Given fixed $\left(\mathbf{v}^{I\star}, \mathbf{P}^\star, \mathbf{f}^\star, \boldsymbol{\rho}^\star\right)$, the subproblem of MUD vector design at HAPs can be rewritten as

$$\max_{\mathbf{U}} \overline{g}_1(\mathbf{U}) = \sum_{k=1}^{K} \mu_k g_k\left(\mathbf{U}, \mathbf{v}^{I\star}, \mathbf{P}^\star\right) \tag{3.79a}$$

$$\text{s.t.} \ \left\|\mathbf{u}_{b,k}\right\|^2 \le 1, \forall b \in \mathcal{B}, \forall k \in \mathcal{K}, \tag{3.79b}$$

where $\mu_k = \left(1 + \rho_k^\star\right) \times \omega$. Since the OF in (3.79) is a high-dimensional sum-of-fractions, the non-convexity of g_k cannot be relaxed by common fractional programming (FP) methods. To work around this non-convex high-dimensional "fractions" problem, we can adopt a method called *multidimensional complex quadratic transform (MCQT)* [35]. By introducing auxiliary variables $\boldsymbol{\xi} = [\xi_1, \xi_2, \ldots, \xi_K]$, problem (3.79) can be rewritten as

$$\max_{\mathbf{U},\boldsymbol{\xi}} \overline{g}_2(\mathbf{U}, \boldsymbol{\xi}) \tag{3.80a}$$

$$\text{s.t.} \ \left\|\mathbf{u}_{b,k}\right\|^2 \le 1, \forall b \in \mathcal{B}, \forall k \in \mathcal{K}, \tag{3.80b}$$

where

$$\begin{aligned}\overline{g}_2(\mathbf{U}, \boldsymbol{\xi}) = &\sum_{k=1}^{K} 2\sqrt{\mu_k P_k}\,\Re\left\{\xi_k^H \mathbf{u}_k^H \mathbf{h}_k\right\} \\ &- \sum_{k=1}^{K} \xi_k^H \left(\sum_{j=1}^{K} P_j \mathbf{u}_k^H \mathbf{h}_j \left(\mathbf{u}_k^H \mathbf{h}_j\right)^H + \Xi_k\right) \xi_k.\end{aligned} \tag{3.81}$$

$\mathbf{U}$ and $\boldsymbol{\xi}$ can be updated alternately. Problem (3.80) can be further divided into the following two independent subproblems.

Fix **U** *and Solve* $\boldsymbol{\xi}$ By setting $\partial \overline{g}_2/\partial \xi_k = 0$, for $\forall k \in \mathcal{K}$, the optimal $\boldsymbol{\xi}$ is given by

$$\xi_k^{\text{opt}} = \sqrt{\mu_k P_k} \left(\sum_{j=1}^{K} P_j \mathbf{u}_k^H \mathbf{h}_j \left(\mathbf{u}_k^H \mathbf{h}_j \right)^H + \Xi_k \right)^{-1} \mathbf{u}_k^H \mathbf{h}_k, \forall k \in \mathcal{K}. \tag{3.82}$$

Fix $\boldsymbol{\xi}$ *and Solve* **U** For convenience, we first define

$$\begin{aligned} &\mathbf{a}_k = \boldsymbol{\xi}_k^H \left(\sum_{j=1}^{K} P_j \mathbf{h}_j \mathbf{h}_j^H \right) \boldsymbol{\xi}_k, \\ &\mathbf{A}_k = \text{diag}(\mathbf{a}_1, \ldots, \mathbf{a}_K), \quad \mathbf{v}_k = \sqrt{\mu_k P_k} \mathbf{h}_k^H \boldsymbol{\xi}_k, \\ &\mathbf{V} = [\mathbf{v}_1, \mathbf{v}_2, \ldots, \mathbf{v}_K]^T, \quad Y = \sum_{k=1}^{K} \boldsymbol{\xi}_k^H \Xi_k \boldsymbol{\xi}_k. \end{aligned} \tag{3.83}$$

Then, problem (3.80) can be simplified as

$$\max_{\{\mathbf{U}\}} \quad \overline{g}_2(\mathbf{U}) = -\mathbf{U}^H \mathbf{A} \mathbf{U} + \Re\{2\mathbf{V}\mathbf{U}\} - Y, \tag{3.84a}$$

$$\text{s.t. } \mathbf{U}^H \mathbf{O}_{b,k} \mathbf{U} \le 1, \forall k \in \mathcal{K}, \tag{3.84b}$$

where $\mathbf{O}_{b,k} = \mathbf{J}_{b,k} \otimes \mathbf{I}_M$, $\mathbf{J} \in \mathbb{C}^{BK \times BK}$ is a matrix whose $((k-1) \times B + b)$-th row and $((k-1) \times B + b)$-th column is 1, and other elements are 0s. Since matrix $\mathbf{A}$ and $\mathbf{O}_{b,k}$ are all positive semidefinite, problem (3.84) is a standard quadratically constrained quadratic program (QCQP) problem, which can be solved by existing CVX tools.

Optimizing $\mathbf{v}^I$ with fixed $(\mathbf{U}, \mathbf{P}, \mathbf{f}, \boldsymbol{\rho})$ Based on the given $(\mathbf{U}^\star, \mathbf{P}^\star, \mathbf{f}^\star, \boldsymbol{\rho}^\star)$, problem (3.77) can be reformulated as the following one

$$\max_{\mathbf{v}^I, \left\{\theta_{i,n}^I\right\}} \quad \overline{g}_3(\mathbf{v}^I, \left\{\theta_{i,n}^I\right\}) \tag{3.85a}$$

$$\text{s.t. } v_{i,n} = \beta_{i,n}\left(\theta_{i,n}\right) e^{\jmath \theta_{i,n}}, \forall i \in \mathcal{I}, \forall n \in \mathcal{N}, \tag{3.85b}$$

$$-\pi \le \theta_{i,n} \le \pi, \forall i \in \mathcal{I}, \forall n \in \mathcal{N}, \tag{3.85c}$$

where

$$\overline{g}_3(\mathbf{v}^I, \left\{\theta_{i,n}^I\right\}) = \sum_{k=1}^{K} \mu_k g_k \left(\mathbf{v}^I, \mathbf{U}^\star, \mathbf{P}^\star\right) - \iota_2 \left\| \mathbf{v}^I - \mathbf{a}^I \right\|^2. \tag{3.86}$$

Next, we define a new auxiliary function with respect to $\mathbf{v}^I$ as

$$\mathbf{F}_{k,j}(\mathbf{v}^I) = \sqrt{P_j}\mathbf{u}_k^H\left(\mathbf{h}_j^d+\mathbf{G}\boldsymbol{\Theta}^I\mathbf{h}_j^r\right). \tag{3.87}$$

Similar to problem (3.79), by introducing an auxiliary variable $\boldsymbol{\varpi} = [\varpi_1, \varpi_2, \cdots, \varpi_K]$, problem (3.85) can be equivalently rewritten as

$$\max_{\mathbf{v}^I,\left\{\theta_{i,n}^I\right\},\boldsymbol{\varpi}} \overline{g}_4(\mathbf{v}^I, \boldsymbol{\varpi})=\sum_{k=1}^{K}\hat{g}_k(\mathbf{v}^I, \boldsymbol{\varpi})-\iota_2\left\|\mathbf{v}^I-\mathbf{a}^I\right\|^2 \tag{3.88a}$$

$$\text{s.t. } v_{i,n} = \beta_{i,n}\left(\theta_{i,n}\right)e^{\jmath\theta_{i,n}}, \forall i \in \mathcal{I}, \forall n \in \mathcal{N}, \tag{3.88b}$$

$$-\pi \leq \theta_{i,n} \leq \pi, \forall i \in \mathcal{I}, \forall n \in \mathcal{N}, \tag{3.88c}$$

where $\hat{g}_k$ is denoted by

$$\begin{aligned}\hat{g}_k(\mathbf{v}^I, \boldsymbol{\varpi}) = {} & 2\sqrt{\mu_k}\Re\left\{\varpi_k^H\mathbf{F}_{k,k}(\boldsymbol{\Theta}^I)\right\} \\ & - \varpi_k^H\left(\sum_{j=1}^{K}\mathbf{F}_{k,j}(\boldsymbol{\Theta}^I)\mathbf{F}_{k,j}^H(\boldsymbol{\Theta}^I) + \Xi_k\right)\varpi_k, \forall k \in \mathcal{K}.\end{aligned} \tag{3.89}$$

Similar to problem (3.80), updating $\mathbf{v}^I$ contains two steps, i.e., updating $\mathbf{v}^I$ and $\boldsymbol{\varpi}$ in turn. Specifically, problem (3.88) is further divided into two subproblems and respectively solved as follows.

Fix $\mathbf{v}^I$ *and Solve* $\boldsymbol{\varpi}$ Given a fixed $\mathbf{v}^I$, the optimal $\boldsymbol{\varpi}$ can be obtained by solving $\partial\overline{g}_4/\partial\varpi_k = 0$, for $\forall k \in \mathcal{K}$, and given by

$$\varpi_k^{\text{opt}}=\sqrt{\mu_k}\left(\sum_{j=1}^{K}\mathbf{F}_{k,j}(\boldsymbol{\Theta})\mathbf{F}_{k,j}^H(\boldsymbol{\Theta})+\Xi_k\right)^{-1}\mathbf{F}_{k,k}(\boldsymbol{\Theta}). \tag{3.90}$$

Fix $\boldsymbol{\varpi}$ *and Solve* $\mathbf{v}^I$ Combining with formula (3.87), we simplify the expression of $\overline{g}_4$ in (3.88) with the auxiliary function $\mathbf{F}_{k,j}$ as follows

$$\begin{aligned}&\varpi_k^H\mathbf{F}_{k,j}(\mathbf{v}^I) \\ &= \varpi_k^H\sqrt{P_j}\mathbf{u}_k^H\mathbf{h}_j^d + \varpi_k^H\sqrt{P_j}\mathbf{u}_k^H\mathbf{G}\boldsymbol{\Theta}^I\mathbf{h}_j^r \\ &= \varpi_k^H\sqrt{P_j}\mathbf{u}_k^H\mathbf{h}_j^d + \varpi_k^H\sqrt{P_j}\mathbf{u}_k^H\mathbf{G}\,\text{diag}\left(\mathbf{h}_j^r\right)\mathbf{v} \\ &= c_{k,j} + \mathbf{g}_{k,j}^H\mathbf{v},\end{aligned} \tag{3.91}$$

where $c_{k,j}$ and $\mathbf{g}_{k,j}$ are defined as

$$c_{k,j} = \varpi_k^H \sqrt{P_j}\mathbf{u}_k^H \mathbf{h}_j^d, \tag{3.92a}$$

$$\mathbf{g}_{k,j} = \left(\varpi_k^H \sqrt{P_j}\mathbf{u}_k^H \mathbf{G}\,\mathrm{diag}\left(\mathbf{h}_j^r\right)\right)^H. \tag{3.92b}$$

Then, substituting (3.91) into (3.89), yields

$$\begin{aligned}\hat{g}_k(\mathbf{v}^I) = {} & 2\sqrt{\mu_k}\Re\left\{c_{k,k} + \mathbf{g}_{k,k}^H \mathbf{v}^I\right\} \\ & - \sum_{j=1}^{K}\left(c_{k,j} + \mathbf{g}_{k,j}^H \mathbf{v}^I\right)\left(c_{k,j}^* + \left(\mathbf{v}^I\right)^H \mathbf{g}_{k,j}\right) - \varpi_k^H \Xi_k \varpi_k.\end{aligned} \tag{3.93}$$

Therefore, $\overline{g}_4$ in (3.88a) can be simplified as

$$\overline{g}_4(\mathbf{v}^I) = -\left(\mathbf{v}^I\right)^H \mathbf{\Lambda}\mathbf{v}^I + \Re\left\{2\boldsymbol{\nu}\mathbf{v}^I\right\} - \zeta - \iota_2\left\|\mathbf{v}^I - \mathbf{a}^I\right\|^2, \tag{3.94}$$

where

$$\begin{aligned}\mathbf{\Lambda} &= \sum_{k=1}^{K}\sum_{j=1}^{K}\mathbf{g}_{k,j}\mathbf{g}_{k,j}^H, \\ \boldsymbol{\nu} &= \sum_{k=1}^{K}\sqrt{\mu_k}\mathbf{g}_{k,k}^H - \sum_{k=1}^{K}\sum_{j=1}^{K}c_{k,j}^*\mathbf{g}_{k,j}^H, \\ \zeta &= \sum_{k=1}^{K}\sum_{j=1}^{K}\left|c_{k,j}\right|^2 + \sum_{k=1}^{K}\varpi_k^H \Xi_k \varpi_k - 2\sum_{k=1}^{K}\sqrt{\mu_k}\Re\left\{c_{k,k}\right\}.\end{aligned} \tag{3.95}$$

As such, the non-convex problem (3.88) has been converted to a convex one, which is given by

$$\min_{\mathbf{v}^I} \left(\mathbf{v}^I\right)^H \mathbf{\Lambda}\mathbf{v}^I - \Re\left\{2\boldsymbol{\nu}\mathbf{v}^I\right\} + \iota_2\left\|\mathbf{v}^I - \mathbf{a}^I\right\|^2 \tag{3.96a}$$

$$\text{s.t.} \left|v_{i,n}^I\right| \le 1, \forall i \in \mathcal{I}, \forall n \in \mathcal{N}. \tag{3.96b}$$

Since matrix $\mathbf{\Lambda}$ is positive semidefinite, problem (3.96) is convex and can be solved by the standard convex optimization tool. Then, based on the obtained $\mathbf{v}^I$, we update $\left\{\theta_{i,n}^I\right\}$ using (3.73).

Optimizing P and f with Fixed $\left(\mathbf{U}, \mathbf{v}^I, \mathbf{f}, \boldsymbol{\rho}\right)$ For given $\left(\mathbf{U}^\star, \mathbf{v}^{I\star}, \mathbf{f}^\star, \boldsymbol{\rho}^\star\right)$ and $\boldsymbol{\xi}^\star$, $\overline{g}_2$ can be reformulated as $\overline{g}_5$,

$$\begin{aligned}\overline{g}_5(\mathbf{P}) &= \sum_{k=1}^{K} 2\sqrt{\mu_k P_k}\Re\left\{\boldsymbol{\xi}_k^H \mathbf{u}_k^H \mathbf{h}_k\right\} - \sum_{k=1}^{K} \boldsymbol{\xi}_k^H \left(\sum_{j=1}^{K} P_j \mathbf{u}_k^H \mathbf{h}_j \left(\mathbf{u}_k^H \mathbf{h}_j\right)^H + \Xi_k\right) \boldsymbol{\xi}_k \\ &= \sum_{k=1}^{K} 2\sqrt{\mu_k}\Re\left\{\boldsymbol{\xi}_k^H \mathbf{u}_k^H \sqrt{P_k}\mathbf{h}_k\right\} \\ &\quad - \sum_{k=1}^{K} \boldsymbol{\xi}_k^H \mathbf{u}_k^H \left(\sum_{j=1}^{K} \sqrt{P_j}\mathbf{h}_j \mathbf{h}_j^H \sqrt{P_j}\right) \mathbf{u}_k \boldsymbol{\xi}_k - \boldsymbol{\xi}_k^H \Xi_k \boldsymbol{\xi}_k.\end{aligned} \tag{3.97}$$

Then, for simplification, we define

$$\begin{aligned}&\mathbf{b} = \sum_{k=1}^{K} \mathbf{u}_k \boldsymbol{\xi}_k \boldsymbol{\xi}_k^H \mathbf{u}_k^H, \quad \mathbf{B} = \mathbf{I}_K \otimes \mathbf{b}, \\ &\mathbf{c}_k = 2\sqrt{\mu_k}\boldsymbol{\xi}_k^H \mathbf{u}_k^H, \quad \mathbf{C} = \left[\mathbf{c}_1, \ldots, \mathbf{c}_K\right], \\ &\mathbf{P}' = \left[\left(\sqrt{P}_1 \mathbf{h}_1\right)^T, \ldots, \left(\sqrt{P}_K \mathbf{h}_K\right)^T\right]^T, \\ &\chi = \boldsymbol{\xi}_k^H \Xi_k \boldsymbol{\xi}_k.\end{aligned} \tag{3.98}$$

By substituting (3.98) to (3.97), we obtain

$$\overline{g}_5(\mathbf{P}) = -\mathbf{P}'^H \mathbf{B} \mathbf{P}' + \Re\left\{\mathbf{C}\mathbf{P}'\right\} - \chi. \tag{3.99}$$

Therefore, the subproblem of uplink transmit power and local computing frequency design at WDs can be formulated as

$$\max_{\mathbf{P},\mathbf{f}} \omega \left(\sum_{k=1}^{K} \ln\left(1+\rho_k\right) - \sum_{k=1}^{K} \rho_k\right) + \overline{g}_5(\mathbf{P}) + \sum_{k=1}^{K} f_k / C_k \tag{3.100a}$$

$$\text{s.t. } 0 \leq f_k \leq f_{k,\max}, \forall k \in \mathcal{K}, \tag{3.100b}$$

$$t_1\left[\kappa f_k^2 + \left(P_k + P_c\right)\right] \leq E_k\left(\tau_2, \mathbf{Q}\right), \forall k \in \mathcal{K}. \tag{3.100c}$$

Since matrix **B** is positive semidefinite, the last term of OF is linear, and constraints (3.100b) and (3.100c) are linear and convex. Therefore, problem (3.100) is a convex optimization problem, which can be solved by the convex optimization tool.

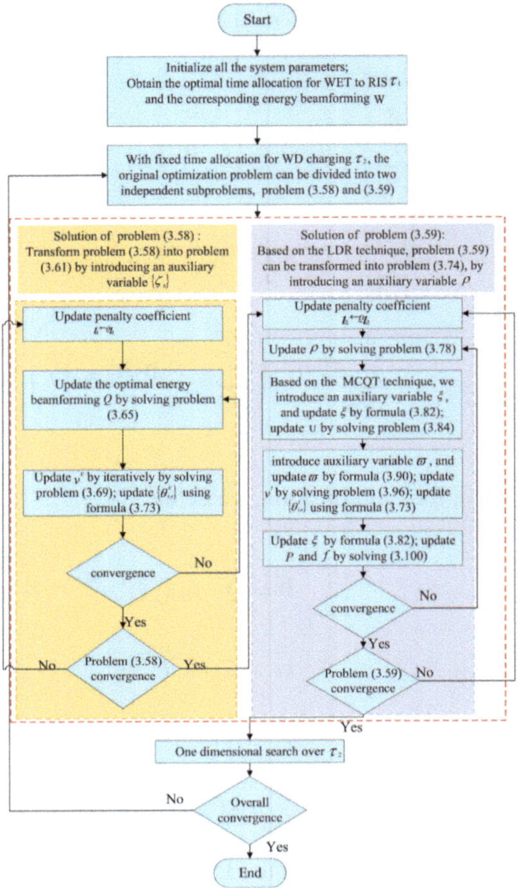

Fig. 3.13 Block diagram of overall algorithm to solve problem (3.53)

Now we have the complete solution for the original optimization problem (3.53), and the corresponding flow diagram is depicted in Fig. 3.13.

As the diagram shows, after obtaining the optimal time allocation for RIS charging and the corresponding energy beamforming, and fixing the time allocation for WD charging, the original optimization problem can be divided into two independent subproblems, i.e., problem (3.58) and (3.59). The first subproblem (3.58) aims to optimize the WD charging setting. To facilitate the solution, problem (3.58) is transformed into problem (3.61) by introducing auxiliary variable $\{\zeta_k\}$. Due to the nonconvex reflecting coefficient constraint of RIS, the reformulated problem (3.61) is still difficult to solve directly. To proceed it, we propose a penalty-based method by adding a penalty term to the OF, and ι_1 is the penalty parameter. Then, problem (3.61) can be solved by our proposed two-layer iterative algorithm, where the inner layer updates energy beamforming $\mathbf{Q}$ and passive beamforming $\mathbf{v}^E$ while the outer layer updates ι_1, until the convergence is achieved. The second subproblem (3.59) aim to optimize the computing setting, and based on the LDR technique, the nonconvex sum-logarithms in its OF is decoupled by introducing an auxiliary variable $\boldsymbol{\rho}$. Similar to problem (3.61), we add the nonconvex reflecting coefficient constraint of RIS as a penalty term to the OF, and ι_2 is the penalty parameter. Similarly, the reformulated subproblem (3.77) can be solved by our proposed two-layer algorithm framework, in which the inner layer algorithm iteratively update auxiliary variable $\boldsymbol{\rho}$, MUD matrix $\mathbf{U}$, passive beamforming $\mathbf{v}^I$, uplink transmit power $\mathbf{P}$ and local computing frequency $\mathbf{f}$, and the outer layer algorithm update penalty coefficient ι_2, until the convergence is achieved. Finally, the optimal time allocation τ_2 is obtained by one dimensional search method.

3.3.3 Performance Evaluation

In this section, numerical results are provided to evaluate the performance of the proposed algorithm [36]. Similar to [37], we consider a three dimensional coordinate system as shown in Fig. 3.14, which consists of five HAPs, two RISs, and four WDs. Here, two RISs are deployed on the user side to improve network capacity. We assume that the b-th HAP is located at $(4\,(b-1)\,\text{m}, -5\,\text{m}, 3\,\text{m})$, two RISs are located at $(6\,\text{m}, 1\,\text{m}, 2\,\text{m})$ and $(10\,\text{m}, 1\,\text{m}, 2\,\text{m})$, and K WDs are uniformly and randomly distributed in a cluster, which is centered at $(L\,\text{m}, 0\,\text{m}, 1\,\text{m})$ with radius $1\,\text{m}$. The simulation parameters are summarized in Table 3.2. As for the communications channel, both the small scale fading and large scale path loss are considered. We define d_{HU}, d_{HI}, and d_{IU} as the distance between HAP and WD, HAP and RIS, RIS and WD. Thus, the distance-dependent large scale path loss model is given by

$$L(d) = C_0 \left(\frac{d}{d_0}\right)^{-\kappa}, \quad d \in \{d_{HU}, d_{HI}, d_{IU}\}, \tag{3.101}$$

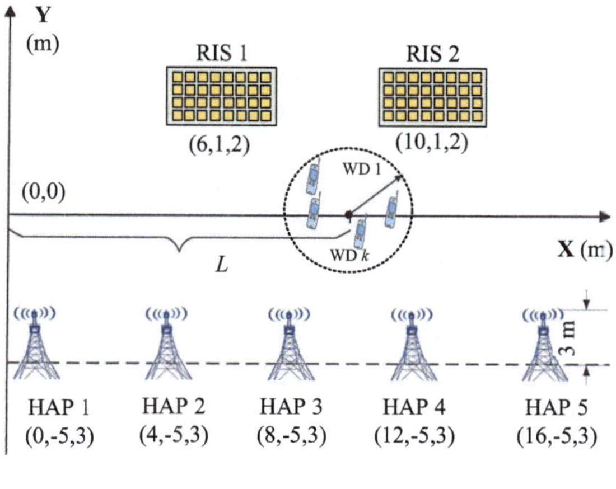

Fig. 3.14 The simulation scenario with five HAPs and two RISs

Table 3.2 Simulation parameters

Parameters	Values
Number of WD, K	4
Number of HAP, B	5
Number of HAP's antennas, M	2
Number of RIS, I	2
Number of RIS reflection element, N	10
Maximum transmit power of HAP	100W
Time block length, T	1s
System bandwidth, ω	1MHz
Local computing capability of the k-th WD, $f_{k,\max}$	1×10^8 cycles/s
Computational complexity, C_k	500 cycles/bit
Energy efficiency coefficient, κ	1×10^{-28}
Energy conversion efficiency, η	0.8
Noise spectral density, N_0	40 dBm
Path loss exponent, $\kappa_{HU}/\kappa_{HI}/\kappa_{IU}$	3.5/2.2/2.8
Power consumption of each reflection element, μ	1mW

where $C_0 = -30\,\text{dB}$ denotes the path loss at a reference distance $d_0 = 1\,\text{m}$. d refers to the individual channel distance, and κ is the path loss exponent. Here we set the path loss exponent of the HAP-WD link, HAP-RIS link, and RIS-WD link to $\kappa_{HU} = 3.5$, $\kappa_{HI} = 2.2$, and $\kappa_{IU} = 2.8$ [37], respectively. For the small scale fading, we consider a Rician fading channel model for all involved channels, and the channel $\mathbf{H}$ is modeled as

$$\mathbf{H} = \sqrt{\frac{\beta_{\text{HU}}}{1+\beta_{\text{HU}}}}\mathbf{H}^{\text{LoS}} + \sqrt{\frac{1}{1+\beta_{\text{HU}}}}\mathbf{H}^{\text{NLoS}}, \tag{3.102}$$

where β_{HU} stands for the Rician factor, $\mathbf{H}^{\text{LoS}}$ and $\mathbf{H}^{\text{NLoS}}$ refer to the LoS deterministic component and the non-LoS Rayleigh fading component, respectively. $\mathbf{H}$ is reduced to a Rayleigh fading channel model when $\beta_{\text{HU}} = 0$, a LoS channel model when $\beta_{\text{HU}} \to \infty$. Then, for the HAP-WD channel, we need to multiply $\mathbf{H}$ by the distance-dependent large scale path loss $L(d)$ in (3.101). Similarly, the HAP-RIS and RIS-WD channels can also be generated by the above procedure with β_{HI} and β_{IU} denoting the Rician factors of them. Here we assume $\beta_{\text{HI}} \to \infty$, $\beta_{\text{IU}} \to \infty$, and $\beta_{\text{HU}} = 0$. Note that the energy efficiency coefficient κ setting follows [16, 30], the local computing capability of the k-th WD $f_{k,max}$ setting follows [18], and the setting of other parameters in Table 3.2 is given by [30] or [37].

For comparison, the following four baseline schemes are considered.

- *Upper bound:* solve problem (3.53) with $\beta_{min} = 1$ using the proposed method.
- *Ideal RIS assumption:* the phase shift design under ideal RIS assumption is applied to the practical RIS model.

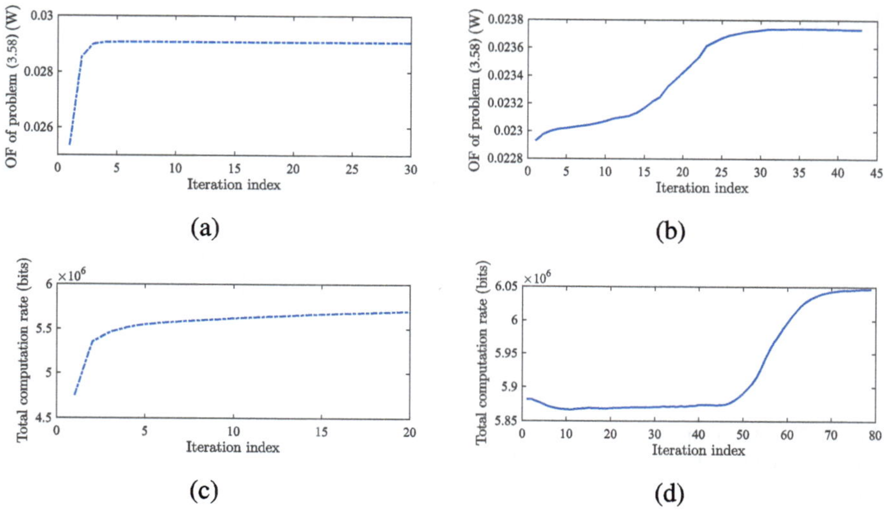

Fig. 3.15 Convergence behavior of the proposed algorithms. (**a**) Inner loop for solving problem (3.58). (**b**) Outer loop for solving problem (3.58). (**c**) Inner loop for solving problem (3.59). (**d**) Outer loop for solving problem (3.59)

- *Full offloading:* all computation tasks of each WD are offloaded to the HAP and performed on the edge server.
- *No RIS:* the conventional communication network without RIS.

1. Convergence Behavior Figure 3.15a–b show the convergence behavior for solving problem (3.58). It is observed that the proposed algorithm for downlink energy beamforming and RIS passive beamforming design converges within 5 iterations, while the outer loops that is related to the initial value of ι_1, converges within 30 iterations. Figure 3.15c–d present the convergence behavior for solving problem (3.59). Similarly, it can be seen that the inner loop for optimizing MUD vector, RIS passive beamforming, offloading power, and local computing frequency can reach convergence within 10 iterations, while the outer loop converges within 70 iterations.

2. Selection of the Time Allocation Combining (3.53b) and (3.54), the time allocation satisfies $\tau_2 + t_1 = T - \tau_1^{\star}$. In order to find an appropriate time allocation, we depict the total computation rate versus the time allocation τ_2 in Fig. 3.16. It is observed that problem (3.57) is convex with respect to τ_2, and this means that, there exists a $\tau_2^{\star}$ that maximizes the total computation bits. Here, we use the one-dimensional search method to find the optimal τ_2.

3. Impact of the Parameter $\beta_{\min}$ In Fig. 3.17, we show the total computation rate against the number of RIS elements N. Specifically, the RIS phase shift design for ideal RIS is applied to the practical RIS with $\beta_{\min} = 0.8$, $\beta_{\min} = 0.5$, and $\beta_{\min} = 0.2$. One can observe that as the number of RIS element N

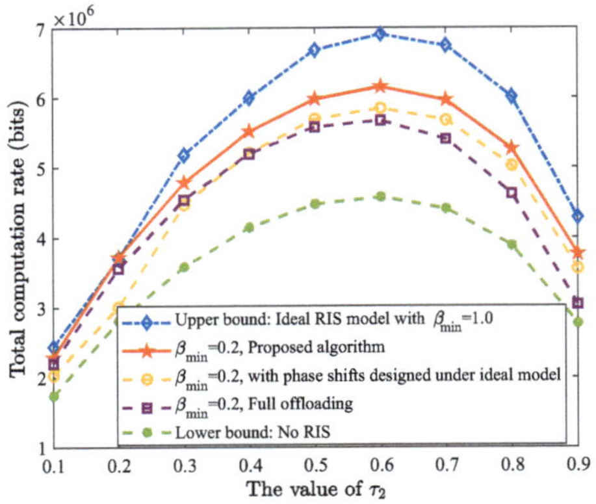

Fig. 3.16 Total computation rate versus τ_2

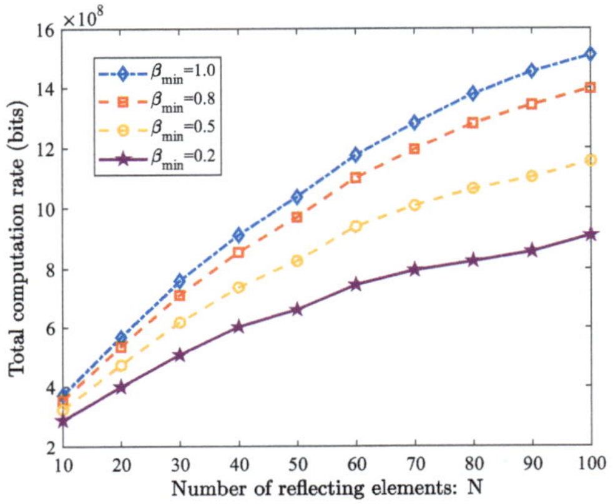

Fig. 3.17 Total computation rate versus under different β_{min}

increases, the performance gap between ideal case ($\beta_{\min} = 1$) and practical cases ($\beta_{\min} = 0.8$, $\beta_{\min} = 0.5$, and $\beta_{\min} = 0.2$) first increases and then approaches a constant, which is determined by $\beta_{\min}$ and α [20]. This is because that when N is moderate, the signal power received from the HAP-WD link is comparable to that of the RIS-WD link, thus the performance loss due to the imperfect hardware of RIS is more pronounced as N increases. Whereas, when N is sufficiently large, the reflection link dominates. Hence the performance loss arising from the RIS reflection imperfection converges to a constant. This observation implies that the promising squared power scaling order, i.e., $O\left(N^2\right)$ unveiled in [14] under the ideal phase shift model, still holds for practical case. Furthermore, this indicates that it is crucial to take into consideration the practical RIS phase shift model for the passive beamforming design in practical RIS-assisted systems.

4. Impact of the Number of RIS Elements N Figure 3.18 presents the total computation rate versus the number of reflecting elements for all considered schemes. It is observed that the performance gap between ideal phase shift model and practical phase shift model increases as the number of reflecting elements increases. This is due to the fact that, with N increases, the RIS-reflected signal power dominates in

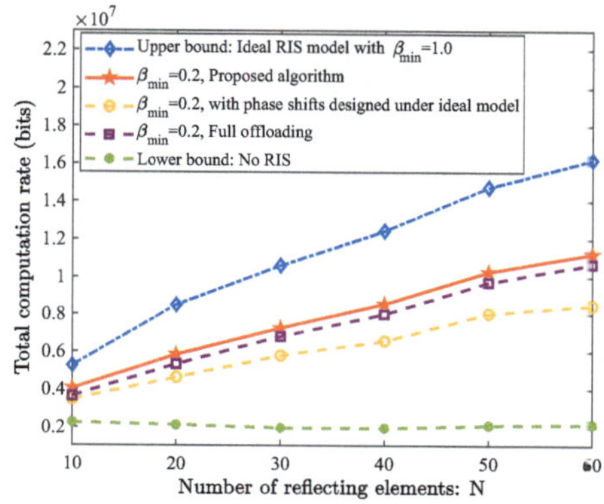

Fig. 3.18 Total computation rate versus the number of RIS elements

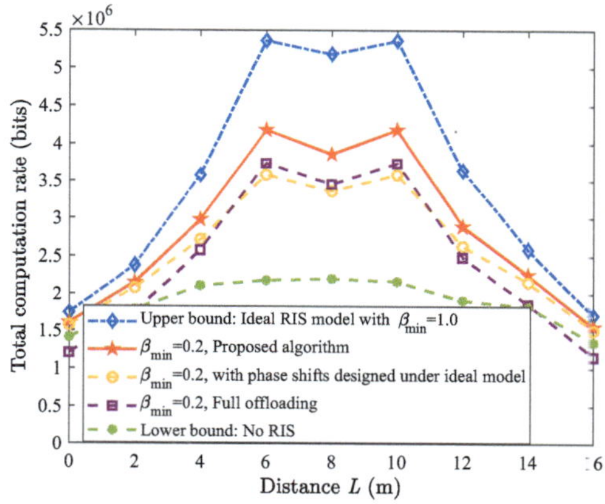

Fig. 3.19 Total computation rate versus the distance L

the total received power of WDs, thus, the performance loss due to the RIS hardware imperfection is more pronounced. Noted that, too more RIS elements will make the channel estimations challenging. Therefore, it is essential to choose an appropriate RIS element number.

5. Impact of the Distance L From Fig. 3.19, we can observe that for the schemes with RIS deployed, there are two obvious peaks at $L = 6$ m and $L = 8$ m. This is because when WDs approach one of the two RISs, WDs can receive strong signals reflected from RISs. While for the conventional scheme without RIS, the two peaks will not appear. When WDs approach one of the two RISs, the performance gap between the ideal RIS case ($\beta_{\min} = 1$) and practical RIS case ($\beta_{\min} = 0.2$) increases. This is because the received signals power reflected from RIS play a dominant role, while when WDs are far from RISs, the contribution of RIS becomes limited.

6. Impact of HAP Maximum Transmit Power $P_{\max}$ By fixing $L = 6$ m, we plot the total computation rate against the maximum transmit power of HAP in Fig. 3.20. We can observe that the total computation rate for all considered schemes increases monotonically with the increase of HAP maximum transmit power. Obviously, this

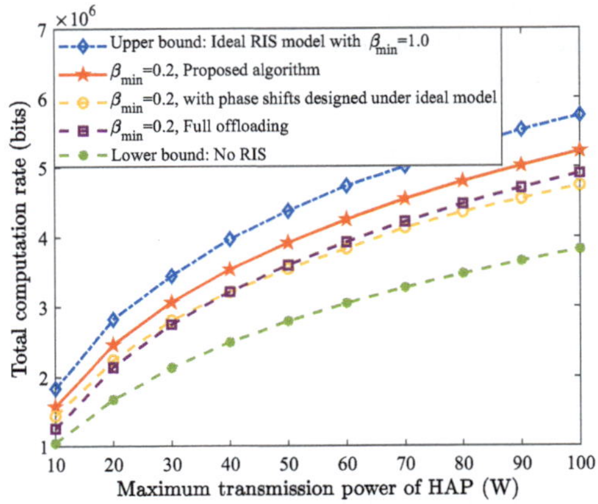

Fig. 3.20 Total computation rate versus maximum transmit power of HAP

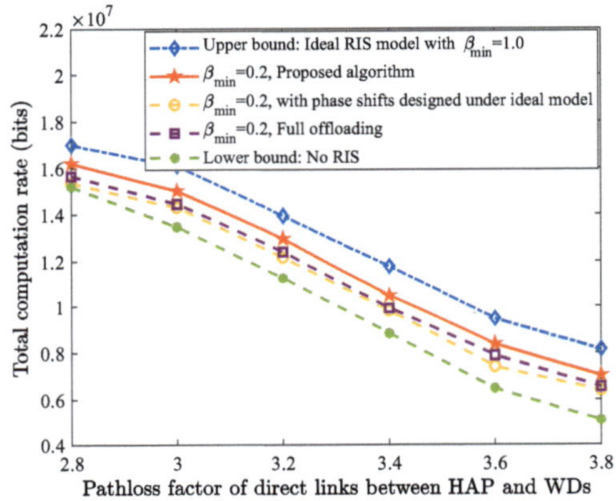

Fig. 3.21 Total computation rate versus path loss exponent κ_{HU}

is due to the fact that WDs will harvest more energy when HAPs adopt a higher transmit power, which will in turn enable WDs to perform more computation data via local computing and task offloading. Furthermore, we see that, compared to the existing schemes, the proposed algorithm can achieve a better performance. Particularly, the performance gain achieved by the proposed algorithm over the conventional scheme without RIS increases with the increase of $P_{\max}$. This indicates that when WDs can harvest more energy with a larger $P_{\max}$, the reflection link gain by employing RIS can improve the task offloading rate significantly.

7. Impact of Path Loss Exponent In Fig. 3.21, we present the total computation rate against the path loss exponent of direct links between WDs and HAPs. We see that the total computation rate decreases with the increase of path loss exponent. This is because that a higher path loss exponent will result in a lower channel gain for the composite channel between HAPs and WDs. Besides, compared to the full offloading scheme and conventional scheme without RIS, the proposed RIS-assisted wireless powered MEC system can achieve 7 % and 38% performance gain, respectively.

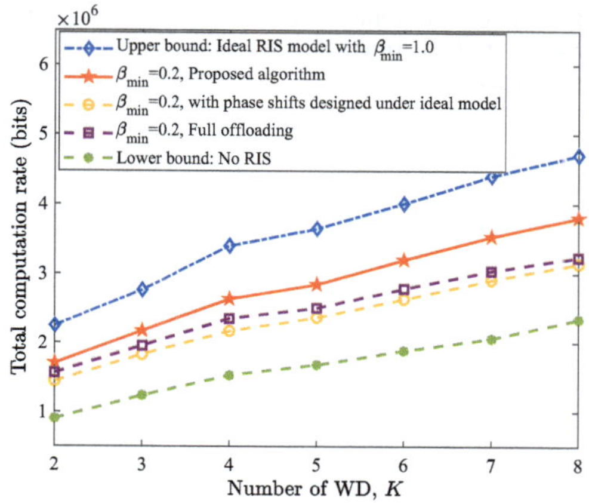

Fig. 3.22 Total computation rate versus the number of WDs K

8. Impact of the Number of WDs In Fig. 3.22, we plot the total computation rate versus the number of WDs. We see that although the total computation rate increases from $K = 2$ to $K = 8$, the increasing slope of the schemes with RIS is larger than the conventional scheme without RIS. This observation corroborates that employing RIS in the wireless communication system can achieve a higher throughput by carefully designing the RIS passive beamforming.

9. Impact of CSI Error Parameter Generally, due to the high-dimensional channels introduced by RIS, the channel estimation is very challenging for the RIS-assisted communication system. We analyze the robustness of the proposed algorithm to CSI error, and model the imperfect channels as

$$\hat{h} = h + e, \tag{3.103}$$

where $\hat{h}$ and h stand for the practically estimated channel and the real channel, respectively. e denotes the estimation error with Gaussian distribution, which satisfy zero mean and variance σ_e^2, i.e., $e \sim CN\left(0, \sigma_e^2\right)$. We define δ as the ratio of error power σ_e^2 to the channel gain $|h|^2$, i.e., $\delta \triangleq \sigma_e^2/|h|^2$, to characterize the level of CSI error. In Fig. 3.23, we depict the total computation rate against the CSI error parameter δ. We see that the performance loss increases with δ. In particular, for the proposed algorithm, compared to the perfect CSI without error ($\delta = 0$), the system performance suffers a loss of 6 % when $\delta = 0.1$, and a loss of 21 % when $\delta = 0.3$. Thereby, the proposed algorithm shows strong robustness to the CSI error.

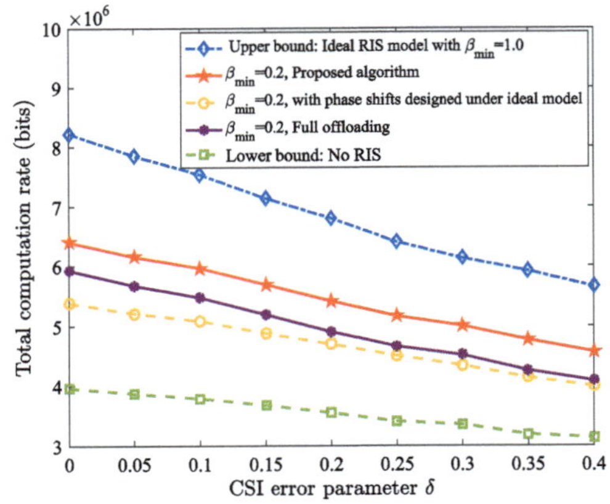

Fig. 3.23 Total computation rate versus CSI error parameter δ

3.4 RIS-Aided Wideband MEC with Practical Reflection Model

3.4.1 System Model and Problem Formulation

As shown in Fig. 3.24, we consider a wideband multi-user orthogonal frequency division multiplexing (MU-OFDM) system with P subcarriers. K single-antenna WDs offload part of computing data to the BS equipped with edge servers with the help of RIS. M and N represent the number of BS antennas and RIS reflection elements, respectively. Denote $\mathcal{P} = \{1, \ldots, P\}$, $\mathcal{K} = \{1, \ldots, K\}$, $\mathcal{M} = \{1, \ldots, M\}$, and $\mathcal{N} = \{1, \ldots, N\}$ as the set of subcarriers, users, transmission antennas, and RIS elements. The edge server and BS are deployed together and connected via a high-speed, low-latency wired fiber. Thus, we ignore the data transmission delay between BS and edge nodes [38, 39].

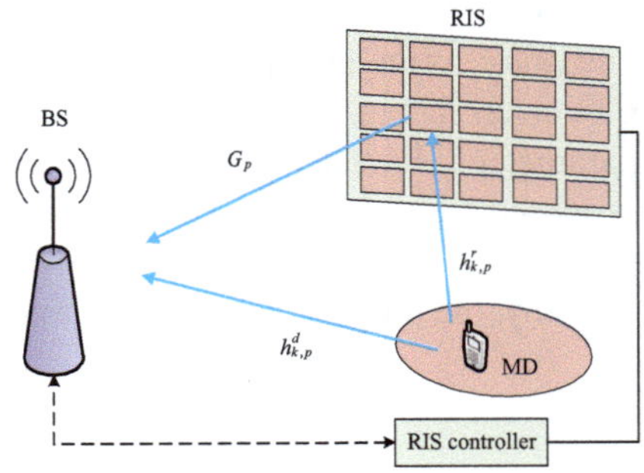

Fig. 3.24 RIS-aided wideband MEC system model

3.4.1.1 RIS Reflection Model

In [40], Cai et al. established a three-dimensional reflection model to accurately describe the variation of RIS amplitude and phase shift with basic phase shift (BPS) and incident signal frequency. This model is so complicated that it may lead to the optimization design of RIS more difficult and complex. Hence, in [41], they further proposed a simplified model based on the actual application. When the relative bandwidth, i.e., B/f_c, is less than 5%, the relationship between reflection amplitudes and phase shifts of RIS elements can be viewed as a quadratic function, and the curves for different frequencies do not have obvious difference. Here, B and f_c represent bandwidth and carrier frequency, respectively. In addition, phase shift can be approximately fitted as a straight line with respect to frequency, whose slope and intercept vary with the BPS θ. Here, BPS θ is defined as the phase shift for carrier frequency f_c. Upon denoting the frequency of incident signal by f, the reflection amplitude $\mathrm{A}(\theta, f)$ and phase shift $\mathrm{B}(\theta, f)$ are given by

$$\begin{aligned}
\mathrm{A}(\theta, f) &= \alpha_1 \mathrm{B}^2(\theta, f) + \beta_1 \mathrm{B}(\theta, f) + \tilde{c}_1, \\
\mathrm{B}(\theta, f) &= \mathcal{F}_1(\theta) f + \mathcal{F}_2(\theta), \\
\mathcal{F}_1(\theta) &= \alpha_2 \sin\left(\beta_2 \theta + \tilde{c}_2\right) + \alpha_3 \sin\left(\beta_3 \theta + \tilde{c}_3\right), \\
\mathcal{F}_2(\theta) &= \alpha_4 \sin\left(\beta_4 \theta + \tilde{c}_4\right) + \alpha_5 \sin\left(\beta_5 \theta + \tilde{c}_5\right),
\end{aligned} \tag{3.104}$$

where $\mathcal{F}_1(\theta)$ represents the slope and $\mathcal{F}_2(\theta)$ represents the intercept of the phase shift-frequency line, respectively. $\{\alpha_i, \beta_i, \tilde{c}_i\}_{i=1}^5$ are RIS parameters related to the specific circuit implementation. For instance, when the carrier frequency $f_c = 2.4$ GHz and bandwidth $B = 100$ MHz, the parameter values are shown in Table 3.3. In addition, the central frequency f_p of each subcarrier is given by $f_p \triangleq f_c + \left(p - \frac{P+1}{2}\right)\frac{B}{P}, \forall p \in \mathcal{P}$.

3.4.1.2 Communication Model

Let $\mathbf{h}_{k,p}^{\mathrm{d}} \in \mathbb{C}^{M\times 1}$, $\mathbf{G}_p \in \mathbb{C}^{M\times N}$, and $\mathbf{h}_{k,p}^{r} \in \mathbb{C}^{N\times 1}$ denote the baseband equivalent channels from the k-th WD to BS, from RIS to BS, and from the k-th WD to RIS on the p-th subcarrier. Let $\mathbf{\Phi}_p = \mathrm{diag}\left(\phi_{p,1}, \ldots, \phi_{p,N}\right)$ denote the reflection matrix of RIS on the p-th subcarrier. Here, $\phi_{p,n}$ is the reflection coefficient of the n-th RIS

Table 3.3 Parameters values for non-ideal RIS models

	i=1	i=2	i=3	i=4	i=5
α_i	0.06	11.27	10.88	89.64	26.11
β_i	0.02	0.008996	0.9799	0.01268	0.9798
$\tilde{c}_i$	0.5736	−1.897	−1.471	0.2899	1.673

element on the p-th subcarrier, which satisfies the following functional relationships

$$\left|\phi_{p,n}\right| = \mathrm{A}\left(\theta_n, f_p\right), \angle\phi_{p,n} = \mathrm{B}\left(\theta_n, f_p\right), \forall p, n, \tag{3.105}$$

where θ_n is the BPS of the n-th RIS element and $\boldsymbol{\theta} = [\theta_1, \ldots, \theta_N]^T$ denotes the BPS vector. Let $\mathbf{s}_p \triangleq \left[s_{1,p}, \ldots, s_{K,p}\right]^T \in \mathbb{C}^K$ represent the transmission signal of the K WDs on the p-th subcarrier, and satisfy $\mathbb{E}\left\{\mathbf{s}_p\mathbf{s}_p^H\right\} = \mathbf{I}_K, \forall p \in \mathcal{P}$. Upon denoting the transmit power of WD by $\widetilde{p}$, the received signal $\mathbf{y}_p \in \mathbb{C}^{M\times 1}$ at BS on the p-th subcarrier can be formulated as

$$\mathbf{y}_p = \sqrt{\widetilde{p}}\sum_{k=1}^{K}\left(\mathbf{h}_{k,p}^{\mathrm{d}} + \mathbf{G}_p\mathbf{\Phi}_p\mathbf{h}_{k,p}^{r}\right)s_{k,p} + \mathbf{n}_p, \tag{3.106}$$

where $\mathbf{n}_p \triangleq \left[n_{p,1}, \ldots, n_{p,M}\right]^T$ is the noise vector, which satisfies $n_{p,m} \sim \mathcal{CN}\left(0, \sigma^2\right), \forall p \in \mathcal{P}, m \in \mathcal{M}$. Upon denoting the BS receiving vectors for the k-th WD on the p-th subcarrier by $\mathbf{u}_{k,p}$, the recovered signal for the k-th WD on the p-th subcarrier is given by

$$\hat{y}_{k,p} = \mathbf{u}_{k,p}^H\left(\sqrt{\widetilde{p}}\sum_{j=1}^{K}\left(\mathbf{h}_{j,p}^{\mathrm{d}} + \mathbf{G}_p\mathbf{\Phi}_p\mathbf{h}_{j,p}^{r}\right)s_{j,p} + \mathbf{n}_p\right). \tag{3.107}$$

Then, the SINR of the k-th WD on the p-th subcarrier can be expressed as

$$\gamma_{k,p}\left(\mathbf{u}_{k,p}, \mathbf{\Phi}_p\right) = \frac{\widetilde{p}\left|\mathbf{u}_{k,p}^H\left(\mathbf{h}_{k,p}^d + \mathbf{G}_p\mathbf{\Phi}_p\mathbf{h}_{k,p}^r\right)\right|^2}{\widetilde{p}\sum_{j=1,j\neq k}^{K}\left|\mathbf{u}_{k,p}^H\left(\mathbf{h}_{j,p}^d + \mathbf{G}_p\mathbf{\Phi}_p\mathbf{h}_{j,p}^r\right)\right|^2 + \sigma^2}. \tag{3.108}$$

Accordingly, we can obtain the offloading rate for the k-th WD on the p-th subcarrier as

$$R_{k,p}\left(\mathbf{u}_{k,p}, \mathbf{\Phi}_p\right) = B\log_2\left[1 + \gamma_{k,p}\left(\mathbf{u}_{k,p}, \mathbf{\Phi}_p\right)\right], \tag{3.109}$$

The total transmission rate for the k-th user is given by

$$R_k(\mathbf{u}_k, \boldsymbol{\theta}) = \sum_{p=1}^{P} R_{k,p}\left(\mathbf{u}_{k,p}, \mathbf{\Phi}_p\right), \forall k, p, \tag{3.110}$$

where $\mathbf{u}_k = [\mathbf{u}_{k,1}^T, \ldots, \mathbf{u}_{k,P}^T]^T$ represents the BS receiving vector for the k-th WD.

3.4.1.3 Computing Model

We consider a partial offloading application model where the computing data is arbitrarily divisible [42]. WD can offload a part of computing data to the edge server for remote processing, and the other part for local computing.

- Local computing: Let D_k, d_k, and c_k denote the total computation data volume, offloading data volume, and computational complexity of the computation data. Upon denoting the computing power of the k-th WD by F_k^l, the local computing latency is given by $T_k^l = (D_k - d_k)c_k / F_k^l$.
- Edge processing: Denote F_{total}^e and F_k^e as the total computing capacity of edge server and the edge computing resource allocated to the k-th WD, respectively, satisfying $\sum_{k=1}^K F_k^e \le F_{\text{total}}^e$. The latency usually consists of three parts: (1) offloading latency for data transmission; (2) computing latency for processing the offloaded data on the edge server; (3) return latency for transmitting the computing result to WD. Generally, due to the small data volume of computing result, the return latency of the last part is usually ignored [11, 36]. Thus, the latency introduced by edge computing is expressed as $T_k^e\left(\mathbf{u}_k, \boldsymbol{\theta}, d_k, F_k^e\right) = d_k / R_k\left(\mathbf{u}_k, \boldsymbol{\theta}\right) + d_k c_k / F_k^e$.

The overall latency of the k-th WD can be expressed as

$$
\begin{aligned}
T_k\left(\mathbf{u}_k,\boldsymbol{\theta},d_k,F_k^e\right) &= \max\left\{T_k^l\left(d_k\right), T_k^e\left(\mathbf{u}_k, \boldsymbol{\theta}, d_k, F_k^e\right)\right\}, \\
&= \max\left\{\frac{(D_k - d_k)c_k}{F_k^l}, \frac{d_k}{R_k(\mathbf{u}_k,\boldsymbol{\theta})} + \frac{d_k c_k}{F_k^e}\right\},
\end{aligned} \tag{3.111}
$$

3.4.1.4 Problem Formulation

In this section, we investigate a weighted computational latency minimization problem by jointly optimizing offloading data volume $\boldsymbol{d} = [d_1, d_2, \ldots, d_K]^T$, edge computing resource $\mathbf{F}^e = \left[F_1^e, \ldots, F_K^e\right]$, BS's receiving vectors $\mathbf{U} = \left[\mathbf{u}_{1,1}^T, \ldots, \mathbf{u}_{K,1}^T, \ldots, \mathbf{u}_{K,P}^T\right]^T$, and RIS BPS $\boldsymbol{\theta}$, which is formulated as

$$\min_{\mathbf{U},\boldsymbol{\theta},\boldsymbol{d},\mathbf{F}^e} \sum_{k=1}^{K} \varpi_k T_k\left(\mathbf{u}_k, \boldsymbol{\theta}, d_k, F_k^e\right) \tag{3.112a}$$

$$\text{s.t. } \left|\phi_{p,n}\right| = \mathrm{A}\left(\theta_n, f_p\right), \forall p, n, \tag{3.112b}$$

$$\angle\phi_{p,n} = \mathrm{B}\left(\theta_n, f_p\right), \forall p, n, \tag{3.112c}$$

$$\theta_n \in [-\pi, \pi], \forall n, \tag{3.112d}$$

$$\left\|\mathbf{u}_{k,p}\right\|^2 \le 1, \forall k, p, \tag{3.112e}$$

$$d_k \in \{0, 1, \ldots, D_k\}, \forall k, \tag{3.112f}$$

$$\sum_{k=1}^{K} F_k^e \leq F_{\text{total}}^e, \tag{3.112g}$$

$$F_k^e \geq 0, \forall k, \tag{3.112h}$$

where ϖ_k denotes the weight of the k-th WD. Equations (3.112b) and (3.112c) are the amplitude and phase-shift constraints of the non-ideal RIS model, respectively. Equation (3.112d) is the phase shift constraint; (3.112e) denotes the unit-norm receiving vector constraint for the k-th WD on the p-th subcarrier; (3.112f) indicates that the offloaded data volume should be an integer between zero and the total computation data.

For the optimization variables of problem (3.112), $\{\boldsymbol{d}, \mathbf{F}^e\}$ are variables related to the computing design, $\{\mathbf{U}, \boldsymbol{\theta}\}$ are variables related to the communication design. It is challenging to solve problem (3.112) due to the following three aspects: 1) the segmented form of objective function; 2) the coupling effect of $\mathbf{U}$ and $\boldsymbol{\theta}$; 3) the non-convex objective function with respect to $\boldsymbol{\theta}$. To proceed, we provide a locally optimal solution by decoupling the communication and computing designs using BCD technique. Then, the segmented form of objective function can be transformed into a more tractable form. Leveraging the equivalence between sum-rate maximization and MSE minimization, the communication design subproblem is converted into a multi-variable problem, which can be solved effectively via BCD technique. To address the non-convexity of $\boldsymbol{\theta}$, we solve the BPS for each RIS reflection element separately, and then update $\boldsymbol{\theta}$ iteratively until it converges.

3.4.2 *Proposed Solution Based on BCD Technique*

Here, we jointly optimize computing and communication resources relying on the BCD technique. We first optimize offloading data volume and edge computing resource, while fixing the communication setting, and then optimize BS receiving vectors and BPS with fixed computing setting. Our goal is to jointly optimize computing and communication resources until convergence.

3.4.2.1 Optimization of Offloading Data and Edge Computing Resources

Given the BS receiving vector $\mathbf{U}$ and BPS $\boldsymbol{\theta}$, the original problem (3.112) can be simplified to

$$\min_{\boldsymbol{d}, \mathbf{F}^e} \sum_{k=1}^{K} \varpi_k T_k \left(d_k, F_k^e\right) \tag{3.113a}$$

$$\text{s.t. } (3.112\text{f}), (3.112\text{g}), (3.112\text{h}) \tag{3.113b}$$

Optimization of *d* Given a set of solutions for $\{\mathbf{U},\boldsymbol{\theta},\mathbf{F}^e\}$, the optimal offloading data volume can be determined by setting $T_k^l(\hat{d}_k) = T_k^e(\hat{d}_k)$, i.e.,

$$\hat{d}_k^* = \frac{D_k c_k R_k F_k^e}{F_k^e F_k^l + c_k R_k \left(F_k^e + F_k^l\right)}. \tag{3.114}$$

Bear in mind that the offloading data volume must be a positive integer, so the optimal d_k^* is given by

$$d_k^* = \underset{\hat{d}_k \in \left\{\left\lfloor \hat{d}_k^* \right\rfloor, \left\lceil \hat{d}_k^* \right\rceil\right\}}{\arg\min} \; T_k\left(\hat{d}_k\right), \tag{3.115}$$

where $\lfloor * \rfloor$ and $\lceil * \rceil$ represent the floor and ceiling operations, respectively.

Proof Upon denoting the relaxation [43] of integer value $d_k \in \{0, 1, \ldots, L_k\}$ by $\hat{d}_k \in [0, L_k]$, the overall latency of the k-th WD is $\hat{T}_k\left(\hat{d}_k\right) \triangleq \max\left\{T_k^l\left(\hat{d}_k\right), T_k^e\left(\hat{d}_k\right)\right\}$, which can be reformulated from (3.111) as the following segmented form

$$\hat{T}_k\left(\hat{d}_k\right) = \begin{cases} \frac{\left(D_k - \hat{d}_k\right) c_k}{F_k^l}, & 0 \le \hat{d}_k \le \frac{D_k c_k R_k F_k^e}{F_k^e F_k^l + c_k R_k \left(F_k^l + F_k^e\right)} \\ \frac{\hat{d}_k}{R_k} + \frac{\hat{d}_k c_k}{F_k^e}, & \frac{D_k c_k R_k F_k^e}{F_k^e F_k^l + c_k R_k \left(F_k^l + F_k^e\right)} < \hat{d}_k \le D_k \end{cases} \tag{3.116}$$

From (3.116), we can observe that when $\hat{d}_k$ increases from 0 to $\frac{D_k c_k R_k F_k^e}{F_k^e F_k^l + c_k R_k \left(F_k^l + F_k^e\right)}$, the latency $\hat{T}_k\left(\hat{d}_k\right)$ decreases, and when $\hat{d}_k$ increases from $\frac{D_k c_k R_k F_k^e}{F_k^e F_k^l + c_k R_k \left(F_k^l + F_k^e\right)}$ to D_k, $\hat{T}_k\left(\hat{d}_k\right)$ increases. Hence, to minimize latency, we should select $\hat{d}_k = \hat{d}_k^* = \frac{D_k c_k R_k F_k^e}{F_k^e F_k^l + c_k R_k \left(F_k^l + F_k^e\right)}$. Since the optimal value of d_k should be a non-negative integer, we can obtain its optimal value after carrying out the following operation $d_k^* = \underset{\hat{d} \in \left\{\left\lfloor \hat{d}_k^* \right\rfloor, \left\lceil \hat{d}_k^* \right\rceil\right\}}{\arg\min} \; T_k\left(\hat{d}_k\right)$.

Optimization of $\mathbf{F}^e$ Next, given a solutions set of $\{\mathbf{U}, \boldsymbol{\theta}, \boldsymbol{d}\}$, we focus on the optimization of edge computing resource. After substituting (3.114) into objective (3.113a), the corresponding computing setting subproblem can be reformulated as

$$\min_{\mathbf{F}^e} \sum_{k=1}^{K} \frac{\varpi_k \left(D_k c_k^2 R_k + D_k c_k F_k^e\right)}{F_k^e F_k^l + c_k R_k \left(F_k^e + F_k^l\right)} \tag{3.117a}$$

$$\text{s.t. } (3.112\text{g}), (3.112\text{h}). \tag{3.117b}$$

Next, we prove that problem (3.117) is a convex problem, and then a solution of $\mathbf{F}^e$ is provided by exploiting the Karush-Kuhn-Tucker (KKT) conditions.

Denote the second derivative of objective function (3.117a) with respect to F_k^e by f'', which is given by

$$f'' = \frac{2\varpi_k D_k c_k^3 R_k^2 \left(F_k^l + c_k R_k\right)}{\left[F_k^e F_k^l + c_k R_k \left(F_k^e + F_k^l\right)\right]^3}. \tag{3.118}$$

Since parameters ϖ_k, c_k, R_k, and F_k^l are all positive and we have $D_k \geq 0$ and $F_k^e \geq 0$, it can be inferred that $f'' \geq 0$. Besides, constraint (3.112g) and (3.112h) are all linear forms. Thus, we can conclude that problem (3.117) is strictly convex, and its optimal solution satisfies KKT conditions. Specifically, the corresponding Lagrangian function is formulated as

$$\mathcal{L}\left(\mathbf{F}^e, \eta\right) = \sum_{k=1}^{K} \frac{\varpi_k \left(D_k c_k^2 R_k + D_k c_k F_k^e\right)}{c_k R_k F_k^l + \left(F_k^l + c_k R_k\right) F_k^e} + \eta \left(\sum_{k=1}^{K} F_k^e - F_{\text{total}}^e\right), \tag{3.119}$$

where $\eta \geq 0$ is the Lagrangian multiplier. The optimal solution of edge resource allocation $\mathbf{F}^{e^*}$ and Lagrangian multiplier η^* should satisfy the related KKT conditions, i.e.,

$$\frac{\partial \mathcal{L}}{\partial F_k^e} = \frac{-\varpi_k D_k c_k^3 R_k^2}{\left[c_k R_k F_k^l + \left(F_k^l + c_k R_k\right) F_k^{e*}\right]^2} + \eta^* = 0, \tag{3.120}$$

$$\eta^* \left(\sum_{k=1}^{K} F_k^{e*} - F_{\text{total}}^e\right) = 0, \tag{3.121}$$

$$F_k^{e*} \geq 0. \tag{3.122}$$

Algorithm 5 Alternating Optimization of $\mathbf{d}$ and $\mathbf{F}^e$, Given $\mathbf{U}$ and $\boldsymbol{\theta}$

Input: $\mathbf{h}_k$, B, p, σ^2, D_k, c_k, K, ϵ_1, l_1^{max}, $\mathbf{U}$, and $\boldsymbol{\theta}$
Output: Optimal $\boldsymbol{d}$ and $\mathbf{F}^e$
1. Initialization
Initialize $l_1 = 0$, calculate $\{R_k\}_{k=1}^K$ using (3.110)
2. Alternating optimization of d and $\mathbf{F}^e$
repeat:
Update η using bisection search method
Update $\mathbf{F}^{e(l_1+1)}$ using (3.123)
Update $\boldsymbol{d}^{(l_1+1)}$ using (3.114)
$\epsilon_1^{(l_1+1)} = \frac{\left|\text{obj}\left(\boldsymbol{d}^{(l_1+1)},\mathbf{F}^{e(l_1+1)}\right)-\text{obj}\left(\boldsymbol{d}^{(l_1)},\mathbf{F}^{e(l_1)}\right)\right|}{\text{obj}\left(\boldsymbol{d}^{(l_1+1)},\mathbf{F}^{e(l_1+1)}\right)}$
$l_1 \leftarrow l_1 + 1$
until $\epsilon_1^{(l_1+1)} \leq \epsilon_1 \parallel l_1 \geq l_1^{max}$
3. Return optimal d^* and $\mathbf{F}^{e*}$

For a given η, the optimal F_k^e can be derived from (3.120), which is given by

$$F_k^e = \frac{\sqrt{\frac{\varpi_k D_k c_k^3 R_k^2}{\eta}} - c_k R_k F_k^l}{F_k^l + c_k R_k}, \forall k. \tag{3.123}$$

To ensure $F_k^e \geq 0$ in (3.112h), the numerator of formula (3.123) must satisfy $\sqrt{\frac{\varpi_k D_k c_k^3 R_k^2}{\eta}} - c_k R_k F_k^l \geq 0$, i.e., $\eta \leq \frac{\varpi_k D_k c_k}{F_k^{l2}}$. Since $\eta \neq 0$ and $\sum_{k=1}^K F_k^e$ monotonically decreases with respect to η, the optimal η^* can be found in the range of $(\eta_l, \eta_u] = \left(0, \min_k \left(\frac{\varpi_k D_k c_k}{F_k^{l2}}\right)\right]$ to ensure (3.121), using the classical bisection search method with the termination coefficient of ϵ_1. Algorithm 1 summarizes the procedure of solving problem (3.113), whose computational complexity is mainly determined by calculating $F^{e(l_1+1)}$ using (3.123) and calculating η using bisection search method. The computational complexity for calculating $F^{e(l_1+1)}$ is $O\left(\log_2\left(\frac{\eta_u-\eta_l}{\epsilon_1}\right)K\right)$. Hence the total complexity of Algorithm 5 is on the order of $O\left(l_1^{\max}\log_2\left(\frac{\eta_u-\eta_l}{\epsilon_1}\right)K\right)$, where $l_1^{\max}$ is the maximum number of iterations. □

3.4.2.2 Joint Optimization of BS Receiving Vector and RIS BPS

With a fixed offloading data volume $\boldsymbol{d}$ and edge computing resource allocation $\mathbf{F}^e$, problem (3.112) can be reduced to

$$\min_{\mathbf{U},\boldsymbol{\theta}} \sum_{k=1}^{K} \varpi_k T_k\left(\mathbf{u}_k, \boldsymbol{\theta}\right) \tag{3.124a}$$

$$\text{s.t. } (3.112\text{b}), (3.112\text{c}), (3.112\text{d}), (3.112\text{e}) \tag{3.124b}$$

Remark 3.3 The challenges of solving problem (3.124) include two aspects: (1) the segmented objective function form caused by the operation of maximization; (2) the objective function is the summation of fractional functions with respect to the BS's receiving vector $\mathbf{U}$ and BPS $\boldsymbol{\theta}$. In order to tackle the first issue and solving the non-convex sum-of-ratios optimization problem caused by the second issue, we transform problem (3.124) as follows.

As explained in Sect. 3.4.2.1, when T_k takes its minimum value, we have $T_k = T_k^l = T_k^e$. Hence we replace T_k with T_k^e and remove the constant terms, problem (3.124) can be reformulated as

$$\min_{\mathbf{U},\boldsymbol{\theta}} \sum_{k=1}^{K} \frac{\varpi_k d_k}{R_k\left(\mathbf{u}_k, \boldsymbol{\theta}\right)} \tag{3.125a}$$

$$\text{s.t. } (3.112\text{b})\text{–}(3.112\text{e}). \tag{3.125b}$$

It can be converted into the following equivalent form by introducing auxiliary variable $\boldsymbol{\xi}$

$$\min_{\mathbf{U},\boldsymbol{\theta},\boldsymbol{\xi}} \sum_{k=1}^{K} \xi_k \tag{3.126a}$$

$$\text{s.t. } \frac{\varpi_k d_k}{R_k\left(\mathbf{u}_k, \boldsymbol{\theta}\right)} \leq \xi_k, \forall k, \tag{3.126b}$$

$$(3.112\text{b})\text{–}(3.112\text{e}). \tag{3.126c}$$

The Lagrangian function related to problem (3.126) is formulated as

$$\mathcal{L}(\mathbf{U}, \boldsymbol{\theta}, \boldsymbol{\xi}, \boldsymbol{\chi}) = \sum_{k=1}^{K} \xi_k + \sum_{k=1}^{K} \chi_k \left[\varpi_k d_k - \xi_k R_k\left(\mathbf{u}_k, \boldsymbol{\theta}\right)\right], \tag{3.127}$$

where $\{\chi_k\} \geq 0$ denotes the Lagrange multiplier. Corresponding, the AL form of problem (3.126) is given by

$$\min_{\mathbf{U},\boldsymbol{\theta},\boldsymbol{\xi},\boldsymbol{\chi}} \mathcal{L}(\mathbf{U}, \boldsymbol{\theta}, \boldsymbol{\xi}, \boldsymbol{\chi}) \tag{3.128a}$$

$$\text{s.t. } (3.112\text{b})\text{–}(3.112\text{e}) \tag{3.128b}$$

Upon denoting the solution of problem (3.126) by $\left(\mathbf{U}^*, \boldsymbol{\theta}^*, \boldsymbol{\xi}^*\right)$, there exist $\boldsymbol{\chi}^*$ satisfying the following KKT conditions for $\forall k \in \mathcal{K}$

$$\frac{\partial \mathcal{L}}{\partial \theta_k} = -\chi_k^* \xi_k^* \nabla R_k \left(\mathbf{u}_k^*, \boldsymbol{\theta}^*\right) = 0, \tag{3.129}$$

$$\frac{\partial \mathcal{L}}{\partial \mathbf{u}_k} = -\chi_k^* \xi_k^* \nabla R_k \left(\mathbf{u}_k^*, \boldsymbol{\theta}^*\right) = 0, \tag{3.130}$$

$$\frac{\partial \mathcal{L}}{\partial \xi_k} = 1 - \chi_k^* R_k \left(\mathbf{u}_k^*, \boldsymbol{\theta}^*\right) = 0, \tag{3.131}$$

$$\chi_k^* \left[\varpi_k d_k - \xi_k^* R_k \left(\mathbf{u}_k^*, \boldsymbol{\theta}^*\right)\right] = 0, \tag{3.132}$$

$$\chi_k^* \geq 0, \tag{3.133}$$

$$\varpi_k d_k - \xi_k^* R_k \left(\mathbf{u}_k^*, \boldsymbol{\theta}^*\right) \leq 0, \tag{3.134}$$

$$0 \leq \theta_k^* \leq 2\pi. \tag{3.135}$$

According to (3.131), (3.132), and $R_k \left(\mathbf{u}_k^*, \boldsymbol{\theta}^*\right) > 0$, we have

$$\chi_k^* = \frac{1}{R_k \left(\mathbf{u}_k^*, \boldsymbol{\theta}^*\right)}, \forall k, \tag{3.136}$$

and

$$\xi_k^* = \frac{\varpi_k d_k}{R_k \left(\mathbf{u}_k^*, \boldsymbol{\theta}^*\right)}, \forall k. \tag{3.137}$$

Next, problem (3.128) will be solved in two steps: (1) obtain $\mathbf{U}^*$ and $\boldsymbol{\theta}^*$ by solving problem (3.128) with fixed $\boldsymbol{\xi}$ and $\boldsymbol{\chi}$; (2) update $\boldsymbol{\xi}$ and $\boldsymbol{\chi}$ using a Newton-like method. $\left\{\mathbf{U}^*, \boldsymbol{\theta}^*\right\}$ and $\{\boldsymbol{\xi}, \boldsymbol{\chi}\}$ are alternately updated until objective (3.125a) converges. The detailed procedures can refer to Algorithm 6. For convenience, we define

$$\Omega_k \left(\chi_k\right) = \chi_k R_k \left(\mathbf{u}_k^*, \boldsymbol{\theta}^*\right) - 1, \forall k, \tag{3.138}$$

$$\psi_k \left(\xi_k\right) = \xi_k R_k \left(\mathbf{u}_k^*, \boldsymbol{\theta}^*\right) - \varpi_k d_k, \forall k. \tag{3.139}$$

Now, we focus our attention on the first step, i.e., optimizing $\mathbf{U}$ and $\boldsymbol{\theta}$. Given a set solution of $\{\boldsymbol{\chi}, \boldsymbol{\xi}, \boldsymbol{d}\}$, problem (3.128) can be reduced to the following weighted sum-rate maximization problem

$$\max_{\mathbf{U}, \boldsymbol{\theta}} \sum_{k=1}^{K} \sum_{p=1}^{P} \chi_k \xi_k R_{k,p} \left(\mathbf{u}_{k,p}, \boldsymbol{\theta}\right) \tag{3.143a}$$

Algorithm 6 Alternating Optimization $\mathbf{U}$ and $\boldsymbol{\theta}$, Given $\boldsymbol{d}$ and $\mathbf{F}^e$

Input: $\boldsymbol{d}, \mathbf{F}^e, \mathbf{h}_{k,p}^d, \mathbf{G}_p, \mathbf{h}_{k,p}^r, \epsilon_2$ and $l_2^{\max}, \forall k \in \mathcal{K}, \forall p \in \mathcal{P}$
Output: Optimal $\mathbf{U}$ and $\boldsymbol{\theta}$

1. Initialization

Initialize $l_2 = 0$, $\tau \in (0, 1)$, $\Gamma \in (0, 1)$, $\boldsymbol{\theta}$ satisfying (3.112d) and $\mathbf{u}_{k,p}$ satisfying (3.112e), $\forall k \in \mathcal{K}, \forall p \in \mathcal{P}$

2. Joint optimization U, $\boldsymbol{\theta}$, $\boldsymbol{\chi}$, [and $\boldsymbol{\xi}$

while $\chi_k^{(l_2)} R_k\left(\mathbf{u}_k^{(l_2)}, \boldsymbol{\theta}^{(l_2)}\right) - 1 > \epsilon_2$ & & $\xi_k R_k\left(\mathbf{u}_k^{(l_2)}, \boldsymbol{\theta}^{(l_2)}\right) - \varpi_k d_k > \epsilon_2$ && $l_2 \le l_2^{\max}$ **do**

Update $\mathbf{u}_{k,p}^{(l_2+1)}$ and $\boldsymbol{\theta}^{(l_2+1)}$ using Algorithm 7, $\forall k \in \mathcal{K}, \forall p \in \mathcal{P}$

Update $\boldsymbol{\chi}^{(l_2+1)}$ and $\boldsymbol{\xi}^{(l_2+1)}$ as follows

$$\chi_k^{(l_2+1)} = \chi_k^{(l_2)} - \frac{\Gamma^{i^{(l_2+1)}} \Omega_k\left(\chi_k^{(l_2)}\right)}{R_k\left(\mathbf{u}_k^{(l_2+1)}, \boldsymbol{\theta}^{(l_2+1)}\right)} \tag{3.140}$$

$$\xi_k^{(l_2+1)} = \xi_k^{(l_2)} - \frac{\Gamma^{i^{(l_2+1)}} \psi_k\left(\xi_k^{(l_2)}\right)}{R_k\left(\mathbf{u}_k^{(l_2+1)}, \boldsymbol{\theta}^{(t_2+1)}\right)} \tag{3.141}$$

where $i^{(l_2+1)}$ is the smallest positive integer that satisfying

$$\sum_{k=1}^{K}\left|\Omega_k\left(\chi_k^{(l_2)} - \frac{\Gamma^i \Omega_k\left(\chi_k^{(l_2)}\right)}{R_k\left(\mathbf{u}_k^{(l_2+1)}, \boldsymbol{\theta}^{(l_2+1)}\right)}\right)\right|^2 + \sum_{k=1}^{K}\left|\psi_k\left(\xi^{(l_2)} - \frac{\Gamma^i \psi_k\left(\xi^{(l_2)}\right)}{R_k\left(\mathbf{u}_k^{(l_2+1)}, \boldsymbol{\theta}^{(l_2+1)}\right)}\right)\right|^2$$
$$\le \left(1 - \tau\Gamma^i\right)^2 \sum_{k=1}^{K}\left[\left|\Omega_k\left(\chi_k^{(l_2)}\right)\right|^2 + \left|\psi_k\left(\xi^{(l_2)}\right)\right|^2\right] \tag{3.142}$$

$l_2 = l_2 + 1$

end while

3. Return $\mathbf{u}_{k,p}^*$ and $\boldsymbol{\theta}^*$, $\forall k \in \mathcal{K}, \forall p \in \mathcal{P}$

$$\text{s.t. (3.112b)–(3.112e).} \tag{3.143b}$$

Leveraging the equivalence between sum-rate maximization and MSE minimization [44], problem (3.143) can be transformed into a modified MSE minimization problem. The latter is convex regarding each optimization variable while fixing others. Specifically, by introducing auxiliary variables $\Upsilon_{k,p} \in \mathbb{C}, \forall k \in \mathcal{K}, \forall p \in \mathcal{P}$, the modified MSE function for the k-th WD on the p-th subcarrier can be formulated as

$$\begin{aligned}\mathrm{MSE}_{k,p} &= \mathbb{E}\left\{\left(\Upsilon_{k,p}^{*} y_{k,p} - s_{k,p}\right)\left(\Upsilon_{k,p}^{*} y_{k,p} - s_{k,p}\right)^{*}\right\} \\ &= \sum_{j=1}^{K}\left|\Upsilon_{k,p}^{*}\sqrt{\widetilde{p}}\mathbf{u}_{k,p}^{H}\left(\mathbf{h}_{j,p}^{\mathrm{d}}+\mathbf{G}_{p}\mathbf{\Phi}_{p}\mathbf{h}_{j,p}^{\mathrm{r}}\right)\right|^{2} \\ &\quad - 2\Re\left\{\Upsilon_{k,p}^{*}\sqrt{\widetilde{p}}\mathbf{u}_{k,p}^{H}\left(\mathbf{h}_{k,p}^{\mathrm{d}}+\mathbf{G}_{p}\mathbf{\Phi}_{p}\mathbf{h}_{k,p}^{\mathrm{r}}\right)\right\} \\ &\quad + \left|\Upsilon_{k,p}\right|^{2}\sigma^{2} + 1, \quad \forall k, p.\end{aligned} \tag{3.144}$$

Next, problem (3.143) can be converted into the following equivalent form by introducing weighting parameters $\rho_{k,p} \in \mathbb{R}^{+}, \forall k \in \mathcal{K}, \forall p \in \mathcal{P}$

$$\max_{\mathbf{U},\boldsymbol{\theta},\boldsymbol{\Upsilon},\boldsymbol{\rho}} \sum_{k=1}^{K}\sum_{p=1}^{P} \chi_k \xi_k \left(\log_2 \rho_{k,p} - \rho_{k,p}\mathrm{MSE}_{k,p} + 1\right) \tag{3.145a}$$

$$\text{s.t. } (3.112\text{b})\text{–}(3.112\text{e}), \tag{3.145b}$$

where $\boldsymbol{\Upsilon}$ and $\boldsymbol{\rho}$ represent the sets of variables $\Upsilon_{k,p}$ and $\rho_{k,p}$, respectively. Compared with problem (3.143), the newly formulated problem (3.145) is more tractable, because the complex SINR term is removed from the $\log(\cdot)$ function. In the following subsection, we will decouple problem (3.145) into four subproblems and provide a solution for each subproblem separately.

1. Optimization of Weighting Parameter $\boldsymbol{\rho}$ Given the BS receiving vector $\mathbf{U}$, BPS $\boldsymbol{\theta}$, and auxiliary variable $\boldsymbol{\Upsilon}$, the subproblem with weighting parameters $\rho_{k,p}$ is formulated as

$$\max_{\rho_{k,p}} \quad \chi_k \xi_k \left(\log_2 \rho_{k,p} - \rho_{k,p}\mathrm{MSE}_{k,p}\right), \tag{3.146}$$

which is a convex problem without constraints. Its solution can be obtained by setting the first-order partial derivative to zero, which is expressed as

$$\rho_{k,p}^{*} = \mathrm{MSE}_{k,p}^{-1} = 1 + \gamma_{k,p}, \forall k, p. \tag{3.147}$$

2. Optimization of Auxiliary Variable $\boldsymbol{\Upsilon}$ Fixing BS's receiving vector $\mathbf{U}$, BPS $\boldsymbol{\theta}$ and weighting parameters $\boldsymbol{\rho}$, the subproblem with respect to the auxiliary variable $\Upsilon_{k,p}$ can be written as

$$\min_{\Upsilon_{k,p}} \quad \chi_k \xi_k \rho_{k,p}\mathrm{MSE}_{k,p}, \forall k, p, \tag{3.148a}$$

similarly, we select $\Upsilon_{k,p}^{\star}$ which ensures the partial derivative with respect to $\Upsilon_{k,p}$ to zero as its optimal solution, i.e.,

$$\Upsilon_{k,p}^{\star} = \frac{\sqrt{\widetilde{p}}\mathbf{u}_{k,p}^{H}\left(\mathbf{h}_{k,p}^{d} + \mathbf{G}_p\mathbf{\Phi}_p\mathbf{h}_{k,p}^{r}\right)}{\sum_{j=1}^{K}\left|\sqrt{\widetilde{p}}\mathbf{u}_{k,p}^{H}\left(\mathbf{h}_{j,p}^{d} + \mathbf{G}_p\mathbf{\Phi}_p\mathbf{h}_{j,p}^{r}\right)\right|^2 + \sigma^2}, \forall k, p \tag{3.149}$$

3. Optimization of BS Receiving Vector U Given the BPS $\boldsymbol{\theta}$, weighting parameters $\boldsymbol{\rho}$, and auxiliary variable $\boldsymbol{\Upsilon}$, the subproblem with respect to the BS's receiving vector $\mathbf{U}$ can be expressed as

$$\min_{\mathbf{U}} \sum_{k=1}^{K}\sum_{p=1}^{P} \chi_k\xi_k\rho_{k,p}[\sum_{j=1}^{K}\left|\Upsilon_{k,p}^{*}\sqrt{\widetilde{p}}\mathbf{u}_{k,p}^{H}\left(\mathbf{h}_{j,p}^{\mathrm{d}}+\mathbf{G}_p\mathbf{\Phi}_p\mathbf{h}_{j,p}^{\mathrm{r}}\right)\right|^2$$

$$-2\Re\left\{\Upsilon_{k,p}^{*}\sqrt{\widetilde{p}}\mathbf{u}_{k,p}^{H}\left(\mathbf{h}_{k,p}^{\mathrm{d}} + \mathbf{G}_p\mathbf{\Phi}_p\mathbf{h}_{k,p}^{\mathrm{r}}\right)\right\}] \tag{3.150a}$$

$$\text{s.t.} \left\|\mathbf{u}_{k,p}\right\|^2 \leq 1. \tag{3.150b}$$

To simplify the expression, we define equivalent channel for the k-th WD on the p-th subcarrier as $\mathbf{h}_{k,p} = \mathbf{h}_{k,p}^{\mathrm{d}} + \mathbf{G}_p\mathbf{\Phi}_p\mathbf{h}_{k,p}^{\mathrm{r}}, \forall k, p$. The objective (3.150a) can be simplified as g_1, which is defined as

$$\begin{aligned} g_1 &= \sum_{k=1}^{K}\sum_{p=1}^{P} \chi_k\xi_k\rho_{k,p}\left(\sum_{j=1}^{K}\left|\Upsilon_{k,p}^{*}\sqrt{\widetilde{p}}\mathbf{u}_{k,p}^{H}\mathbf{h}_{j,p}\right|^2 - 2\Re\left\{\Upsilon_{k,p}^{*}\sqrt{\widetilde{p}}\mathbf{u}_{k,p}^{H}\mathbf{h}_{k,p}\right\}\right) \\ &= \sum_{k=1}^{K}\sum_{p=1}^{P}\left[\mathbf{u}_{k,p}^{H}\left(\sum_{j=1}^{K}\chi_k\xi_k\rho_{k,p}\widetilde{p}\left|\Upsilon_{k,p}\right|^2\mathbf{h}_{j,p}\mathbf{h}_{j,p}^{H}\right)\mathbf{u}_{k,p}\right] \\ &- \sum_{k=1}^{K}\sum_{p=1}^{P} 2\chi_k\xi_k\rho_{k,p}\Re\left\{\Upsilon_{k,p}^{*}\sqrt{\widetilde{p}}\mathbf{u}_{k,p}^{H}\mathbf{h}_{k,p}\right\}. \end{aligned} \tag{3.151}$$

To further simplify the expression of g_1, we define

$$\mathbf{a}_{k,p} = \sum_{j=1}^{K}\chi_k\xi_k\rho_{k,p}\widetilde{p}\left|\Upsilon_{k,p}\right|^2\mathbf{h}_{j,p}\mathbf{h}_{j,p}^{H}, \tag{3.152}$$

$$\mathbf{A}_p = \mathrm{diag}\left[\mathbf{a}_{1,p}, \ldots, \mathbf{a}_{K,p}\right], \mathbf{A} = \mathrm{diag}\left(\mathbf{A}_1, \cdots, \mathbf{A}_P\right), \tag{3.153}$$

$$\mathbf{v}_{k,p} = \chi_k\xi_k\rho_{k,p}\Upsilon_{k,p}^{*}\sqrt{\widetilde{p}}\mathbf{h}_{k,p}, \tag{3.154}$$

$$\mathbf{V} = \left[\mathbf{v}_{1,1}^{T}, \mathbf{v}_{2,1}^{T}, \ldots, \mathbf{v}_{K,1}^{T}, \mathbf{v}_{1,2}^{T}, \mathbf{v}_{2,2}^{T}, \ldots, \mathbf{v}_{K,P}^{T}\right]^{T}, \tag{3.155}$$

By substituting (3.152)–(3.155) into g_1, g_1 can be rewritten as

$$g_2(\mathbf{U}) = \mathbf{U}^H \mathbf{A} \mathbf{U} - \Re\left\{2\mathbf{U}^H \mathbf{V}\right\}. \tag{3.156}$$

So far, problem (3.150) is reduced to

$$\min_{\mathbf{U}} \quad \mathbf{U}^H \mathbf{A} \mathbf{U} - \Re\left\{2\mathbf{U}^H \mathbf{V}\right\} \tag{3.157a}$$

$$\text{s.t.} \mathbf{U}^H \mathbf{D}_{k,p} \mathbf{U} \leq 1, \forall k, p, \tag{3.157b}$$

where $\mathbf{D}_{k,p} = \mathbf{O}_{k,p} \otimes \mathbf{I}_M$, $\mathbf{O}_{k,p}$ is a $K \times P$ matrix whose (k, p)-th element is one, and other elements are zeros. Since matrices $\mathbf{A}$ and $\mathbf{D}_{k,p}$ are all positive semidefinite, the simplified subproblem (3.157) is a standard convex optimization problem, which can be optimally solved using the existing convex optimization toolbox [45].

4. Optimization of BPS Vector $\boldsymbol{\theta}$ When the BS receiving vector $\mathbf{U}$, weighting parameters $\boldsymbol{\rho}$, and auxiliary variable $\boldsymbol{\Upsilon}$ are all fixed, the subproblem regarding BPS $\boldsymbol{\theta}$ can be written as

$$\min_{\boldsymbol{\theta}} \sum_{k=1}^{K} \sum_{p=1}^{P} \chi_k \xi_k \rho_{k,p} J_1(\theta) \tag{3.158a}$$

$$\text{s.t. (3.112b)–(3.112d)}, \tag{3.158b}$$

where

$$J_1(\theta) = \sum_{j=1}^{K} \left| \Upsilon_{k,p}^* \sqrt{\bar{p}} \mathbf{u}_{k,p}^H \left(\mathbf{h}_{j,p}^{\mathrm{d}} + \mathbf{G}_p \boldsymbol{\Phi}_p \mathbf{h}_{j,p}^{\mathrm{r}} \right) \right|^2 - 2\Re\left\{ \Upsilon_{k,p}^* \sqrt{\bar{p}} \mathbf{u}_{k,p}^H \left(\mathbf{h}_{k,p}^{\mathrm{d}} + \mathbf{G}_p \boldsymbol{\Phi}_p \mathbf{h}_{k,p}^{\mathrm{r}} \right) \right\} \tag{3.159}$$

Upon defining $\boldsymbol{\phi}_p \triangleq [\phi_{p,1}, \ldots, \phi_{p,N}]^T$, $\bar{h}_{k,j,p}^{\mathrm{d}} \triangleq \mathbf{u}_{k,p}^H \mathbf{h}_{j,p}^{\mathrm{d}}$ and $\mathbf{g}_{k,j,p} \triangleq \mathbf{u}_{k,p}^H \mathbf{G}_p \operatorname{diag}\left(\mathbf{h}_{j,p}^{r}\right)$, $\forall k, j \in \mathcal{K}, \forall p \in \mathcal{P}$, problem (3.158) can be reformulated as

$$\min_{\boldsymbol{\theta}} \sum_{p=1}^{P} \sum_{k=1}^{K} \chi_k \xi_k \rho_{k,p} J_2(\theta) \tag{3.160a}$$

$$= \min_{\boldsymbol{\Theta}} \sum_{p=1}^{P} \left(\boldsymbol{\phi}_p^H \boldsymbol{\Lambda}_p \boldsymbol{\phi}_p - 2\Re\left\{ \boldsymbol{\phi}_p^H \boldsymbol{v}_p \right\} + \zeta_p \right) \tag{3.160b}$$

$$\text{s.t. (3.112b)–(3.112d)}, \tag{3.160c}$$

where

$$J_2(\theta) = \sum_{j=1}^{K} \left| \Upsilon_{k,p}^{*} \sqrt{\widetilde{p}} \left(\bar{h}_{k,j,p}^{\mathrm{d}} + \mathbf{g}_{k,j,p} \boldsymbol{\phi}_p \right) \right|^2 - 2\Re \left\{ \Upsilon_{k,p}^{*} \sqrt{\widetilde{p}} \left(\bar{h}_{k,k,p}^{\mathrm{d}} + \mathbf{g}_{k,k,p} \boldsymbol{\phi}_p \right) \right\} \tag{3.161}$$

Matrix $\boldsymbol{\Lambda}_p$, vector $\boldsymbol{v}_p$ and scalar ζ_p, $\forall p \in \mathcal{P}$, are respectively defined as

$$\boldsymbol{\Lambda}_p \triangleq \sum_{k=1}^{K} \chi_k \xi_k \rho_{k,p} \left| \Upsilon_{k,p} \right|^2 \widetilde{p} \sum_{j=1}^{K} \mathbf{g}_{k,j,p}^{H} \mathbf{g}_{k,j,p}, \forall p, \tag{3.162}$$

$$\boldsymbol{v}_p \triangleq \sum_{k=1}^{K} \chi_k \xi_k \rho_{k,p} \left(\Upsilon_{k,p} \sqrt{\widetilde{p}} \mathbf{g}_{k,k,p}^{H} - \left| \Upsilon_{k,p} \right|^2 \widetilde{p} \sum_{j=1}^{K} \mathbf{g}_{k,j,p}^{H} \bar{h}_{k,j,p}^{d} \right), \forall p \tag{3.163}$$

$$\zeta_p \triangleq \sum_{k=1}^{K} \chi_k \xi_k \rho_{k,p} \left(\left| \Upsilon_{k,p} \right|^2 \widetilde{p} \sum_{j=1}^{K} \left| \bar{h}_{k,j,p}^{d} \right|^2 - 2\Re \left\{ \Upsilon_{k,p}^{*} \sqrt{\widetilde{p}} \bar{h}_{k,k,p}^{d} \right\} \right), \forall p \tag{3.164}$$

It is challenging to solve problem (3.160) directly because of BPS $\boldsymbol{\theta}$ is embedded into P complicated functions. To handle this issue, one feasible scheme is to decouple the original problem to N subproblems, only one element of BPS $\boldsymbol{\theta}$ is optimized each time.

To proceed, the objective function (3.160b) is divided element-by-element as

$$\sum_{p=1}^{P} \left(\boldsymbol{\phi}_p^{H} \boldsymbol{\Lambda}_p \boldsymbol{\phi}_p - 2\Re \left\{ \boldsymbol{\phi}_p^{H} \boldsymbol{v}_p \right\} \right) \tag{3.165}$$

$$= \sum_{p=1}^{P} \sum_{n=1}^{N} \left(\sum_{n'=1}^{N} \boldsymbol{\Lambda}_p(n, n') \phi_{p,n}^{*} \phi_{p,n'} - 2\Re \left\{ \phi_{p,n}^{*} \boldsymbol{v}_p(n) \right\} \right). \tag{3.166}$$

Fixing the other elements, the objective function regarding the n-th element can be expressed as

$$\sum_{p=1}^{P} \Bigg(\sum_{n' \neq n} \left(\boldsymbol{\Lambda}_p(n, n') \phi_{p,n}^{*} \phi_{p,n'} + \boldsymbol{\Lambda}_p(n', n) \phi_{p,n'}^{*} \phi_{p,n} \right)$$

$$+ \boldsymbol{\Lambda}_p(n, n) \left| \phi_{p,n} \right|^2 - 2\Re \left\{ \phi_{p,n}^{*} \boldsymbol{v}_p(n) \right\} \Bigg)$$

$$\overset{(a)}{=} \sum_{p=1}^{P} \Bigg(\sum_{n' \neq n} \left(\boldsymbol{\Lambda}_p(n, n') \phi_{p,n}^{*} \phi_{p,n'} + \boldsymbol{\Lambda}_p^{*}(n, n') \phi_{p,n} \phi_{p,n'}^{*} \right) + \boldsymbol{\Lambda}_p(n, n) \left| \phi_{p,n} \right|^2$$

$$- 2\Re\left\{\phi_{p,n}^{*}\boldsymbol{v}_{p}(n)\right\}\Bigg)$$

$$= \sum_{p=1}^{P}\left(2\Re\left\{\left(\sum_{n'\neq n}\boldsymbol{\Lambda}_{p}(n,n')\phi_{p,p'} - \boldsymbol{v}_{p}(n)\right)\phi_{p,n}^{*}\right\} + \boldsymbol{\Lambda}_{i}(n,n)\left|\phi_{p,n}\right|^{2}\right), \tag{3.167}$$

in which (a) holds since $\boldsymbol{\Lambda}_p = \boldsymbol{\Lambda}_p^H, \forall p \in \mathcal{P}$. The subproblem with respect to the n-th element θ_n is given by

$$\min_{\theta_n}\sum_{p=1}^{P}\left(2\Re\left\{\left(\sum_{n'\neq n}\boldsymbol{\Lambda}_{p}(n,n')\phi_{p,n'} - \boldsymbol{v}_{p}(n)\right)\phi_{p,n}^{*}\right\} + \boldsymbol{\Lambda}_{p}(n,n)\left|\theta_{p,n}\right|^{2}\right) \tag{3.168a}$$

$$\text{s.t. (3.112b)–(3.112d).} \tag{3.168b}$$

For convenience, we further define $\omega_{p,n} \triangleq \sum_{n'\neq n}\boldsymbol{\Lambda}_p(n,n')\phi_{p,n'} - \boldsymbol{v}_p(n), \forall p \in \mathcal{P}, \forall n \in \mathcal{N}$. Upon substituting constraints (3.112b) and (3.112c) into objective (3.168a), problem (3.168) can be rewritten as

$$\min_{\theta_n} \quad g_3\left(\theta_n\right) \tag{3.169a}$$

$$\text{s.t. } \theta_n \in [-\pi, \pi], \forall n, \tag{3.169b}$$

where

$$g_3\left(\theta_n\right) = \sum_{p=1}^{P}\Big(2\left|\omega_{p,n}\right|\mathrm{A}\left(\theta_n, f_p\right)\cos\left(\angle\omega_{p,n} - \mathrm{B}\left(\theta_n, f_p\right)\right) + \boldsymbol{\Lambda}_p(n,n)\mathrm{A}^2\left(\theta_n, f_p\right)\Big). \tag{3.170}$$

Problem (3.169) is still difficult to solve because the complicated objective function (3.169a). A large number of numerical simulations indicates that function (3.169a) behaves like a smooth curve with two peak-trough. Thereby, there is only one minimum point within the range $[-\pi, \pi]$. Inspired by this observation, we adopt the following three-phase search method to search its optimal solution.

Step 1: We first focus our attention on narrowing the search range. Initialize the start point within the range $[-\pi, \pi]$ and search step length $l > 0$. If $g_3\left(\theta_n^0 + l\right) < g_3\left(\theta_n^0\right)$, search forward; otherwise search reversely, until the value of g_3 rises.

Step 2: Determine the minimum point $\widetilde{\theta}$ by continuously sectioning the search range, until a predetermined threshold is met.

Step 3: The minimum value of g_3 and the corresponding phase shift is determined by comparing the objective value at the points $\widetilde{\theta}_n$, $-\pi$ and π.

In order to reduce hardware consumption and cost, we can use finite discrete phases to realized RISs in realistic applications. Assuming that these discrete phases of BPS θ_n is controlled by b bits, which is given by

$$\theta_n \in \mathcal{S} \triangleq \left\{ \frac{2\pi}{2^b} i - \pi \mid i = 0, 1, \ldots, 2^b - 1 \right\}, \forall n. \tag{3.171}$$

Accordingly, the RIS optimization subproblem for discrete phases is expressed as

$$\min_{\theta_n} \sum_{p=1}^{P} \left(2 \left| \omega_{p,n} \right| \mathrm{A} \left(\theta_n, f_p \right) \cos \left(\angle \omega_{p,n} - \mathrm{B} \left(\theta_n, f_p \right) \right) + \mathbf{\Lambda}_p(n,n) \mathrm{A}^2 \left(\theta_n, f_p \right) \right) \tag{3.172a}$$

$$\text{s.t. } \theta_n \in \mathcal{S}, \forall n. \tag{3.172b}$$

It can be seen that except for constraint (3.172b), the discrete RIS design subproblem is almost identical to that of continuous phases case. To find the optimal $\boldsymbol{\theta}$, the one-dimensional exhaustive search can be performed over the feasible set $\mathcal{S}$ due to the application of low-resolution phase shifter. Specifically, we alternately optimize each element in the BPS $\boldsymbol{\theta}$, while fixing the others until convergence. To determine the optimal BPS θ_n^*, we check all the feasible solution from set $\mathcal{S}$ and calculate the corresponding reflection coefficients for each subcarrier using the non-ideal phase shift model. Subsequently, the optimal θ_n^* is selected.

Up to now, we provide the detailed approaches for solving the above four subproblems with respect to $\mathbf{U}$, $\boldsymbol{\theta}$, $\boldsymbol{\Upsilon}$ and $\boldsymbol{\rho}$, the overall procedure for solving problem (3.145) is summarized in Algorithm 7. Given appropriate initial values for $\mathbf{U}$ and $\boldsymbol{\theta}$, we alternately update the four variables until the objective converges.

3.4.3 Performance Evaluation

In this section, we will evaluate the proposed algorithm by a large number of simulation results. As illustrated in Fig. 3.25, we consider a single-cell MEC system

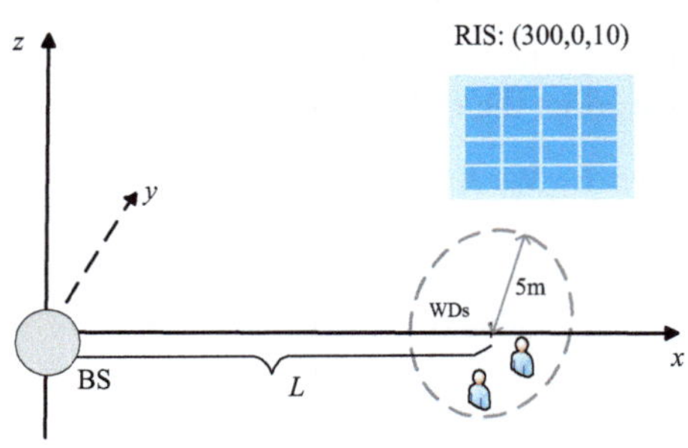

Fig. 3.25 The simulation scenario setup

Table 3.4 System parameters

Description	Parameter and value
Location setting	BS: (0 m, 0 m, 0 m), RIS: (300 m, 0 m, 10 m), $L = 290$ m, $r = 5$ m
Communication setting	$K = 2$, $\widetilde{p} = 1$ mW, $M = 4$, $N = 20$, $f_c = 2.4$ GHz, $B = 100$ MHz $P = 8$, $b = 3$, $\varpi_k = 1/K$, $\sigma^2 = 3.98 \times 10^{-15}$ W, $\Gamma = 0.5\tau = 0.1$, $\kappa_{\mathrm{BW}} = 3.5$, $\kappa_{\mathrm{BI}} = 2.2$, $\kappa_{\mathrm{IW}} = 2.2$
Computing setting	$D_k = [250, 350] \times 10^3$ bit, $c_k = [700, 800]$ cycle/bit $F_k^l = [4, 6] \times 10^8$ cycle/s, $F_{\mathrm{total}}^e = 50 \times 10^{11}$ cycle/s

Algorithm 7 Alternating Optimization $\mathbf{U}$ and $\boldsymbol{\theta}$, Given χ and ξ

Input: $B, \mathbf{h}_{k,p}^d, \mathbf{G}_p, \mathbf{h}_{k,p}^r, \forall p \in \mathcal{P}, \forall k \in \mathcal{K}$
Output: $\mathbf{U}$ and $\boldsymbol{\theta}$
1. Initialization
$\boldsymbol{\theta}$ and $\mathbf{u}_{k,p}, \forall p \in \mathcal{P}, \forall k \in \mathcal{K}$
2. Alternating optimization $\mathbf{U}, \boldsymbol{\theta}, \boldsymbol{\rho}, \boldsymbol{\Upsilon}$
repeat:
  Update $\rho_{k,p}$ using (3.147), $\forall k \in \mathcal{K}, \forall p \in \mathcal{P}$
  Update $\Upsilon_{k,p}$ using (3.149), $\forall k \in \mathcal{K}, \forall p \in \mathcal{P}$
  Update $\mathbf{u}_{k,p}$ by solving problem (3.157), $\forall k \in \mathcal{K}, \forall p \in \mathcal{P}$
  repeat
    for $n = 1$ to N **do**
      Continuous phase case: update θ_n by three-phase one-dimensional search method
      Low-resolution phases case: update θ_n by exhaustive search
    end for
  until BPS $\boldsymbol{\theta}$ converges
until objective (3.145a) converges
3. Return optimal $\mathbf{u}_{k,p}^*$ **and** $\boldsymbol{\theta}^*$, $\forall k \in \mathcal{K}, \forall p \in \mathcal{P}$

in which the BS coverage radius is 300 meters [46]. To improve the communication capacity, an RIS is deployed at the cell edge, which is high enough to construct a additional reflection link to assist the data offloading. Two WDs are randomly distributed in a circle centered at $(L, 0, 0)$ m with radius $r = 5$ m. The detailed location information for BS and RIS is presented in the "Location setting" block of Table 3.4.

We assume that the number of subcarriers is $P = 8$. The carrier frequency and bandwidth setting follows [41] and are given by $f_c = 2.4$ GHz and $B = 100$ MHz, respectively, and the noise power is $\sigma^2 = 3.98 \times 10^{-15}$ W. Upon denoting the distance between BS and WD, BS and RIS, as well as RIS and WD by d_{BW}, d_{BI} and d_{IW}, respectively, the distance-dependent large-scale fading model is given by

$$L(d) = C_0 \left(\frac{d}{d_0}\right)^{-\kappa}, \quad d \in \{d_{BW}, d_{BI}, d_{IW}\}, \tag{3.172}$$

Algorithm 8 The Method for Solving Problem (3.112)

Input: D_k, c_k, F^e_{total}, ϵ, and $l_3^{\max}$
Output: Optimal $\boldsymbol{d}$, $\mathbf{F}^e$, $\mathbf{u}_{k,p}$ and $\boldsymbol{\theta}$, $\forall k \in \mathcal{K}, \forall p \in \mathcal{P}$

1. Initialization
Initialize $l_3 = 0$ and $\epsilon_3^{(0)} = 1$
Initialize $\boldsymbol{\theta}^{(0)}$ satisfying (3.112d), $\mathbf{u}_{k,p}^{(0)}$ satisfying (3.112e), and $\mathbf{F}^{e(0)}$ satisfying (3.112g) and (3.112h)

2. Alternating optimization of $\boldsymbol{d}$ and $\mathbf{F}^e$, $\mathbf{u}_{k,p}$ and $\boldsymbol{\theta}$
repeat
Updating $\boldsymbol{d}^{(l_3+1)}$ and $\mathbf{F}^{e(l_3+1)}$ using Algorithm 1
Updating $\mathbf{u}_{k,p}^{(l_3+1)}$ and $\boldsymbol{\theta}^{(l_3+1)}$ using Algorithm 6
$\epsilon_3^{(l_3)} = \frac{\text{obj}\left(\mathbf{d}^{(l_3+1)},\mathbf{F}^{e(l_3+1)},\mathbf{U}^{(l_3+1)},\boldsymbol{\theta}^{(l_3+1)}\right)-\text{obj}\left(\mathbf{d}^{(l_3)},\mathbf{F}^{e(l_3)},\mathbf{U}^{(l_3)},\boldsymbol{\theta}^{(l_3)}\right)|}{\text{obj}\left(\mathbf{d}^{(l_3+1)},\mathbf{F}^{e(l_3+1)},\mathbf{U}^{(l_3+1)},\boldsymbol{\theta}^{(l_3+1)}\right)}$
$l_3 = l_3 + 1$
until $\epsilon_3^{(l_3)} < \epsilon \ \|\|\ l_3 > l_3^{\max}$

3. Output the optimal $\boldsymbol{d}^*$, $\mathbf{F}^{e*}$, $\mathbf{u}_{k,p}^*$ and $\boldsymbol{\theta}^*$, $\forall k \in \mathcal{K}, \forall p \in \mathcal{P}$

where κ represents the path loss exponent, and C_0 denotes the path loss at the reference distance $d_0 = 1$ m. Here, we set $C_0 = -30$ dB. Besides, we assume that the path loss exponent of the BS-WD link, BS-RIS link, and RIS-WD link are $\kappa_{\text{BW}} = 3.5$, $\kappa_{\text{BI}} = 2.2$ and $\kappa_{\text{IW}} = 2.2$, respectively [46]. For the small-scale fading, we consider a Rice fading channel model, thus the channel $\mathbf{H}$ of BS-WD can be expressed as

$$\mathbf{H} = \sqrt{\frac{\beta_{\text{BW}}}{1+\beta_{\text{BW}}}}\mathbf{H}^{\text{LoS}} + \sqrt{\frac{1}{1+\beta_{\text{BW}}}}\mathbf{H}^{\text{NLoS}}, \tag{3.174}$$

where β_{BW} is the Rician factor, $\mathbf{H}^{\text{LoS}}$ and $\mathbf{H}^{\text{NLoS}}$ represent the LoS and non-LoS Rayleigh fading components, respectively. Note that $\mathbf{H}$ is equivalent to a LoS channel when $\beta_{\text{BW}} \to \infty$, and a Rayleigh fading channel when $\beta_{\text{BW}} = 0$. Here, let β_{BW}, β_{BI}, and β_{IW} denote the Rician factors of the BS-WD link, BS-RIS link and RIS-WD link, respectively. We further set $\beta_{\text{BW}} = 0$, $\beta_{\text{BI}} \to \infty$ and $\beta_{\text{IW}} = 0$ as [14]. The complete BS-WD channel can be obtained by multiplying the small scale fading $\mathbf{H}$ by the square root of the large scale path loss $L(d)$. Likewise, the BS-RIS channel and the RIS-WD channel can also be generated through the aforementioned procedure. The default setting of "Communication setting" are presented in Table 3.4. In addition, the computation-related settings are provided in the "Computing setting" block of Table 3.4 and the value of these parameter are referenced from [46].

In Fig. 3.26, we first demonstrate the convergence of the proposed algorithm by depicting latency versus the number of iterations. Numerical results show that Algorithms 8 and 6 can achieve convergence within 2 iterations and 10 iterations, respectively, regardless of using continuous phase shifters or low-resolution phase shifters. Additionally, simulation results show that Algorithm 7 can achieve con-

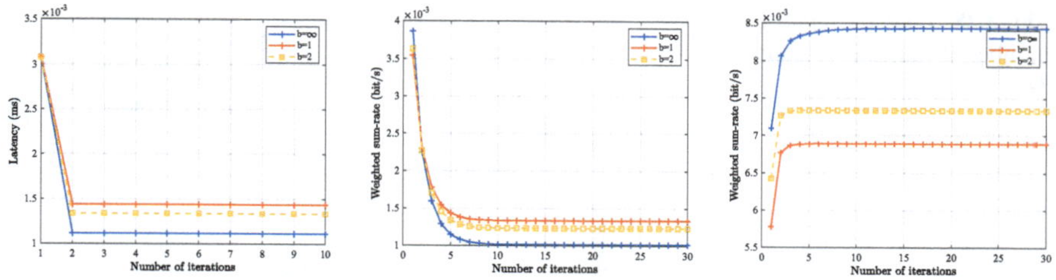

(a) (b) (c)

Fig. 3.26 Convergence behavior of the proposed algorithm. (**a**) Convergence of Algorithm 8. (**b**) Convergence of Algorithm 6. (**c**) Convergence of Algorithm 7

Fig. 3.27 Latency versus the resolution b

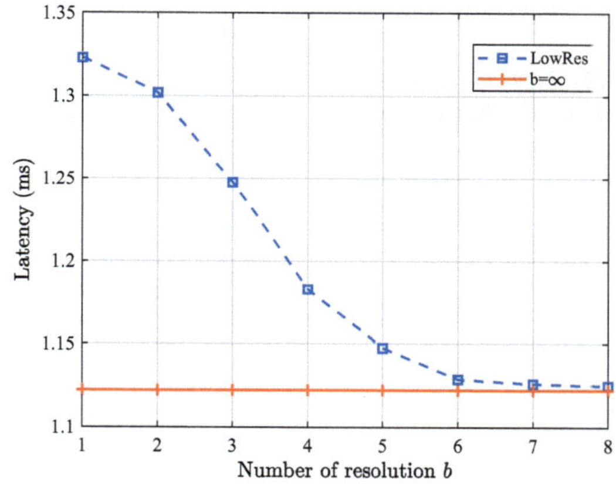

vergence within 10 iterations for continuous phases case and within 5 iterations for low-resolution phases case. Figure 3.27 depicts the latency versus resolution b. It is observed that a resolution level of $b = 5$ is deemed adequate, with only marginal performance enhancements when the value of b is greater than 5. Examining both the convergence behavior illustrated in Fig. 3.26c and the impact of resolution b presented in Fig. 3.27, it is more cost-effective to apply low-resolution phase shifters at RISs.

Next, the performance of the proposed algorithm is evaluated for the continuous phases case and discrete phases case (i.e., $b = 3$ bits) under different system settings. The following three benchmark schemes are taken into consideration for a fair comparison.

- *w/RIS, Proposed:* The latency optimization by our proposed algorithm based on the practical RIS reflection model.
- *w/RIS, Ideal:* The RIS optimization design based on the ideal reflection model.
- *w/o, RIS:* Traditional MEC systems without RIS.
- *w/RIS, Random:* Set the value of BPS $\boldsymbol{\theta}$ randomly within the range $[-\pi, \pi]$.

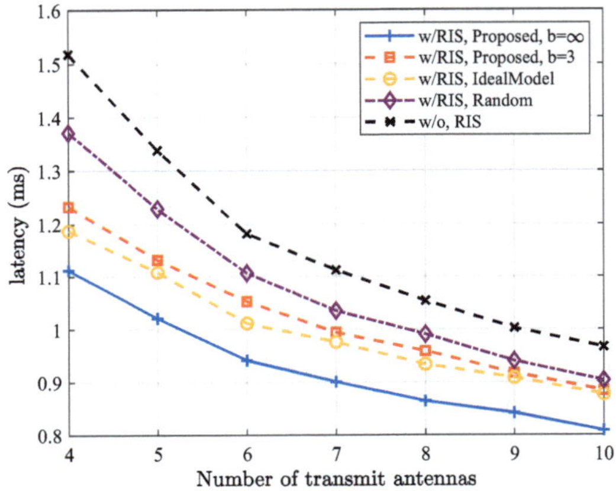

Fig. 3.28 Latency versus the number of transmit antennas M

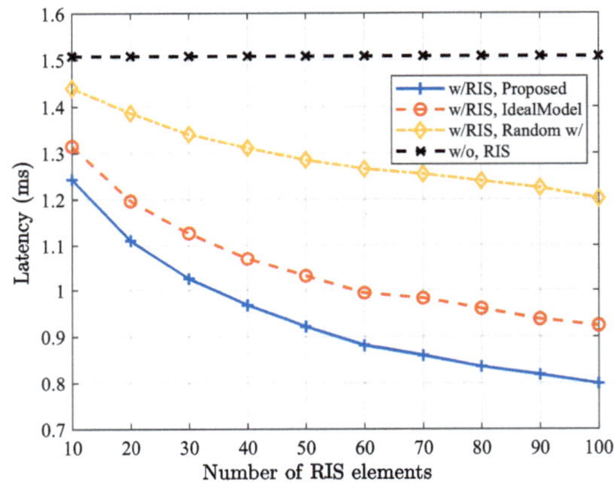

Fig. 3.29 Latency versus the number of RIS elements N

Figure 3.28 shows the latency versus the number of BS transmit antennas. The "w/o, RIS" scheme achieves the highest latency, illustrating the benefits of introducing RIS into MEC systems. The latency gap between the "w/RIS, Ideal" and the "w/RIS, Proposed" schemes demonstrates the significance of considering the non-ideal RIS reflection model.

The latency as a function of the number of RIS elements is presented in Fig. 3.29. The same conclusion can be drawn from Fig. 3.29 that the proposed algorithm outperforms its competitors in term of latency performance. Moreover, the performance gap between the schemes "w/RIS, Proposed" and the "w/RIS, Ideal" becomes higher upon increasing the number of RIS elements. The reason is that the signal power received by BS from the direct link dominates when N is of a small value, whereas the power received from the WD-RIS-BS link becomes dominant as the value of N increases. Consequently, the performance degradation resulting from hardware circuit defects of RIS becomes more significant.

Figure 3.30 illustrates the latency as a function of the edge computing capability F_{total}. It is evident that, for all schemes, the latency drastically reduces upon

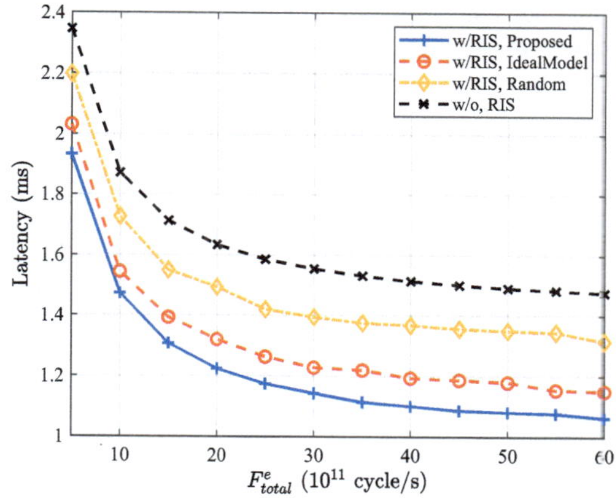

Fig. 3.30 Latency versus the edge computing capability F^e_{total}

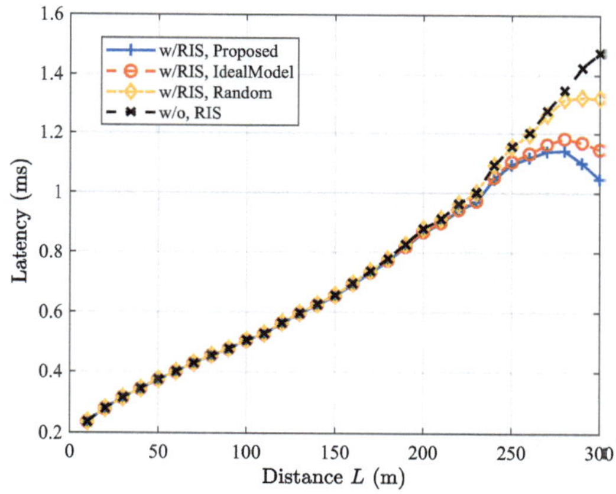

Fig. 3.31 Latency versus the distance L

increasing F_{total} when the value of F_{total} is small, while the rate of latency reduction diminishes as F_{total} approaches a specific threshold, specifically 30×10^{11} cycle/s. The reason for this phenomenon is that the edge computing latency dominates when the value of F_{total} is small, whereas the data transmission latency becomes dominant when F_{total} reaches a sufficiently large level. This indicates that adding appropriate computing capability to edge server is a more economical method for latency minimization.

Figure 3.31 shows the latency versus the distance L. Our observations are as follows. Firstly, for the conventional scheme without RIS, the latency increases upon increasing the distance L. Secondly, when WDs move away from BS to the RIS, the latency increases and reaches its maximum value at $d = 280$ m, because the signal power received by BS from WDs becomes weaker, and then decreases thanks to the reflecting signal from RIS. Thirdly, for the "w/RIS, Proposed" scheme, the advantages of employing RIS become notable when the distance between WD and RIS is less than 100 m, whereas the beneficial role of RIS becomes visible only when the distance is less than 20 m for the "w/RIS, Random" scheme. It is important to

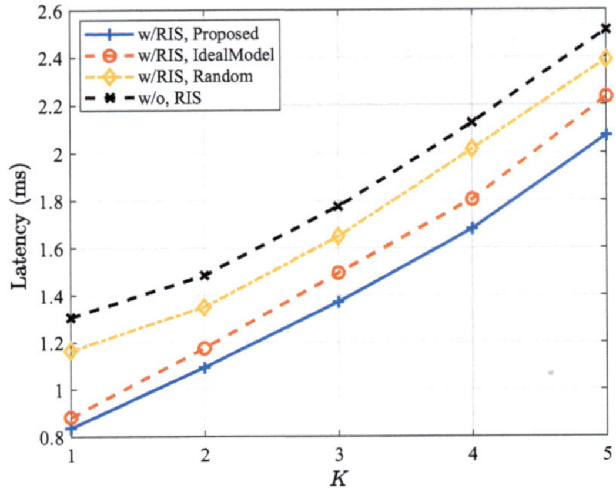

Fig. 3.32 Latency versus the number of users K

note that our proposed algorithm can achieve better latency performance compared with others under different distance settings.

Finally, Fig. 3.32 illustrates the latency as a function of the number of WDs. It is evident that the average latency rises as the number of WDs increases. This can be attributed to the diminished beamforming gain achieved at each WD and the reduced edge computing resources allocated to each WD. The former problem may be relieved by deploying more RIS to form stronger beams, and the latter issue can be solved by enhancing the computing capabilities of edge servers. Moreover, when $K = 5$, the proposed algorithm can reduce latency from 2.24 to 2.07 ms, compared to the "w/RIS, Ideal" scheme. This further validates the benefits of the proposed algorithm.

References

1. J. Lin, G. Wang, R. Fan, T.A. Tsiftsis, C. Tellambura, Channel estimation for wireless communication systems assisted by large intelligent surfaces (2019). arXiv:1911.02158
2. C. You, B. Zheng, R. Zhang, Channel estimation and passive beamforming for intelligent reflecting surface: discrete phase shift and progressive refinement. IEEE J. Sel. Areas Commun. **38**(11), 2604–2620 (2020)
3. Q. Sun, P. Qian, W. Duan, J. Zhang, J. Wang, K.-K. Wong, Ergodic rate analysis and IRS configuration for multi-IRS dual-hop DF relaying systems. IEEE Commun. Lett. **25**(10), 3224–3228 (2021)
4. H. Lu, Y. Zeng, S. Jin, R. Zhang, Single-carrier delay alignment modulation for multi-IRS aided communication. IEEE Trans. Wireless Commun. https://doi.org/10.1109/TWC.2023.3306899
5. S. Zhang, R. Zhang, Capacity characterization for intelligent reflecting surface aided MIMO communication. IEEE J. Sel. Areas Commun. **38**(8), 1823–1838 (2020)
6. T. Bai, C. Pan, Y. Deng, M. Elkashlan, A. Nallanathan, Latency minimization for intelligent reflecting surface aided mobile edge computing. IEEE J. Sel. Areas Commun. **38**(11), 2666–2682 (2020)

7. J. Wang, D. Feng, S. Zhang, A. Liu, X. Xia, Joint computation offloading and resource allocation for MEC-enabled IoT systems with imperfect CSI. IEEE Internet Things J. **8**(5), 3462–3475 (2021)
8. H. Hu, Q. Wang, R.Q. Hu, H. Zhu, Mobility-aware offloading and resource allocation in a MEC-enabled IoT network with energy harvesting. IEEE Internet Things J. **8**(24), 17541–17556 (2021)
9. M. Grant, S. Boyd, CVX: MATLAB software for disciplined convex programming (2016) [Online] Available: http://cvxr.com/cvx
10. Z. Luo, W. Ma, A.M. So, Y. Ye, S. Zhang, Semidefinite relaxation of quadratic optimization problems. IEEE Signal Process. Mag. **27**(3), 20–34 (2010)
11. N. Li et al., Min–max latency optimization for IRS-aided cell-free mobile edge computing systems. IEEE Internet Things J. **11**(5), 8757–8770 (2024)
12. G. Interdonato, E. Bjöornson, H.Q. Ngo, P. Frenger, E.G. Larsson, Ubiquitous cell-free massive MIMO communications. EURASIP J. Wirel. Commun. Netw. 197–206 (2019)
13. Z. Zhang, L. Dai, A joint precoding framework for wideband reconfigurable intelligent surface-aided cell-free network. IEEE Trans. Signal Process. **69**, 4085–4101 (2021)
14. Q. Wu, R. Zhang, Intelligent reflecting surface enhanced wireless network via joint active and passive beamforming. IEEE Trans. Wirel. Commun. **18**(11), 5394–5409 (2019)
15. C. You, K. Huang, H. Chae, Energy efficient mobile cloud computing powered by wireless energy transfer. IEEE J. Sel. Areas Commun. **34**(5), 1757–1771 (2016)
16. F. Wang, J. Xu, X. Wang, S. Cui, Joint offloading and computing optimization in wireless powered mobile-edge computing systems. IEEE Trans. Wirel. Commun. **17**(3), 1784–1797 (2018)
17. S. Mao, S. Leng, S. Maharjan, Y. Zhang, Energy efficiency and delay tradeoff for wireless powered mobile-edge computing systems with multi-access schemes. IEEE Trans. Wirel. Commun. **19**(3), 1855–1867 (2020)
18. T. Bai, C. Pan, H. Ren, Y. Deng, M. Elkashlan, A. Nallanathan, Resource allocation for intelligent reflecting surface aided wireless powered mobile edge computing in OFDM systems. IEEE Trans. Wirel. Commun. **20**(8), 5389–5407 (2021). https://doi.org/10.1109/TWC.2021.3067709
19. Q. Wu, R. Zhang, Towards smart and reconfigurable environment: intelligent reflecting surface aided wireless network. IEEE Commun. Mag. **58**(1), 106–112 (2020)
20. S. Abeywickrama, R. Zhang, Q. Wu, C. Yuen, Intelligent reflecting surface: practical phase shift model and beamforming optimization. IEEE Trans. Commun. **68**(9), 5849–5863 (2020). https://doi.org/10.1109/TCOMM.2020.3001125
21. Y. Zeng, B. Clerckx, R. Zhang, Communications and signals design for wireless power transmission. IEEE Trans. Commun. **65**(5), 2264–2290 (2017)
22. S. Bi, C.K. Ho, R. Zhang, Wireless powered communication: opportunities and challenges. IEEE Commun. Mag. **53**(4), 117–125 (2015)
23. J. Xu, L. Liu, R. Zhang, Multiuser MISO beamforming for simultaneous wireless information and power transfer. IEEE Trans. Signal Process. **62**(18), 4798–4810 (2014)
24. F. Wang, T. Peng, Y. Huang, X. Wang, Robust transceiver optimization for power-splitting based downlink MISO SWIPT systems. IEEE Signal Process. Lett. **22**(9), 1492–1496 (2015)
25. F. Wang, C. Xu, Y. Huang, X. Wang, X.-Q. Gao, REEL-BF design: achieving the SDP bound for downlink beamforming with arbitrary shaping constraints. IEEE Trans. Signal Process. **65**(10), 2672–2685 (2017)
26. J. Xu, R. Zhang, Energy beamforming with one-bit feedback. IEEE Trans. Signal Process. **62**(20), 5370–5381 (2014)
27. Y. Wang, M. Sheng, X. Wang, L. Wang, J. Li, Mobile edge computing: partial computation offloading using dynamic voltage scaling. IEEE Trans. Commun. **64**(10), 4268–4282 (2016)
28. L. Ji, S. Guo, Energy-efficient cooperative resource allocation in wireless powered mobile edge computing. IEEE Internet Things J. **6**(3), 4744–4754 (2019)

29. L. Huang, S. Bi, Y.-J.A. Zhang, Deep reinforcement learning for online computation offloading in wireless powered mobile-edge computing networks. IEEE Trans. Mobile Comput. **19**(11), 2581–2593 (2020)
30. S. Mao et al., Computation rate maximization for intelligent reflecting surface enhanced wireless powered mobile edge computing networks. IEEE Trans. Veh. Technol. **70**(10), 10820–10831 (2021)
31. X. Hu, K.K. Wong, Y. Zhang, Wireless-powered edge computing with cooperative UAV: task, time scheduling and trajectory design. IEEE Trans. Wirel. Commun. **19**(12), 8083–8098 (2020)
32. X. Hu, K. Wong, K. Yang, Z. Zheng, UAV-assisted relaying and edge computing: Scheduling and trajectory optimization. IEEE Trans. Wirel. Commun. **18**(10), 4738–4752 (2019)
33. B. Lyu, P. Ramezani, D.T. Hoang, S. Gong, Z. Yang, A. Jamalipour, Optimized energy and information relaying in self-sustainable IRS-empowered WPCN. IEEE Trans. Commun. **69**(1), 619–633 (2021)
34. Y. Zou, S. Gong, J. Xu, W. Cheng, D.T. Hoang, D. Niyato, Wireless powered intelligent reflecting surfaces for enhancing wireless communications. IEEE Trans. Veh. Technol. **69**(10), 12369–12373 (2020)
35. K. Shen, W. Yu, Fractional programming for communication systems—Part I: power control and beamforming. IEEE Trans. Signal Process. **66**(10), 2616–2630 (2018)
36. N. Li, W. Hao, F. Zhou, Z. Chu, S. Yang, P. Xiao, Resource management for IRS-assisted WP-MEC networks with practical phase shift model. IEEE Internet Things J. **11**(4), 6677–6691 (2024)
37. Z. Zhang, L. Dai, A joint precoding framework for wideband reconfigurable intelligent surface-aided cell-free network. IEEE Trans. Signal Process. **69**, 4085–4101 (2021). https://doi.org/10.1109/TSP.2021.3088755
38. L. Li, T.Q.S. Quek, J. Ren, H.H. Yang, Z. Chen, Y. Zhang, An incentive-aware job offloading control framework for multi-access edge computing. IEEE Trans. Mobile Comput. **20**(1), 63–75 (2021)
39. J. Zheng, Y. Cai, Y. Wu, X. Shen, Dynamic computation offloading for mobile cloud computing: a stochastic game-theoretic approach. IEEE Trans. Mobile Comput. **18**(4), 771–786 (2019)
40. W. Cai, H. Li, M. Li, Q. Liu, Practical modeling and beamforming for intelligent reflecting surface aided wideband systems. IEEE Commun. Lett. **24**(7), 1568–1571 (2020)
41. H. Li, W. Cai, Y. Liu, M. Li, Q. Liu, Q. Wu, Intelligent reflecting surface enhanced wideband MIMO-OFDM communications: from practical model to reflection optimization. IEEE Trans. Commun. **69**(7), 4807–4820 (2021)
42. Y. Wang, M. Sheng, X. Wang, L. Wang, J. Li, Mobile-edge computing: partial computation offloading using dynamic voltage scaling. IEEE Trans. Commun. **64**(10), 4268–4282 (2016)
43. M.L. Fisher, The Lagrangian relaxation method for solving integer programming problems. Manage. Sci. **27**(1), 1–18 (1981)
44. Q. Shi, M. Razaviyayn, Z.-Q. Luo, C. He, An iteratively weighted MMSE approach to distributed sum-utility maximization for a MIMO interfering broadcast channel. IEEE Trans. Signal Process. **59**(9), 4331–4340 (2011)
45. M. Grant, S. Boyd, CVX: MATLAB software for disciplined convex programming (2016) [Online]. Available: http://cvxr.com/cvx
46. T. Bai et al., Latency minimization for intelligent reflecting surface aided mobile edge computing. IEEE J. Sel. Areas Commun. **38**(11), 2666–2682 (2020)

Chapter 4
Cooperative Cloud and Mobile Edge Computing

4.1 Introduction

The development of the internet has brought significant transformations to human life and production. Over the past decade, smart terminal devices (such as smartphones, laptops, automotive devices, and wearable devices) have gradually become the main access platforms for the internet. With the massive proliferation of smart terminal devices, there has been an emergence of large-scale and diverse applications on the user side. These applications are often computationally intensive, delay-sensitive, or energy-sensitive, including image processing, facial recognition, augmented reality, autonomous driving, computer vision, interactive games, and panoramic live streaming. Consequently, handling delay-sensitive and computationally intensive applications has become a primary task for terminal devices. However, due to the limitations of the hardware in these devices, such as limited battery capacity, storage capacity, and computing resources, they are unable to independently support the operation of these applications. To address the rapid growth of wireless terminal devices and the challenges posed by the demand for powerful computational capabilities by emerging applications, cloud computing technology has emerged. Cloud computing effectively alleviates the limitations of terminal devices by extending their computational and storage capabilities [1].

Although the rapid development of cloud computing has enriched people daily lives, it has also raised several issues that cannot be overlooked, such as information security, long transmission delays, and limited spectrum resources [2]. Therefore, there is an urgent need for a computational model that supports multiple modes, integrates multi-dimensional spatially distributed data sources, and provides various novel services. MEC has emerged as a solution to mitigate these problems to some extent. It decentralizes centralized cloud computing resources to the network edge, closer to the terminal devices. By meeting the computational demands of applications while significantly reducing transmission delays, MEC greatly enhances the Quality of Experience (QoE) for users [3–5]. Although the edge cloud, deployed

W. Hao et al., *Intelligent Mobile Edge Computing and Sensing*, Wireless Networks,
https://doi.org/10.1007/978-981-96-9400-6_4

in close proximity, can effectively reduce transmission delays, its limited and homogeneous computational resources still cannot meet the demands of massive and diverse data requests in the future. The delay-sensitive and computationally intensive applications place higher demands on MEC technologies in terms of balancing energy consumption and latency[6]. By combining the advantages of cloud computing and MEC, collaborative cloud computing (CCC) has emerged as a model that, to some extent, satisfies the latency and energy consumption requirements of delay-sensitive and computationally intensive applications. In this computing model, cloud computing acts as a complement to MEC capabilities. For CCC, each playing to its strengths, maximizing the advantages of cloud computing and MEC, and ultimately maximizing their combined value [7, 8].

The structure of this chapter is organized as follows. Section 4.2 investigates Q-learning-based offloading for CCC[9] . Section 4.3 focuses on maximizing the energy time cost in the multi-user multi-edge CCC[10]. Section 4.4 explores the weighted costs minimization in the subtask dependency CCC [11].

4.2 Q-Learning-based CCC

4.2.1 System Model

This subsection presents the local computation model, the CCC model, and the subtask dependency model, offering concise explanations and analyses of each. In this context, we assume a CCC system consisting of a central cloud server with virtually unlimited computational capacity, complemented by several edge servers, each with constrained computational resources. As a result, only one user (terminal device) can be connected at any given time. The terminal device hosts a computation-intensive application, which can offload its subtasks to the edge cloud via a wireless channel, while the edge cloud subsequently forwards the data to the central cloud via an optical backhaul link.

Each computation-intensive application is assumed to consist of I subtasks organized in a single-chain structure, denoted as $\mathcal{I} = 1, \ldots, I$. The offloading decision for each subtask is represented by a_i, where $a_i = 1$ signifies that subtask i is processed locally, while $a_i = 0$ indicates that it is offloaded to the collaborative cloud. Due to the dependencies among adjacent subtasks, each subtask must be executed sequentially in the order defined by the single-chain structure. To model these dependency relationships, this study employs a Directed Acyclic Graph (DAG), $G = (V, E)$, where $i \in V$ represents a subtask, and a directed edge $e(i, j)$ signifies the precedence relationship between subtasks i and j [12]. As depicted in Fig. 4.1, the system model for this chapter is presented.

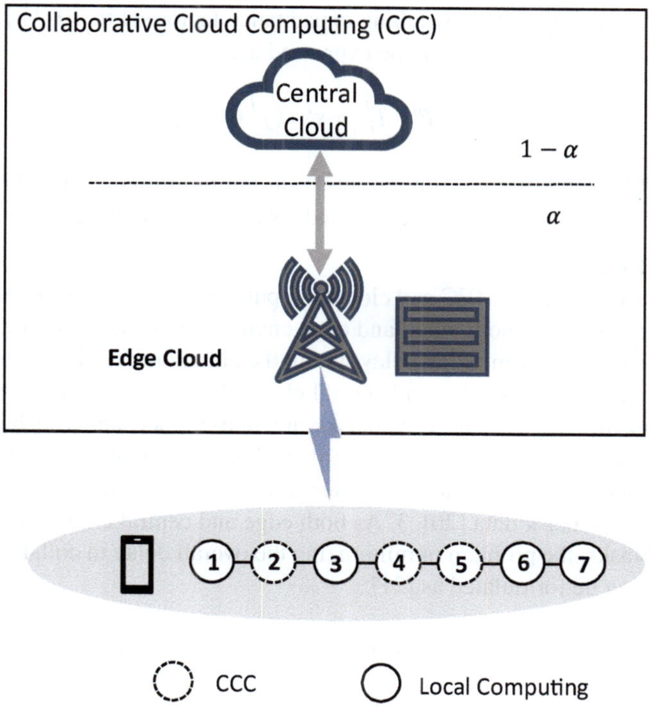

Fig. 4.1 System model for subtask dependency-based computation offloading

(1) Local Computing Model

The i-th subtask of a single-chain application is denoted as $ST_i = L_i, C_i$, where L_i represents the input data, including system configurations, program code, and input parameters, and C_i denotes the number of CPU cycles required per unit of data. Each subtask can be executed either locally or offloaded to the collaborative cloud for computation [13]. The terminal device can dynamically adjust its computational frequency, denoted as f^l, based on the complexity of the application using dynamic voltage and frequency scaling technology [14]. Consequently, the local computation delay can be expressed as:

$$T_i^l = \frac{C_i L_i}{f^l} \tag{4.1}$$

Since the CPU power is a nonlinear function of the computation frequency f^l [15–17], it can be expressed as:

$$P^l = \kappa^l \cdot (f^l)^\gamma \tag{4.2}$$

where $\gamma = 2$, and κ^l is the switching capacitance factor set to 10^{-11} [15, 17], the terminal energy consumption can be expressed as:

$$E_i^l = P^l \cdot T_i^l = \kappa^l \cdot (f^l)^{\gamma-1} C_i L_i \tag{4.3}$$

From Eqs. (4.1) and (4.3), it can be observed that the local computation delay T_i^l and energy consumption E_i^l are determined solely by the input data size L_i and C_i.

(2) CCC Model

The CCC leverages both MEC and cloud computing to optimize available computational resources across both cloud and edge environments. Subtasks are partitioned to minimize the total computing delay within the collaborative cloud, enabling concurrent operation of both edge and central clouds [17]. The following assumptions are made in this subsection: 1. Subtasks are fine-grained and can be divided in arbitrary proportions [16, 18, 19]. 2. To ensure the accuracy of the partitioning ratio, the edge cloud is permitted to split a subtask only after it has fully received the corresponding subtask data [20]. 3. As both edge and central clouds collaboratively process subtasks, the problem of minimizing the overall delay in collaborative cloud computing can be formulated as [21]:

$$T_i^{exe} = \min \max\{T_i^e, T_i^{ed-ce} + T_i^{cent}\} \tag{4.4}$$

The overall delay in collaborative cloud computing can be minimized when $T_i^e = T_i^{ed-ce} + T_i^{cent}$, where $T_i^e = \frac{\alpha_i L_i C_i}{f_i^e}$ represents the edge cloud computation delay, $T_i^{ed-ce} = \frac{(1-\alpha_i)L_i}{W}$ denotes the fiber backhaul transmission delay [22–24], and $T_i^{cent} = \frac{(1-\alpha_i)L_i C_i}{f^c}$ is the central cloud computation delay. After analyzing T_i^{exe}, the collaborative cloud computing delay is minimized when $T_i^e = T_i^{ed-ce} + T_i^{cent}$, and the optimal partition ratio is given by:

$$\alpha_i = \frac{f_i^e(f^c + C_i W)}{f_i^e(f^c + C_i W) + f^c C_i W} \tag{4.5}$$

where f_i^e is the computation frequency allocated by the edge cloud for subtask i, f^c is the computation frequency of the central cloud, and W is the communication capacity of the optical backhaul link, the total collaborative cloud computing delay under the optimal split ratio can be expressed as:

$$T_i^{exe} = \frac{\alpha_i L_i C_i}{f_i^e} \tag{4.6}$$

Since the central cloud is assumed to have infinite computational resources, its energy consumption is not included in the total system energy consumption [12, 13]. Additionally, the energy consumption of the optical backhaul link is negligible and can be ignored. Therefore, the energy consumption in collaborative cloud computing is solely dependent on the energy consumption of the edge cloud, which can be expressed as:

$$E_i^{exe} = T_i^e \cdot P_i^e = \kappa^e \cdot \alpha_i L_i C_i f_i^e \tag{4.7}$$

where κ^e is the switch capacitance factor set to 10^{-12} [12].

(3) Transmission Model

For delay-sensitive and computation-intensive applications, the transmission of subtasks over wireless channels introduces additional latency and energy consumption. When the computation locations of adjacent subtasks differ, the terminal device must allocate an appropriate uplink transmission power to offload the subtask data to the collaborative cloud. Similarly, the edge cloud must allocate a downlink transmission power to send the processed data back to the terminal device. The wireless channel gain between the terminal device and the edge cloud is represented by H_i, B is the user bandwidth, and N_0 denotes the noise power. Furthermore, $p_i^{t,U}$ indicates the uplink transmission power allocated by the terminal device under the maximum power constraint, and $p_i^{t,D}$ represents the downlink transmission power allocated by the edge cloud for the subtask, which is assumed to be known. According to Shannon theorem, the data transmission rate from the terminal device to the edge cloud is given by:

$$R_i(p_i^{t,U}) = B \cdot \log_2(1 + \frac{p_i^{t,U} H_i}{N_0}) \tag{4.8}$$

This section assumes that the channel between the terminal device and the edge cloud operates under quasi-static fading conditions [25, 26]. Given the relatively short duration of the offloading transmission delay, it is reasonable to neglect the mobility of the terminal device during this period. Thus, the CSIs remain constant while the terminal device offloads subtasks, and can be estimated and obtained in advance by the scheduler. As a result, the transmission delay and energy consumption can be expressed as follows:

$$T_i^{trans,U} = \frac{L_i}{R_i(p_i^{t,U})} \tag{4.9}$$

$$E_i^{trans,U} = p_i^{t,U} \cdot T_i^{trans} = \frac{L_i p_i^{t,U}}{R_i(p_i^{t,U})} \tag{4.10}$$

Similarly, the downlink transmission rate $R_i(p_i^{t,D})$, transmission delay $T_i^{trans,D}$, and transmission energy consumption $E_i^{trans,D}$ can be derived. For the convenience of constructing the subtask dependency model and the optimization problem, we first define the Task Energy-Time Cost ($TETC$).

Definition 4.1 $TETC$ is defined as the weighted sum of the ratio between the delay and energy consumption for computing or transmitting the subtask, compared to the delay and energy consumption under a fully local (local only) computing scheme for the entire application, as follows:

$$TETC_i = \gamma^t \frac{T_i}{\sum_{i=1}^{I} T_i^l} + \gamma^e \frac{E_i}{\sum_{i=1}^{I} E_i^l}, \tag{4.11}$$

where γ^t and γ^e represent the delay and energy weight factors, respectively. If $\gamma^t > \gamma^e$, the application is considered delay-sensitive; otherwise, it is energy-sensitive. The constraint $\gamma^e + \gamma^t = 1$ is imposed to balance delay and energy consumption, preventing excessive loss due to overly large weight factors. $\sum_{i=1}^{I} T_i^l$ and $\sum_{i=1}^{I} E_i^l$ represent the total delay and energy consumption required to complete the application under the fully local scheme. Thus, the $TETC$ for local computating, collaborative cloud computing, and uplink/downlink transmission can be expressed as follows:

$$TETC_i^l = \gamma^t \frac{T_i^l}{\sum_{i=1}^{I} T_i^l} + \gamma^e \frac{E_i^l}{\sum_{i=1}^{I} E_i^l}, \tag{4.12}$$

$$TETC_i^{exe} = \gamma^t \frac{T_i^{exe}}{\sum_{i=1}^{I} T_i^l} + \gamma^e \frac{E_i^{exe}}{\sum_{i=1}^{I} E_i^l}, \tag{4.13}$$

$$TETC_i^{trans,U} = \gamma^t \frac{T_i^{trans,U}}{\sum_{i=1}^{I} T_i^l} + \gamma^e \frac{E_i^{trans,U}}{\sum_{i=1}^{I} E_i^l}, \tag{4.14}$$

$$TETC_i^{trans,D} = \gamma^t \frac{T_i^{trans,D}}{\sum_{i=1}^{I} T_i^l} + \gamma^e \frac{E_i^{trans,D}}{\sum_{i=1}^{I} E_i^l}, \tag{4.15}$$

(4) Subtask Dependency Model

As applications become more complex and diverse, they are often composed of multiple subtasks with specific topological structures, resulting in dependencies between subtasks. For instance, the computation location of a previous subtask can influence the computation location of the subsequent subtask. Therefore, the topological structure of complex application subtasks imposes higher demands on the modeling of the computation offloading problem.

This subsection describes subtask dependencies based on the transmission cost between two adjacent subtasks. When two adjacent subtasks are computed on the same side (e.g., both locally or both offloaded to the collaborative cloud), the data only needs to be transmitted within the same server, so transmission delay and energy consumption can be ignored. However, when the adjacent subtasks are computed on different sides (i.e., one locally and the other offloaded), additional transmission delay and energy consumption due to wireless channel transmission must be considered. Therefore, three cases are discussed:

1. $a_i = a_{i+1} = 0/1$: When two adjacent subtasks are computed on the same side, meaning both are either computed locally or both are offloaded, the data is transmitted within the same processor, so transmission losses do not need to be considered.
2. $a_i = 0, a_{i+1} = 1$: When subtask i is computed locally and subtask $i+1$ is offloaded to the collaborative cloud, the terminal device must configure the uplink transmission power $p_i^{t,U}$ to offload the required data to the collaborative cloud via a wireless channel. In this case, the uplink transmission energy-time cost is $TETC_{i+1}^{trans,U}$.
3. $a_i = 1, a_{i+1} = 0$: When subtask i is offloaded to the collaborative cloud and subtask $i+1$ is computed locally, the edge cloud must configure the downlink transmission power $p_i^{t,D}$ to send the processed data back to the terminal device via a wireless channel. In this case, the downlink transmission energy-time cost is $TETC_i^{trans,D}$.

Therefore, the transmission energy-time cost between two adjacent subtasks can be expressed as:

$$
\begin{aligned}
&TETC_i^{trans} \\
&= \frac{1-(-1)^{a_i-a_{i+1}}}{2} \\
&\cdot \frac{[1-(a_i-a_{i+1})]TETC_{i+1}^{trans,U} + [1+(a_i-a_{i+1})]TETC_i^{trans,D}}{2} \\
&i = 1, 2, \ldots, I-1
\end{aligned}
\tag{4.16}
$$

4.2.2 Problem Formulation

With the rapid development of the internet, a multitude of new intelligent applications has emerged, many of which impose stringent requirements on both latency and energy consumption. For instance, autonomous driving systems not only need to process and analyze complex road condition data but also require the ability to respond in real-time. However, due to their size constraints, terminal devices lack the computational resources needed to meet these demands within the limited time available, thereby impacting QoE.

In response, this subsection formulates an optimization problem that simultaneously addresses latency and energy consumption. The goal is to optimize transmission power, edge cloud computing frequency, and offloading decisions in a collaborative manner.

Definition 4.2 (Application Energy-Time Cost (AETC)) This is defined as the cumulative sum of the computation energy-time cost and transmission energy-time cost required to complete all subtasks of the application, as follows:

$$AETC = \sum_{i=1}^{I}[a_i TETC_i^{exe} + (1-a_i)TETC_i^{l}] + \sum_{i=1}^{I-1} TETC_i^{trans} \tag{4.17}$$

Therefore, the optimization problem can be formulated as minimization of $AETC$.

$$\begin{aligned} P4-1: \quad & \min_{a_i, p_i^{t,U}, f_i^e} \; AETC \\ s.t. \; & C_1 : a_i \in \{0,1\}, \forall i \in \mathcal{I} \\ & C_2 : 0 \le p_i^{t,U} \le p^{max}, \forall i \in \mathcal{I} \\ & C_3 : f_{min}^e \le f_i^e \le f_{max}^e, \forall i \in \mathcal{I} \end{aligned} \tag{4.18}$$

where C_1 indicates that the subtask ST_i can either be computed locally or offloaded to the collaborative cloud. If computed locally, $a_i = 0$, and if offloaded, $a_i = 1$. C_2 constrains the bounds of the offloading transmission power that the terminal device can configure. Specifically, if subtask ST_i is offloaded, the offloading transmission power configured by the terminal device must be greater than 0 and cannot exceed the maximum transmission power p^{max} that the terminal device can configure. C_3 constrains the bounds of the edge cloud computing frequency. If subtask ST_i is offloaded, the edge cloud must configure computational resources for this subtask such that the computing frequency is no less than f_{min}^e and no greater than the maximum computing frequency f_{max}^e that the edge cloud server can provide.

4.2.3 Propose Q-Learning Algorithm

As for $P4-1$, since the offloading decision a_i is an integer variable, while the transmission power $p_i^{t,U}$ and edge cloud computing frequency f_i^e are continuous variables, the optimization problem $P3$ is a Mixed-Integer Nonlinear Programming (MINLP) problem [27], which is a non-convex NP-hard problem that is difficult to solve in polynomial time [28]. Therefore, we decompose the original optimization problem *P4 – 1* into three subproblems, each independently optimizing the offloading transmission power, edge cloud computing frequency, and offloading decision. When $a_i = 1$, the terminal device needs to configure the corresponding offloading transmission power and edge cloud computing frequency for subtask ST_i. By substituting Eq. (4.17), the optimization problem *P4 – 1* can be further transformed into:

$$\begin{aligned} P4-2: \quad & \min_{a_i, p_i^{t,U}, f_i^e} \sum_{i=1}^{I} TETC_i^{exe} + \sum_{i=1}^{I-1} TETC_i^{trans} \\ & s.t. \;\; C_1, C_2, C_3 \end{aligned} \tag{4.19}$$

Since the transmission power $p_i^{t,U}$ of the offloaded subtasks is only related to $TETC_i^{trans,U}$, and the edge cloud computing frequency f_i^e is only related to $TETC_i^{exe}$, the two are independent of each other. Therefore, we can first optimize the offloading transmission power $p_i^{t,U}$ by minimizing $TETC_i^{trans,U}$, and then independently optimize the edge cloud computing frequency f_i^e by minimizing $TETC_i^{exe}$.

(1) Optimization of Transmission Power

This subsection focuses on optimizing the terminal device's offloading transmission power $p_i^{t,U}$. In the optimization problem *P4 – 2*, $p_i^{t,U}$ is only related to $TETC_i^{trans,U}$, so the optimization problem *P4 – 2* can be simplified to the form of *P4 – 3*:

$$\begin{aligned} P4-3: \quad & \min_{p_i^{t,U}} TETC_i^{trans,U} \\ & s.t. \;\; C_2. \end{aligned} \tag{4.20}$$

Substituting (4.14) into *P4 – 3*:

$$\begin{aligned} P4-4: \quad & \min_{p_i^{t,U}} \gamma^t \frac{T_i^{trans}}{\sum_{i=1}^{I} T_i^l} + \gamma^e \frac{E_i^{trans}}{\sum_{i=1}^{I} E_i^l} \\ & s.t. \;\; C_2. \end{aligned} \tag{4.21}$$

By substituting (4.1), (4.3), (4.9), and (4.10), *P4 – 4* can be expressed as:

$$\begin{aligned} P4-5: \quad & \min_{p_i^{t,U}} f(p_i^{t,U}) \\ & s.t. \;\; C_2, \end{aligned} \tag{4.22}$$

where

$$f(p_i^{t,U}) = \frac{\theta_i + \lambda_i p_i^{t,U}}{\log_2(1 + \mu_i p_i^{t,U})} \tag{4.23}$$

In (4.23), $\theta_i = \gamma^t L_i/(B \cdot \sum_{i=1}^{I} T_i^l)$, $\lambda_i = \gamma^e L_i/(B \cdot \sum_{i=1}^{I} E_i^l)$, $\mu_i = H_i/N_0$. The second derivative of $f(p_i^{t,U})$ can be expressed as:

$$\begin{aligned} f''(p_i^{t,U}) = & \frac{\mu_i \left[\mu_i(\theta_i + \lambda_i p_i^{t,U}) - 2\lambda_i(1 + \mu_i p_i^{t,U})\right]}{\ln 2(1 + \mu_i p_i^{t,U})^2 \log_2^3(1 + \mu_i p_i^{t,U})} \\ & \cdot \frac{\log_2(1 + \mu_i p_i^{t,U})}{\ln 2(1 + \mu_i p_i^{t,U})^2 \log_2^3(1 + \mu_i p_i^{t,U})} \\ & + \frac{2\mu_i^2(\theta_i + \lambda_i p_i^{t,U})/\ln 2}{\ln 2(1 + \mu_i p_i^{t,U})^2 \log_2^3(1 + \mu_i p_i^{t,U})} \end{aligned} \tag{4.24}$$

By analyzing (4.24), it can be concluded that $f''(p_i^{t,U})$ is not always positive within the domain of $p_i^{t,U}$. Therefore, $f(p_i^{t,U})$ is not a convex function. If $f(\cdot)$ is twice differentiable on $\mathbf{R}$ and there exists an x_0 such that $f'(x_0) = 0$ and $f''(x_0) \geq 0$, then $f(\cdot)$ is a quasi-convex function on $\mathbf{R}$ [29]. The first derivative of $f(p_i^{t,U})$ is then given as follows:

$$f'(p_i^{t,U}) = \frac{\lambda_i \log_2(1 + \mu_i p_i^{t,U}) - \mu_i/\ln 2(\frac{\theta_i + \lambda_i p_i^{t,U}}{1 + \mu_i p_i^{t,U}})}{\log_2^2(1 + \mu_i p_i^{t,U})} \tag{4.25}$$

When $f'(p_0) = 0$, the numerator equals 0. Here, we denote the numerator as $\psi(p_i^{t,U})$, which can be expressed as:

$$\psi(p_0) = \lambda_i \log_2(1 + \mu_i p_0) - \frac{\mu_i}{\ln 2} \cdot \frac{\theta_i + \lambda_i p_0}{1 + \mu_i p_0} = 0 \tag{4.26}$$

Substituting (4.26) into (4.24):

$$f''(p_0) = \frac{\mu_i^3}{\lambda_i \ln^2 2} \frac{(\theta_i + \lambda_i p_0)^2}{(1 + \mu_i p_0)^3 \log_2^3(1 + \mu_i p_0)} \geq 0 \tag{4.27}$$

Therefore, $f(p_i^{t,U})$ is quasi-convex within $\mathbf{R}$, and the bisection method is generally used to solve quasi-convex functions [29]. The first derivative of (4.26) can be written as:

$$\psi'(p_i^{t,U}) = \frac{\mu_i^2}{\ln 2} \frac{\theta_i + \lambda_i p_i^{t,U}}{(1 + \mu_i p_i^{t,U})^2} > 0 \tag{4.28}$$

Algorithm 9 Bisection Method for Transmission Power Optimization

---

Input $0 < p_i^{t,U} < p^{max}$ and $\psi(p_i^{t,U})$
Output p_i^*
if $\psi(p^{max}) \leq 0$ **then**
  $p_i^* = p^{max}$
else
  $p_i^s = 0$ and $p_i^{t,U} = p^{max}$
  repeat
    $p_i^l = (p_i^s + p_i^{t,U})/2$
    if $\psi(p_i^l) \leq 0$ **then**
      $p_i^s = p_i^l$
    else
      $p_i^{t,U} = p_i^l$
    end if
  until $(p_i^{t,U} - p_i^s) \leq \epsilon$
  $p_i^* = (p_i^s + p_i^{t,U})/2$
end if

Since (4.28) is greater than 0 and $\psi(0) = -\frac{\mu_i \theta_i}{\ln 2} < 0$, through simple analysis, it can be concluded that $\psi(p_i^{t,U})$ is monotonically increasing and less than 0 at the starting point $p_i^{t,U} = 0$. Therefore, $f'(p_i^{t,U})$ is also monotonically increasing, satisfying $f'(0) < 0$. Consequently, when $0 < p_i^{t,U} < p_0$ (where p_0 satisfies $f'(p_i^{t,U}) = 0$), $f(p_i^{t,U})$ initially decreases and then increases when $p_i^{t,U} \geq p_0$, reaching its minimum value at $p_i^{t,U} = p_0$.

Next, we need to analyze whether p_0 lies within the domain of $p_i^{t,U}$, and we will consider two cases. If p_0 is within the domain of $p_i^{t,U}$, then the optimal offloading transmission power is $p_i^* = p_0$. If p_0 is not within the domain of $p_i^{t,U}$, then the optimal offloading transmission power is $p_i^* = p^{max}$. To determine the optimal offloading transmission power, this subsection uses the bisection method to minimize $f(p_i^{t,U})$ and find the optimal offloading transmission power. The pseudocode for this approach is shown in Algorithm 9.

(2) Edge Cloud Computing Frequency Allocation

When a subtask is offloaded, the edge cloud needs to allocate corresponding computing resources for the task. Therefore, in this subsection, we optimize the edge cloud computing resources. Since in problem P, MEC resources are only related to

$TETC_i^{exe}$, the optimization problem $P3$ can be simplified as follows:

$$\begin{aligned} P4-6: &\min_{f_i^e} \ TETC_i^{exe} \\ &s.t.\ \ C_3. \end{aligned} \tag{4.29}$$

By substituting (4.13) into $P4-6$, it can be simplified as:

$$\begin{aligned} P4-7: &\min_{f_i^e} \ y(_i^e) \\ &s.t.\ \ C_3, \end{aligned} \tag{4.30}$$

where

$$y(f_i^e) = \frac{Am + Bm(f_i^e)^2}{mf_i^e + n} \tag{4.31}$$

Here$A = \gamma^t L_i C_i / \sum_{i=1}^{I} T_i^l$, $B = \gamma^e \kappa^e L_i C_i / \sum_{i=1}^{I} E_i^l$,$m = f^c + C_i W$, $n = f^c \cdot C_i W$. The first-order derivative of $y(f_i^e)$ is expressed as:

$$y'(f_i^e) = \frac{-Am^2 + 2Bmnf_i^e + Bm^2(f_i^e)^2}{(mf_i^e + n)^2} \tag{4.32}$$

By analysis, it can be concluded that the sign of $y'(f_i^e)$ is determined by the sign of its numerator. Therefore, it is sufficient to analyze the properties of its numerator $\Psi(f_i^e)$, which can be expressed as:

$$\begin{aligned} \Psi(f_i^e) &= -Am^2 + 2Bmnf_i^e + Bm^2(f_i^e)^2 \\ &= m[-Am + 2Bnf_i^e + Bm(f_i^e)^2] \end{aligned} \tag{4.33}$$

Since $m > 0$, in order to simplify the subsequent analysis, it can be further simplified as:

$$N(f_i^e) = -Am + 2Bnf_i^e + Bm(f_i^e)^2 \tag{4.34}$$

By analyzing the (4.34), $N(\cdot) = 0$ has two roots. Since the formula (4.34) is an upward-opening parabola and $N(0) = -Am$, it is easy to get that the left root f^l is negative and the right root f^r is positive. Therefore, now we only need to analyze whether f^r is within the domain of f_i^e.

1. $f^r < f^e_{min}$, in the definition domain $\Psi(f^e_{min}) > 0$. $y(f_i^e)$ is monotonically increasing in the domain and has a minimum value at f^e_{min}. Therefore, $(f_i^e)^* = f^e_{min}$.
2. $f^e_{min} < f^r < f^e_{max}$, when $f_i^e < f^r$, Ψ is less than 0, and when $f_i^e > f^r$, Ψ is greater than 0, so $y(f_i^e)$ first decreases monotonically and then increases monotonically, and has a minimum value at f^r. Therefore, $(f_i^e)^* = f^r$.
3. $f^r > f^e_{max}$, within the definition domain, $\Psi(f^e_{max}) < 0$. $y(f_i^e)$ is always monotonically decreasing and reaches its minimum at f^e_{max}. Therefore, the optimal edge cloud computing frequency $(f_i^e)^* = f^e_{max}$.

(3) Optimization of Offloading Decisions

For a single-chain application composed of multiple subtasks, due to the dependencies between each subtask, the offloading process is a sequential decision-making process where the terminal device must sequentially determine the computation location for each subtask. However, the optimal offloading decision for an application subtask not only depends on its inherent characteristics but is also influenced by the computation locations and data information of other subtasks. Therefore, it is necessary to consider the global offloading scheme of the application.

In this subsection, we model the offloading process of a task-dependent single-chain application as a Markov Decision Process (MDP), with the Markov property serving as the link. We propose the QLOF algorithm to obtain the optimal offloading scheme. The Markov property states that the conditional probability distribution of future states depends only on the current state, meaning the future state is influenced only by the present state [30–32]. MDP is an optimal decision-making process for a random dynamic system based on the Markov property, consisting of two entities: the agent and the environment. The agent is also the decision-maker [32, 33]. Through repeated trials in the environment, the agent adjusts its strategy based on feedback received, ultimately generating an optimal policy. This policy dictates what action should be taken in a given state, thereby achieving the goal of the decision-making process [33].

In this subsection, we model the sequential offloading process of a task-dependent single-chain application as an MDP by defining the state, action, policy, and reward.

1. State S: A finite set of all states. The MDP state space is a finite-dimensional space that can be viewed as an observation of the environment. In the model established in this section, four states are assigned to each subtask to form a sub-state space $\mathcal{S}_i$, expressed as:

$$\begin{aligned} \mathcal{S}_i &= \{00, 01, 10, 11\} \\ i &= \{1, 2, \cdots, I-1\} \end{aligned} \tag{4.35}$$

where i is the index of the subtask in the single-chain application, and I is the number of subtasks in the single-chain application. The states are defined as $s_i^1 = 00$, $s_i^2 = 01$, $s_i^3 = 10$, and $s_i^4 = 11$. Since the Markov property emphasizes the dependency of the next state on the current state, two-bit binary numbers are used to establish the connection between two adjacent subtasks. The first bit represents the computation location of the current subtask, and the second bit represents the computation location of the next subtask. Local computation is represented by 0, and collaborative cloud computation is represented by 1. For example, $s_i^2 = 01$ means that subtask i is executed on the terminal device, i.e., local computation, while subtask $i+1$ is offloaded to the collaborative cloud for execution. The entire system state space consists of the initial state $\mathcal{S}_0$, the terminal state $0\mathcal{T}$, and all substate spaces $\mathcal{S}_i$. Note that $\mathcal{S}_0$ and $0\mathcal{T}$ satisfy the requirement that the initial and terminal subtasks must be computed locally [34]. Therefore, the system state space $\mathcal{S}$ can be represented as:

$$\mathcal{S} = \{\mathcal{S}0, \mathcal{S}_1\mathcal{S}_2, \mathcal{S}_3, \ldots, \mathcal{S}_{I-1}, 0\mathcal{T}\} \tag{4.36}$$

2. Action A: The action space refers to the set of actions that the decision-maker can take in a particular state to reach the next state [35]. In the model presented in this section, the decision-maker is the terminal device, which has two actions to choose from, represented as:

$$A = \{0, 1\} \tag{4.37}$$

where 0 and 1 represent local computation and collaborative cloud computation, respectively. Based on the model's definition of states, a particular state contains both the execution location of the current subtask and the execution location of the next subtask. Therefore, the action taken by the terminal device is not directed toward the next subtask but rather toward the second subtask adjacent to the current one. To explain the state transition process accurately, a specific example is given. Suppose the current state of the application is $s_i^2 = 01$, meaning the current subtask i is computed locally, and the next subtask $i + 1$ is computed in the collaborative cloud. Therefore, the subtask $i + 1$ can only transition to state $s_{i+1}^3 = 10$ or $s_i^4 = 11$. At this point, when the terminal device issues the offloading decision, i.e., the action $a = 1$, the system will transition from state $s_i^2 = 01$ to state $s_{i+1}^4 = 11$. This illustrates that there is a correlation between the subtask states. As shown in Fig. 4.2, the state transition diagram for a single-chain application illustrates the correlation between the subtask states, where the current subtask state is influenced by the previous subtask state.

3. Strategy π: The strategy π refers to the distribution of actions [35], i.e., the probability of selecting a particular action in a specific state, expressed as:

$$\pi(a|s_i^j) = \mathrm{P}\left[A = a|S_i = s_i^j\right] \tag{4.38}$$

In our model, action selection is either offloaded or locally computed with unknown probabilities.

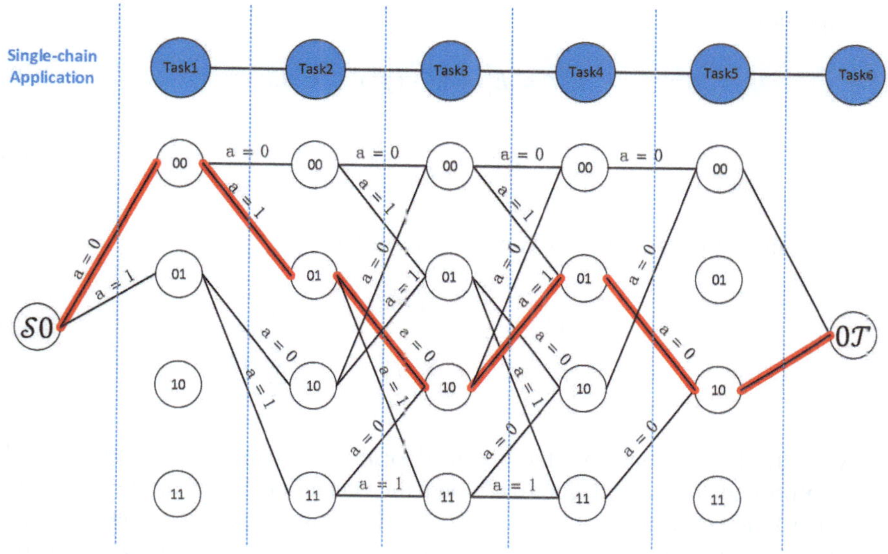

Fig. 4.2 State transition

4. Reward R: The decision-maker, i.e., the terminal device, interacts with the environment to learn and make optimal decisions, thereby receiving rewards. The goal of MDP is to maximize the accumulated reward under uncertainty [28, 35].

This subsection first designs two loss functions: the state loss function $STLF$ and the system loss function $SYLF$. Then, the negative value of R is used to replace $STLF$, thereby transforming the problem of minimizing $SYLF$ into a standard MDP problem of maximizing the accumulated reward.

Definition 4.3 (State Loss Function (*STLF*)) It is defined as the weighted sum of the ratio of the delay and energy consumption of the subtask in a certain state to the delay and energy consumption of the application under the Local Only scheme. The normalized form of $STLF$ can be expressed as:

$$STLF_i^{s_i^j} = \gamma^e \cdot \frac{E_i^{s_i^j}}{\sum\limits_{i=1}^{I} E_i^l} + \gamma^t \cdot \frac{T_i^{s_i^j}}{\sum\limits_{i=1}^{I} T_i^l}, \quad j = \{1, 2, 3, 4\} \tag{4.39}$$

where i is the index of the subtask, and j is the state index. $\gamma^e, \gamma^t \in [0, 1]$ are the delay loss weight factor and the energy loss weight factor, respectively. The specific expressions of $STLF$ for different states are given below.

1. $s_i^1 = 00$: Since both adjacent subtasks are executed on the terminal device, only the local computation consumption of the current subtask i needs to be considered. Therefore, the energy consumption and delay for $s_i^1 = 00$ can be

expressed as:

$$E_i^{00} = E_i^l = \kappa^l \cdot (f^l)^{\gamma-1} C_i L_i \tag{4.40}$$

$$T_i^{00} = T_i^l = \frac{C_i L_i}{f^l} \tag{4.41}$$

Thus, the $STLF$ for $s_i^1 = 00$ can be expressed as:

$$STLF_i^{00} = \gamma^e \cdot \frac{E_i^{00}}{\sum\limits_{i=1}^{I} E_i^l} + \gamma^t \cdot \frac{T_i^{00}}{\sum\limits_{i=1}^{I} T_i^l} \tag{4.42}$$

2. $s_i^2 = 01$: The current subtask is executed locally, while the adjacent next subtask is offloaded to the collaborative cloud for execution. Since the two adjacent subtasks are executed at different locations, the terminal device not only needs to execute the current subtask but also needs to transmit the data of the adjacent next subtask to the edge cloud. Due to the task dependency, the data of the subsequent subtask can only be transmitted after the current subtask is completed. Therefore, the energy consumption and delay for $s_i^2 = 01$ can be expressed as:

$$E_i^{01} = E_i^l + E_{i+1}^{trans} \quad = \kappa^l \cdot (f^l)^{\gamma-1} C_i L_i + \frac{L_{i+1} p_{i+1}^{t,U}}{R_{i+1}(p_{i+1}^{t,U})} \tag{4.43}$$

$$T_i^{01} = T_i^l + T_{i+1}^{trans} \quad = \frac{C_i L_i}{f^l} + \frac{L_{i+1}}{R_{i+1}(p_{i+1}^{t,U})} \tag{4.44}$$

Thus, the $STLF$ for $s_i^2 = 01$ can be expressed as:

$$STLF_i^{01} = \gamma^e \cdot \frac{E_i^{01}}{\sum\limits_{i=1}^{I} E_i^l} + \gamma^t \cdot \frac{T_i^{01}}{\sum\limits_{i=1}^{I} T_i^l} \tag{4.45}$$

3. $s_i^3 = 10$: The current subtask is executed on the collaborative cloud, and the next subtask is executed locally. Since the two adjacent subtasks are executed at different locations, the wireless channel transmission loss needs to be considered. The edge cloud must configure the downlink transmission power to send the data of subtask i back to the terminal device. Therefore, the energy consumption and delay for $s_i^3 = 10$ can be expressed as:

$$E_i^{10} = E_i^{exe} + E_i^{trans} \quad = \kappa^e \cdot \alpha_i L_i C_i f_i^e + \frac{L_i p_i^{t,D}}{R_i(p_i^{t,D})} \tag{4.46}$$

$$T_i^{10} = T_i^{exe} + T_i^{trans} = \frac{\alpha_i L_i C_i}{f_i^e} + \frac{L_i}{R_i(p_{i+1}^{t,D})} \tag{4.47}$$

Thus, the $STLF$ for $s_i^3 = 10$ can be expressed as:

$$STLF_i^{10} = \gamma^e \cdot \frac{E_i^{10}}{\sum\limits_{i=1}^{I} E_i^l} + \gamma^t \cdot \frac{T_i^{10}}{\sum\limits_{i=1}^{I} T_i^l} \tag{4.48}$$

4. $s_i^4 = 11$: Both adjacent subtasks are executed on the collaborative cloud, so only the computation loss of the current subtask on the collaborative cloud is considered. Therefore, the energy consumption and delay for $s_i^4 = 11$ can be expressed as:

$$E_i^{11} = E_i^{exe} = \kappa^e \cdot \alpha_i L_i C_i f_i^e \tag{4.49}$$

$$T_i^{11} = T_i^{exe} = \frac{\alpha_i L_i C_i}{f_i^e} \tag{4.50}$$

Thus, the $STLF$ for $s_i^4 = 11$ can be expressed as:

$$STLF_i^{11} = \gamma^e \cdot \frac{E_i^{11}}{\sum\limits_{i=1}^{I} E_i^l} + \gamma^t \cdot \frac{T_i^{11}}{\sum\limits_{i=1}^{I} T_i^l} \tag{4.51}$$

Definition 4.4 The System Loss Function ($SYLF$) is defined as the sum of the $STLF$ of each subtask, expressed as:

$$SYLF = \sum_{i=1}^{I} STLF_i^{s_i^j} \tag{4.52}$$

Therefore, the original optimization problem $P4-7$ can be transformed into the form of minimizing $SYLF$:

$$P4-8 ::\ \min_j SYLF = \sum i = 1^I STLF_i^{s_i^j}\ s.t.; ;\quad s_i^j \in \mathcal{S}i \tag{4.53}$$

By substituting $-Ri^{s_i^j}$ for $STLF_i^{s_i^j}$, the optimization problem $P4-8$ can be transformed into a standard MDP reward maximization problem:

$$P4-9 ::; \max_j R = \sum i = 1^I R_i^{s_i^j} \; s.t.;; \quad s_i^j \in S_i \tag{4.54}$$

The sequential offloading process of a single-chain application has been modeled as an MDP. By observing the environment, the terminal device can take the optimal action to determine the best offloading decision [36–39]. Subsequently, we propose the QLOF algorithm based on Q-learning to assist the terminal device in learning and solving the optimal offloading decision. Q-learning is the most widely used technique for solving MDPs, combining Monte Carlo and dynamic programming, and it performs offline learning without requiring prior knowledge [40].

In this section, under the optimal transmission power of the terminal device and the computation frequency of the edge cloud, the QLOF algorithm is employed to find the state of each subtask by minimizing $SYLF$, thereby obtaining the optimal offloading decision. When the decision-maker adopts the strategy π, it is essential to consider the potential reward that can be obtained. In general, the expected cumulative reward can be used to evaluate the policy in the current state, represented by the value function $v_\pi(s_i^j)$ as:

$$v_\pi(s_i^j) = \mathbb{E}[R_i^{s_i^j} + \gamma R_{i+1}^{s_{i+1}^j} + \gamma^2 R_{i+2}^{s_{i+2}^j} + \cdots + \gamma^{I-i} R_I^{s_I^j} | s_i^j] \tag{4.55}$$

The expectation in (4.55) depends on the policy π, indicating whether the terminal device performs an offloading action in the current state. Equation (4.55) can be further written as:

$$v_\pi(s_i^j) = \mathbb{E}[R_i^{s_i^j} + \gamma v(s_{i+1}^j) | S_i = s_i^j] \tag{4.56}$$

Since a standard MDP aims to maximize cumulative rewards [38–40], the optimal value function can be expressed as:

$$v^*(s_i^j) = \max \pi \mathbb{E}[Ri^{s_i^j} + \gamma v(s_{i+1}^j) | S_i = s_i^j] \tag{4.57}$$

Equation (4.57) can be further written as:

$$v^*(s_i^j) = \max a[Ri^{s_i^j} + \gamma \sum p(s_{i+1}^j, a_i) v(s_{i+1}^j) | S_i = s_i^j] \tag{4.58}$$

Since the state transition probabilities in certain environments are not easily obtainable, directly learning the optimal policy $\pi : s \rightarrow a$ is challenging. Q-learning solves the MDP without requiring knowledge of the state transition

Table 4.1 Q-table

i		Q-value	i+1
$s_i^1 = 00$	0	$Q(s_i^1, 0)$	$s_{i+1}^1 = 00$
	1	$Q(s_i^1, 1)$	$s_{i+1}^2 = 01$
$s_i^2 = 01$	0	$Q(s_i^2, 0)$	$s_{i+1}^3 = 10$
	1	$Q(s_i^2, 1)$	$s_{i+1}^4 = 11$
$s_i^3 = 10$	0	$Q(s_i^3, 0)$	$s_{i+1}^1 = 00$
	1	$Q(s_i^3, 1)$	$s_{i+1}^2 = 01$
$s_i^4 = 11$	0	$Q(s_i^4, 0)$	$s_{i+1}^3 = 10$
	1	$Q(s_i^4, 1)$	$s_{i+1}^4 = 11$

probabilities [41–44]. In the Q-learning algorithm, the Q-value is redefined as an evaluation function:

$$Q_{k+1}(s_i^j, a_i) = R_i^{s_i^j} + \gamma \max Q_k(s_{i+1}^j, a_{i+1}) \tag{4.59}$$

Here, k is the iteration count, $R_i^{s_i^j}$ represents the reward of the current state, γ is the discount factor that measures the influence of the observed next state, and $Q_k(s_{i+1}^j, a_{i+1})$ is the Q-value of the next subtask state. A Q-table is designed to associate actions with states, storing the Q-values for each subtask, as shown in Table 4.1. The QLOF algorithm learns the optimal offloading decision by iteratively updating the Q-value for each state using (4.59), with the pseudocode provided in Algorithm 10.

1. First, initialize all Q-values in the Q-table and set them to 0;
2. Randomly select an initial state s_i^j of a subtask and start the loop;
3. In the current state s_i^j, choose the action that yields the maximum Q-value for the next state, interact with the environment, and obtain the reward $R_i^{s_i^j}$. Update the current state Q-value based on (4.59);
4. Set the new state as the current state, completing the state transition;
5. Repeat steps 2–4 until the Q-values in the Q-table of all subtasks stabilize, and the loop ends;
6. Starting from the initial state $0\mathcal{S}$, choose the action that leads to the maximum Q-value state according to the stable Q-table, until the current state transitions to the terminal state $0\mathcal{T}$, at which point the algorithm ends.

It can be seen that the outer loop of QLOF is for each *Episode*, i.e., one training session, and the inner loop corresponds to each step of the *Episode*, until the Q-values of all subtasks converge, at which point the outer loop of the *Episode* ends. Finally, the stable Q-values in the Q-table can be used to guide the decision-making process of the decision-maker, i.e., the terminal device, in order to obtain the optimal offloading decision for the entire application. Thus, the learning process of QLOF is essentially the process of updating the Q-values in the Q-table.

Algorithm 10 QLOF

/ * **Q-value Update** * /
Initialization: Set all Q-values in the Q-table of each subtask to 0;
for *Episode* **do**
  1. Randomly select the initial state s_1^j of a subtask;
  repeat
    2. Choose the action that gives the maximum Q-value of the next state in the current state;
Interact with the environment and receive reward R;
    3. Update the current state Q-value according to Eq. (4.59);
    4. Set the new state as the current state, completing the state transition;
  until The current state = terminal state $0\mathcal{T}$;
  if All subtask state Q-values are stable **then**
    break *Episode*
  end if
end for
/***/
/ * **Optimal Offloading Decision** * /
5. Current state = initial state $\mathcal{S}0$;
repeat
  6. Based on the stable Q-table, choose the action that leads to the maximum Q-value state;
  7. Set the new state as the current state, completing the state transition;
until The current state = terminal state $0\mathcal{T}$

4.2.4 *Performance Evaluation*

This section evaluates the performance of the QLOF algorithm under different parameters through simulation experiments and compares it with other offloading schemes.

(1) Parameter Setting

This chapter sets the simulation environment as a single edge cloud and single user environment. All subtasks of the same application share the same values of γ^t and γ^e. The input data for each subtask and the CPU cycles required per unit of data follow uniform distributions $L_i \sim [0.1, 0.5]$ and $C_i \sim [500, 2500]$, respectively. The wireless channel gain between the terminal device and the edge cloud is modeled as a series of Rayleigh random variables with unit variance. Other simulation parameters are shown in Table 4.2.

(2) Comparison of Different Execution Schemes

This subsection compares the performance of delay-sensitive applications ($\gamma^t > \gamma^e$) under the QLOF scheme and different execution schemes. Figure 4.3 first compares the $SYLF$ of the QLOF scheme with the baseline execution schemes: Local Only and Cloud Only. From the observation, it can be seen that the $SYLF$ for applications with different numbers of subtasks in the Local Only scheme remains consistently at 1, so this scheme is set as the baseline for evaluating the other two schemes. Since both the Cloud Only and QLOF algorithms are influenced by

Table 4.2 Parameter settings

Parameter	Setting
System bandwidth B	20 MHz
Backhaul link communication capacity W	5 Mbps
Noise power spectral density	− 174 dBm/Hz
Maximum transmission power of the terminal p^{max}	23 dBm
Input data L_i	[0.1, 0.5] Mbits
Unit data computation complexity C_i	[500, 2500] cycles/bit
Central cloud computing capacity f^c	[150, 300] GHz
Local computing capacity f^l	[0.1, 0.5] GHz
Edge cloud computing capacity f^e	[20, 80] GHz
Weight factors γ^e, γ^t	[0,1]

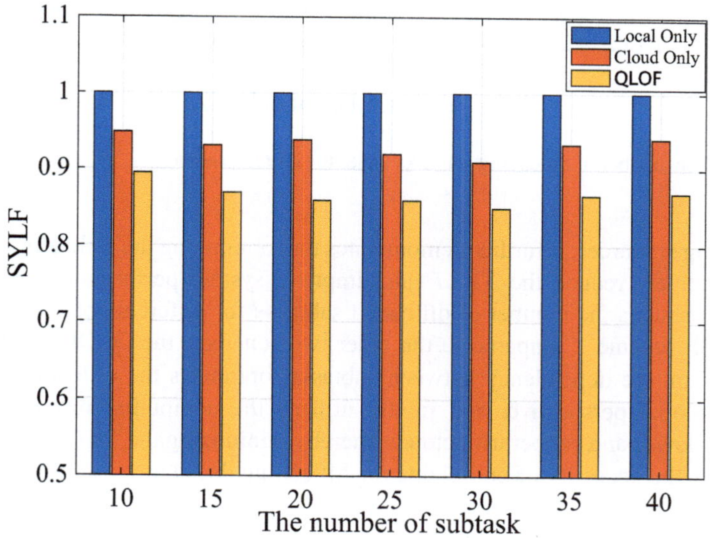

Fig. 4.3 Comparison of $SYLF$ under different execution schemes

wireless channel conditions, terminal transmission power, and the computing capabilities of edge and central clouds, the $SYLF$ for different applications under the same execution scheme exhibits some fluctuation. For delay-sensitive applications, the performance of the Cloud Only scheme is always superior to the Local Only scheme. This is because the Cloud Only scheme can fully exploit the computing resources of both the edge and central clouds, which work collaboratively to provide sufficient computational resources and significantly reduce latency. Furthermore, the proposed QLOF scheme consistently outperforms the other two basic execution schemes. This is due to the fact that the QLOF scheme comprehensively considers factors such as channel conditions, terminal device computing capability, and transmission power. By offloading and jointly utilizing three-layer network

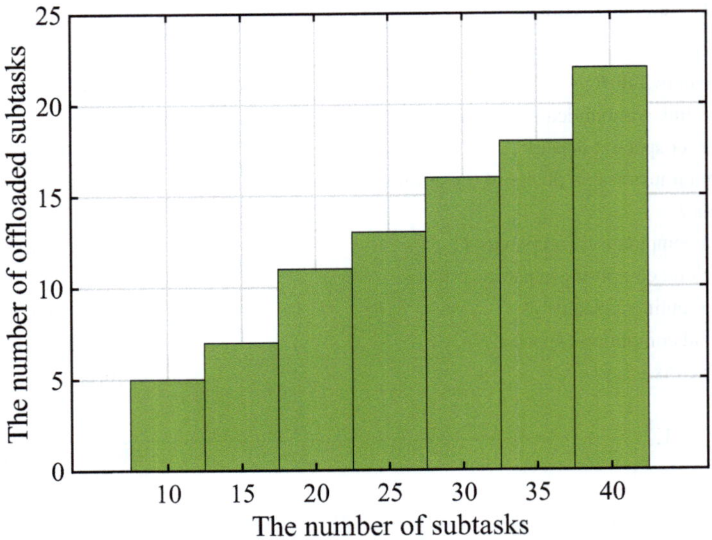

Fig. 4.4 The number of offloading subtasks under the QLOF scheme

computing resources, it further demonstrates that optimizing the offloading decision can effectively reduce the $SYLF$ and improve system performance. Figure 4.4 visually presents the number of offloaded subtasks for different applications under the QLOF scheme. Compared to the other two schemes, the QLOF scheme takes into account the dependency between subtasks, optimizes the offloading decision from a global perspective, and jointly utilizes the computing resources of the terminal device and cooperative clouds, thereby minimizing the $SYLF$. This further highlights the necessity of optimizing the offloading decision.

Figure 4.5 compares the performance of the QLOF scheme with other offloading schemes: ARHOS[45], One Climb[46], and eDors[12]. As shown in Fig. 4.5, applications with different numbers of subtasks always perform better under the QLOF scheme compared to the other three offloading schemes. This is because One Climb and ARHOS are one-time offloading schemes, where ARHOS adjusts the offloading window length based on the adaptability of subtask data. The eDors scheme, on the other hand, makes a single decision by comparing whether the current subtask should be computed locally or offloaded to collaborative cloud computing, and then continues to make decisions for the next subtask, without considering the dependency of offloading decisions between subtasks. It does not make a global plan for offloading decisions across all subtasks of the application. The proposed QLOF scheme, however, takes the inter-task state coupling into account, and the terminal device minimizes $SYLF$ as the goal by interacting with the environment multiple times, learning the globally optimal offloading decisions. Figure 4.6 shows the impact of local computing frequency f^l on the QLOF and eDors schemes. As f^l increases, the $SYLF$ for the QLOF scheme consistently

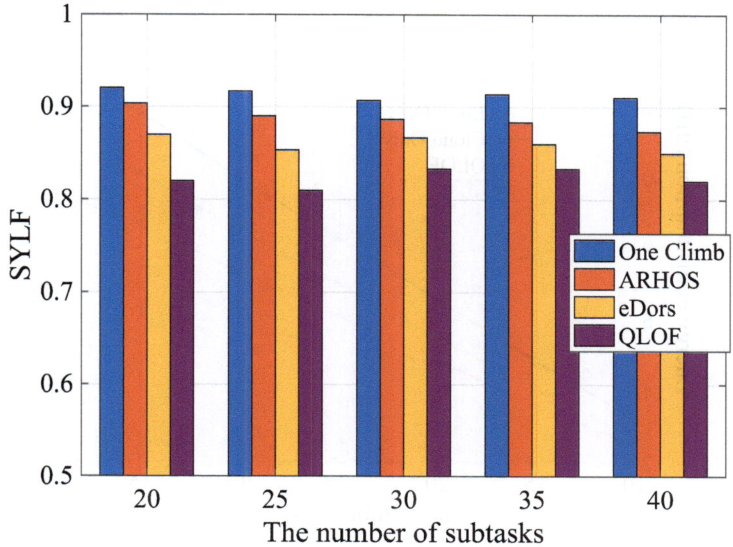

Fig. 4.5 Comparison of $SYLF$ between QLOF and One Climb, ARHOS and eDors

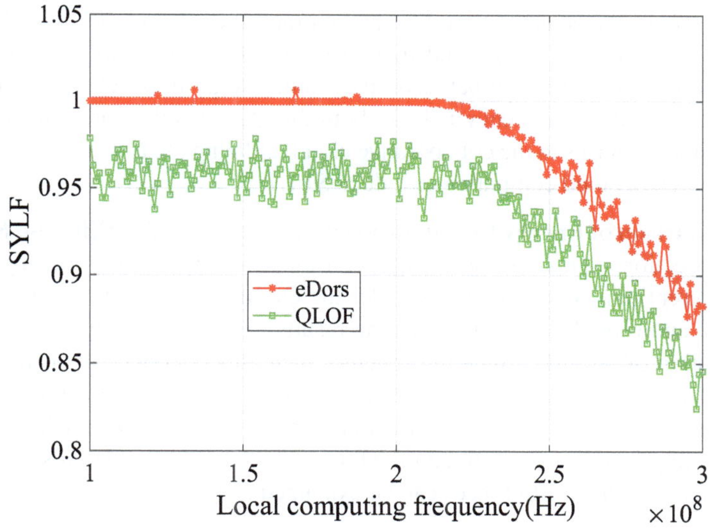

Fig. 4.6 QLOF and $SYLF$ under the scheme change with local calculation frequency

remains lower than that of the eDors scheme. When f^l is below 2.2×10^8, the $SYLF$ of both QLOF and eDors schemes fluctuates around 0.96 and 1, respectively. When f^l exceeds 2.2×10^8, both schemes show a significant downward trend in $SYLF$. This is because as the local computing frequency increases and approaches the edge cloud computing frequency, local computation no longer has a significant advantage

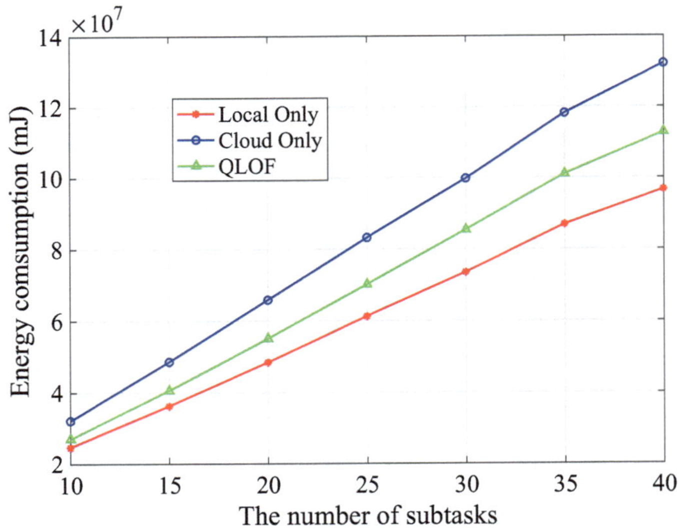

Fig. 4.7 Comparison of energy consumption under different execution schemes

in terms of energy consumption. On the contrary, the edge cloud offloads part of the data to the central cloud, and their parallel computation not only minimizes latency to the greatest extent but also saves some energy in MEC. Therefore, when the local computing frequency is high, both the QLOF and eDors schemes opt to offload more subtasks to the collaborative cloud, utilizing the low-latency advantage of collaborative cloud computing to reduce $SYLF$.

(3) Comparison of Energy Consumption and Latency Under Different Schemes This subsection compares the energy consumption and latency of applications with different numbers of subtasks under the QLOF, Local Only, and Cloud Only schemes, and provides an analysis of the results. As shown in Fig. 4.7, the energy consumption of all three execution schemes increases continuously as the number of subtasks increases. The Local Only scheme consistently shows a significant advantage in terms of energy consumption, while the Cloud Only scheme has the highest energy consumption among the three. The QLOF scheme falls in between. The reasons for these differences can be explained as follows:

1. Energy consumption is mainly determined by the computational frequency: Although the edge cloud's computing frequency is limited, it is still much higher than the terminal device's computing frequency. Therefore, the Cloud Only scheme performs worse in terms of energy consumption compared to the Local Only scheme, as it requires more energy to offload all tasks to the cloud and perform computations there.
2. Local Only scheme energy advantage: In the Local Only scheme, all subtasks are processed locally on the terminal device. This results in lower energy

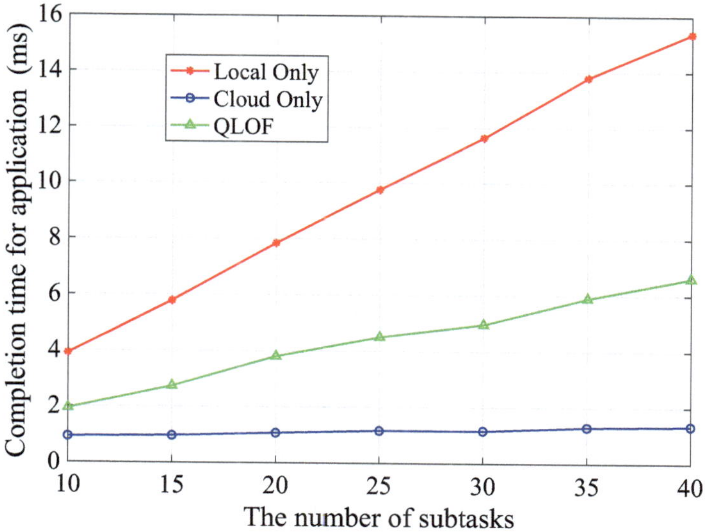

Fig. 4.8 Latency comparison under different execution schemes

consumption compared to offloading tasks to the collaborative cloud, as it avoids the energy cost of transmitting data from the terminal device to the edge cloud.

3. QLOF scheme's energy and latency trade-off: The QLOF scheme minimizes the system loss function $(SYLF)$ by balancing energy consumption and latency. It optimizes the offloading decisions from a global perspective, allowing the terminal device to selectively offload some subtasks to the collaborative cloud while keeping others for local computation. This selective offloading leads to energy consumption that is positioned between the Local Only and Cloud Only schemes.

Thus, the energy consumption results confirm that the QLOF scheme effectively balances energy efficiency with latency reduction by intelligently managing task offloading, while the Local Only scheme benefits from lower transmission energy costs, and the Cloud Only scheme incurs the highest energy costs due to full reliance on the cloud. As shown in Fig. 4.8, the application completion latency under different execution schemes is compared. The latency of the Local Only scheme increases sharply as the number of subtasks grows, while the Cloud Only scheme shows a slight increase in latency, which remains much lower than the other two schemes. There are two main reasons for this: First, the central cloud, as a supplement to edge cloud computing capabilities, provides powerful computational resources. The collaborative operation of both clouds allows for parallel processing of subtasks, effectively reducing task computation latency. Second, the edge cloud processor is deployed closer to the terminal device, significantly reducing transmission latency. It is evident that the advent of collaborative cloud computing greatly meets the needs of latency-sensitive and computationally intensive applications for low latency and

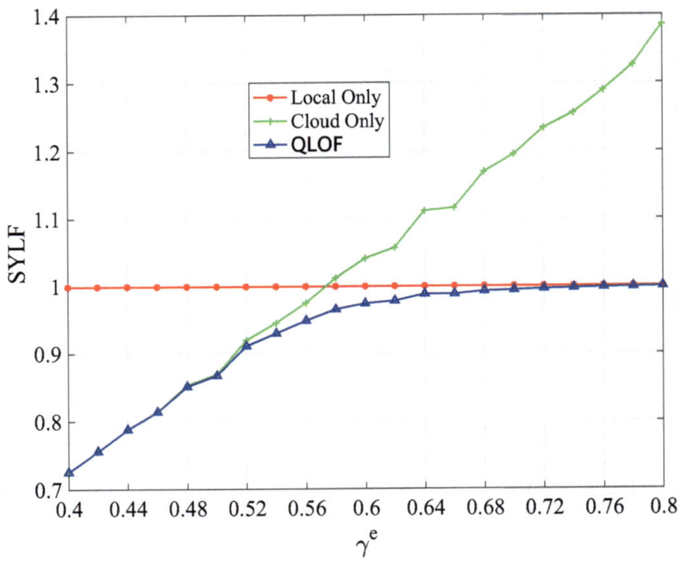

Fig. 4.9 The impact of weight factor γ^e on different execution schemes $SYLF$

powerful computational capabilities. The QLOF scheme proposed in this chapter effectively combines the low energy consumption of local computation and the low latency of collaborative cloud computing. By balancing latency and energy consumption based on application types, it minimizes the $SYLF$ through optimized offloading decisions.

(4) The Impact of Weight Factors

This subsection presents the impact of the weight factor γ^e on the $SYLF$ of different execution schemes. To obtain relatively accurate experimental results, the range of variation for γ^e is set from 0.4 to 0.8, with a step size of 0.02. For each value of γ^e, 1000 simulations are conducted, and the average result is taken. As shown in Fig.4.9, the Cloud Only scheme is highly sensitive to changes in γ^e, with its $SYLF$ increasing almost linearly as γ^e increases. In contrast, the Local Only scheme, as the baseline, remains constant at a value of 1. When $\gamma^e < 0.58$, the performance of the Cloud Only scheme is better than that of the Local Only scheme; however, when $\gamma^e > 0.58$, the performance of the Cloud Only scheme is worse than that of the Local Only scheme. This is because collaborative cloud computing can effectively reduce latency, making it more suitable for delay-sensitive applications, while the Local Only scheme has a more significant advantage in energy consumption, making it better suited for energy-sensitive applications. The QLOF scheme proposed in this chapter consistently outperforms the other two schemes. When $\gamma^e < 0.52$, its $SYLF$ curve closely follows that of the Cloud Only scheme, increasing almost linearly. When $0.52 < \gamma^e < 0.66$, its $SYLF$ increases more slowly. When $\gamma^e > 0.66$, its $SYLF$ gradually

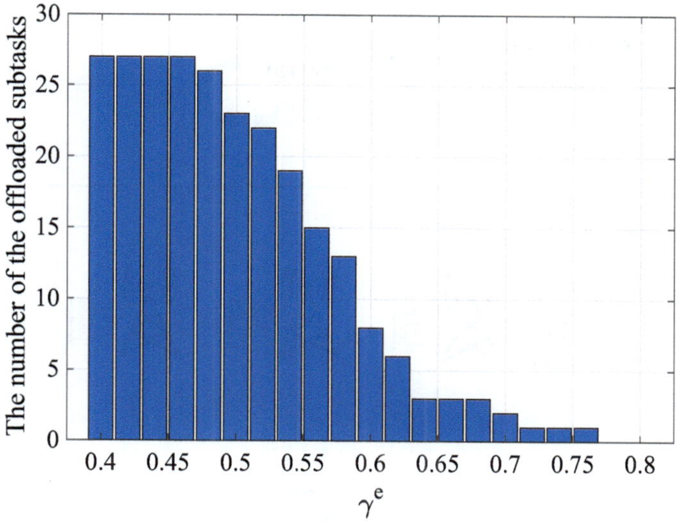

Fig. 4.10 The influence of weight factor γ^e for the QLOF scheme

approaches that of the Local Only scheme, becoming flatter. This is because the QLOF scheme effectively leverages the advantages of local computation to save energy and collaborative cloud computing to save time. By optimizing offloading decisions, it fully utilizes the available computational resources across the three-layer network, thereby reducing $SYLF$. As shown in Fig. 4.10, the number of offloaded subtasks in the QLOF scheme changes with γ^e. In the QLOF scheme, for delay-sensitive applications ($\gamma^t > \gamma^e$), the terminal device offloads relatively more subtasks to the collaborative cloud, improving performance by reducing latency. For energy-sensitive applications ($\gamma^e > \gamma^t$), the terminal device prefers to perform more computations locally, thereby improving performance by reducing energy consumption.

4.3 Multi-User Multi-Edge CCC

4.3.1 System Model

We consider a system consisting of M MUs, denoted by $\mathcal{M} = \{1, 2, \cdots, M\}$, and N edge cloud servers denoted by $\mathcal{N} = \{1, 2, 3, \cdots, N\}$. Each MU can be served by one edge cloud, and each edge cloud can serve multiple MUs within its maximum computing capacity Cap_n, which can be obtained by pre-scheduler. The system model is shown in Fig. 4.11. We assume that an MU offloads a computation-intensive application to the edge cloud via the wireless channel. Different edge clouds transmit data to the central cloud through different backhaul links. Similar to

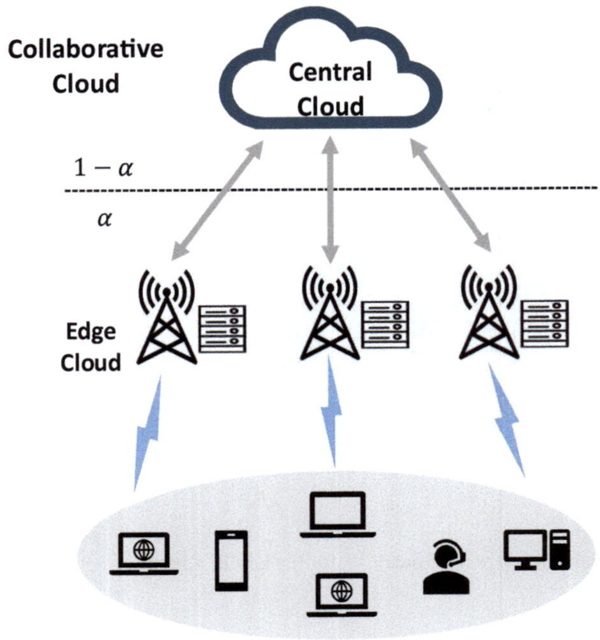

Fig. 4.11 System model for multi-user multi-edge CCC

the previous work [12], [26], we assume a quasi-static scenario, and the channel states during the offloading period are constant. We adopt a two-filed notation $\mathcal{A}pplication_m = \{L_m, C_m\}$ to represent the computation-intensive application of MU m, where L_m (bit) is the input data size, including system settings, program codes, and input parameters. C_m represents the required CPU cycles/bit to accomplish the application.

(1) Local Computing

We use $\mathcal{A}pp_m = \{L_m, C_m\}$ to represent user application m, where L_m is the amount of input data, including system settings, program code, and input parameters, and C_m represents the number of CPU cycles required per unit of data. Therefore, the latency and energy consumption of local computing for user application m can be expressed as [12, 26]:

$$T_m^l = C_m L_m / f_m^l \tag{4.60}$$

$$E_m^l = \kappa^l f_m^l C_m L_m \tag{4.61}$$

where f_m^l is local computing capacity of MU m, and κ^l is the effective switched capacity [12].

(2) CCC Model

For general analysis, we give two reasonable assumptions: (1) Each computation application can be arbitrarily split without considering the inherent content, which corresponds to the scenarios like video compression and speech recognition [18], [16], [19]. (2) The edge cloud and the central cloud work in parallel, and the central cloud allocates its complete computation resource to all MDs for parallel computing. According to [9], each edge cloud determines whether the offloaded applications should be executed by themselves or edge cloud and central cloud collaboratively. For latter, the edge cloud should determine the proportion of each application that needs to be executed on the central cloud server after it is completely received. We first consider how to design the optimal splitting ratio $\alpha_m^n \in [0, 1]$ for achieving the lowest delay. Since edge cloud and central cloud process applications in parallel, the overall time consumption for executing an application of MU m by edge cloud n can be expressed as:

$$T_m^{n,exe} = \min \max\{T_m^{n,e}, T_m^{n,ed-ce} + T_m^{cent}\}, \tag{4.62}$$

where $T_m^{n,e} = \frac{\alpha_m^n L_m C_m}{f_m^{n,e}}$ is computation delay of edge cloud n executing application of MU m, $T_m^{n,ed-ce} = \frac{(1-\alpha_m^n)L_m}{W}$ is transmission delay through a backhaul link, where W is the backhaul communication capacity. $T_m^{cent} = \frac{(1-\alpha_m^n)L_m C_m}{f^c}$ is the computation delay of central cloud, where F^{cent} is the ultra-high frequency of central cloud. By analyzing the monotonicity[9], the minimum value of $T_m^{n,exe}$ is achieved when $T_m^{n,e} = T_m^{n,ed-ce} + T_m^{cent}$, therefore the optimal splitting ratio can be derived as:

$$\alpha_m^n = \frac{f_m^{n,e}(f^c + C_m W)}{f_m^{n,e}(f^c + C_m W) + f^c C_m W}, \tag{4.63}$$

where $f_m^{n,e}$ is the computing frequency allocated by edge cloud n to MU m. The overall delay and energy consumption of the collaborative cloud computing at an optimal splitting ratio can be expressed as:

$$T_m^{n,exe} = \frac{\alpha_m^n L_m C_m}{f_m^{n,e}} \tag{4.64}$$

$$E_m^{n,exe} = \alpha_m^n \kappa^e f_m^{n,e} C_m L_m \tag{4.65}$$

where κ^e is the effective swatch capacity [9].

(3) Transmission Model

Computation-intensive applications are offloaded through the wireless channel. Here, $a_m \in \{0, 1\}$ denotes the offloading decision of MU m, where $a_m = 0$ means local computing, and $a_m = 1$ means collaborative cloud computing. Hence, we can formulate an offloading decision profile as $\mathbf{a} = (a_1, a_2, \cdots, a_m)$, and the accumulation of offloading decisions $K(\mathbf{a}) = \sum_{m=1}^{M} a_m$ expresses the number of the offloaded applications. Based on the OFDMA technology, the total bandwidth B is equally divided among $K(\mathbf{a})$ offloaded devices [47]. Based on the Shannon principle, the wireless transmission rate can be expressed as:

$$R_m^n(p_m^{n,t}, \mathbf{a}) = \frac{B}{K(\mathbf{a})} \log_2(1 + \frac{p_m^{n,t} H_m^n}{BN_0/K(\mathbf{a})}) \tag{4.66}$$

where $p_m^{n,t}$ indicates the transmission power of MU m to edge cloud n, which can be configured by the MU subject to a maximum transmission power constraint. H_m^n is the wireless channel gain between MU m and edge cloud n. B and N_0 denote the total channel bandwidth and noise power spectral density, respectively. The transmission energy consumption and time consumption are affected by $\mathbf{a}$ and can be represented by:

$$T_m^{n,trans}(p_m^{n,t}, K(\mathbf{a})) = \frac{L_m}{R_m^n(p_m^{n,t}, K(\mathbf{a}))} \tag{4.67}$$

$$E_m^{n,trans}(p_m^{n,t}, K(\mathbf{a})) = p_m^{n,t} \cdot T_m^{trans,n}(p_m^{n,t}, K(\mathbf{a})) \tag{4.68}$$

Equations (4.67) and (4.68) show that transmission time consumption and energy consumption of transmission are affected by the offloading decision and transmission power. Combined with (4.64), (4.65), (4.67) and (4.68), the latency and energy consumption required for the entire collaborative cloud computing can be expressed as:

$$T_m^{n,c} = T_m^{n,exe} + T_m^{n,trans} \tag{4.69}$$

$$E_m^{n,c} = E_m^{n,exe} + E_m^{n,trans} \tag{4.70}$$

4.3.2 Problem Formulation

The massive growth of user applications has led to diversity and heterogeneity, and different applications have different properties. Taking autonomous driving as an example, in order to ensure driving safety, the overall response time of the system generally cannot exceed 10 milliseconds, so there are high requirements for latency. In addition, some applications need to improve their energy efficiency from a technical level to achieve green communication in order to reduce operating costs. This section comprehensively considers the two most important attributes of latency and energy consumption, and proposes $AETC$ as the main indicator for measuring user experience and application performance.

Definition 4.5 *Application Energy-Time Cost* ($AETC$) is defined as the weighted sum of the latency and energy required to complete the application. which is expressed as:

$$AETC_m = \gamma_m^e E_m + \gamma_m^t T_m \tag{4.71}$$

γ_m^e and $\gamma_m^t \in [0, 1]$ are weight factors that measure the preference of the application

The $AETC$ corresponding to local computing and collaborative cloud computing can be expressed as:

$$AETC_m^l = \gamma_m^e E_m^l + \gamma_m^t T_m^l, \tag{4.72}$$

$$AETC_m^{n,c} = \sum\nolimits_{n=1}^{N} b_m^n (\gamma_m^e E_m^{n,c} + \gamma_m^t T_m^{n,c}) \tag{4.73}$$

where b_m^n represents the user and edge cloud matching strategy. If user m offloads its application to edge cloud n for computation, then $b_m^n = 1$, otherwise $b_m^n = 0$. Taking the offloading decision a_m into account, the combined (4.72) and (4.73), the $AETC$ of user m can be expressed as:

$$AETC_m = a_m AETC_m^{n,c} + (1 - a_m) AETC_m^l \tag{4.74}$$

Definition 4.6 System Energy-Time Cost ($SETC$): It is defined as the cumulative sum of all applications $AETC$ in the system, so $SETC$ can be expressed as:

$$SETC = \sum_{m=1}^{M} AETC_m \tag{4.75}$$

Our goal is to minimize $SETC$ by optimizing the offloading decision a_m, matching strategy b_m^n, edge cloud computing resources $f_m^{n,e}$, and offloading transmission power $p_m^{n,t}$. Therefore, the optimization problem can be expressed as:

$$\begin{aligned}
P4-10: \quad & \min_{a_m, b_m^n, p_m^{n,t}, f_m^{n,e}} \quad SETC \\
s.t.\ & C_1: a_m \in \{0,1\}, m \in \mathcal{M}, n \in \mathcal{N} \\
& C_2: b_m^n \in \{0,1\}, m \in \mathcal{M}_{off}, n \in \mathcal{N}, \\
& C_3: \sum\nolimits_{n=1}^{N} b_m^n = 1, m \in \mathcal{M}_{off} \\
& C_4: 0 \le p_m^{n,t} \le p_m^{max}, m \in \mathcal{M}_{off}, n \in \mathcal{N} \\
& C_5: f_{min}^{n,e} \le f_m^{n,e} \le f_{max}^{n,e}, m \in \mathcal{M}_{off}, n \in \mathcal{N} \\
& C_6: 0 \le \sum\nolimits_{m=1}^{M} b_m^n \le Cap_n, n \in \mathcal{N}
\end{aligned} \tag{4.76}$$

where $\mathcal{M}_{off}$ is the set of offload users, and Cap_n is the upper limit of the number of users that can be simultaneously connected to the edge cloud n. C_1 indicates that each user application can choose to compute locally or offload to collaborative cloud computing. $C_2 \sim C_6$ is a constraint for offload users in $\mathcal{M}_{off}$. $C_2 \sim C_3$ ensures that each offload application can only be processed by one edge cloud. C_4 and C_5 represent the upper and lower limits of the offload transmission power and edge cloud computing frequency, respectively. C_6 indicates that the number of users that can be simultaneously connected to the edge cloud cannot exceed the upper limit Cap_n.

4.3.3 Proposed Semi-Distributed Algorithm

Since the a_m and b_m^n of $P4-10$ are integer variables, while $f_m^{n,e}$ and $p_m^{n,t}$ are continuous variables, and the offloading decision a_m is coupled with $p_m^{n,t}$, $P4-10$ is MINLP [26] and cannot be solved in polynomial time. This section uses a semi-distributed algorithm to decompose the problem into multiple sub-problems and solve them separately. Due to the limited system bandwidth, there is spectrum competition between multiple offloading user applications. In order to achieve efficient offloading transmission process, the terminal is required to provide higher transmission power. Therefore, the transmission power $p_m^{n,t}$ is coupled with the offloading decision **a**. In addition, different offloading decisions will also cause different matching strategies between terminal devices and edge clouds, so the offloading decision **a** is coupled with the matching strategy b_m^n. The coupling between optimization variables makes the problem $P4-10$ challenging, so this section proposes two offloading algorithms based on heuristic search, GS-MOA and GS-SOA, and combines the GS-MEMA algorithm to iteratively update $p_m^{n,t}$ and b_m^n to find the optimal offloading decision **a**. The solution process is described in detail below.

When the user application is offloaded, that is, $a_m = 1$, the terminal device needs to configure the corresponding offloading transmission power $p_m^{n,t}$ for the offloaded application according to the channel conditions, available bandwidth and weight factors; the edge cloud needs to configure the corresponding computing resources for the offloaded application according to the application input data volume, complexity and weight factors. First, optimize the offloading transmission power $p_m^{n,t}$ and edge cloud computing frequency $f_m^{n,e}$ for all possible matching strategies. Since the offloading transmission power configuration and edge cloud computing frequency configuration between each application are independent of each other, they can be solved by minimizing the $AETC_m$ of each application. When $a_m = 1$, $AETC_m = AETC_m^{n,c}$. Substituting (4.69) and (4.70), the original optimization problem can be simplified to:

$$\begin{aligned} P4-11: &\min_{p_m^{n,t}, f_m^{n,e}} \gamma_m^t T_m^{n,exe} + \gamma_m^e E_m^{n,exe} + \gamma_m^t T_m^{n,trans} + \gamma_m^e E_m^{n,trans} \\ s.t.\ & C_4, C_5 \end{aligned} \tag{4.77}$$

Substituting (4.64), (4.65), (4.67), (4.68), $P4-11$ can be expressed as:

$$\begin{aligned} P4-12: \min_{p_m^{n,t}, f_m^{n,e}} & \frac{\gamma_m^t L_m K(\mathbf{a})/B + \gamma_m^e L_m K(\mathbf{a}) p_m^{n,t}/B}{\log_2(1+\frac{p_m^{n,t} H_m^n K(\mathbf{a})}{BN_0})} \\ + & \frac{\gamma_m^t L_m C_m (f^c + C_m) f_m^{n,e} + \gamma_m^e \kappa^e L_m C_m (f^c + C_m)(f_m^{n,e})^3}{(f^c + C_m)(f_m^{n,e})^2 + f^c \cdot C_m W f_m^{n,e}} \\ s.t.\quad & C4, C5 \end{aligned} \tag{4.78}$$

By analyzing (4.78), the offloading transmission power $p_m^{n,t}$ and the edge cloud computing frequency $f_m^{n,e}$ are independent of each other, so they can be optimized independently.

(1) Offloading Transmission Power Optimization

For offloading data, the terminal device needs to determine the offloading transmission power based on the current channel conditions and available bandwidth, subject to its own configurable maximum power constraints, to ensure that the application can be successfully offloaded to the edge cloud. For the system model designed in this chapter, the channel bandwidth is shared equally among multiple offloading applications. According to Shannon theorem, it can be analyzed that the offloading decisions **a** in the system are coupled with the terminal device transmission power $p_m^{n,t}$. By analyzing Eq. (4.78), the offloading transmission power and edge cloud computing frequency are independent. Therefore, in this section, we first optimize $p_m^{n,t}$ with respect to **a**, which simplifies the original optimization problem to $P4-13$:

$$\begin{aligned} P4-13: &\min_{p_m^{n,t}} f(p_m^{n,t}) \\ s.t.\ & C_4 \end{aligned} \tag{4.79}$$

where

$$f(p_m^{n,t}) = \frac{\theta_m + \lambda_m^n p_m^{n,t}}{\log_2(1+\mu_m^n p_m^{n,t})} \tag{4.80}$$

In (4.80), we have the following definitions: $\theta_m = \frac{\gamma_m^t L_m K(\mathbf{a})}{B}$, $\lambda_m^n = \frac{\gamma_m^e L_m K(\mathbf{a}) p_m^{n,t}}{B}$, $\mu_m^n = \frac{H_m^n K(\mathbf{a})}{B N_0}$. The second derivative of $f(p_m^{n,t})$ can be expressed as:

$$f''(p_m^{n,t}) = \frac{\mu_m^n \left[\mu_m^n(\theta_m + \lambda_m^n p_m^{n,t}) - 2\lambda_m^n(1+\mu_m^n p_m^{n,t})\right]}{\ln 2(1+\mu_m^n p_m^{n,t})^2 \log_2^3(1+\mu_m^n p_m^{n,t})} \cdot \frac{\log_2(1+\mu_m^n p_m^{n,t})}{\ln 2(1+\mu_m^n p_m^{n,t})^2 \log_2^3(1+\mu_m^n p_m^{n,t})} + \frac{2(\mu_m^n)^2(\theta_m + \lambda_m^n p_m^{n,t})/\ln 2}{\ln 2(1+\mu_m^n p_m^{n,t})^2 \log_2^3(1+\mu_m^n p_m^{n,t})} \tag{4.81}$$

Analyzing Eq. (4.81), it can be concluded that $f''(p_m^{n,t})$ is not always positive within the domain of $p_m^{n,t}$, and therefore, $f(p_m^{n,t})$ is non-convex. If $f(\cdot)$ is twice differentiable on $\mathbf{R}$ and there exists a point x_0 satisfying $f'(x_0) = 0$ and $f''(x_0) \geq 0$, then $f(\cdot)$ is a quasi-convex function on $\mathbf{R}$ [29]. Hence, the first derivative of $f(p_m^{n,t})$ is given by:

$$f'(p_m^{n,t}) = \frac{\lambda_m^n \log_2(1+\mu_m^n p_m^{n,t}) - \mu_m^n/\ln 2\left(\frac{\theta_m + \lambda_m^n p_m^{n,t}}{1+\mu_m^n p_m^{n,t}}\right)}{\log_2^2(1+\mu_m^n p_m^{n,t})} \tag{4.82}$$

After analyzing, we can get that when $f'(p_m^{n,t}) = 0$, its numerator is equal to 0. To simplify the analysis, the numerator is recorded as ψ:

$$\psi(p_0) = \lambda_m^n \log_2(1+\mu_m^n p_0) - \frac{\mu_m^n}{\ln 2} \cdot \frac{\theta_m + \lambda_m^n p_0}{1+\mu_m^n p_0} = 0 \tag{4.83}$$

Substituting Eq. (4.83) into (4.81), we get:

$$f''(p_0) = \frac{(\mu_m^n)^3}{\lambda_m^n \ln^2 2} \frac{(\theta_m + \lambda_m^n p_0)^2}{(1+\mu_m^n p_0)^3 \log_2^3(1+\mu_m^n p_0)} \geq 0 \tag{4.84}$$

If (4.84) is greater than or equal to 0, then $f(p_m^{n,t})$ is quasi-convex. The bisection method is generally used to solve quasi-convex functions [29]. The first derivative of Eq. (4.83) can be expressed as:

$$\psi'(p_m^{n,t}) = \frac{(\mu_m^n)^2}{\ln 2} \frac{\theta_m + \lambda_m^n p_m^{n,t}}{(1+\mu_m^n p_m^{n,t})^2} > 0 \tag{4.85}$$

Since $\psi(0) = -\frac{\mu_m^n \theta_m}{\ln 2} < 0$, simple analysis shows that $\psi(p_m^{n,t})$ is monotonically increasing and less than 0 at the starting point $p_m^{n,t} = 0$. Therefore, $f'(p_m^{n,t})$ is also monotonically increasing and satisfies $f'(0) < 0$. Thus, the behavior of $f(p_m^{n,t})$ in $\mathbf{R}$

can be derived. Specifically, when $0 < p_m^{n,t} < p_0$ (where p_0 satisfies $f'(p_m^{n,t}) = 0$), $f(p_m^{n,t})$ is monotonically decreasing. When $p_m^{n,t} \geq p_0$, $f(p_m^{n,t})$ is monotonically increasing. Therefore, $f(p_m^{n,t})$ reaches its minimum at $p_m^{n,t} = p_0$. Next, we need to analyze whether p_0 is within the domain of $p_m^{n,t}$. This requires classification into two cases: If p_0 is within the domain of $p_m^{n,t}$, the optimal transmission power is $p_m^{n,t*} = p_0$. Otherwise, the optimal transmission power is $p_m^{n,t*} = p_m^{max}$. We apply the bisection method to minimize $f(p_m^{n,t})$ for finding the optimal transmission power. The pseudocode is shown in Algorithm 11.

Algorithm 11 Bisection Method for Transmission Power Optimization

Input: $0 < p_m^{n,t} < p_m^{max}$ and $\psi(p_m^{n,t})$
Output: $p_m^{n,t*}$
if $\psi(p_m^{max}) \leq 0$ **then**
  $p_m^{n,t*} = p_m^{max}$
else
  $p^s = 0$ and $p^t = p_m^{max}$
  repeat
    $p^l = (p^s + p^t)/2$
    if $\psi(p^l) \leq 0$ **then**
      $p^s = p^l$
    else
      $p^t = p^l$
    end if
  until $(p^t - p^s) \leq \epsilon$
  $p_m^{n,t*} = (p^s + p^t)/2$
end if

(2) Edge Cloud Computing Frequency Allocation

The edge cloud servers, due to the distributed deployment in close proximity, significantly alleviate the issue of insufficient computational resources at the terminal devices. They also help mitigate the high transmission latency associated with central cloud computing, thus providing effective computational support for latency-sensitive applications that require timely responses. However, due to the limited computational resources of the edge cloud servers, they need to configure the corresponding computational frequency for offloading users under the constraint of the available maximum computational resources. According to Eq. (4.78), MEC resources are independent of offloading transmission power, so the optimization problem can be simplified to *P4 − 14*:

$$\begin{aligned} P4-14: \ & \min_{f_m^{n,e}} \ y(f_m^{n,e}) \\ & s.t. \ \ C_5 \end{aligned} \tag{4.85}$$

where

$$y(f_m^{n,e}) = \frac{Am + Bm(f_m^{n,e})^2}{mf_m^{n,e} + n} \tag{4.87}$$

where $A = \gamma_m^t L_m C_m$, $B = \gamma_m^e \kappa^e L_m C_m$, $m = f^c + C_m$, $n = f^c \cdot C_m W$. First, we take the first derivative of $y(f_m^{n,e})$, as follows:

$$y'(f_m^{n,e}) = \frac{-Am^2 + 2Bmnf_m^{n,e} + Bm^2(f_m^{n,e})^2}{(mf_m^{n,e} + n)^2} \tag{4.88}$$

Observing (4.88), we can see that the sign of $y(f_m^{n,e})$ is determined only by the sign of its molecule, so we can only analyze its molecule, that is:

$$\begin{aligned} \Psi(f_m^{n,e}) &= -Am^2 + 2Bmnf_m^{n,e} + Bm^2(f_m^{n,e})^2 \\ &= m[-Am + 2Bnf_m^{n,e} + Bm(f_m^{n,e})^2] \end{aligned} \tag{4.89}$$

From (4.89), we can see that $\Psi(\cdot) = 0$ has two roots in the real domain and is determined by the univariate quadratic polynomial in the brackets. Here, $Q(f_m^{n,e})$ is used to represent the contents of the brackets:

$$Q(f_m^{n,e}) = Bm(f_m^{n,e})^2 + 2Bnf_m^{n,e} - Am \tag{4.90}$$

By analyzing the (4.90), $Q(\cdot) = 0$ has two roots and is a parabola that opens upward. Since $Q(0) = -Am$, it is easy to get that the left root f^l is negative and the right root f^r is positive. Therefore, now we only need to analyze whether f^r is within the domain of $f_m^{n,e}$.

1. $f^r < f_{min}^{n,e}$, $\Psi(f_{min}^{n,e}) > 0$. Since Ψ is positive in the domain, $y(f_m^{n,e})$ is monotonically increasing in the domain, and $y(f_m^{n,e})$ has a minimum value at $f_{min}^{n,e}$. Therefore, $(f_m^{n,e})^* = f_{min}^{n,e}$.
2. $f_{min}^{n,e} < f^r < f_{max}^{n,e}$, $\Psi(f^r) = 0$. Ψ is negative to the left of f^r and positive to the right of f^r, so $y(f_m^{n,e})$ first decreases and then increases. The minimum value of $y(f_m^{n,e})$ occurs at f^r, so $(f_m^{n,e})^* = f^r$.
3. $f^r > f_{max}^{n,e}$, $\Psi(f^c) < 0$. Since Ψ is negative in the domain, $y(f_m^{n,e})$ is monotonically decreasing in the domain, and $y(f_m^{n,e})$ achieves a minimum value at $f_{max}^{n,e}$. Therefore, the optimal edge cloud computing frequency is $(f_m^{n,e})^* = f_{max}^{n,e}$.

(3) Matching Strategy Optimization

This subsection uses the Gale-Shapley matching algorithm to find the optimal matching strategy between multiple users and multiple edge clouds in the system. The Gale-Shapley matching algorithm, also known as the Deferred Acceptance Algorithm, is a market mechanism designed by Gale and Shapley to find a stable match [48]. In the market, one side proposes invitations to the objects on the other side, and the objects receiving the invitations consider them, then "grab" the ones they favor and reject the others. The key point of this algorithm is that agreeable invitations are not immediately accepted but are only "grabbed," meaning they are "deferred" [49]. After an invitation is rejected, a new invitation can be made, and the entire process continues until both sides are fully matched. The optimization of the matching problem in this chapter needs to consider three constraints: (1) Each user application can only offload to one edge cloud, but each edge cloud can connect to multiple users at the same time. (2) The maximum number of users that each edge cloud can connect to cannot exceed its maximum capacity. (3) The total number of users that all edge clouds can connect to must be at least equal to the total number of users in the network, i.e., $\sum_{n=1}^{N} Cap_n \geq M$. Since the matching strategy b_m^n and offloading decisions $\mathbf{a}$ are interdependent, it is difficult to directly optimize b_m^n. This subsection proposes the GS-MEMA algorithm, assuming that the optimal resource allocation and offloading decisions are known. The matching problem between terminal devices and edge clouds is modeled as a many-to-one bipartite matching problem [50], and the optimization problem can be expressed as $P4-15$:

$$\begin{aligned} P4-15:\ &\min_{b_m^n} \sum\nolimits_{m=1}^{M} a_m b_m^n (AETC_m^{n,exe} + AETC_m^{n,trans}) \\ &s.t.\ \ C_2, C_3, C_6 \end{aligned} \tag{4.91}$$

Algorithm 12 GS-MEMA

Input: $\mathcal{M}_{off}, \mathcal{N}, Cap_n$
Output: Matching strategy for offloading users and edge clouds b_m^n
Initialize: $\mathcal{PL}_{user}^m, \mathcal{PL}_{edge}^n$, unmatched user set $\mathcal{M}_{unmatch} = \mathcal{M}_{off}$
while $\mathcal{M}_{unmatch} \neq \emptyset$ **do**
  for all $m \in \mathcal{M}_{unmatch}$ **do**
    1. Each unmatched user sends a connection request to the edge clouds that they have not yet made a request to, based on their preference list $\mathcal{PL}_{user}^m$;
  end for
  for $n \in \mathcal{N}$ **do**
    if $\sum_{m=1}^{M} b_m^n \leq Cap_n$ **then**
      2. The edge cloud temporarily accepts all user connection requests $b_m^n = 1$;
    else
      3. The edge cloud accepts Cap_n users based on its preference list $\mathcal{PL}_{edge}^n$ and rejects the others, updating b_m^n;
      4. Remove the Cap_n accepted users from $\mathcal{M}_{unmatch}$ and set their connection status to $b_m^n = 1$;
      5. Rejected users return to an unmatched state and join $\mathcal{M}_{unmatch}$, updating $b_m^n = 0$;
    end if
  end for
end while

The core of the GS-MEMA algorithm is deferred acceptance, aiming to maximize bilateral preferences [51–53]. First, the participants are divided into two separate sets: terminal users and edge clouds. Each member of these sets ranks the members of the other set according to their preference and constructs a preference list. Based on these preference lists, multiple rounds of selection are performed until all members from both sides are matched. During this process, if the required number of users received by an edge cloud exceeds its maximum capacity, the edge cloud will select the most preferred users within its capacity and reject the rest. Therefore, the algorithm first constructs preference lists (Preference List, $\mathcal{PL}$): The preference lists for the edge clouds and terminals are designed as $\mathcal{PL}_{edge}^{n}$ and $\mathcal{PL}_{user}^{m}$, respectively.

$\mathcal{PL}_{edge}^{n}$: For each edge cloud $n \in \mathcal{N}$, the users offloading tasks are ranked strictly in descending order according to the size of $AETC_{m}^{n,exe}$, $m \in \mathcal{M}_{off}$.

$\mathcal{PL}_{user}^{m}$: For each offloading user $m \in \mathcal{M}_{off}$, all edge clouds are ranked strictly in descending order according to the size of $AETC_{m}^{n,trans}$, $n \in \mathcal{N}$.

For example, if $\mathcal{PL}_{edge}^{n}(m_1) > \mathcal{PL}_{edge}^{n}(m_2)$, it indicates that edge cloud n prefers user m_1 over user m_2, i.e., $AETC_{m_1}^{n,exe} < AETC_{m_2}^{n,exe}$.

Definition 4.7 (Blocking Pair) $Pair(m_i, n_j)$ is a blocking pair in the matching set ($\mathcal{MS}$) if the following conditions are met relative to $\mathcal{MS}$:

(1) $Pair(m_i)$ prefers n_j over its current match,
(2) $Pair(n_j)$ prefers m_i over its current match,

where $Pair(*)$ represents the element that has already been matched with the element inside the parentheses. If there are no blocking pairs in $\mathcal{MS}$, it is called a stable matching [49, 53].

Lemma 4.1 *GS-MEMA is a stable matching algorithm*

Proof Since each user initially chooses the edge cloud they prefer the most, and the edge cloud considers whether to replace a paired user based on their preferences and capacity, there are no blocking pairs. For example, if user m_2 is paired with edge cloud n_2, and user m_1 prefers edge cloud n_2 and edge cloud n_2 also prefers user m_1 over user m_2, then edge cloud n_2 will prioritize accepting user m_1 and either delay accepting or reject user m_2 based on its capacity. Therefore, there are no blocking pairs in GS-MEMA, and the matching is stable.

Based on this, *P4 – 15* can be transformed into a many-to-one bilateral preference maximization problem based on the Gale-Shapley algorithm.

$$P4-16: \max_{b_m^n} \sum\nolimits_{m=1}^{M} a_m b_m^n (\mathcal{PL}_{edge}^{n}(m) + \mathcal{PL}_{user}^{m}(n)) \qquad (4.92)$$
$$s.t.\ C_2, C_3, C_6$$

The GS-MEMA pseudocode is shown in the Algorithm 12, which can be simply described as the following five steps:

1. Each unmatched user selects the top-ranked edge cloud from their preference list and sends a request for access.
2. If the number of users already connected to the edge cloud is less than Cap_n, the edge cloud accepts the user access request.
3. If the number of users already connected to the edge cloud equals Cap_n, the edge cloud refers to its preference list and retains the top Cap_n most preferred users in the connected state, replacing users with lower preferences.
4. Users who are replaced return to the unmatched state.
5. Steps 1–4 are repeated when all offloading users are matched.

□

(4) Offloading Decisions Optimization

When optimizing offloading transmission power and matching strategies, the offloading decision **a** is considered as a fixed value. Consequently, the obtained optimal solutions are functions of the offloading decision. Therefore, this section incorporates the coupling between the offloading decision and transmission power, as well as the matching strategy. Based on heuristic search, two offloading algorithms, GS-MOA and GS-SOA, are proposed. These algorithms iteratively update the offloading transmission power and matching strategy by minimizing $SETC$ until the optimal offloading decision is found. The optimization problem can thus be expressed as *P4 – 17*:

$$P4-17: \min_{a_m} \sum_{m=1}^{M} a_m AETC_m^{n,c}(b_m^n) + (1-a_m)AETC_m^l \\ s.t.\ C_1 \tag{4.93}$$

Before introducing the GS-MOA algorithm, the following definitions are given.

Definition 4.8 Relatively Optimal Offloading Decision: An offloading decision **a** is relatively optimal compared to $\mathbf{a}^*$, denoted as $\mathbf{a} \rhd \mathbf{a}^*$, if and only if $SETC(\mathbf{a})$ is less than $SETC(\mathbf{a}^*)$, i.e., $SETC(\mathbf{a}) < SETC(\mathbf{a}^*)$.

Definition 4.9 Non-Expandable Local Set: A local computation set $\mathcal{M}_{local}$ is non-expandable if and only if the number of elements in the set equals the total number of users in the system, $|\mathcal{M}_{local}| = \mathcal{M}$, or there does not exist a local computation set $\mathcal{M}_{local} \cup \{k\}$ such that $\mathbf{a}_{\mathcal{M}_{local} \cup \{k\}} \rhd \mathbf{a}_{\mathcal{M}_{local}}$.

Definition 4.10 Local Optimal Offloading Decision: An offloading decision **a** is locally optimal if and only if **a** is relatively optimal among all offloading sets with the same number of elements, i.e., $\mathbf{a}_{|\mathcal{M}_{off}|} \rhd \mathbf{a}_{|\mathcal{M}'_{off}|}$, where $\mathcal{M}_{off}$ and $\mathcal{M}'_{off}$ are offloading sets with the same number of elements. Note that determining whether **a** is locally optimal requires comparisons among all offloading sets with the same number of elements, and the number of such offloading sets is $C_{|\mathcal{M}|}^{|\mathcal{M}_{off}|}$.

Definition 4.11 Marginal Value Δ_k: defined as $SETC(\mathbf{a}^*) - SETC(\mathbf{a})$, where the local computation set corresponding to $\mathbf{a}^*$ is $\mathcal{M}_{local} \cup \{k\}$, and the local computation set corresponding to $\mathbf{a}$ is $\mathcal{M}_{local}$. If $\Delta_k \leq 0$, then application k should be computed locally; otherwise, application k should adopt collaborative cloud computing. Δ_k can be simplified as:

$$
\begin{aligned}
\Delta_k &= SETC(\mathbf{a}^*) - SETC(\mathbf{a}) \\
&= AETC_k^l - (\sum_{m=1}^{M} a_m^* AETC_m^{n,c}(\mathbf{b}^*) - \sum_{m=1}^{M} a_m AETC_m^{n,c}(\mathbf{b})),
\end{aligned}
\tag{4.94}
$$

(1) GS-MOA: This algorithm determines whether to expand the local computation set $\mathcal{M}_{local}$ based on whether Δ_k is less than 0, until the system $SETC$ can no longer be reduced, at which point the algorithm converges. The initialization involves offloading all users for computation in the collaborative cloud, i.e., $\mathcal{M}_{off} = \mathcal{M}$. In each iteration process, according to Definitions 4.4–4.8, the local computation set $\mathcal{M}_{local}$ is continuously expanded until it becomes non-expandable, at which point the algorithm terminates. The pseudocode for GS-MOA is shown in Algorithm 13. From Step 1 to Step 2, it can be seen that $\mathbf{a}$ is coupled with offloading transmission power $p_m^{n,t}$ and matching strategy b_m^n; during each iteration, both $p_m^{n,t}$ and b_m^n are continuously updated. Steps 5 to 6 represent the process of finding a local optimal offloading decision.

Lemma 4.2 *The offloading decision obtained by GS-MOA is a local optimal solution to the original optimization problem P4−4.*

Proof The offloading decision $\mathbf{a}$ obtained under the GS-MOA scheme is a local optimal solution to *P4−4* if and only if $\mathcal{M}_{local}$ cannot be further expanded, i.e., $\mathcal{M}_{off}$ cannot be decomposed further. GS-MOA initializes the offloading set as $\mathcal{M}_{off} = \mathcal{M}$, then the offloading set $\mathcal{M}_{off}$ contracts due to bandwidth limitations while $\mathcal{M}_{local}$ gradually expands. Since the local optimal offloading decision search is performed according to Definition 4.6 in each expansion process of the local set, an optimal offloading decision corresponding to a fixed number of offloaded users can always be found. When $\mathcal{M}_{local}$ cannot be further expanded, the result of GS-MOA is also non-expandable and thus represents a local optimal solution to *P4−4*, which concludes the proof. Next, we analyze the time complexity of GS-MOA. The GS-MOA consists of two loops: an inner loop for finding a local optimal offloading decision and an outer loop for updating transmission power, matching strategy, and offloading decisions. □

First, let's analyze the inner loop. In GS-MOA, assume there are K user applications that are computed locally, i.e., $|\mathcal{M}_{local}| = K$. For the k-th local computation user application, since searching for a local optimal decision requires $(M-k+1)$ transmission power calculations, with each calculation involving $M-k$ user applications, the time complexity is $O((M-k)(M-k+1))$.

Algorithm 13 GS-MOA

Input: Matching strategy b_m^n, $\mathcal{M}$, $\mathcal{N}$, Cap_n
Output: Offloading decision **a**
Initialize: $\mathbf{a} = \{1, \cdots, 1\}$, $SETC(\mathbf{a})$, $\mathcal{M}_{off} = \mathcal{M}$, $\mathcal{M}_{local} = \emptyset$
repeat
  for $\forall k \in \mathcal{M}_{off}$ **do**
    1. For each user in the new offloading set $m \in \mathcal{M}_{off}/\{k\}$, $n \in \mathcal{N}$, compute and update $p_m^{n,t}$ and $AETC_m^{n,trans}$;
    2. Update the matching strategy b_m^n for the new offloading set $\mathcal{M}_{off}/\{k\}$ using the GS-MEMA matching algorithm;
    3. Based on the updated matching strategy, compute $SETC(\mathbf{a}_{\mathcal{M}_{off}}/\{k\})$;
    4. For the offloading decision $\mathbf{a}_{\mathcal{M}_{off}/\{k\}}$, compute $\triangle_k$ based on Eq. (4.94);
    if $\triangle_k \leq 0$ **then**
      5. $\triangle_{\mathbf{readylocal}} = \{\triangle_k\}$;
    end if
  end for
  6. Select the marginal value corresponding to the locally optimal offloading decision $\triangle_{k,opt} = \min \triangle_{\mathbf{readylocal}}$;
  7. Update the offloading decision $\mathbf{a}^*$, and set $a_k = 0$;
  8. Compute and update $SETC(\mathbf{a}^*) = SETC(\mathbf{a}) + \triangle_{k,opt}$;
  9. Update the local computation set $\mathcal{M}_{local} = \mathcal{M}_{local} \cup \{k\}$;
  10. Update the offloading set $\mathcal{M}_{off} = \mathcal{M}_{off}/\{k\}$;
  11. Update the offloading decision $\mathbf{a} = \mathbf{a}^*$;
until The local computation set becomes a non-expandable set

For the outer loop, considering K locally computed user applications, the time complexity can be expressed as $O(K(M-k)(M-k+1))$. This can be simplified to $O(M^2)$. As M increases, the time complexity of GS-MOA grows quadratically with respect to M. Therefore, if the number of users in the system is too large, it will result in a very high time complexity.

To address this issue, this chapter designs a suboptimal algorithm with lower time complexity called GS-SOA.

(2) GS-SOA: Compared to GS-MOA, GS-SOA does not require searching for a local optimal offloading decision; therefore, its time complexity is $O(m)$. GS-SOA first randomly numbers all users in the network and then sequentially determines whether $\triangle_k$ is less than 0 according to their numbers to expand the local computation set. During each determination process, it still needs to iteratively update the offloading transmission power $p_m^{n,t}$ and matching strategy b_m^n. The pseudocode of GS-SOA is shown in Algorithm 14.

Algorithm 14 GS-SOA

Input: Matching strategy b_m^n, $\mathcal{M}$, $\mathcal{N}$, Cap_n;
Output: Offloading decision **a**;
Initialize: $\mathbf{a} = \{1, \cdots, 1\}$, $SETC(\mathbf{a})$, $\mathcal{M}_{off} = \mathcal{M}$, $\mathcal{M}_{local} = \emptyset$, randomly number the users in the system;
for $k = 1 : M$ **do**
  1. For each user application $m \in \mathcal{M}_{off}/\{k\}$ and $n \in \mathcal{N}$ in the new offloading set, calculate and update $p_m^{n,t}$ and $AETC_m^{n,trans}$;
  2. For the new $\mathcal{M}_{off}/\{k\}$ and $n \in \mathcal{N}$, update b_m^n using GS-MEMA;
  3. Based on the existing matching strategy, calculate and update $SETC(\mathbf{a}_{\mathcal{M}_{off}}/\{k\})$;
  4. Calculate $\triangle_k$ for the offloading decision $\mathbf{a}_{\mathcal{M}_{off}/\{k\}}$ according to Eq. (4.94);
  if $\triangle_k \leq 0$ **then**
    5. Set $a_k = 0$, and update the offloading decision $\mathbf{a}^*$;
  end if
  6. Calculate and update $SETC(\mathbf{a}^*) = SETC(\mathbf{a}) + \triangle_k$;
  7. Update the local computation set $\mathcal{M}_{local} = \mathcal{M}_{local} \cup \{k\}$;
  8. Update the offloading user application set $\mathcal{M}_{off} = \mathcal{M}_{off}/\{k\}$;
  9. Update the offloading decision $\mathbf{a} = \mathbf{a}^*$;
end for

4.3.4 Performance Evaluation

This section simulates and analyzes the performance of the proposed algorithms GS-MEMA, GS-MOA and GS-SOA under different parameters and compares them with other algorithms.

(1) Parameters Setting

In this chapter, the simulation environment is set as a single central cloud, multiple edge clouds, and multiple users. Each user carries a computation-intensive application, with input data and the CPU cycles required for each unit of data following uniform distributions $L_m \sim [1, 5]$ Mbits and $C_m \sim [500, 2500]$ cycles/bit, respectively. In consideration of a scenario with multiple densely deployed edge clouds, the radius of coverage for each edge cloud is 500 m, and the coverage areas of the multiple edge clouds overlap. Users are randomly distributed within the coverage areas of the edge clouds and can communicate with multiple edge clouds. Communication between terminal users and edge clouds is carried out through wireless networks, where the channel gain is a series of Rayleigh random variables with unit variance. The system bandwidth is shared among multiple offloading applications. Other simulation parameters are shown in Table 4.3.

This section sets up a simulation environment with a single central cloud, multiple edge clouds, and multiple users. Each user carries one computation-intensive application, where the input data L_m and the CPU cycles required per unit of data C_m follow uniform distributions $L_m \sim [1, 5]$ Mbits and $C_m \sim [500, 2500]$ cycles/bit, respectively. The scenario considers a dense deployment of multiple edge clouds, with each edge cloud covering an area with a radius of 500 meters, and the coverage areas of different edge clouds may overlap. Users are randomly distributed

Table 4.3 Parameter settings

Parameter	Setting
System bandwidth B	200 MHz
Backhaul link capacity W	5 Mbps
Noise power spectral density	− 174 dBm/Hz
Maximum transmission power of terminal p^{max}	23 dBm
Input data L_m	[1, 5] Mbits
Computation complexity per unit data C_m	[500, 2500] cycles/bit
Central Cloud computing capacity f^c	[400, 600] GHz
Local computing capacity f^l	[0.2, 0.5] GHz
Edge cloud computing capacity $f_m^{n,e}$	[10, 80] GHz
Weight factors γ^e, γ^t	[0,1]

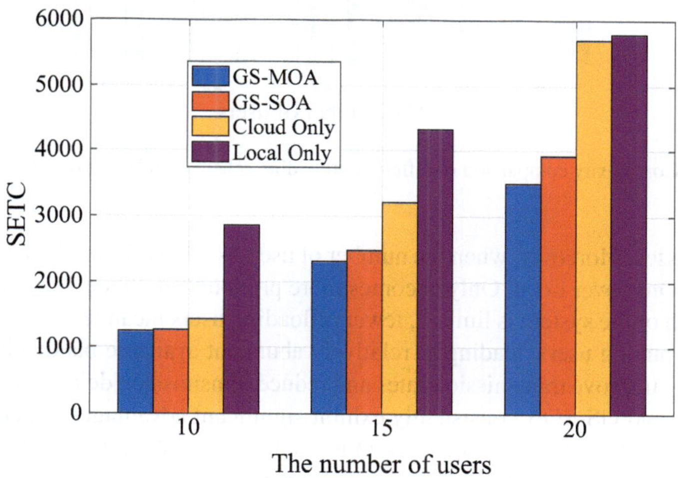

Fig. 4.12 Performance comparison among different schemes

within these overlapping areas and can communicate with multiple edge clouds. Transmission between users and edge clouds occurs over wireless networks, where channel gains are modeled as Rayleigh random variables with unit variance. The system bandwidth is evenly divided among multiple offloaded applications. Other simulation parameters are shown in Table 4.3.

(2) Performance Comparison Among Different Schemes

This subsection first compares GS-MOA, GS-SOA with two baseline schemes: Local Only and Cloud Only. As shown in Fig. 4.12, as the number of users in the system increases, the SETC under each scheme shows a stepwise increase. The performance of the Cloud Only scheme is consistently better than that of the Local Only scheme, with its SETC always being lower than that of the Local Only scheme. This is because CCC uses MEC and MCC technologies in parallel to fully exploit cloud and MEC resources, thereby reducing computational delay and lowering overall

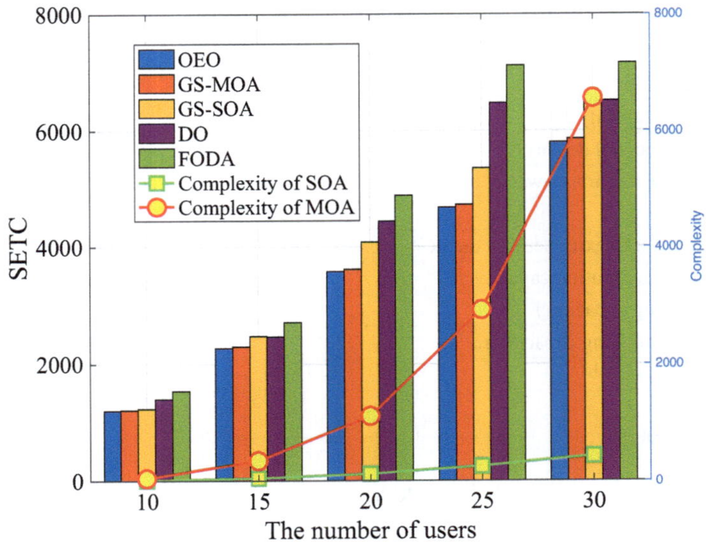

Fig. 4.13 Complexity comparison of different offloading schemes and GS-MOA/GS-SOA

system losses. Moreover, when the number of users is relatively small, the advantage of Cloud Only over Local Only becomes more pronounced. Since the total available bandwidth of the system is limited, fewer offloading users mean less competition for spectrum among users, leading to relatively abundant available bandwidth that can effectively improve transmission rates and reduce transmission delays. Additionally, GS-MOA and GS-SOA consistently exhibit significant advantages in performance; when the number of users in the system is small, GS-MOA performs slightly better than GS-SOA, while with an increasing number of users, GS-MOA's performance becomes notably superior to that of GS-SOA. This is because as the number of users increases, combined offloading schemes become more diverse, and GS-MOA trades time complexity for a more thorough search to achieve higher performance. This further highlights the importance of optimizing offloading decisions in reducing SETC and enhancing system performance.

Figure 4.13 compares the performance of GS-MOA, GS-SOA with Dynamic Offloading (DO) schemes [12], Fixed Number Offloading (FNO) scheme [26], and Optimal Enumerate Offloading (OEO) scheme, as well as the time complexity of GS-MOA and GS-SOA. As the number of users increases, input data size and complexity also increase, leading to a stepwise rise in SETC for all three schemes. However, the SETC of GS-MOA and GS-SOA remains consistently lower than that of other offloading schemes, with the performance of the GS-MOA algorithm being very close to that of OEO, further demonstrating the effectiveness of our proposed algorithms. Additionally, it can be observed that the time complexity of GS-SOA is always lower than that of GS-MOA, which further illustrates that GS-MOA sacrifices time complexity for deeper search and improved performance.

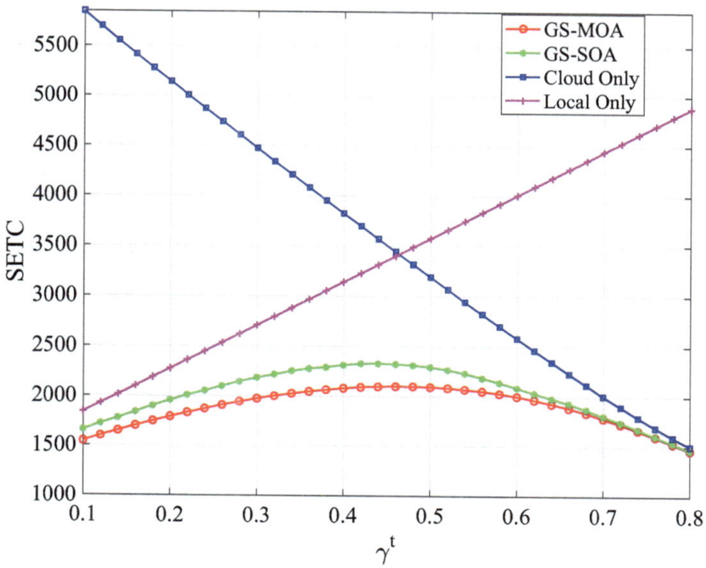

Fig. 4.14 The impact of delay weight factor γ^t on different schemes $SETC$

(3) The Impact of Weight Factor

This subsection analyzes the impact of the weight factor γ^t on different execution schemes. In this simulation experiment, it is assumed that all user applications within the system are the same type, meaning they have the same time weight factor. To obtain relatively accurate experimental results, the range of variation for γ^t is from 0.1 to 0.8, with values taken at intervals of 0.02. For each value of γ^t, simulations are conducted 1000 times and the average result is taken. As shown in Fig. 4.14, the $SETC$ of the Local Only and Cloud Only schemes is highly sensitive to changes in γ^t, showing completely different trends. As γ^t increases, the $SETC$ of the Local Only scheme shows a sharp linear rise, while the $SETC$ of the Cloud Only scheme decreases linearly with increasing γ^t. When $\gamma^t \leq 0.46$, the performance of the Local Only scheme is significantly better than that of the Cloud Only scheme; however, as γ^t increases, user application types shift from being energy consumption-sensitive to delay-sensitive, at which point the Cloud Only scheme demonstrates a clear advantage. This is because that the Local Only scheme is limited by the weak computational capabilities of terminal devices, leading to significantly higher computational delays compared to the Cloud Only scheme, making it unsuitable for delay-sensitive applications; conversely, while the strong computing capability of the Cloud Only scheme can handle such demands, it comes with a higher energy consumption, making it less suitable for energy-consumption-sensitive applications. The performance of the GS-MOA and GS-SOA schemes consistently shows significant advantages as γ^t varies. When $\gamma^t \leq 0.46$, the performance of the GS-MOA and GS-SOA schemes is close to that of the Local Only scheme, but it gradually approaches that of the Cloud Only scheme

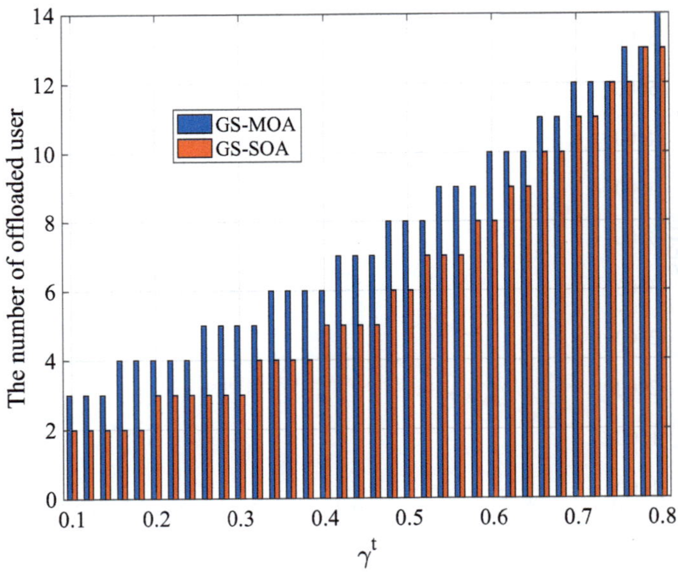

Fig. 4.15 The impact of the delay weight factor γ^t on the number of users offloaded by GS-MOA and GS-SOA

as γ^t increases. This indicates that for energy-consumption-sensitive applications, most users under the GS-MOA and GS-SOA schemes perform computations locally, reducing $SETC$ by decreasing energy consumption; for delay-sensitive applications, these schemes offload most users to reduce delays and achieve high performance. These analyses further prove that optimizing offloading decisions can effectively reduce system losses. Additionally, the performance of GS-MOA is consistently better than GS-SOA, indicating that under different parameters, GS-MOA optimizes offloading decisions by sacrificing time complexity through deep searches, thus improving performance.

Figure 4.15 shows the number of users offloading tasks under the GS-MOA and GS-SOA schemes as a function of γ^t. From the analysis of the figure, it can be concluded that for delay-sensitive applications, collaborative cloud computing can improve overall performance by reducing computation latency. On the other hand, for energy-sensitive applications, local computation can enhance overall performance by saving energy.

(4) The Impact of Local Computing Frequency

This subsection analyzes the impact of local computing resources f^l on the GS-MOA, GS-SOA, Cloud Only, and Local Only schemes. As shown in Fig. 4.16, the $SETC$ of the Cloud Only scheme remains constant, while the $SETC$ of the Local Only scheme almost linearly increases with the increase in local computing frequency. When $f^l < 0.95 \times 10^9$, the performance of the Local Only scheme is better than that of the Cloud Only scheme. This is because when the local computing

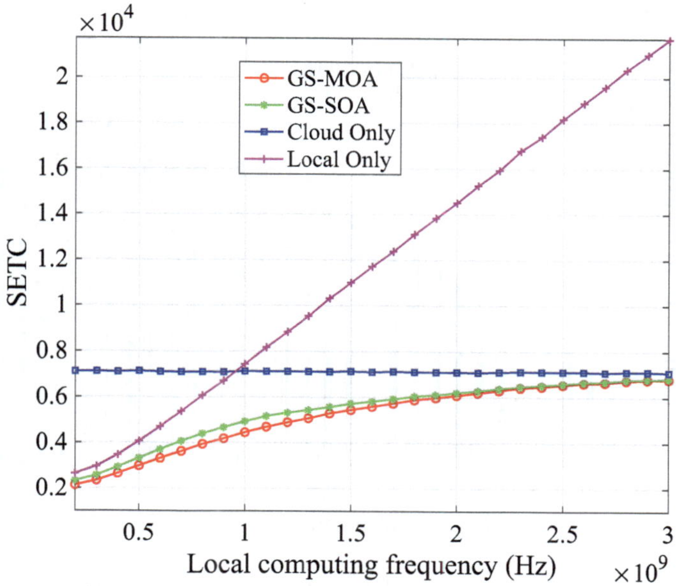

Fig. 4.16 The impact of local computing frequency on $SETC$ of different schemes

frequency is significantly lower than the edge cloud computing frequency, the Local Only scheme can reduce energy consumption and thereby decrease $SETC$, making it suitable for energy-consumption-sensitive applications. As f^l gradually increases, the gap between local computing frequency and edge cloud computing frequency narrows. The advantage of the Local Only scheme becomes less pronounced, and its $SETC$ gradually exceeds that of the Cloud Only scheme.

This is because that the Cloud Only scheme fully utilizes cloud and edge computing resources by offloading all user applications. The strong computational capability of the central cloud complements that of the edge cloud, with both working in parallel to significantly reduce computation delays without causing excessively high energy consumption, thus having a clear advantage. For GS-MOA and GS-SOA schemes, when $f^l < 0.95 \times 10^9$, their $SETC$ shows a steady upward trend, closely resembling that of the Local Only scheme. Then, as f^l increases further, their performance gradually levels off and approaches that of the Cloud Only scheme. This indicates that when f^l is relatively low, most users under GS-MOA and GS-SOA schemes perform local computations to reduce energy consumption and lower $SETC$, thereby enhancing system performance. In cases where f^l is relatively high, these schemes offload more users to the collaborative cloud to decrease delays and further reduce $SETC$ and improve system performance. These analyses further demonstrate that optimizing offloading decisions can effectively lower $SETC$ and enhance system performance. Additionally, the $SETC$ of GS-MOA consistently remains below that of GS-SOA, indicating that

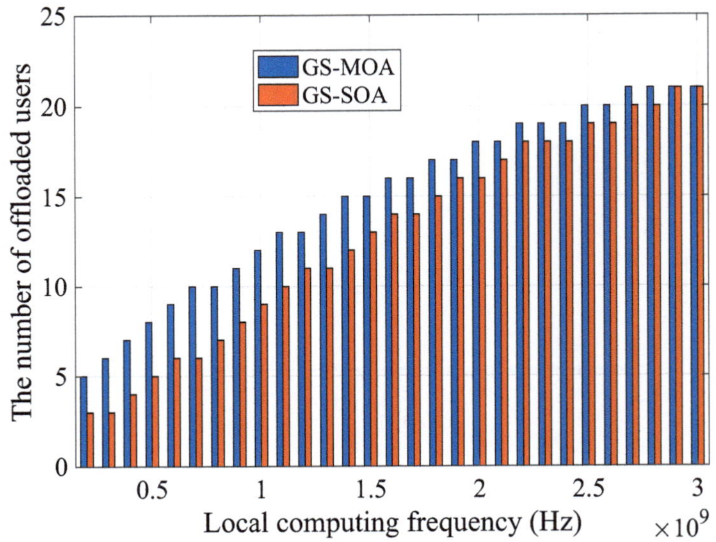

Fig. 4.17 The impact of local computing frequency on the number of users offloaded under GS-MOA and GS-SOA

GS-MOA improves system performance by sacrificing time complexity through deeper searches.

As shown in Fig. 4.17, the number of offloaded users increases with f^l for both the GS-MOA and GS-SOA schemes, which validates the above analysis.

4.4 Dependent Subtask-based CCC

4.4.1 System Model

We assume that there are M terminal devices, and each one is equipped with a computation-intensive application denoted as $\mathcal{M} = \{1, 2, 3, \ldots, M\}$. Each application consists of I_m dependent subtasks, represented by $\mathcal{I}_m = \{1, 2, 3, \ldots, I_m\}$. The system model is shown as Fig. 4.18. We employ a directed acyclic graph $G = (V, E)$ to depict the relationships among subtasks, where each node $i \in V$ represents a subtask. A directed edge $e(i, j)$ signifies the precedence constraint between subtasks i and j, indicating that subtask j cannot start before completing subtask i. Each subtask can either be executed locally or offloaded to the CCC system. Let $\mathcal{A}_m$ denote the offloading decisions for subtasks in application m, that is, $\mathcal{A}_m = \{a_{m,1}, a_{m,2}, \cdots, a_{m,I_m}\}$, where $a_{m,i} = 0$ represents local computing and $a_{m,i} = 1$ represents CCC. Furthermore, our CCC system comprises a multi-

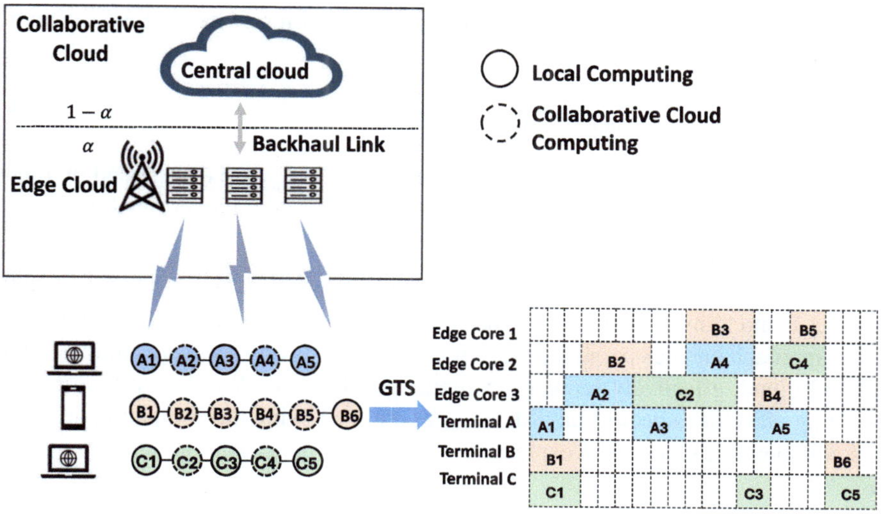

Fig. 4.18 System model for subtask dependency-based computation offloading and scheduling for CCC with multi-core server

core edge server and a remote central cloud. Each core is configured with a virtual machine tailored to provide a computing environment for specific types of subtasks, denoted as $\mathcal{N} = \{1, 2, 3, \cdots, N\}$. In general, the computing resources of each core are limited, so we assume that each core can only execute a subtask within the same time interval. As an extension of the edge cloud, the remote central cloud generally possesses substantial computing resources. Moreover, owing to the constraint on edge cloud computing resources, the allocation of computing resources for each application is restricted. Let $\mathcal{F}_m^{edge}$ represent the MEC resources allocation for offloaded subtasks in application m, expressed as $\mathcal{F}_m^{edge} = \{f_{m,i}^{n,e} | i \in \mathcal{S}_m^{off}, n \in \mathcal{N}\}$, where $\mathcal{S}_m^{off}$ represents the offloaded subtasks set for application m.

(1) Local Computing Model

For ease of reference, let $ST_{m,i}$ represent the i-th subtask within the m-th application. We assume that the input data size for $ST_{m,i}$ is $D_{m,i}$ bits, and the required CPU cycles per bit is $C_{m,i}$ cycles/bit. Typically, terminal devices dynamically adjust their computing frequency through Dynamic Voltage and Frequency Scaling (DVFS) technology based on the complexity of the application [14]. Let f_m^l denote the local computing frequency of terminal device, and thus the time consumption can be expressed as:

$$T_{m,i}^l = \frac{D_{m,i} C_{m,i}}{f_m^l}. \tag{4.95}$$

According to [15–17], the consumed power of CPU is a super-linear function about f_m^l and can be expressed as $P_m^l = \kappa^l (f_m^l)^2$, where κ^l is the switch capacitance factor and is usually set as 10^{-11} [54]. The energy consumed for processing $ST_{m,i}$ can be computed as:

$$E^l_{m,i} = P^l_m \times T^l_{m,i} = \kappa^l f^l_m D_{m,i} C_{m,i}. \tag{4.96}$$

From (4.95) and (4.96), it can be found that $T^l_{m,i}$ and $E^l_{m,i}$ are determined by input data size, required CPU cycles, and computing capability of the terminal device.

(2) CCC Model

When a subtask is offloaded to the collaborative cloud, the edge cloud immediately divides it and transfers a portion to the central cloud through the backhaul link [21]. This approach enables parallel processing of the subtask by the edge cloud and the central cloud, effectively reducing computing delay [21]. We denote the optimal splitting ratio for a specific subtask $ST_{m,i}$ as $\alpha_{m,i}$, allowing the computing delay on the collaborative cloud to be expressed as:

$$T^{c,exe}_{m,i} = \min_{\alpha} \max \left\{ T^{edge}_{m,i}, T^{ed-ce}_{m,i} + T^{cent}_{m,i} \right\}, \tag{4.97}$$

where $T^{edge}_{m,i} = \frac{\alpha_{m,i} D_{m,i} C_{m,i}}{f^{n,e}_{m,i}}$ is edge core computing delay , $T^{ed-ce}_{m,i} = \frac{(1-\alpha_{m,i}) D_{m,i}}{W}$ is the subtask transmission delay from the edge cloud to the central cloud, and W bits/s is the backhaul link capacity, and $T^{cent}_{m,i} = \frac{(1-\alpha_{m,i}) D_{m,i} C_{m,i}}{f^c}$ is the central cloud computing delay, f^c is the central cloud computing capability. Therefore, (4.97) represents the process of minimizing the maximum delay for a subtask by optimizing parameter α, where maximum CCC delay is determined by the computation delay on the edge cloud or the combined delay of transmitting data to the central cloud and completing the computation at the central cloud. By analyzing monotonicity of $T^{edge}_{m,i}$ and $T^{ed-ce}_{m,i} + T^{cent}_{m,i}$ [9], we can observe that when $T^{edge}_{m,i} = T^{ed-ce}_{m,i} + T^{cent}_{m,i}$, $T^{c,exe}_{m,i}$ reaches the minimum value. Therefore, the optimal splitting ratio can be expressed as:

$$\alpha_{m,i}(f^{n,e}_{m,i}) = \frac{f^{n,e}_{m,i}(f^c + C_{m,i} W)}{f^{n,e}_{m,i}(f^c + C_{m,i} W) + f^c C_{m,i} W}. \tag{4.98}$$

From (4.98), it is evident that $\alpha_{m,i}$ is solely determined by the edge core computing frequency $f^{n,e}_{m,i}$. As the central cloud is typically powered by an intelligent grid, the energy consumption associated with computing can be disregarded [13, 54]. The time and energy consumption of the collaborative cloud can be formulated as:

$$T^{c,exe}_{m,i} = \frac{\alpha_{m,i} D_{m,i} C_{m,i}}{f^{n,e}_{m,i}}, \tag{4.99}$$

$$E^{c,exe}_{m,i}(f^{n,e}_{m,i}) = \kappa^e P_n T^{c,exe}_{m,i}, \tag{4.100}$$

where κ^e is switch capacity of the edge cloud, P_n is the power of the edge core which is configured by the edge cloud.

(3) Transmission Model

Let $H_{m,i}$ represent the channel gain, and $p^t_{m,i}$ denotes the transmission power configured by the terminal device for $ST_{m,i}$. The data transmission rate can be expressed as:

$$R_{m,i}(p^t_{m,i}) = B \cdot \log_2(1 + \frac{p^t_{m,i} H_{m,i}}{N_0}), \tag{4.101}$$

where N_0 represents the noise power, and B stands for the bandwidth allocated to each terminal device. Accordingly, the transmission time and energy can be expressed as follows:

$$T^{trans}_{m,i} = \frac{D_{m,i}}{R_{m,i}(p^t_{m,i})}, \tag{4.102}$$

$$E^{trans}_{m,i} = p^t_{m,i} \cdot T^{trans}_{m,i} = \frac{D_{m,i} p^t_{m,i}}{R_{m,i}(p^t_{m,i})}. \tag{4.103}$$

According (4.99), (4.100), (4.102), and (4.103), the time and energy consumptions for a subtask offloaded to the CCC system can be written as:

$$T^c_{m,i} = T^{trans}_{m,i} + T^{c,exe}_{m,i}, \tag{4.104}$$

$$E^c_{m,i} = E^{trans}_{m,i} + E^{c,exe}_{m,i}. \tag{4.105}$$

(4) Subtask Dependency Model

Subtask dependency implies that the execution of a particular subtask relies on the output from all preceding interconnected subtasks. In this study, we exclusively examine the subtask dependency within a single-chain application. Moving forward, we construct the subtask dependency model by defining $BeginT$ and $EndT$:

Definition 4.12 *BeginT* is defined as the earliest possible initiation time for the computation of a subtask.

Definition 4.13 *EndT* is defined as the latest possible completion time for the computation of a subtask.

For local computing, $BeginT^l_{m,i}$ cannot be earlier than $EndT_{m,i-1}$. Therefore, $BeginT^l_{m,i}$ can be expressed as follows:

$$BeginT^l_{m,i} = EndT_{m,i-1}, \tag{4.106}$$

$EndT^l_{m,i}$ can be expressed as:

$$EndT^l_{m,i} = BeginT^l_{m,i} + T^l_{m,i}. \tag{4.107}$$

For CCC, $BeginT^{c}_{m,i}$ denotes the maximum time among $EndT_{m,i-1}$ of the preceding interconnected subtasks, the transmission time of $ST_{m,i}$, and the available time slot of the pre-scheduled edge core. This can be expressed as:

$$BeginT^{c}_{m,i} = \max\left\{EndT_{m,i-1}, T^{trans}_{m,i}, SpareT_n\right\}, \tag{4.108}$$

where $SpareT_n$ represents the earliest available time on edge core n. By analyzing (4.108), we can deduce that each subtask in CCC must satisfy three conditions: The preceding subtasks of the offloaded subtask must have been completed due to the subtask dependency. The transmission of the subtask's data must be completed. The edge core must have finished executing the previously scheduled subtask. Due to subtask dependency, when a subtask's data is offloaded, its preceding subtask must be fully computed. When a subtask receives an offloading instruction, its data can be offloaded. Since the offloading time of a subtask is relatively short, the offloading completion time is earlier than the completion time of the previous subtask, and is thus omitted from this formula. Thus, $BeginT^{c}_{m,i}$ is primarily determined by $EndT_{m,i-1}$ and $SpareT_n$, which can be expressed as:

$$BeginT^{c}_{m,i} = \max\left\{EndT_{m,i-1}, SpareT_n\right\}. \tag{4.109}$$

$EndT^{c}_{m,i}$ can be represented as:

$$EndT^{c}_{m,i} = BeginT^{c}_{m,i} + T^{c,exe}_{m,i}. \tag{4.110}$$

Combining (4.107) and (4.110), we can formulate the expression of $EndT_{m,i}$ as:

$$EndT_{m,i} = a_{m,i}EndT^{c}_{m,i} + (1 - a_{m,i})EndT^{l}_{m,i}. \tag{4.111}$$

(5) Subtask Scheduling Model

Considering that edge cores have limited computing capabilities and are specialized for specific task types, they can compute only one subtask within the same time interval. Arranging the processing order of subtasks from multiple applications across multiple edge cores in a logical manner can mitigate the idle periods in edge cores and thereby substantially reduce the overall delay within the CCC system. Given J subtasks allocated to a specific edge core n from various applications, the sequence in which these subtasks are executed on that core can be described as follows:

$$seq^{n} = \left\{st^{n}_{1}, st^{n}_{2} \cdots st^{n}_{j}, \cdots st^{n}_{J}\right\}, \tag{4.112}$$

where st_j^n represents the j-th subtask processed on the n-th edge core. It's important to note that st_j^n may pertain to distinct applications, and this relationship can be articulated as:

$$st_j^n = ST_{m,i}, \quad i \in \mathcal{I}_m, m \in \mathcal{M}. \tag{4.113}$$

The scheduling of subtasks from multiple applications across the N edge cores can be formulated as:

$$\mathbf{Seq} = \begin{bmatrix} seq^1 \\ seq^2 \\ \vdots \\ seq^N \end{bmatrix} = \begin{bmatrix} st_1^1 & \cdots & st_j^1 & \cdots st_J^1 \\ st_1^2 & \cdots & st_j^2 & \cdots st_J^2 \\ \vdots & \cdots & \vdots & \cdots \\ st_1^N & \cdots & st_j^N & \cdots st_J^N \end{bmatrix}. \tag{4.114}$$

4.4.2 Problem Formulation

In this section, we formulate the problem of minimizing $SETC$ by jointly optimizing transmission power, edge core computing frequency, combined offloading decisions, and subtask scheduling. First of all, we define the concepts of Task Energy-Time Cost ($TETC$) and Application Energy-Time Cost ($AETC$).

Definition 4.14 $TETC$ is defined as the weighted sum of the time consumption and energy consumption required to compute a specific subtask.

$$TETC_{m,i} = \gamma_m^t T_{m,i} + \gamma_m^e E_{m,i}, \tag{4.115}$$

where γ_m^t and γ_m^e represent the weight factors of time consumption and energy consumption, respectively, reflecting the application's sensitivity to delay and energy. If $\gamma_m^t \geq \gamma_m^e$, it indicates that application m is delay-sensitive, and vice versa. The values of γ_m^t and γ_m^e lie within the range of [0, 1] to balance time consumption and energy consumption, preventing disproportionately large weight factors from causing excessive $TETC$. As such, the $TETC$ of local computing, collaborative cloud computing, and transmission can be expressed as follows:

$$TETC_{m,i}^l = \gamma_m^t T_{m,i}^l + \gamma_m^e E_{m,i}^l, \tag{4.116}$$

$$TETC_{m,i}^{c,exe} = \gamma_m^t T_{m,i}^{c,exe} + \gamma_m^e E_{m,i}^{c,exe}, \tag{4.117}$$

$$TETC_{m,i}^{trans} = \gamma_m^t T_{m,i}^{trans} + \gamma_m^e E_{m,i}^{trans}. \tag{4.118}$$

Therefore, the $TETC$ of a subtask offloaded to the collaborative cloud can be formulated as follows:

$$\begin{aligned} TETC^c_{m,i} &= TETC^{c,exe}_{m,i} + TETC^{trans}_{m,i} \\ &= \gamma^t_m (T^{c,exe}_{m,i} + T^{trans}_{m,i}) + \gamma^e_m (E^{c,exe}_{m,i} + E^{trans}_{m,i}). \end{aligned} \tag{4.119}$$

Definition 4.15 $AETC$ is defined as the sum of all $TETC$ values for a specific application:

$$AETC_m = \sum_{i=1}^{I_m} a_{m,i} TETC^c_{m,i} + (1 - a_{m,i}) TETC^l_{m,i}, \tag{4.120}$$

Definition 4.16 $SETC$ is defined as the total sum of delay and energy consumption required for computing all applications in the system:

$$SETC = \sum_{m=1}^{M} [\gamma^t_m EndT_{m,I_m} + \gamma^e_m \sum_{i=1}^{I} a_{m,i} E^c_{m,i} + (1 - a_{m,i}) E^l_{m,i}]. \tag{4.121}$$

which can be rewritten as:

$$SETC = \sum_{m=1}^{M} AETC_m + \tau_m \tag{4.122}$$

where τ_m represents the cumulative waiting time of all subtasks within a specific application. Note that $AETC$ is the sum of $TETC$ of each subtask and does not consider the potential waiting time on edge cores. On the other hand, $SETC$ is defined as the total accumulation of all $AETC$ within the system, while also incorporating the idle time of edge cloud cores and the interdependencies among subtasks. By substituting (4.120) into (4.122), the expression for $SETC$ can be reformulated as:

$$SETC = \sum_{m=1}^{M} \sum_{i=1}^{I_m} a_{m,i} TETC^c_{m,i} + (1 - a_{m,i}) TETC^l_{m,i} + \tau_m \tag{4.123}$$

Hence, the $SETC$ minimization problem can be formulated as:

$$
\begin{aligned}
P4-17: \quad & \min_{\mathcal{A},\mathcal{P}^t,\mathcal{F}^{edge},\mathbf{Seq}} \quad SETC, \\
\text{s.t.} \quad & C_1: a_{m,i} \in \{0,1\}, i \in \mathcal{I}_m, m \in \mathcal{M} \\
& C_2: \sum_{m=1}^{M}\sum_{i=1}^{I_m} a_{m,i}(n,t) = 1, i \in \mathcal{S}_m^{off}, m \in \mathcal{M} \\
& C_3: 0 \le p_{m,i}^t \le p_m^{max}, i \in \mathcal{S}_m^{off}, m \in \mathcal{M} \\
& C_4: f_{m,i}^{n,e} \ge 0, i \in \mathcal{S}_m^{off}, m \in \mathcal{M}, n \in \mathcal{N} \\
& C_5: 0 \le \sum_{i \in \mathcal{S}_m^{off}} f_{m,i}^{n,e} \le f_m^{max}, i \in \mathcal{S}_m^{off}, m \in \mathcal{M}.
\end{aligned}
\tag{4.124}
$$

$\mathcal{S}_m^{off}$ represents the set of subtasks offloaded for application m. $C1$ indicates that a subtask can either be locally computed or offloaded to the collaborative cloud. C_2 ensures that each edge core can only execute one subtask at a time. C_3 is the constraint on the transmission power. C_4 ensures that all offloaded subtasks are assigned the corresponding edge core computing resources. C_5 specifies that the available edge cloud computing resources for each application are constrained and must remain below f_m^{max}.

4.4.3 Proposed Iterative Algorithm

To solve the original optimization problem, we design a distributed algorithm to decompose it into three subproblems firstly:

(1) Optimization of transmission power.
(2) Joint optimization of edge core computing frequency and combined offloading decisions.
(3) Optimization of subtask scheduling for multiple applications across multiple edge cores.

(1) Optimization of Transmission Power
When subtask $ST_{m,i}$ is offloaded, the offloading decision is set to 1, i.e., $a_{m,i} = 1$. Since the transmission power of a specific subtask is independent of other offloaded subtasks, the $SETC$ minimization problem can be reformulated as a $TETC_{m,i}^{c}$ minimization problem. By substituting (4.117) and (4.118) into the expression for $TETC_{m,i}^{c}$, the original problem can be reformulated as:

$$P4-18: \min_{p^t_{m,i}} \gamma^t_m(T^{c,exe}_{m,i} + T^{trans}_{m,i}) + \gamma^e_m(E^{c,exe}_{m,i} + E^{trans}_{m,i}) \\ s.t. \quad C_3. \tag{4.125}$$

Based on (4.5) and (4.6), it can be observed that $p^t_{m,i}$ is not influenced by $T^{c,exe}_{m,i}$ and $E^{c,exe}_{m,i}$. As a result, $P4-18$ can be simplified as:

$$P4-19: \quad \min_{p^t_{m,i}} \gamma^t_m T^{trans}_{m,i} + \gamma^e_m E^{trans}_{m,i} \\ s.t. \quad C_3. \tag{4.126}$$

By substituting (4.102), (4.103) into (4.126), $P4-19$ can be simplified as:

$$P4-20: \quad \min_{p^t_{m,i}} f(p^t_{m,i}) \\ s.t. \quad C_3. \tag{4.127}$$

and

$$f(p^t_{m,i}) = \frac{\theta_{m,i} + \lambda_{m,i} p^t_{m,i}}{\log_2(1 + \mu_{m,i} p^t_{m,i})}, \tag{4.128}$$

where $\theta_{m,i} = \gamma^t_m D_{m,i}/W$, $\lambda_{m,i} = \gamma^e_m D_{m,i}/B$, $\mu_{m,i} = H_{m,i}/N_0$. The second derivative of $f(p^t_{m,i})$ can be expressed as:

$$\begin{aligned} f''(p^t_{m,i}) = & \frac{\mu_{m,i}\left[\mu_{m,i}(\theta_{m,i} + \lambda_{m,i})p^t_{m,i} - 2\lambda_{m,i}(1 + \mu_{m,i}p^t_{m,i})\right]}{\ln 2(1 + \mu_{m,i}p^t_{m,i})^2 \log_2^3(1 + \mu_{m,i}p^t_{m,i})} \\ & \times \frac{\log_2(1 + \mu_{m,i}p^t_{m,i})}{\ln 2(1 + \mu_{m,i}p^t_{m,i})^2 \log_2^3(1 + \mu_{m,i}p^t_{m,i})} \\ & + \frac{2\mu^2_{m,i}(\theta_i + \lambda_i p^{up}_i)/\ln 2}{\ln 2(1 + \mu_{m,i}p^t_{m,i})^2 \log_2^3(1 + \mu_{m,i}p^t_{m,i})}. \end{aligned} \tag{4.129}$$

By analyzing (4.129), it can be observed that $f''(p^t_{m,i})$ might not always be positive across **R**. Consequently, $f(p^t_{m,i})$ is not guaranteed to be a convex function. According to [29], when $f(\cdot)$ is twice differentiable and there exists x_0 such that

$f''(x_0) \geq 0$ and $f'(x_0) = 0$, $f(\cdot)$ can be regarded as quasiconvex in $\mathbf{R}$. The first-order derivative of $f(p_{m,i}^t)$ is:

$$f'(p_{m,i}^t) = \frac{\lambda_i \log_2(1 + \mu_{m,i} p_{m,i}^t) - \mu_{m,i}/\ln 2(\frac{\theta_{m,i}+\lambda_{m,i} p_{m,i}^t}{1+\mu_{m,i} p_{m,i}^t})}{\log_2^2(1 + \mu_{m,i} p_{m,i}^t)}. \tag{4.130}$$

If $f'(p_0^t)$ equals 0, denoted as $f'(p_0^t) = 0$, its numerator becomes 0. We use ψ to represent its numerator:

$$\psi(p_0^t) = \lambda_{m,i} \log_2(1 + \mu_{m,i} p_0^t) - \frac{\mu_{m,i}}{\ln 2} \cdot \frac{\theta_{m,i} + \lambda_{m,i} p_0^t}{1 + \mu_{m,i} p_0^t} = 0. \tag{4.131}$$

By substituting (4.35) into (4.33), the second derivative $f''(p_0^t)$ can be expressed as:

$$f''(p_0^t) = \frac{\mu_{m,i}^3}{\lambda_{m,i} \ln^2 2} \frac{(\theta_{m,i} + \lambda_{m,i} p_0^t)^2}{(1 + \mu_{m,i} p_0^t)^3 \log_2^3(1 + \mu_{m,i} p_0^t)} \geq 0. \tag{4.132}$$

Since $f''(p_0^t)$ is greater than or equal to 0, i.e., $f''(p_0^t) \geq 0$, the function $f(p_{m,i}^t)$ is quasiconvex in $\mathbf{R}$. For solving it, we can utilize the bisection method [29]. The first-order derivative of (4.131) can be expressed as:

$$\psi'(p_{m,i}^t) = \frac{\mu_{m,i}^2}{\ln 2} \frac{\theta_{m,i} + \lambda_{m,i} p_{m,i}^t}{(1 + \mu_{m,i} p_{m,i}^t)^2} > 0. \tag{4.133}$$

We can observe that $\psi(0) = -\frac{\mu_{m,i}\theta_{m,i}}{\ln 2} < 0$ and $\psi'(p_{m,i}^t) \geq 0$. This implies that $\psi(p_{m,i}^t)$ is monotonically increasing and negative when $p_{m,i}^t = 0$. Consequently, $f'(p_{m,i}^t)$ is also monotonically increasing and negative at $p_{m,i}^t = 0$. Thus, for $0 < p_{m,i}^t \leq p_0^t$, $f(p_{m,i}^t)$ monotonically decreases, and for $p_{m,i}^t > p_0^t$, it monotonically increases. Now, we should analyze whether the domain of $p_{m,i}^t$ includes p_0^t. If $p_0^{max} > p_0^t$, the optimal transmission power $p_{m,i}^{t*} = p_0^t$, leading to the minimum value of $f(p_{m,i}^t)$. If $p_0^{max} \leq p_0^t$, then $p_{m,i}^{t*} = p_m^{max}$. Algorithm 15 outlines the bisection method for optimizing transmission power.

(2) Edge Core Computing Frequency Optimization

Since the computation resources of all offloaded subtasks within the application are kept within f_m^{max}, the combined offloading decisions and MEC resources allocation are coupled, which poses a challenge for edge core computing frequency allocation. To tackle it, we leverage the Lagrangian algorithm to deduce the non-closed form of the available MEC resources $f_{m,i}^{n,e}$ for each offloaded subtask, expressed as a function of combined offloading decision. Considering that the edge core computing frequency allocation of an application is independent of other applications, we can

Algorithm 15 Bisection Method of Transmission Power Optimization

Initialize: $0 < p^t_{m,i} < p^{max}_m$, $\psi(p^t_{m,i})$
Output: $p^{t*}_{m,i}$
  if $\psi(p^{max}_m) \leq 0$ **then**
    $p^*_{m,i} = p^{max}_m$
  else
    $p^s_{m,i} = 0$, $p^e_{m,i} = p^{max}_m$
    repeat
      $p^l_{m,i} = (p^s_{m,i} + p^e_{m,i})/2$
      if $\psi(p^l_{m,i}) \leq 0$ **then**
        $p^s_{m,i} = p^l_{m,i}$
      else
        $p^e_{m,i} = p^l_{m,i}$
      end if
    until $(p^e_{m,i} - p^s_{m,i}) \leq \epsilon$
    $p^*_{m,i} = (p^s_{m,i} + p^e_{m,i})/2$
  end if

optimize them independently by minimizing $AETC$. By substituting (4.120) into the original problem, this optimization problem can be structured as follows:

$$P4-20: \min_{f^{n,e}_{m,i}} \sum_{i\in S^{off}_m} \gamma^t_m (T^{c,exe}_{m,i} + T^{trans}_{m,i}) + \gamma^e_m (E^{c,exe}_{m,i} + E^{trans}_{m,i}) \tag{4.134}$$

$$s.t. \quad C_4, C_5$$

Upon analyzing (4.102) and (4.103), it becomes evident that $T^{trans}_{m,i}$ and $E^{trans}_{m,i}$ are independent of $f^{n,e}_{m,i}$. Consequently, $P4-20$ can be formulated as:

$$P4-21: \min_{f^{n,e}_{m,i}} \sum_{i\in S^{off}_m} (\gamma^t_{m,i} T^{c,exe}_{m,i} + \gamma^e_m E^{c,exe}_{m,i}). \tag{4.135}$$

$$s.t. \quad C_4, C_5$$

By substituting (4.99) and (4.100) into (4.135), the expression for $P4-22$ can be simplified to:

$$P4-22: \min_{f^{n,e}_{m,i}} \quad h(\mathbf{f}) \tag{4.136}$$

$$s.t. \quad C_4, C_5,$$

and

$$h(\mathbf{f})_{S^{off}_m} = \sum_{i\in S^{off}_m} \frac{A_{m,i} + B_{m,i}}{Z_{m,i} f^{n,e}_{m,i} + Q_{m,i}}, \tag{4.137}$$

where $Z_{m,i} = f^c + C_{m,i}W$, $Q_i = f^c C_{m,i} W$, $A_{m,i} = \gamma_m^t Z_{m,i} C_{m,i} L_{m,i}$, and $B_{m,i} = \gamma_m^e Z_{m,i} C_{m,i} L_{m,i} P_n \kappa^e$. Moving forward, we utilize the Lagrangian multiplier to solve for the optimal $f_{m,i}^{n,e}$. Given that $\frac{\mathrm{d}^2 h}{\mathrm{d}(f_{m,i}^{n,e})^2} > 0$, the Hessian matrix of $h(\mathbf{f})$ is positive definite, rendering $h(\mathbf{f})$ convex within the specified domain. The Lagrangian function for *P4 − 23* can be expressed as:

$$L(\mathbf{f}, \lambda) = \sum_{i \in \mathcal{S}_m^{off}} \frac{A_{m,i} + B_{m,i}}{Z_{m,i} f_{m,i}^{n,e} + Q_{m,i}} + \lambda(\sum_{i \in \mathcal{S}_m^{off}} f_{m,i}^{n,e} - f_m^{max}). \tag{4.138}$$

According to KKK conditions, since $C4$ is slack and eliminated in (4.138), we can deduce the dual problem for *P4 − 23* as follows:

$$\begin{aligned} &\max_{\lambda > 0} \min_{f \succ 0} L(\mathbf{f}, \lambda) \\ &= \sum_{i \in \mathcal{S}_m^{off}} \frac{A_{m,i} + B_{m,i}}{Z_{m,i} f_{m,i}^{n,e} + Q_{m,i}} + \lambda(\sum_{i \in \mathcal{S}_m^{off}} f_{m,i}^{n,e} - f_m^{max}). \end{aligned} \tag{4.139}$$

Let $\frac{\partial L}{\partial f_{m,i}^{n,e}} = 0$, the optimal edge core computing frequency can be expressed as:

$$f_{m,i}^{n,e*} = \sqrt{\frac{A_{m,i} + B_{m,i}}{Z_{m,i}\lambda}} - \frac{Q_{m,i}}{Z_{m,i}}. \tag{4.140}$$

By substituting (4.140) into (4.138), we can obtain the Lagrangian dual function:

$$\begin{aligned} \varphi(\lambda) &= \min_{f \succ 0} L(\mathbf{f}, \lambda) \\ &= \min_{f \succ 0} 2\sqrt{\lambda} \sum_{i \in \mathcal{S}_m^{off}} \sqrt{\frac{A_{m,i} + B_{m,i}}{Z_{m,i}}} - \lambda(\frac{Q_{m,i}}{Z_{m,i}} + f_m^{max}). \end{aligned} \tag{4.141}$$

Let $\frac{\partial \varphi}{\partial \lambda} = 0$, the optimal Lagrange multiplier is:

$$\lambda^* = (\frac{\sum_{i \in \mathcal{S}_m^{off}} \sqrt{\frac{A_{m,i} + B_{m,i}}{Z_{m,i}}}}{\frac{Q_{m,i}}{Z_{m,i}} + f_m^{max}})^2. \tag{4.142}$$

Substituting λ into $f_{m,i}^{n,e}$, we can obtain the non-closed form of the optimal edge core computing frequency:

$$f_{m,i}^{n,e*} = \frac{\sqrt{\tau_{m,i} + \theta_{m,i}}}{\sum_{i \in \mathcal{S}_m^{off}} \sqrt{\tau_{m,i} + \theta_{m,i}}} (\beta_{m,i} + f_m^{max}) - \beta_{m,i}, \tag{4.143}$$

where $\tau_{m,i} = \frac{A_{m,i}}{Z_{m,i}}$, $\theta_{m,i} = \frac{B_{m,i}}{Z_{m,i}}$, $\beta_{m,i} = \frac{Z_{m,i}}{Q_{m,i}}$. By analyzing (4.143), we can deduce that the allocation of edge core computing frequency for a subtask is not only influenced by the combined offloading decisions but also affected by the computing frequency allocation of other subtasks within the same application. By substituting (4.143) into (4.137), the minimum value of $h(\mathbf{f})$ can be expressed as:

$$h(\mathbf{f})^{min}_{\mathcal{S}_m^{off}} = \sum_{i \in \mathcal{S}_m^{off}} \left(\frac{\sqrt{\tau_{m,i} + \theta_{m,i}} \sum_{i \in \mathcal{S}_m^{off}} \sqrt{\tau_{m,i} + \theta_{m,i}}}{\beta_{m,i} + f_m^{max}}\right). \tag{4.144}$$

(3) Optimization of Combined Offloading Decisions

Based on the closed-form expression of edge core computing frequency obtained in the previous subsection, we first propose an offloading algorithm based on heuristic search, namely MLSO. Given that the computational complexity of the MLSO algorithm is $O(I^2)$, it might not be well-suited for applications with numerous subtasks. Therefore, we introduce a suboptimal offloading algorithm, namely SSO. Since the combined offloading decisions for each application are not influenced by other applications, the optimization problem *P4 − 18* can be simplified as follows:

$$\begin{aligned} &P4-23: \min_{a_{m,i}} \ AETC_m \\ &s.t. \quad C_1. \end{aligned} \tag{4.145}$$

By substituting (4.120) into (4.145), *P4 − 23* can be expressed as:

$$\begin{aligned} &P4-24: \min_{a_{m,i}} \sum_{i=1}^{I_m} a_{m,i} TETC^c_{m,i} + (1 - a_{m,i}) TETC^l_{m,i} \\ &s.t. \quad C_1. \end{aligned} \tag{4.146}$$

Utilizing the optimal transmission power and optimal allocation of edge core computing resources from (4.127) and (4.144), and substituting them into (4.146), *P4 − 23* can be represented as:

$$\begin{aligned} &P4-25: \min_{a_{m,i}} h(\mathbf{f})^{min}_{S_{off}} + \sum_{i \in \mathcal{S}_m^{off}} f(p^{t*}_{m,i}) + \sum_{i \in \mathcal{S}_m^{local}} TETC^l_{m,i} \\ &s.t. \quad C_1. \end{aligned} \tag{4.147}$$

Since $\mathcal{S}_m^{off}$ is the set of offloading subtasks in (4.147), the number of offloaded subtasks for application m is equal to $\sum_{i=1}^{I_m} a_{m,i} = |\mathcal{S}_m^{off}|$. Additionally, $\mathcal{S}_m^{local}$ in the same equation stands for the set of subtasks that are scheduled for local computing. Hence, we have $|\mathcal{S}_m^{off}| + |\mathcal{S}_m^{local}| = |\mathcal{I}_m|$. Drawing on the heuristic search algorithm, we introduce the MLSO and SSO algorithms to attain local optimal combined offloading decisions. Let's commence by outlining the following definitions.

Definition 4.17 (Heuristic Information Function (*HIF*)) This function is defined as the disparity between $AETC(\mathbf{a}_m^{\#})$ and $AETC(\mathbf{a}_m)$, where $\mathbf{a}_m^{\#}$ represents the updated combined offloading decisions, and $\mathbf{a}_m$ is the initial set of combined offloading decisions. It can be expressed as:

$$HIF(\mathbf{a}_m^{\#}|\mathbf{a}_m) = AETC(\mathbf{a}_m^{\#}) - AETC(\mathbf{a}_m), \tag{4.148}$$

or written as:

$$HIF(\mathcal{S}_m^{off\#}|\mathcal{S}_m^{off}) = AETC(\mathcal{S}_m^{off\#}) - AETC(\mathcal{S}_m^{off}), \tag{4.149}$$

where $\mathcal{S}_m^{off\#}$ denotes the collection of offloaded subtasks associated with the updated combined offloading decisions $\mathbf{a}_m^{\#}$, and $\mathcal{S}_m^{off}$ denotes the set of offloaded subtasks associated with the original combined offloading decisions $\mathbf{a}_m^{\#}$. Therefore, by substituting (4.147) into $HIF(\mathcal{S}_m^{off}/\{k\}|\mathcal{S}_m^{off})$, we can obtain that:

$$\begin{aligned} HIF(\mathcal{S}_m^{off}/\{k\}|\mathcal{S}_m^{off}) &= -f(p_{m,k}^{t*}) + h(\mathbf{f})_{i\in\mathcal{S}_{off}/k}^{min} \\ &\quad - h(\mathbf{f})_{i\in\mathcal{S}_{off}}^{min} + TETC_{m,k}^{l}, \end{aligned} \tag{4.150}$$

where $h(\mathbf{f})_{i\in\mathcal{S}_{off}/\{k\}}^{min} - h(\mathbf{f})_{i\in\mathcal{S}_{off}}^{min}$ can be simplified as:

$$\begin{aligned} & h(\mathbf{f})_{\mathcal{S}_{off}/\{k\}}^{min} - h(\mathbf{f})_{\mathcal{S}_{off}}^{min} \\ &= - \sum_{i\in\mathcal{S}_m^{off}/\{k\}} \frac{\sqrt{\tau_{m,i}+\theta_{m,i}}\sqrt{\tau_{m,k}+\theta_{m,k}}}{\beta_{m,i} f_m^{max}} \\ &\quad - \frac{\sqrt{\tau_{m,i}\theta_{m,k}}\sum_{i\in\mathcal{S}_m^{off}}\sqrt{\tau_{m,i}+\theta_{m,i}}}{\beta_{m,k}+f_m^{max}}. \end{aligned} \tag{4.151}$$

Definition 4.18 (Relative Optimal Offloading Decisions) $\mathbf{a}_m^{\#}$ is considered optimal relative to $\mathbf{a}_m$, denoted as $\mathbf{a}_m^{\#} \rhd \mathbf{a}_m$, if and only if $AETC(\mathbf{a}_m^{\#})$ is smaller than $AETC(\mathbf{a}_m)$, or $HIF(\mathbf{a}_m^{\#}|am) < 0$.

Definition 4.19 (Local Optimal Offloading Decisions) Let's assume that $\mathcal{S}_m^{off} \in \mathbf{S}_m^{off}$, where $\mathbf{S}_m^{off}$ represents the collection of all offloading sets $\mathcal{S}_m^{off}$ with the same number of elements. If there exists an $\mathcal{S}_m^{off}$ for which $AETC(\mathcal{S}_m^{off})$ is the smallest among $\mathcal{S}_m^{off} \in \mathbf{S}_m^{off}$, then $\mathcal{S}_m^{off}$ is a local optimal offloading set, denoted as $\mathcal{S}_m^{off,opt}$. The corresponding combined offloading decisions are referred to as the local optimal combined offloading decisions, denoted as $\mathbf{a}_m^{opt}$.

Definition 4.20 (Unexpandable Local Computing Set) $\mathcal{S}_m^{local}$ is an unexpandable local computing set if and only if either the number of elements $|\mathcal{S}_m^{local}|$ equals the total number of subtasks of an application, or if there exists no set $\mathcal{S}_m^{local*} = \mathcal{S}_m^{local} \cup k$ where $k \in \mathcal{S}_m^{off}$ that satisfies $HIF(\mathcal{S}_m^{local*}|\mathcal{S}_m^{local}) < 0$.

1. **Maximum Local Searching Offloading (MLSO)** The key idea of the MLSO algorithm is to iteratively expand the local computing set to gradually find the optimal combined offloading decision for each application. The algorithm calculates the $AETC$ of different offloaded subtask sets and selectively adds subtasks to the local computing set to obtain the best offloading decision for each application, thereby achieving the goal of reducing the $AETC$. The algorithm is described in detail as follows. Initially, we assume that all subtasks within the application are offloaded to the collaborative cloud, which implies an empty local computing set denoted as $\mathcal{S}_m^{local} = \emptyset$. The MLSO algorithm progressively achieves the optimal combined offloading decisions by iteratively expanding the local computing set. For each episode, according to Definitions 6 to 7, we systematically explore all relatively optimal offloading decisions $\mathbf{a}_m^{\#}$ by evaluating whether $HIF(\mathbf{a}_m/a_{m,k}|\mathbf{a}_m) = AETC(\mathbf{a}_m/a_{m,k}) - AETC(\mathbf{a}_m)$ is less than 0 or not. Then, according to Definition 8, the local optimal offloading decisions can be derived from all the relatively optimal offloading decisions. According to Definition 9, iterative process continues until $\mathcal{S}_m^{local}$ is unexpandable. The pseudocode for the MLSO algorithm is outlined in Algorithm 16.

Algorithm 16 MLSO algorithm

Input: Initial offloading decision $\mathbf{a}_m = \{1, \cdots, 1\}$, $AETC(\mathbf{a})$, offloading set $\mathcal{S}_m^{off} = \mathcal{I}_m$, empty local computing set $\mathcal{S}_m^{local} = \emptyset$
Output: Optimized offloading decision $\mathbf{a}$
repeat
  for each k in $\mathcal{S}_m^{off}$ **do**
    1. Calculate the Heuristic Information Function $HIF(\mathcal{S}_m^{off}/\{k\}|\mathcal{S}_m^{off})$ for all k in $\mathcal{S}_{off}$, searching for all relatively optimal offloading sets and decisions $\mathbf{a}_m^{\#}$, collect all $\mathbf{a}_m^{\#}$.
    2. Search for the locally optimal combined offloading decisions $\mathbf{a}^{opt}$ and offloading set $\mathcal{S}^{off,opt}$ according to Definition 8.
  end for
  Update $AETC(\mathbf{a}^{opt})$.
  Update $\mathcal{S}_m^{local} = \mathcal{S}_m^{local} \cup \{k\}$.
  Update $\mathcal{S}_m^{off} = \mathcal{S}_m^{off}/\{k\}$.
  Set $\mathbf{a} = \mathbf{a}^{opt}$.
until $|\mathcal{S}_m^{local}| = |\mathcal{I}_m|$ or $\mathcal{S}_m^{local}$ is unexpandable

2. **Sequential Searching Offloading (SSO)** Compared to the MLSO algorithm, the SSO algorithm achieves a reduction in time complexity by not requiring local optimal offloading decisions. In SSO, we begin with the assumption that all subtasks are offloaded to the collaborative cloud, denoted as $\mathcal{S}_m^{local} = \emptyset$. The algorithm then evaluates the feasibility of local execution for each subtask based

on their execution sequence. Specifically, it checks whether $HIF(\mathcal{S}_m^{off}/k|\mathcal{S}_m^{off})$ is less than 0. If this condition is met, subtask k can be executed locally. Following the evaluation, the algorithm updates the combined offloading decisions $\mathbf{a}_m$, the offloading set $\mathcal{S}_m^{off}$, and the local computing set $\mathcal{S}_m^{local}$. The pseudocode for the SSO algorithm is presented in Algorithm 17.

Algorithm 17 SSO algorithm

Input: Initial offloading decision $\mathbf{a}_m = \{1, \cdots, 1\}$, $AETC(\mathbf{a})$, offloading set $\mathcal{S}_m^{off} = \mathcal{I}_m$, empty local computing set $\mathcal{S}_m^{local} = \emptyset$
Output: Optimized offloading decision **a**
for $k = 1 : I_m$ **do**
  1. Calculate $HIF(\mathcal{S}_m^{off}/\{k\}|\mathcal{S}_m^{off})$;
  2. Determine if $HIF(\mathcal{S}_m^{off}/\{k\}|\mathcal{S}_m^{off}) < 0$.
  if $HIF(\mathcal{S}_m^{off}/\{k\}|\mathcal{S}_m^{off}) < 0$ **then**
    3. Update $\mathbf{a}_m$ and set $a_{m,k} = 0$;
    4. Update $\mathcal{S}_m^{off} = \mathcal{S}_m^{off}/\{k\}$;
    5. Update $\mathcal{S}_m^{local} = \mathcal{S}_m^{local} \cup \{k\}$;
    6. Update $AETC(\mathbf{a}_m)$;
  end if
end for

(4) Optimization of Subtask Scheduling on Multi-core Edge Cloud

By leveraging the optimal transmission power, combined offloading decisions, and edge core computing frequency, we optimize the subtasks scheduling for multiple applications across multiple edge cores to further minimize *P4 – 18*. As mentioned before, each edge core is capable of processing a single subtask at a time and different execution sequences of subtasks will lead to varying time consumption. Therefore, it is necessary to methodically arrange the execution sequence of subtasks for multiple applications on a multi-core edge server, while satisfying the subtask dependency within each application. Given that the order of subtasks execution on the edge core primarily impacts delay, the optimization objective *P4 – 18* can be simplified to:

$$P4-26: \quad \min_{\mathbf{Seq}} \sum_{m=1}^{M} \gamma_m^t EndT_{m,I} \quad (4.152)$$
$$s.t. \quad C2.$$

To optimize *P4 – 26*, we propose a Genetic-based Task Scheduling (GTS) algorithm. In this approach, we model the subtask scheduling across multiple edge cores for multiple applications as a Job Shop Scheduling Problem (JSSP). The JSSP involves M machines, N jobs, and each job includes T tasks. These tasks are characterized by predetermined execution sequences and corresponding machines, along with known execution times. The main objective of JSSP is to optimize the task execution sequence on each machine, ensuring minimal total completion time while adhering to the predefined task order within each job. A genetic algorithm achieves optimization through successive iterations, involving the selection, crossover, and mutation of a set of potential initial solutions [55, 56]. Thus, our initial step involves designing a chromosome, representing a potential solution.

1. **Chromosomes and population** Chromosomes are representative of potential solutions, and populations denote sets of these solutions or chromosomes [57]. To optimize the subtasks scheduling, we configure the chromosome to correspond to the execution order of subtasks for all applications that satisfy the subtask dependencies within each application. It can be expressed as:

$$v_j = \{ST_{m,i} | m \in \mathcal{M}, i_m \in \mathcal{I}_m\}, \tag{4.153}$$

   In (4.153), j is the index of chromosome. Chromosomes are encoded using a Genetic Algorithm to meet the constraint C_2 and maintain subtask dependencies within an application.

   For better clarification, we consider a scenario where the system encompasses three applications, each having three subtasks. These subtasks are assigned to specific edge cores as illustrated in Table 4.4. If the chromosome is represented as $v_j = \{ST_{1,1}, ST_{3,1}, ST_{1,2}, ST_{2,1}, ST_{3,2}, ST_{2,2}, ST_{3,3}, ST_{1,3}, ST_{2,3}\}$, the corresponding sequence of edge cores would be: {2, 3, 3, 1, 2, 3, 1, 1, 2}. The population can be defined as:

$$\mathcal{P} = \{v_1, v_2, v_3, \cdots, v_P\}, \tag{4.154}$$

   where P represents the population size of chromosomes.
2. **Fitness** Fitness indicates the level of adaptability of a chromosome to the environment. A chromosome with a higher fitness value stands a better chance of survival, thus it is employed to assess the quality of each chromosome in the population. Typically, the fitness function aligns with the objective function [55]. In this context, we use the negative value of the system delay to measure the excellence of chromosomes, which can be mathematically expressed as:

$$fitness(v_j) = -\sum_{m=1}^{M} \gamma_m^t EndT_{m,I_m}, \tag{4.155}$$

Table 4.4 The example for subtasks execution across multiple cores

Edge core/Time			
App_m	$ST_{m,1}$	$ST_{m,2}$	$ST_{m,3}$
App_1	2/3	3/3	1/2
App_2	1/3	3/2	2/4
App_3	3/2	2/3	1/4

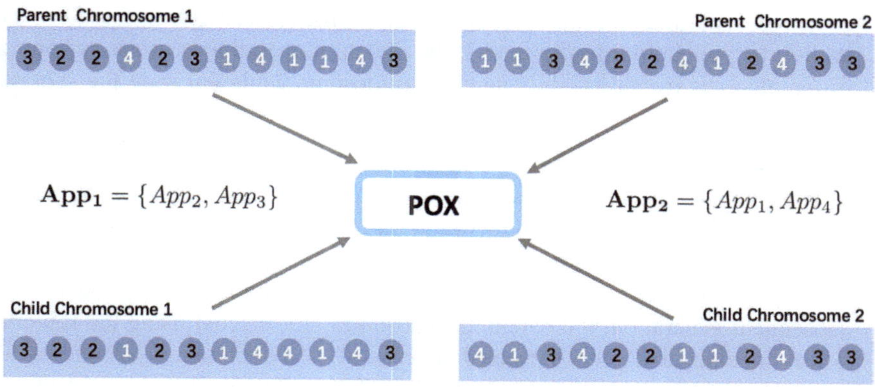

Fig. 4.19 POX

3. **Genetic Operator** Three fundamental genetic operators are conventionally employed in genetic algorithms: Selection, Crossover, and Mutation [57].

   Selection The selection operator chooses a set of chromosomes from the current population to pass on to the next generation based on a certain probability. Typically, the roulette wheel method is employed for selection, assigning a specific genetic probability to each chromosome according to its fitness within the population. The selection probability is calculated by:

$$p_n(v_j) = fitness(v_j) / \sum_{j=1}^{P} fitness(v_j), \tag{4.156}$$

   Crossover Incorporating the constraint of subtask dependency, our problem employs the Precedence Operation Crossover (POX) technique, which can be better understood through an example. Here, P_c represents the frequency of the crossover operator's application, which typically falls within the range of 0.25 and 1.00.

   a. Let's consider a scenario with 4 applications in the system. We randomly divide these applications into two sets: $\mathbf{App}_1 = \{App_2, App_3\}$ and $\mathbf{App}_2 = \{App_1, App_4\}$ as shown in Fig. 4.19.
   b. For the offspring chromosome v_1, copy the subtasks (genes) associated with $\mathbf{App}_1$ from the parent chromosome v_1. Similarly, for the offspring chromosome v_2, copy the subtasks associated with $\mathbf{App}_1$ from the parent chromosome v_2, while preserving their positions.
   c. Now, copy the subtasks related to $\mathbf{App}_2$ from the parent chromosome v_2 to the offspring chromosome v_1. Also, copy the subtasks linked to $\mathbf{App}_2$ from the parent chromosome v_1 to the offspring chromosome v_2, maintaining their original order. The steps outlined above constitute a complete POX operation.

Mutation The mutation operator plays a vital role in preserving the diversity within the population. In our model, the mutation operation involves swapping different genes (subtasks) on a single chromosome while ensuring the subtask dependency within each application.

4. **Genetic-based Task Scheduling (GTS)** Initially, the chromosomes are encoded to meet subtask dependency within each application and establish the initial parent population. As indicated by (4.59), the fitness value of each chromosome in $\mathcal{P}$ is computed. The chromosome with the highest fitness value is retained, and this value is continuously updated during each iteration. To produce the subsequent generation, the parent chromosomes are selected using the roulette wheel method, and then subjected to crossover and mutation operations to generate new offspring chromosomes. The GTS algorithm stops either when the number of genetic generations reaches or surpasses G_{max}, or when the maximum fitness variance within each generation becomes smaller than σ. The pseudocode for the GTS algorithm is presented in Algorithm 18.

Algorithm 18 GTS algorithm

Input: $T_{m,i}^{c,exe}$, $ST_{m,i}$ for $m \in \mathcal{M}$, $i \in \mathcal{I}_m$, Maximum Generation G_{max}.
Output: Optimal chromosome v_j^*, $fitness(v_j^*)$.
1. Encode $ST_{m,i}$ for $m \in \mathcal{M}$, $i \in \mathcal{I}_m$ into chromosome v_j.
2. Create a random population $\mathcal{P} = \{v_1, v_2, v_3, \cdots, v_P\}$.
3. Evaluate each chromosome in $\mathcal{P}$ by calculating its fitness.
4. Initialize $fitness_{max}(t)$ in $\mathcal{P}$.
repeat
  5. Update $fitness_{max}(t-1) = fitness_{max}(t)$.
  6. Select parent chromosomes using the roulette wheel method and update the population $\mathcal{P}$.
  7. Perform crossover and mutation with probability p_c.
  8. Perform mutation with probability p_m.
  9. Evaluate each chromosome in $\mathcal{P}$ by calculating fitness values.
  10. Update $fitness_{max}(t)$ as the maximum fitness in $\mathcal{P}$.
  if $|fitness_{max}(t-1) - fitness_{max}(t)| < \sigma$ **then**
    break.
  end if
until $t \geq G_{max}$.

4.4.4 Performance Evaluation

In this section, we conduct a comparative evaluation of our proposed offloading schemes against baseline offloading schemes under different parameter settings. Additionally, we compare the proposed GTS algorithm with an existing subtask scheduling algorithm. First, we provide an overview of the experimental parameter configurations.

Table 4.5 Parameter settings

Parameter	Settings
User bandwidth B	1 MHz
Backhaul link capacity W	15×10^6 Mbps
Noise N_0	– 174 dBm/Hz
Maximum transmission power p_m^{max}	36 dBm
Subtask input data $D_{m,i}$	[0.1, 0.5]Mbits
Required CPU cycles/bit $C_{m,i}$	[500, 1500]cycles/bit
Central cloud computing frequency f^c	[20, 40] GHz
Local computing frequency f_m^l	[0.1, 0.5] GHz
Edge core computing frequency $f^{n,edge}$	[10, 15] GHz
Weight factor γ^t, γ^e	[0,1]

(1) Parameter Setting

The CCC system consists of a central cloud, a multi-core edge cloud, and multiple users. Users are randomly distributed across a 50 m × 50 m area, with the multi-core edge cloud positioned at the periphery of this region. The central cloud is remotely deployed and provides substantial computing capacity, fixed at 20 GHz. The edge core's computing frequency is constrained and randomly selected within the range of [10, 15] GHz, while the computing frequency of the terminal devices falls within the range of [0.1, 0.5] GHz. The maximum user bandwidth is set at 1 MHz. The wireless channel gain between the terminal devices and the edge core follows a series of Rayleigh-distributed random variables with unit variance [12]. Additional parameter settings are listed in Table 4.5. The parameters for our simulations are selected based on several references, including [12, 26], which are widely used in similar studies.

(2) Analysis of Different Offloading Schemes

Since offloading decisions for different applications are independent, we focused on scenarios involving a single application with multiple subtasks, allowing us to concentrate on the performance of offloading schemes. Figure 4.20 illustrates the $AETC$ comparison for different offloading schemes as the number of subtasks increases. The schemes compared include Local Only, Cloud Only, MLSO, SSO, and OEO (Optimal Enumeration Offloading). The x-axis represents the number of subtasks, ranging from 0 to 25, while the y-axis denotes the $AETC$ value. As the number of subtasks increases, the $AETC$ values also rise for all strategies, indicating the increased computational burden. When the number of subtasks is small, the performance of the Cloud Only scheme is better than that of the Local Only scheme. However, as the number of subtasks keeps increasing, the competition for limited MEC resources intensifies, resulting in the performance degradation of the Cloud Only scheme. When the number of subtasks is less than 10 ($I \leq 10$), both the MLSO and SSO schemes exhibit similar performance. As the number of subtasks increases, the MLSO scheme shows significant advantages over the SSO scheme and approaches the OEO scheme, which implies that the MLSO scheme can

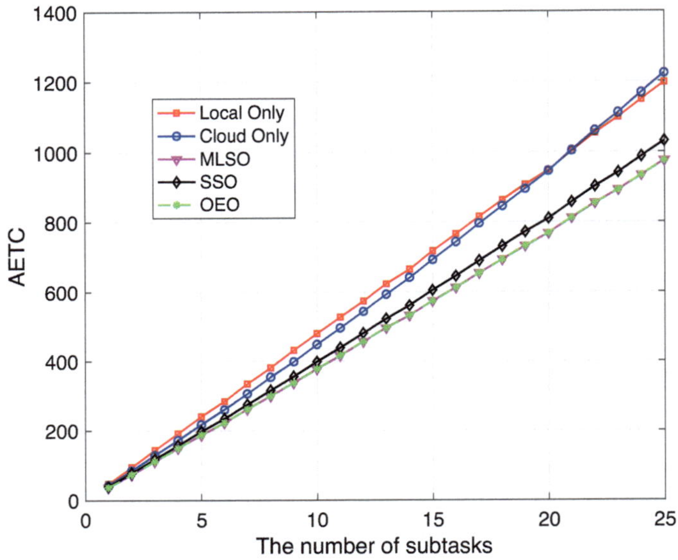

Fig. 4.20 Analysis of different offloading algorithms

find the optimal combined offloading decision through deep search. Additionally, although both the SSO scheme and the MLSO scheme optimize the combined offloading decision to reduce $AETC$, the performance of the SSO scheme never reaches that of the OEO scheme and the MLSO scheme, suggesting that the MLSO scheme sacrifices time complexity for better performance. These results further emphasize the importance of optimizing combined offloading decisions to reduce the overall loss of the application.

(3) The Impact of Weight Factors

To focus on studying the impact of weight factors on the execution scheme, we focus on the scenarios involving a single-chain application with multiple subtasks. Figure 4.21 illustrates the influence of γ^t on various execution schemes. In the experiment, it is assumed that the application consists of 28 subtasks in a single chain. It is observed that γ^t has a minimal impact on the Cloud Only scheme. As γ^t increases, the $AETC$ of the Local Only scheme exhibits a steep linear rise, while the $AETC$ of the Cloud Only scheme gradually increases. This suggests that the Cloud Only scheme significantly reduces time consumption in comparison to the Local Only scheme. When $\gamma^t \leq 0.4$, the Local Only scheme outperforms the Cloud Only scheme, indicating its suitability for applications with limited sensitivity to delay. Conversely, for delay-sensitive applications characterized by a larger γ^t, the Cloud Only scheme offers superior performance. Moreover, the performance of the MLSO, SSO, and OEO schemes surpasses that of the baseline schemes, i.e., the Cloud Only and Local Only schemes, demonstrating the effectiveness of optimizing combined offloading decisions in reducing $AETC$. When $\gamma^t \leq 0.4$, the

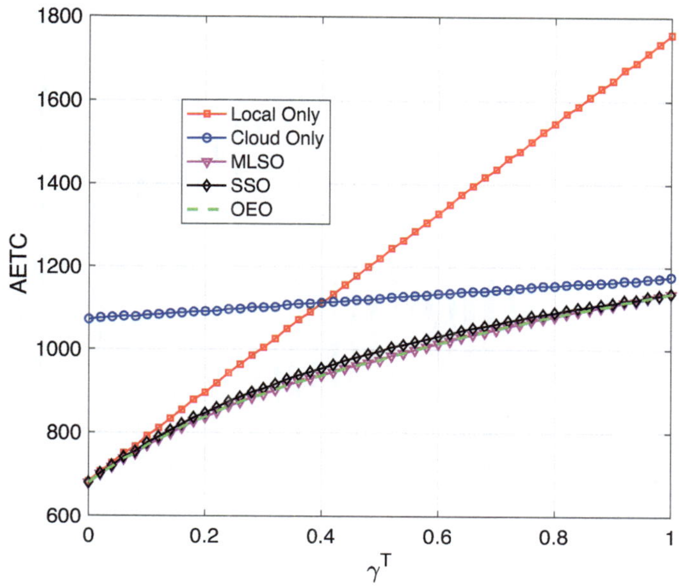

Fig. 4.21 The impact of γ^t on different offloading schemes

performance of MLSO, SSO, and OEO approximates that of the Local Only scheme, indicating the suitability of local computing for non-delay-sensitive applications. As γ^t gradually increases, the performance of MLSO, SSO, and OEO converges toward that of the Cloud Only scheme, suggesting that CCC is more suitable for delay-sensitive applications. Furthermore, MLSO outperforms SSO and closely aligns with the performance of OEO, indicating that MLSO balances time complexity with enhanced performance by performing in-depth searches. Figure 4.22 visually illustrates how γ^t influences the number of offloaded subtasks in MLSO and SSO.

(4) The Impact of MEC Resources

Since the impact of available MEC resources on the performance of offloading algorithms is independent across different applications, we consider the influence of MEC resource configurations on the proposed MLSO algorithm by focusing solely on scenarios involving a single application with multiple subtasks. Figure 4.23 depicts the impact of f_m^{max} on the MLSO scheme. As f_m^{max} increases, the performance of the MLSO scheme steadily improves, leading to a gradual decrease in $AETC$. This suggests that sufficient MEC resources not only alleviate the competition for these resources among subtasks but also introduce more diversity to the combined offloading decisions. Figure 4.24 depicts the system maximum completion time of the GTS algorithm as the number of subtasks increases from 10 to 26 for three different edge core configurations (2, 4, and 6 cores). Assume that there are 4 applications in this scenario. It can be seen that when the number of subtasks is large, the more edge cores there are, the more obvious the advantage of GTS is. Moreover, as the number of subtasks increases, the maximum completion

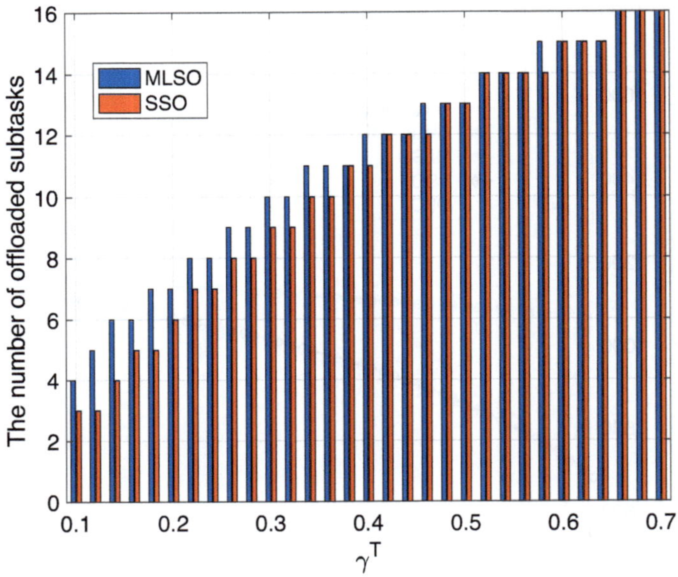

Fig. 4.22 The impact of γ^t on the number of offloaded subtasks for MLSO and SSO schemes

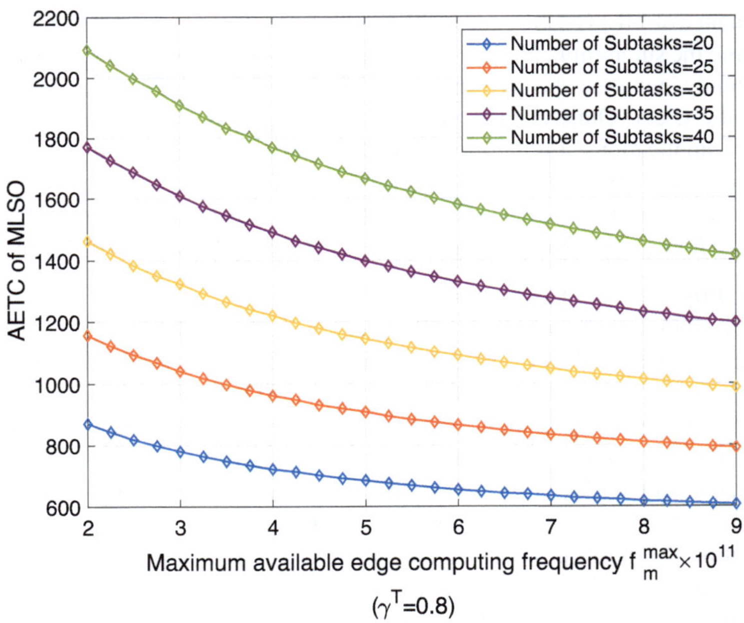

Fig. 4.23 The impact of maximum available MEC resources

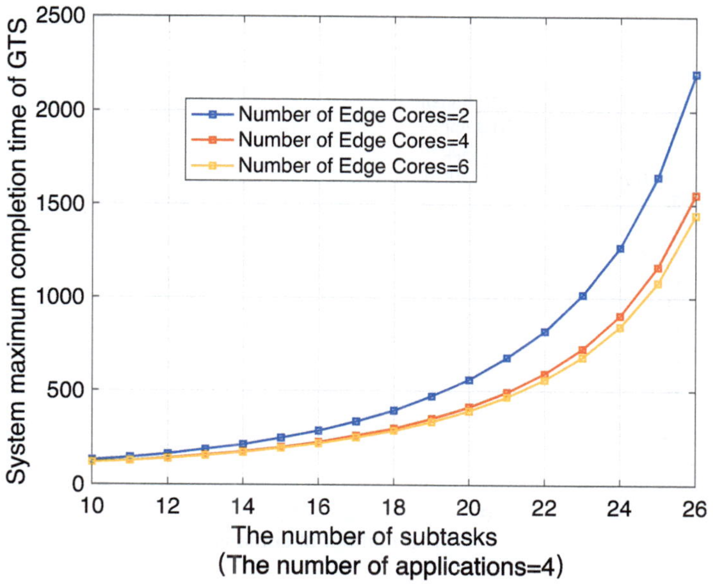

Fig. 4.24 The impact of the number of edge cores on subtask scheduling under the GTS algorithm

time experiences a gentle increase followed by a sharp escalation, which indicates that a large number of subtasks intensifies the competition for MEC resources, reducing the performance of the GTS algorithm.

(5) Comparison of Subtask Scheduling Schemes

Figure 4.25 illustrates the system maximum completion time as a function of the number of subtasks for two different algorithms, SEF and GTS. These results are based on an MEC environment with 4 edge cores. The x-axis represents the number of subtasks, ranging from 2 to 20, while the y-axis shows the system maximum completion time in milliseconds (ms). As the number of subtasks increases, the system maximum completion time rises across all configurations. This trend reflects the growing computational load and resource contention with more subtasks. For both algorithms, an increase in the number of applications (from 4 to 6) leads to higher completion times, highlighting the additional computational burden introduced by more applications. The difference in performance between SEF and GTS becomes more pronounced as the number of subtasks increases, particularly in scenarios with 6 applications, indicating that GTS is more suitable for scheduling subtasks with higher complexity.

Figure 4.26 compares the performance of three different task timing scheduling schemes under the MLSO offloading scheme. GTS scheme, the literature [58] proposed a scheme that prioritizes subtasks with short computational delays (Shortest Execution First, SEF) and a first come first serve (First Come First Serve, FCFS) [59] scheme. As shown in the Fig. 4.26, as the number of tasks increases, the

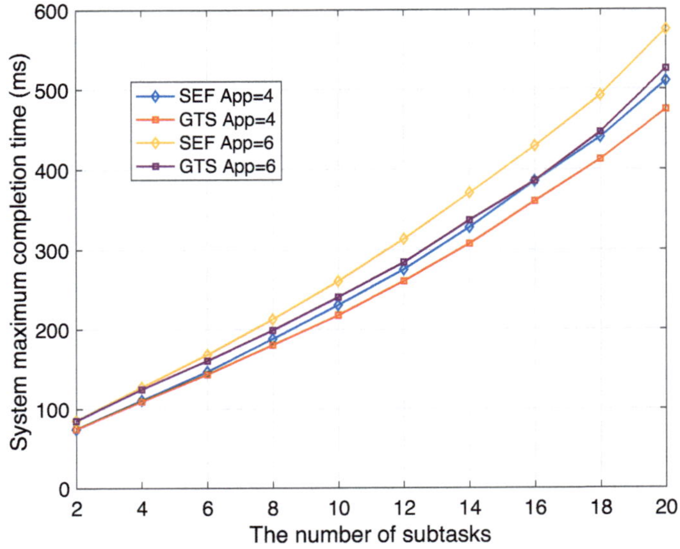

Fig. 4.25 The performance comparison between GTS and SEF

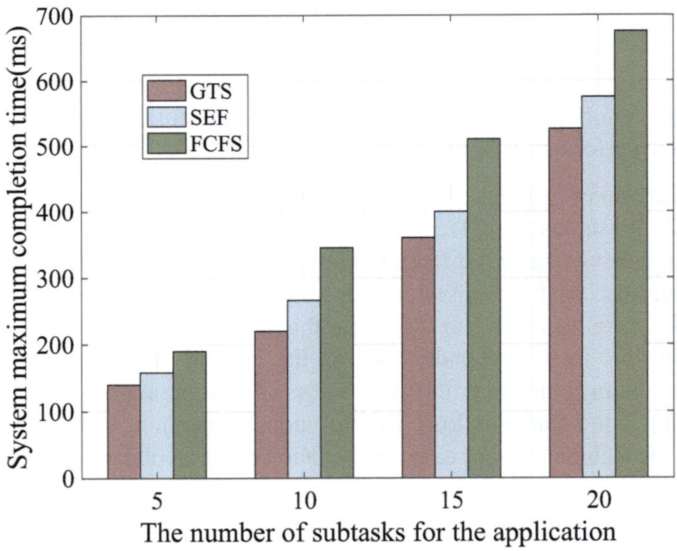

Fig. 4.26 Comparison of subtask scheduling schemes GTS, SEF and FCFS under MLSO scheme

maximum completion time of different scheduling schemes also increases, and the performance of the GTS scheme has always been better than the SEF and FCFS scheduling schemes, and the advantage becomes more obvious as the number of

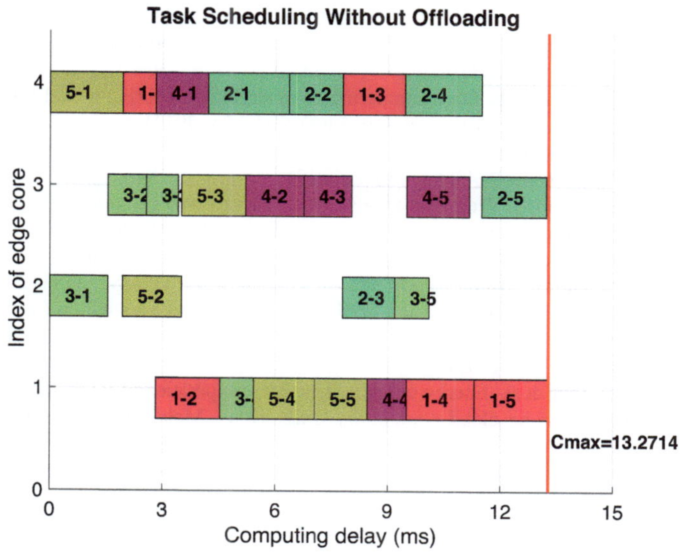

Fig. 4.27 Gantt chart of subtask scheduling under GTS algorithm without considering offloading decisions

subtasks increases. This is because the increase in the number of subtasks will increase the diversity and complexity of task scheduling, and the GTS algorithm gradually converges to the optimal scheduling scheme through multiple iterations of genetic selection optimization.

Figure 4.27 shows the Gantt chart of subtask scheduling without considering offloading decisions, with different colors used to distinguish between multiple applications.

References

1. H. Wu, Multi-objective decision-making for mobile cloud offloading: a survey. IEEE Access **6**, 3962–3976 (2018)
2. P. Voigt, A. Von dem Bussche, The eu general data protection regulation (gdpr). *A Practical Guide*, 1st edn. (Springer International Publishing, Cham, 2017). **10**(3152676), 10–5555.
3. T. Taleb, K. Samdanis, B. Mada et al., On multi-access edge computing: a survey of the emerging 5G network edge cloud architecture and orchestration. IEEE Commun. Surv. Tutor. **19**(3), 1657–1681 (2017)
4. M. Zeng, W. Hao, O. A. Dobre, Z. Ding and H. V. Poor, Massive MIMO-assisted mobile edge computing: exciting possibilities for computation offloading. IEEE Veh. Technol. Magaz. **15**(2), 31–38 (2020)
5. Q.-V. Pham, L. B. Le, S.-H. Chung and W.-J. Hwang, Mobile edge computing with wireless backhaul: joint task offloading and resource allocation. IEEE Access, **7**, 16444–16459 (2019)

6. Z. Gao, W. Hao, R. Zhang, Shouyi Y, Markov decision process-based computation offloading algorithm and resource allocation in time constraint for mobile cloud computing. IET Commun. **14**(13), 2068–2078 (2020)
7. W. Shi, H. Sun, J. Cao et al., Edge computing-an emerging computing model for the internet of everything era. J. Comput. Res. Develop. **54**(5), 907–924 (2017)
8. X. Li, C. Zhang, B. Gu et al., Optimal pricing and service selection in the mobile cloud architectures. IEEE Access **7**, 43564–43572 (2019)
9. Z. Gao, W. Hao, Z. Han, S. Yang, Q-learning-based task offloading and resources optimization for a collaborative computing system. IEEE Access **8**, 149011–149024 (2020)
10. Z. Gao, W. Hao, S. Yang, Joint offloading and resource allocation for multi-user multi-edge collaborative computing system. IEEE Trans. Veh. Technol. **71**(3), 3383–3388 (2022)
11. Z. Gao, P. Zheng, W. Hao, S. Yang, Joint offloading and resource allocation for collaborative cloud computing with dependent subtask scheduling on multi-core server. IEEE Trans. Cloud Comput. **12**(4), 1401–1414 (2024)
12. S. Guo, J. Liu, Y. Yang et al., Energy-efficient dynamic computation offloading and cooperative task scheduling in mobile cloud computing. IEEE Trans. Mobile Comput. **18**(2), 319–333 (2018)
13. X. Chen, Decentralized computation offloading game for mobile cloud computing. IEEE Trans. Parallel and Distributed Sys. **26**(4), 974–983 (2015)
14. X. Lin, Y. Wang, Q. Xie et al., Task scheduling with dynamic voltage and frequency scaling for energy minimization in the mobile cloud computing environment. IEEE Trans. Services Comput. **8**(2), 175–186 (2014)
15. S. Sardellitti, G. Scutari, S. Barbarossa, Joint optimization of radio and computational resources for multicell mobile-edge computing. IEEE Trans. Signal Inf. Process. Netw. **1**(2), 89–103 (2015)
16. C. You, K. Huang, H. Chae et al., Energy-efficient resource allocation for mobile-edge computation offloading. IEEE Trans. Wirel. Commun. **16**(3), 1397–1411 (2016)
17. X. Sun, N. Ansari, Latency aware workload offloading in the cloudlet network. IEEE Commun. Lett. **21**(7), 1481–1484 (2017)
18. Y. Mao, C. You, J. Zhang et al., A survey on mobile edge computing: the communication perspective. IEEE Commun. Surv. Tutor. **19**(4), 2322–2358 (2017)
19. X. Meng, W. Wang, Z. Zhang, Delay-constrained hybrid computation offloading with cloud and fog computing. IEEE Access **5**, 21355–21367 (2017)
20. Y. Wang, M. Sheng, X. Wang et al., Mobile-edge computing: Partial computation offloading using dynamic voltage scaling. IEEE Trans. Commun. **64**(10), 4268–4282 (2016)
21. J. Ren, G. Yu, Y. He et al., Collaborative cloud and edge computing for latency minimization. IEEE Trans. Veh. Technol. **68**(5), 5031–5044 (2019)
22. G. Zhang, T.Q.S. Quek, M. Kountouris et al., Fundamentals of heterogeneous backhaul design—analysis and optimization. IEEE Trans. Commun. **64**(2), 876–889 (2016)
23. A. Al-Shuwaili, O. Simeone, A. Bagheri et al., Joint uplink/downlink optimization for backhaul-limited mobile cloud computing with user scheduling. IEEE Trans. Signal Inf. Process. Netw. **3**(4), 787–802 (2017)
24. X. Peng, J. Zhang, S.H. Song et al., Cache size allocation in backhaul limited wireless networks, in *2016 IEEE International Conference on Communications (ICC)* (IEEE, 2016), pp. 1–6.
25. F. Guo, H. Zhang, H. Ji et al., An efficient computation offloading management scheme in the densely deployed small cell networks with mobile edge computing. IEEE/ACM Trans. Netw. **26**(6), 2651–2664 (2018)
26. X. Lyu, H. Tian, C. Sengul et al., Multiuser joint task offloading and resource optimization in proximate clouds. IEEE Trans. Veh. Technol. **66**(4), 3435–3447 (2016)
27. Y. Pochet, L.A. Wolsey, *Production Planning by Mixed Integer Programming* (Springer, New York, 2006)
28. R. Bellman, Dynamic programming. Science **153**(3731), 34–37 (1966)

29. S. Boyd, L. Vandenberghe, *Convex Optimization* (Cambridge University Press, Cambridge, 2004)
30. Y. Wang, R. Xu, B. Liu et al., Machine learning and cybernetics. Commun. Comput. Inf. Sci **481** (2014)
31. Y. Ephraim, N. Merhav, Hidden markov processes. IEEE Trans. Inf. Theory **48**(6), 1518–1569 (2002)
32. J.A. Whittaker, M.G. Thomason, A Markov chain model for statistical software testing. IEEE Trans. Software Eng. **20**(10), 812–824 (1994)
33. Y. Liu, D. Lu, G. Zhang et al., Q-learning based content placement method for dynamic cloud content delivery networks. IEEE Access **7**, 66384–66394 (2019)
34. W. Zhang, Y. Wen, Energy-efficient task execution for application as a general topology in mobile cloud computing. IEEE Trans. Cloud Comput. **6**(3), 708–719 (2015)
35. M.L. Puterman, *Markov Decision Processes: Discrete Stochastic Dynamic Programming* (John Wiley & Sons, Hoboken, 2014)
36. L.V. Zhou, A. Swain, A. Ukil, Q-learning and dynamic fuzzy Q-learning based intelligent controllers for wind energy conversion systems, in *2018 IEEE Innovative Smart Grid Technologies-Asia (ISGT Asia)* (IEEE, 2018), pp. 103–108
37. Q. Wei, F.L. Lewis, Q. Sun et al., Discrete-time deterministic Q-learning: a novel convergence analysis. IEEE Trans. Cybern. **47**(5), 1224–1237 (2016)
38. X. Zhang, J. Zhang, Z. Liu et al., MDP-based task offloading for vehicular edge computing under certain and uncertain transition probabilities. IEEE Trans. Veh. Technol. **69**(3), 3296–3309 (2020)
39. C. Tang, X. Chen, Y. Chen et al., A MDP-based network selection scheme in 5G ultra-dense network, in *2018 IEEE 24th International Conference on Parallel and Distributed Systems (ICPADS)* (IEEE, 2018), pp. 823–830
40. K. Arulkumaran, M.P. Deisenroth, M. Brundage et al., Deep reinforcement learning: a brief survey. IEEE Signal Process. Mag. **34**(6), 26–38 (2017)
41. N.C. Luong, D.T. Hoang, S. Gong et al., Applications of deep reinforcement learning in communications and networking: a survey. IEEE Commun. Surv. Tutor. 2019(4), 3133–3174 (2019)
42. A. Galindo-Serrano, L. Giupponi, Distributed q-Learning for aggregated interference control in cognitive radio networks. IEEE Trans. Veh. Technol. **59**(4),1823–1834 (2010)
43. B. Luo, D. Liu, T. Huang et al., Model-free optimal tracking control via critic-only Q-learning. IEEE Trans. Neural Netw. Learn. Syst. **27**(10), 2134–2144 (2016)
44. J. Zhu, Y. Song, D. Jiang et al., A new deep-Q-learning-based transmission scheduling mechanism for the cognitive Internet of Things. IEEE Internet Things J. **5**(4), 2375–2385 (2017)
45. X. Lyu and H. Tian, Adaptive receding horizon offloading strategy under dynamic environment. IEEE Commun. Lett., **20**(5), 878–881 (2016)
46. W. Zhang, Y. Wen, D.O. Wu, Collaborative task execution in mobile cloud computing under a stochastic wireless channel. IEEE Trans. Wirel. Commun. **14**(1), 81–93 (2014)
47. Z. Kuang, Y. Shi, S. Guo, J. Dan, B. Xiao, Multi-user offloading game strategy in OFDMA mobile cloud computing system. IEEE Trans. Veh. Technol. **68**(12), 12190–12201 (2019)
48. M. Abououf, S. Singh, H. Otrok et al., Gale-shapley matching game selection—A framework for user satisfaction. IEEE Access **7**, 3694–3703 (2018)
49. H. Lee, H. Lee, S. Jung et al., Stable marriage matching for traffic-aware space-air-ground integrated networks: a gale-shapley algorithmic approach, in *2022 International Conference*
50. Y. Zhang, Y. Mao, S. Zhong, Joint differentially private Gale–Shapley mechanisms for location privacy protection in mobile traffic offloading systems. IEEE J. Selected Areas Commun. **34**(10), 2738–2749 (2016)
51. Z. Zhou, K. Ota, M. Dong et al., Energy-efficient matching for resource allocation in D2D enabled cellular networks. IEEE Trans. Veh. Technol. **66**(6), 5256–5268 (2016)
52. Z. Zhou, J. Feng, B. Gu et al., When mobile crowd sensing meets UAV: Energy-efficient task assignment and route planning. IEEE Trans. Commun. **66**(11), 5526–5538 (2018)

53. Z. Zhou, C. Gao, C. Xu et al., Energy-efficient stable matching for resource allocation in energy harvesting-based device-to-device communications. IEEE Access **5**, 15184–15196 (2017)
54. J. Guo, Z. Song, Y. Cui et al., Energy-efficient resource allocation for multi-user mobile edge computing, in *GLOBECOM 2017-2017 IEEE Global Communications Conference* (IEEE, 2017), pp. 1–7
55. L.D. Chambers, *The Practical Handbook of Genetic Algorithms: Applications* (Chapman and Hall/CRC, Boca Raton, 2000)
56. M. Srinivas, L.M. Patnaik, Genetic algorithms: a survey. Computer **27**(6), 17–26 (1994)
57. S.C. Liu, Z.G. Chen, Z.H. Zhan et al., Many-objective job-shop scheduling: a multiple populations for multiple objectives-based genetic algorithm approach. IEEE Trans. Cybern. **53**(3), 1460–1474 (2021)
58. Y. Liu, M.J. Lee, An effective dynamic programming offloading algorithm in mobile cloud computing system, in *2014 IEEE Wireless Communications and Networking Conference (WCNC)* (IEEE, 2014), pp. 1868–1873
59. F. Alhaidari, T. Balharith, A.L.Y. Eyman, Comparative analysis for task scheduling algorithms on cloud computing, in *2019 International Conference on Computer and Information Sciences (ICCIS)* (IEEE, 2019), pp. 1–6
60. J. Yan, S. Bi, Y. J. Zhang and M. Tao, Optimal task offloading and resource allocation in mobile-edge computing with inter-user task dependency. IEEE Trans. Wireless Commun., **19**(1), 235–250 (2020)
61. C. Shu, Z. Zhao, Y. Han et al., Multi-user offloading for edge computing networks: a dependency-aware and latency-optimal approach. IEEE Internet Things J. **7**(3), 1678–1689 (2019)
62. M.A. Awad, H.M. Abd-Elaziz, An efficient modified genetic algorithm for integrated process planning-job scheduling, in *2021 International Mobile, Intelligent, and Ubiquitous Computing Conference (MIUCC)* (IEEE, 2021), pp. 319–323

Chapter 5
Integrated Communications, Computing and Sensing

5.1 Introduction

With the development of science and technology, emerging scenarios have put forward higher requirements for resource utilization efficiency, real-time performance, and system coordination. However, the communication, computing and sensing functions in traditional wireless networks are designed and developed independently, making it difficult to efficiently utilize system resources. Therefore, it is necessary for us to explore the possibility of ICCS functions into wireless edge networks. And this research field with great potential is ICCS. However, the existing research on ICCS still faces several challenges. First, in order to achieve the expected performance of the three different functions of communication, computing and sensing under limited system resources, it is necessary to design corresponding beamforming algorithms to coordinate interference and consider how to balance the performance between these three functions. Secondly, the current research on ICCS assumes an ideal communication environment, which will inevitably suffer serious performance loss in the actual communication environment. Finally, considering the mobility of users in actual situations, it is difficult to obtain perfect CSI.

In response to the above challenges, this chapter thoroughly studies the resource optimization problem for ICCS, which is organized as follows. Section 5.2 constructs a weighted performance maximization problem for the ICCS system. Section 5.3 studies the RIS-assisted ICCS system. Section 5.4 considers the resource optimization of the RIS-assisted ICCS system with imperfect CSIs.

W. Hao et al., *Intelligent Mobile Edge Computing and Sensing*, Wireless Networks,
https://doi.org/10.1007/978-981-96-9400-6_5

5.2 Resource Optimization for ICCS

5.2.1 System Model and Problem Formulation

As shown in Fig. 5.1, we consider an ICCS system, which consists of a multi-antenna three-function BS, K randomly distributed communication users (CM-UEs), M randomly distributed computing users (CP-UEs) and a sensing target. In addition, the BS is equipped with N antennas, while each CM-UE and CP-UE are equipped with single antenna, respectively. Let $\mathcal{K} = \{1, \ldots, K\}$ and $\mathcal{M} = \{1, \ldots, M\}$ denote the index of CM-UEs, CP-UEs. In order to realize synchronous transmission of downlink and uplink signals, the BS antennas are divided into two groups. One group with N_s antennas is used for transmitting communication and sensing signals, and the other group with N_r antennas is used for receiving echo signals and offloading signals from CP-UEs, where $N = N_r + N_s$. We assume that the self interference from the transmit antennas to receive antennas at the BS can be perfectly canceled by the physical isolation of antennas and advanced signal processing techniques [1, 2].

5.2.1.1 Signal Model

Let s_k^{cm} represent the downlink communication signal, $\mathbf{w}_k \in \mathbb{C}^{N_s \times 1}$ represent the corresponding transmit beamforming vector, and $\mathbf{s}_0^r$ represent the sensing signal. $\{s_k^{cm}\}_{k=1}^K$ are independent random variables with zero mean and unit variance, and $\mathbf{s}_0^r$ has zero mean and covariance matrix $\mathbf{S} = \mathbb{E}[\mathbf{s}_0^r \mathbf{s}_0^{r\,H}] \succeq 0$, where $\mathbb{E}[s_k^{cm} s_0^r] = 0, \forall k$.

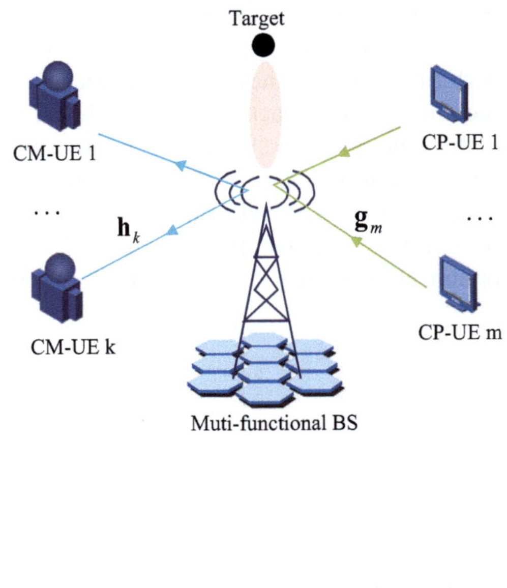

Fig. 5.1 The system model of ICCS

Then, the transmit signals at the BS can be expressed as

$$\mathbf{x} = \sum_{k=1}^{K} \mathbf{w}_k s_k^{cm} + \mathbf{s}_0^r, \tag{5.1}$$

where the transmit power can be calculated as $Q = \sum_{k=1}^{K} \|\mathbf{w}_k\|^2 + \mathrm{Tr}(\mathbf{S})$.

The signals received at the BS are composed of two parts, the computation offloading signals and the echo signal from a desired sensing target in the θ direction, and computation offloading signals can be expressed as

$$\mathbf{y}^{cp} = \sum_{m=1}^{M} \sqrt{P_m} \mathbf{g}_m s_m^{cp}, \tag{5.2}$$

where $\mathbf{g}_m \in \mathbb{C}^{N_r \times 1}$ represents the channel vector from CP-UE m to BS, $\sqrt{P_m} s_m^{cp}$ represents the transmit signal of CP-UE m to BS with transmit power P_m, and the information streams $\{s_m^{cp}\}_{m=1}^{M}$ are independent random variables with zero mean and unit variance.

The sensing echo signals received at the BS is expressed as

$$\mathbf{y}^r = \varpi \mathbf{a}_r(\theta) \mathbf{a}_s(\theta)^T \mathbf{x}, \tag{5.3}$$

where $\varpi = \Phi_r^{-1/2} \widehat{\varpi}$ denotes the sensing channel gain including the path loss $\Phi_r^{-1/2}$ and the radar cross section $\widehat{\varpi}$ of sensing target [3]. $\mathbf{a}_r(\theta) \in \mathbb{C}^{N_r \times 1}$ and $\mathbf{a}_s(\theta) \in \mathbb{C}^{N_s \times 1}$ represent the steering vectors of the antenna array at the BS. We assume that a uniform linear array (ULA) is deployed at the BS, d and λ represent the antenna spacing and signal wavelength, respectively. Then the steering vectors are expressed as

$$\mathbf{a}_s(\theta) = \left[1, e^{j2\pi \frac{d}{\lambda} \sin(\theta)}, \ldots, e^{j2\pi (N_s-1)\frac{d}{\lambda} \sin(\theta)}\right]^T, \tag{5.4}$$

$$\mathbf{a}_r(\theta) = \left[1, e^{j2\pi \frac{d}{\lambda} \sin(\theta)}, \ldots, e^{j2\pi (N_r-1)\frac{d}{\lambda} \sin(\theta)}\right]^T. \tag{5.5}$$

Thus, the overall signals received at the BS is expressed as

$$\mathbf{y} = \mathbf{y}^{cp} + \mathbf{y}^r + \mathbf{n}_b, \tag{5.6}$$

where $\mathbf{n}_b \sim \mathcal{CN}\left(0, \sigma_b^2 \mathbf{I}_{N_r}\right)$ represents the additive white Gaussian noise (AWGN).

5.2.1.2 Communication Model

The signal received by CM-UE k can be expressed as

$$y_k^{cm} = \mathbf{h}_k^H \mathbf{x} + n_k = \mathbf{h}_k^H \left(\sum_{k'=1}^{K} \mathbf{w}_{k'} s_{k'}^{cm} + \mathbf{s}_0^r \right) + n, \tag{5.7}$$

where $\mathbf{h}_k \in \mathbb{C}^{N_s \times 1}$ represents the communication channel vector from BS to CM-UE k, $n \sim \mathcal{CN}(0, \sigma^2)$ denotes the AWGN. Thus, the received SINR at CM-UE k can be calculated as

$$r_k^{cm} = \frac{|\mathbf{h}_k^H \mathbf{w}_k|^2}{\sum\limits_{k' \in \mathcal{K}, k' \neq k} |\mathbf{h}_k^H \mathbf{w}_{k'}|^2 + \mathbf{h}_k^H \mathbf{S} \mathbf{h}_k + \sigma_k^2}, \tag{5.8}$$

the achievable communication rate from BS to CM-UE k is thus expressed as

$$R_k^{cm} = B \log_2 \left(1 + r_k^{cm}\right), \tag{5.9}$$

where B represents the transmission bandwidth.

5.2.1.3 Computation Model

1. Local Computing We assume that $\varepsilon_{l,m}$ represents the CPU cycle required by the m-th CP-UE to process a bit of raw data, l_m represents the computation task size at the m-th CP-UE, and $f_{l,m}$ denotes the local CPU computing frequency of the m-th CP-UE. Then the computation rate and energy consumption at each CP-UE can be expressed as

$$R_{l,m} = \frac{f_{l,m}}{\varepsilon_{l,m}}, \tag{5.10}$$

and

$$E_{l,m} = \bar{\sigma} l_m \varepsilon_{l,m} f_{l,m}^2, \tag{5.11}$$

respectively, where $\bar{\sigma}$ represents the constant related to the hardware architecture.

2. Offloading Computing The offloading signal at the BS via the receiving beamforming vector $\mathbf{z}_m \in \mathbb{C}^{N_r \times 1}$ is expressed as

$$\hat{s}_m^{cp} = \mathbf{z}_m^H \sum_{m'=1}^{M} \sqrt{P_m} \mathbf{g}_{m'} s_{m'}^{cp} + \mathbf{z}_m^H \left(\mathbf{H}^r \mathbf{x} + \mathbf{n}_b\right), \tag{5.12}$$

then the SINR of the m-th CP-UE offloading signal can be written

$$r_m^{cp} = \frac{P_m \left|\mathbf{z}_m^H \mathbf{g}_m\right|^2}{\sum\limits_{m' \neq m}^{M} P_m \left|\mathbf{z}_m^H \mathbf{g}_{m'}\right|^2 + \left|\mathbf{z}_m^H \mathbf{H}^r \mathbf{x}\right|^2 + \left|\mathbf{z}_m^H\right|^2 \sigma_b^2}, \tag{5.13}$$

and the maximum achievable offloading rate and transmission energy consumption can be expressed as

$$R_m^{cp} = B\log_2(1 + r_m^{cp}), \tag{5.14}$$

and

$$E_{o,m} = \frac{l_m}{R_m^{cp}} P_m, \tag{5.15}$$

respectively.

In addition, the computation rate at the BS is expressed as

$$R_{b,m} = \frac{f_{b,m}}{\varepsilon_{b,m}}, \tag{5.16}$$

where $f_{b,m}$ represents the CPU computing frequency allocated by BS to the m-th CP-UE, and $\varepsilon_{b,m}$ represents the CPU cycle required by BS to process one bit raw data. The computing power consumption at the BS can be calculated as

$$Q' = \sum_{m}^{M} \kappa f_{b,m}^3, \tag{5.17}$$

where κ is the computing power factor on the BS.

5.2.1.4 Sensing Model

After the receiver decodes the offloading signal, the successive interference cancellation (SIC) is used to remove the offloading signal from the observed waveform to obtain a clean sensing echo signal [4]. Hence at the BS, the effective echo signal via the receiving beamforming vector $\mathbf{u} \in \mathbb{C}^{N_r \times 1}$ can be expressed as

$$\tilde{y}^r = \mathbf{u}^H \mathbf{y} = \mathbf{u}^H \mathbf{H}^r \mathbf{x} + \mathbf{u}^H \mathbf{n}_b, \tag{5.18}$$

where $\mathbf{H}^r = \varpi \mathbf{a}_r(\theta) \mathbf{a}_s(\theta)^T$ denotes the sensing channel.

The signal noise ratio of the echo signal at the BS can be written as

$$r_0 = \frac{\left|\mathbf{u}^H \mathbf{H}^r \mathbf{x}\right|^2}{|\mathbf{u}|^2 {\sigma_b}^2}. \tag{5.19}$$

5.2.1.5 Problem Formulation

To evaluate the performance of the system, we define the WSR of the system as follows:

$$R = \gamma^r R^r + \sum_{k=1}^{K} \gamma_k^{cm} {R_k}^{cm} + \sum_{m=1}^{M} \gamma_m^{cp} \left(c_m \left(R_m^{cp} + R_{b,m}\right) + (1 - c_m) R_{l,m}\right), \tag{5.20}$$

where $c_m \in \{0, 1\}$ represents the offloading strategy of the CP-UE m. Specifically, if $c_m = 0$, CP-UE m performs the task locally. Otherwise, CP-UE m offloads the task to BS. $R^r = B \log(1 + r_0)$ is used to characterize the sensing ability, and $\gamma^r, \gamma^{cm}, \gamma^{cp} \in (0, 1]$ represent the weights of sensing, communication, and computation, respectively.

We aim to maximize WSR by jointly optimizing the information beamforming, sensing covariance matrix, sensing echo receiving beamforming, offloading signal receiving beamforming, local computing resources, edge computing resources and offloading strategy. Mathematically, the optimization problem can be expressed as follows

$$\mathcal{P}^0 : \max_{\mathbf{w}_k, \mathbf{S}, \mathbf{u}, \mathbf{z}_m, \mathbf{f}_b, \mathbf{f}_l, \mathbf{c}} R \tag{5.21}$$

$$s.t.\ \mathrm{C1} : \mathrm{Q} + \sum_{m}^{\mathcal{M}} \kappa c_m f_{b,m}^3 \leq \mathrm{P}_b, \tag{5.21a}$$

$$\mathrm{C2} : \mathbf{S} \succeq 0, \tag{5.21b}$$

$$\mathrm{C3} : \mathrm{Tr}\left(\mathbf{u}\mathbf{u}^H\right) \leq 1, \tag{5.21c}$$

$$\mathrm{C4} : \mathrm{Tr}\left(\mathbf{z}_m \mathbf{z}_m^H\right) \leq 1, \tag{5.21d}$$

$$\mathrm{C5} : (1 - c_m) E_{l,m} + c_m E_{o,m} \leq E_m^{\max}, \tag{5.21e}$$

$$\mathrm{C6} : f_{l,m} \geq 0, \tag{5.21f}$$

$$\mathrm{C7} : \sum_{m=1}^{M} f_{b,m} \leq f_b, \tag{5.21g}$$

$$\mathrm{C8} : c_m \in \{0, 1\}, \tag{5.21h}$$

where P_b represents the maximum transmission power budget at the BS, f_b represents the total computing resources of the edge server, $E_m^{\max}$ represents the maximum energy budget of the m-th CP-UE. $\mathbf{c} = [c_1, c_2, \cdots, c_M]^T$ represents the offloading strategy vector, $\mathbf{f}_b = \left[f_{b,1}, f_{b,2}, \cdots, f_{b,M}\right]^T$ and $\mathbf{f}_l = \left[f_{l,1}, f_{l,2}, \cdots, f_{l,M}\right]^T$ represent vectors of edge computing resources and local computing resources respectively. C1 denotes the transmit power constraint at the BS. C3 denotes the constraint of sensing echo receiving beamforming. C4, C5, C6, and C7 denote the offloading signal receiving beamforming constraint, CP-UE m energy consumption constraint, local computing resource constraint, and the edge maximum computing resource constraint, respectively.

5.2.2 *Proposed AO-Based Algorithm*

Due to the existence of nonlinear fractional terms and binary variables, problem $\mathcal{P}^0$ is non-convex, and thus it is difficult to find its global optimal solution. To solve this problem, we propose an alternating iterative optimization algorithm, in which the original problem is decomposed into four subproblems, and each one is alternatively solved until convergence, the detailed steps are as follows.

Algorithm 19 for Solving $\mathcal{P}^1$-4 and $\mathcal{P}^1$-5

1: **Initialization:**
Given $\mathbf{z}_m, \mathbf{f}_l$ and $\mathbf{c}$, Initialize $\mathbf{w}_k^{(0)}, \mathbf{S}^{(0)}, \mathbf{u}^{(0)}, \mathbf{f}_b^{(0)}$ into feasible values.
Set maximum number of iterations: N_{max} and n=0.
2: **Repeat**
3: Given $\mathbf{w}_k^{(n)}, \mathbf{S}^{(n)}, \mathbf{u}^{(n)}, \mathbf{f}_b^{(n)}$, update μ and υ by Eqs. (5.29a), (5.29b), (5.29c), (5.29d), (5.29e) and (5.29f), respectively.
4: Obtain $\mathbf{w}_k^{(n+1)}, \mathbf{S}^{(n+1)}$ and $\mathbf{f}_b^{(n+1)}$ by solving problem (5.36).
5: Obtain $\mathbf{u}^{(n+1)}$ by solving problem (5.37).
6: Set $n = n + 1$.
7: **Until:** $n = N_{max}$ or the objective of problem (5.22) converges.

5.2.2.1 Fix ($\mathbf{z}_m, \mathbf{f}_l, \mathbf{c}$) and Solve ($\mathbf{w}_k$,$\mathbf{S}$,$\mathbf{u}$,$\mathbf{f}_b$)

For given $\mathbf{z}_m, \mathbf{f}_l, \mathbf{c}$, we need to solve the information beamforming $\mathbf{w}_k$, the sensing covariance matrix $\mathbf{S}$, the sensing echo receiving beamforming $\mathbf{u}$ and the edge computing resources $\mathbf{f}_b$, and thus $\mathcal{P}^0$ can be reduced to the following subproblem

$$\mathcal{P}^1\text{-}1 : \max_{\mathbf{w}_k,\mathbf{S},\mathbf{u},\mathbf{f}_b} \tilde{R} + \sum_{m=1}^{M} \gamma_m^{cp} c_m R_{\mathrm{b},m} \tag{5.22}$$

$$s.t.\ \text{C1, C2, C3, C5, C7,} \tag{5.22a}$$

where $\tilde{R} = \gamma^r R^r + \sum_{k=1}^{K} \gamma_k^{cm} R_k{}^{cm} + \sum_{m=1}^{M} \gamma_m^{cp} c_m R_m^{cp}$.

Considering the complexity of logarithm in $\mathcal{P}^1$-1, we transform the objective function into a more tractable form by introducing auxiliary variables μ_0, μ_j^{cm}, μ_m^{cp}, as follows

$$\tilde{R} = \alpha^r + \frac{\chi^r r_0}{1+r_0} + \sum_{j=1}^{K} \left[\alpha_j^{cm} + \frac{\chi_j^{cm} r_j^{cm}}{1+r_j^{cm}} \right] \\ + \sum_{m=1}^{M} c_m \left[\alpha_m^{cp} + \frac{\chi_m^{cp} r_m^{cp}}{1+r_m^{cp}} \right], \tag{5.23}$$

where

$$\chi^r = \gamma^r (1+\mu_0), \tag{5.24a}$$

$$\alpha^r = \gamma^r \left[\log(1+\mu_0) - \mu_0 \right], \tag{5.24b}$$

$$\chi_j^{cm} = \gamma_j^{cm} \left(1+\mu_j^{cm}\right), \tag{5.24c}$$

$$\alpha_j^{cm} = \gamma_j^{cm} \left[\log\left(1+\mu_j^{cm}\right) - \mu_j^{cm} \right], \tag{5.24d}$$

$$\chi_m^{cp} = \gamma_m^{cp} \left(1+\mu_m^{cp}\right), \tag{5.24e}$$

$$\alpha_m^{cp} = \gamma_m^{cp} \left[\log\left(1+\mu_m^{cp}\right) - \mu_m^{cp} \right], \tag{5.24f}$$

Then, according to [5], the objective function (5.23) is further transformed by using the fractional programming method as follows

$$\frac{\chi^r r_0}{1+r_0} = \frac{\chi^r |A^r|^2}{B^r} = 2\sqrt{\chi^r} \Re \left\{ \upsilon_0^* A^r \right\} - \upsilon_0^* B^r \upsilon_0, \tag{5.25a}$$

$$\frac{\chi_j^{cm} r_j^{cm}}{1+r_j^{cm}} = \frac{\chi_j^{cm} \left| A_j^{cm} \right|^2}{B_j^{cm}} \\ = 2\sqrt{\chi_j^{cm}} \Re \left\{ (\upsilon_j^{cm})^* A_j^{cm} \right\} - (\upsilon_j^{cm})^* B_j^{cm} \upsilon_j^{cm}, \tag{5.25b}$$

$$\frac{\chi_m^{cp} r_m^{cp}}{1+r_m^{cp}} = \frac{\chi_m^{cp} |A_m^{cp}|^2}{B_m^{cp}} \\ = 2\sqrt{\chi_m^{cp}} \Re \left\{ (\upsilon_m^{cp})^* A_m^{cp} \right\} - (\upsilon_m^{cp})^* B_m^{cp} \upsilon_m^{cp}, \tag{5.25c}$$

where υ_0, υ_j^{cm}, υ_m^{cp} are auxiliary variables, and

$$A^r = \mathbf{u}^H \mathbf{H}^r \mathbf{x}, \tag{5.26a}$$

$$B^r = \left|\mathbf{u}^H \mathbf{H}^r \mathbf{x}\right|^2 + |\mathbf{u}|^2 \sigma_b^2, \tag{5.26b}$$

$$A_j^{cm} = \mathbf{h}_j^H \mathbf{w}_j, \tag{5.26c}$$

$$B_j^{cm} = \sum_{k \in \mathcal{K}} \left|\mathbf{h}_j^H \mathbf{w}_k\right|^2 + \mathbf{h}_j^H \mathbf{S} \mathbf{h}_j + \sigma_j^2,\ j \in \mathcal{K}, \tag{5.26d}$$

$$A_m^{cp} = \mathbf{z}_m^H \mathbf{g}_m \sqrt{P_m}, \tag{5.26e}$$

$$B_m^{cp} = \sum_{m' \in \mathcal{M}} P_m \left|\mathbf{z}_m^H \mathbf{g}_{m'}\right|^2 + \left|\mathbf{z}_m^H \mathbf{H}^r \mathbf{x}\right|^2 + \left|\mathbf{z}_m^H\right|^2 \sigma_b^2. \tag{5.26f}$$

Thus, $\mathcal{P}^1$-1 can be rewritten as

$$\mathcal{P}^1\text{-2:} \max_{\mathbf{w}_k, \mathbf{S}, \mathbf{u}, \mathbf{f}_b, \mu, \upsilon} g\left(\mathbf{w}_k, \mathbf{S}, \mathbf{u}, \mu, \upsilon\right) + \sum_{m=1}^{M} \gamma_m^{cp} c_m R_{\mathrm{b},m} \tag{5.27}$$

$$s.t.\ \text{C1, C2, C3, C5, C7} \tag{5.27a}$$

$$\text{C9: } \mu_0 \geq 0,\ \mu_j^{cm} \geq 0,\ \mu_m^{cp} \geq 0, \tag{5.27b}$$

where

$$\begin{aligned} & g\left(\mathbf{w}_k, \mathbf{S}, \mathbf{u}, \mu, \upsilon\right) \\ & = \alpha^r + 2\sqrt{\chi^r} \Re\left\{\upsilon_0^* A^r\right\} - \upsilon_0^* B^r \upsilon_0 \\ & + \sum_{j=1}^{K} \begin{bmatrix} \alpha_j^{cm} + 2\sqrt{\chi_j^{cm}} \Re\left\{(\upsilon_j^{cm})^* A_j^{cm}\right\} \\ - (\upsilon_j^{cm})^* B_j^{cm} \upsilon_j^{cm} \end{bmatrix} \\ & + \sum_{m=1}^{M} c_m \begin{bmatrix} \alpha_m^{cp} + 2\sqrt{\chi_m^{cp}} \Re\left\{(\upsilon_m^{cp})^* A_m^{cp}\right\} \\ - (\upsilon_m^{cp})^* B_m^{cp} \upsilon_m^{cp} \end{bmatrix}. \end{aligned} \tag{5.28}$$

Then, to deal with $\mathcal{P}^1$-2, we apply the alternate optimization algorithm.

1. Optimizing μ *and* υ
For fixed $\mathbf{w}_k, \mathbf{S}, \mathbf{u}, \mathbf{f}_b$, the optimal solution of μ, υ can be obtained by solving $\partial g/\partial \mu_0 = 0$, $\partial g/\partial \upsilon_0 = 0$, $\partial g/\partial \mu_j^{cm} = 0$, $\partial g/\partial \upsilon_j^{cm} = 0$, $\partial g/\partial \mu_m^{cp} = 0$, $\partial g/\partial \upsilon_m^{cp} = 0$, which can be respectively written as

$$\hat{\mu}_0 = r_0, \tag{5.29a}$$

$$\hat{\upsilon}_0 = \sqrt{\chi^r}(B^r)^{-1}A^r, \tag{5.29b}$$

$$\hat{\mu}_j^{cm} = r_j^{cm}, \tag{5.29c}$$

$$\hat{\upsilon}_j^{cm} = \sqrt{\chi_j^{cm}}(B_j^{cm})^{-1}A_j^{cm}, j \in \mathcal{K}, \tag{5.29d}$$

$$\hat{\mu}_m^{cp} = r_m^{cp}, \tag{5.29e}$$

$$\hat{\upsilon}_m^{cp} = \sqrt{\chi_m^{cp}}(B_m^{cp})^{-1}A_m^{cp}, m \in \mathcal{M}. \tag{5.29f}$$

2. Optimizing $\mathbf{w}_k$, $\mathbf{S}$ *and* $\mathbf{f}_b$
Based on the obtained μ, υ, $\mathbf{u}$, $\mathcal{P}^1$-2 can be reduced to

$$\mathcal{P}^1\text{-}3: \max_{\mathbf{w}_k,\mathbf{S},\mathbf{f}_b} \; g(\mathbf{w}_k, \mathbf{S}) + \sum_{m=1}^{M} \gamma_m^{cp} c_m R_{\mathrm{b},m} \tag{5.30}$$

$$s.t. \; \text{C1, C2, C3, C5, C7,} \tag{5.30a}$$

where

$$\begin{aligned} & g(\mathbf{w}_k, \mathbf{S}) \\ & = 2\sqrt{\chi_r}\Re\left\{\upsilon_0^*\mathbf{u}^H\mathbf{H}^r\left(\sum_{k=1}^{K}\mathbf{w}_k s_k^{cm} + \mathbf{s}_0^r\right)\right\} \\ & - \upsilon_0^*\left|\mathbf{u}^H\mathbf{H}^r\left(\sum_{k=1}^{K}\mathbf{w}_k s_k^{cm} + \mathbf{s}_0^r\right)\right|^2\upsilon_0 \\ & + \sum_{j=1}^{K}\begin{bmatrix} 2\sqrt{\chi_j^{cm}}\Re\left\{(\upsilon_j^{cm})^*\mathbf{h}_j^H\mathbf{w}_j\right\} \\ - (\upsilon_j^{cm})^*\left[\sum_{k\in\mathcal{K}}\left|\mathbf{h}_j^H\mathbf{w}_k\right|^2 + \mathbf{h}_j^H\mathbf{S}\mathbf{h}_j\right]\upsilon_j^{cm}\end{bmatrix} \\ & - \sum_{m=1}^{M} c_m\left[(\upsilon_m^{cp})^*\left|\mathbf{z}_m^H\mathbf{H}^r\left(\sum_{k=1}^{K}\mathbf{w}_k s_k^{cm} + \mathbf{s}_0^r\right)\right|^2\upsilon_m^{cp}\right], \end{aligned} \tag{5.31}$$

then, we transform $g(\mathbf{w}_k, \mathbf{S})$ into the following form

$$2\Re\left\{\upsilon_0^* \mathbf{u}^H \mathbf{H}^r \left(\sum_{k=1}^{K} \mathbf{w}_k s_k^{cm} + \mathbf{s}_0^r\right)\right\} = \text{Tr}\left(\Psi_0 \left(\sum_{k=1}^{K} \tilde{\mathbf{W}}_k + \tilde{\mathbf{S}}\right)\right), \tag{5.32a}$$

$$\upsilon_0^* \left|\mathbf{u}^H \mathbf{H}^r \left(\sum_{k=1}^{K} \mathbf{w}_k s_k^{cm} + \mathbf{s}_0^r\right)\right|^2 \upsilon_0 = \text{Tr}\left(|\upsilon_0|^2 (\mathbf{H}^r)^H \mathbf{U} \mathbf{H}^r \left(\sum_{k=1}^{K} \mathbf{W}_k + \mathbf{S}\right)\right), \tag{5.32b}$$

$$2\Re\left\{(\upsilon_j^{cm})^* \mathbf{h}_j^H \mathbf{w}_j\right\} = \text{Tr}\left(\Psi_j \tilde{\mathbf{W}}_j\right), \tag{5.32c}$$

$$(\upsilon_j^{cm})^* \left[\sum_{k\in\mathcal{K}} \left|\mathbf{h}_j^H \mathbf{w}_k\right|^2 + \mathbf{h}_j^H \mathbf{S} \mathbf{h}_j\right] \upsilon_j^{cm} = \text{Tr}\left(\left|\upsilon_j^{cm}\right|^2 \mathbf{h}_j \mathbf{h}_j^H \left(\sum_{k=1}^{K} \mathbf{W}_k + \mathbf{S}\right)\right), \tag{5.32d}$$

$$\sum_{m=1}^{M} \left[-(\upsilon_m^{cp})^* \left|\mathbf{z}_m^H \mathbf{H}^r \left(\sum_{k=1}^{K} \mathbf{w}_k s_k^{cm} + \mathbf{s}_0^r\right)\right|^2 \upsilon_m^{cp}\right]$$
$$= \sum_{m=1}^{M} \text{Tr}\left[-|\upsilon_m^{cp}|^2 (\mathbf{H}^r)^H \mathbf{z}_m \mathbf{z}_m^H \mathbf{H}^r \left(\sum_{k=1}^{K} \mathbf{W}_k + \mathbf{S}\right)\right], \tag{5.32e}$$

where $\mathbf{W}_k = \mathbf{w}_k \mathbf{w}_k^H$, $\tilde{\mathbf{W}}_k = \tilde{\mathbf{w}}_k \tilde{\mathbf{w}}_k^H$, $\mathbf{U} = \mathbf{u}\mathbf{u}^H$, and

$$\Psi_0 = \begin{bmatrix} 0 & (\upsilon_0^* \mathbf{u}^H \mathbf{H}^r)^H \\ \upsilon_0^* \mathbf{u}^H \mathbf{H}^r & 0 \end{bmatrix}, \tag{5.33a}$$

$$\Psi_j = \begin{bmatrix} 0 & ((\upsilon_j^{cm})^* \mathbf{h}_j^H)^H \\ (\upsilon_j^{cm})^* \mathbf{h}_j^H & 0 \end{bmatrix}, \tilde{\mathbf{w}}_k = \begin{bmatrix} \mathbf{w}_k \\ 1 \end{bmatrix}. \tag{5.33b}$$

Similarly to problem (5.23), based on the Lagrangian dual transformation and the quadratic transformation, we can reform constraint C5 as follows

$$(1 - c_m) E_{l,m} + c_m E_{o,m} \le E_m^{\max} \Leftrightarrow$$
$$\frac{l_m P_m}{E_m^{\max} - (1 - c_m) E_{l,m}} - c_m \tilde{R}_m^{cp}(\mathbf{W}, \mathbf{S}) \le 0, \tag{5.34}$$

Algorithm 20 Algorithm for Solving $\mathcal{P}^2$-2

1: **Initialization:**
Given $\mathbf{w}_k$, $\mathbf{S}$, $\mathbf{u}$, $\mathbf{f}_b$, $\mathbf{f}_l$, $\mathbf{c}$, Initialize $\mathbf{z}_m^{(0)}$ into feasible values.
Set maximum number of iterations: Q_{max} and q=0.
2: **Repeat**
3: Given $\mathbf{z}_m^{(q)}$, update $p(m)$ by Eq. (5.51).
4: Initialize Lagrange multipliers $\{\theta_m(0)\}_{m\in\mathcal{M}}$, $\{\omega_m(0)\}_{m\in\mathcal{M}}$,
set $i = 0$ and maximum number of iterations: I_{max}.
5: **Repeat**
6: Obtain the optimal $\mathbf{z}_m^{(opt)}$ by solving (5.47).
7: Update Lagrange multipliers $\{\theta_m(i+1)\}_{m\in\mathcal{M}}$, $\{\omega_m(i+1)\}_{m\in\mathcal{M}}$
by solving Eqs. (5.52), (5.52).
8: Set $i = i + 1$.
9: **Until:** $i = I_{max}$ or the objective function of problem (5.43) converges.
10: Denote the optimal solution of problem (5.40) by $\mathbf{z}_m^{(q+1)}$.
11: Set $q = q + 1$.
12: **Until:** $q = Q_{max}$ or the objective function of problem (5.21) converges.

where

$$\begin{aligned}\tilde{R}_m^{cp}(\mathbf{W},\mathbf{S}) &= \tilde{\alpha}_m^{cp} + 2\sqrt{\tilde{\chi}_m^{cp}}\,\Re\left\{(\upsilon_m^{cp})^* A_m^{cp}\right\}\\ &- (\upsilon_m^{cp})^*\left(\sum_{m'\in\mathcal{M}} P_u\left|\mathbf{z}_m^H\mathbf{g}_{m'}\right|^2 + \sigma_b^2\left|\mathbf{z}_m^H\right|^2\right)\upsilon_m^{cp}\\ &- \sum_{m=1}^{M}\mathrm{Tr}\left[\upsilon_m^{cp}(\upsilon_m^{cp})^H(\mathbf{H}^r)^H\mathbf{z}_m\mathbf{z}_m^H\mathbf{H}^r\left(\sum_{k=1}^{K}\mathbf{W}_k+\mathbf{S}\right)\right],\end{aligned} \tag{5.35}$$

and $\tilde{\alpha}_m^{cp} = \log\left(1+\mu_m^{cp}\right) - \mu_m^{cp}$, $\tilde{\chi}_m^{cp} = 1 + \mu_m^{cp}$.

Finally, $\mathcal{P}^1$-3 is reformulated as

$$\begin{aligned}\mathcal{P}^1\text{-4}:\ \max_{\tilde{\mathbf{W}}_k,\,\tilde{\mathbf{S}},\,\tilde{\mathbf{f}}_b}\ &\mathrm{Tr}\left(\Psi_0\left(\sum_{k=1}^{K}\tilde{\mathbf{W}}_k+\tilde{\mathbf{S}}\right)\right)\\ &- \mathrm{Tr}\left(|\upsilon_0|^2(\mathbf{H}^r)^H\mathbf{U}\mathbf{H}^r\left(\sum_{k=1}^{K}\mathbf{W}_k+\mathbf{S}\right)\right)\\ &+\sum_{j=1}^{K}\left[\begin{array}{l}\sqrt{\chi_j^{cm}}\,\mathrm{Tr}\left(\Psi_j\tilde{\mathbf{W}}_j\right)\\ -\mathrm{Tr}\left(\left|\upsilon_j^{cm}\right|^2\mathbf{h}_j\mathbf{h}_j^H\left(\sum_{k=1}^{K}\mathbf{W}_k+\mathbf{S}\right)\right)\end{array}\right]\end{aligned} \tag{5.36}$$

$$-\sum_{m=1}^{M} c_m \mathrm{Tr}\left[\left|\upsilon_m^{cp}\right|^2 (\mathbf{H}^r)^H \mathbf{z}_m \mathbf{z}_m^H \mathbf{H}^r \left(\sum_{k=1}^{K} \mathbf{W}_k + \mathbf{S}\right)\right]$$

$$+\sum_{m=1}^{M} \gamma_m^{cp} c_m R_{\mathrm{b},m}$$

$$s.t.\ \mathrm{C1}: \sum_{k=1}^{K} \mathbf{tr}(\mathbf{W}_k) + \mathbf{tr}\,(\mathbf{S}) + \sum_{m}^{M} \kappa c_m f_{b,m}^3 \leq \mathrm{P}_b\,, \tag{5.36a}$$

$$\mathrm{C7}: \sum_{m=1}^{M} f_{b,m} \leq f_b, \tag{5.36b}$$

$$\mathrm{C10}: \frac{l_m P_m}{E_m^{\max} - (1 - c_m)\, E_{l,m}} - c_m \tilde{R}_m^{cp}\,(\mathbf{W}, \mathbf{S}) \leq 0\,, \tag{5.36c}$$

$$\mathrm{C11}: \left[\tilde{\mathbf{W}}_k\right]_{N_s+1, N_s+1} = 1, k \in \mathcal{K}, \tag{5.36d}$$

$$\mathrm{C12}: \left[\tilde{\mathbf{S}}\right]_{N_s+1, N_s+1} = 1, \tag{5.36e}$$

$$\mathrm{C13}: \tilde{\mathbf{W}}_k \succeq 0, k \in \mathcal{K}, \tilde{\mathbf{S}} \succeq 0\,, \tag{5.36f}$$

$$\mathrm{C14}: \mathrm{rank}\left(\tilde{\mathbf{W}}_k\right) = 1\,. \tag{5.36g}$$

Due to the rank-one constraints, $\mathcal{P}^1$-4 is still intractable. Next, we apply the SDR technique to obtain the solution by removing the rank-one constraint C14. If the optimal solution $\tilde{\mathbf{W}}_k$ of the problem satisfies the rank-one condition, we can directly use the eigenvalue decomposition to obtain the feasible $\mathbf{w}_k$. Otherwise, Gaussian randomization techniques can be used to obtain an approximate solution [6, 7].

3. Optimizing $\mathbf{u}$
Based on the obtained μ, υ, $\mathbf{w}_k$, $\mathbf{S}$, $\mathbf{f}_b$, $\mathcal{P}^1$-2 can be reduced to

$$\mathcal{P}^1\text{-5}: \min_{\mathbf{u}}\ \mathbf{u}^H \mathbf{Y} \mathbf{u} - 2\sqrt{\chi^r} \Re\left\{\mathbf{u}^H \mathbf{q}\right\} \tag{5.37}$$

$$s.t.\ \mathrm{C3}, \tag{5.37a}$$

where

$$\mathbf{Y} = \upsilon_0^* \upsilon_0 \mathbf{H}^r \mathbf{x} \mathbf{x}^H \left(\mathbf{H}^r\right)^H + \upsilon_0^* \upsilon_0 \sigma_b^2 \mathbf{I}_{Nr}, \tag{5.38}$$

$$\mathbf{q} = \upsilon_0^* \mathbf{H}^r \mathbf{x}, \tag{5.39}$$

we can solve $\mathcal{P}^1$-5 directly using the CVX toolbox.

For fixed $\mathbf{z}_m$, $\mathbf{f}_l$, $\mathbf{c}$, the optimal solutions of $\mathbf{w}_k$, $\mathbf{S}$, $\mathbf{f}_b$ and $\mathbf{u}$ are obtained by solving $\mathcal{P}^1$-4 and $\mathcal{P}^1$-5, and the detailed procedure is summarized in Algorithm 19.

5.2.2.2 Fix ($\mathbf{w}_k$, $\mathbf{S}$, $\mathbf{u}$, $\mathbf{f}_b$, $\mathbf{f}_l$, $\mathbf{c}$) and Solve $\mathbf{z}_m$

For given $\mathbf{w}_k$, $\mathbf{S}$, $\mathbf{u}$, $\mathbf{f}_b$, $\mathbf{f}_l$, $\mathbf{c}$, $\mathcal{P}^0$ can be reformulated as

$$\mathcal{P}^2\text{-1} : \max_{\mathbf{z}_m} \sum_{m=1}^{M} \gamma_m^{cp} c_m R_m^{cp} \tag{5.40}$$

$$s.t.\ \text{C4, C5}. \tag{5.40a}$$

Next, we apply the minimum mean square error (MMSE)-based algorithm to solve the objective function [8]. The mean square error (MSE) matrix of CP-UE m can be expressed as

$$\begin{aligned} e_m =& \mathbb{E}\left[\left(\hat{s}_m^{cp} - s_m^{cp}\right)\left(\hat{s}_m^{cp} - s_m^{cp}\right)^H\right] \\ =& \left|\mathbf{z}_m^H \mathbf{g}_m \sqrt{P_u} - 1\right|^2 + \sum_{m' \neq m} P_u \left|\mathbf{z}_m^H \mathbf{g}_{m'}\right|^2 \\ &+ \left|\mathbf{z}_m^H \mathbf{H}^r \mathbf{x}\right|^2 + \sigma_b^2 \|\mathbf{z}_m\|^2. \end{aligned} \tag{5.41}$$

By using e_m and introducing a set of auxiliary variables $\{p_m \geq 0 | \forall m \in \mathcal{M}\}$, R_m^{cp} can be equivalently recast as

$$\tilde{R}_m^{cp} = \frac{B}{\ln 2}\left(\ln(p_m) - p_m e_m + 1\right), \tag{5.42}$$

Thus, $\mathcal{P}^2$-1 can be reformulated as

$$\mathcal{P}^2\text{-2} : \max_{\mathbf{z}_m, \mathbf{p}} \sum_{m=1}^{M} \gamma_m^{cp} c_m \tilde{R}_m^{cp} \tag{5.43}$$

$$s.t.\ \text{C4},\ p_m \geq 0, \forall m \in \mathcal{M}, \tag{5.43a}$$

$$\breve{C}5 : \frac{l_m P_m}{E_m^{\max} - (1 - c_m) E_{l,m}} - c_m \tilde{R}_m^{cp} \leq 0, \tag{5.43b}$$

where $\mathbf{p} = [p_1, \cdots, p_M]$. It can be proved that $\mathcal{P}^2$-2 is convex and satisfies the Slater's condition [9]. Therefore, the dual gap between $\mathcal{P}^2$-2 and its dual problem is 0. Next, we apply the Lagrangian dual method to solve $\mathcal{P}^2$-2. The Lagrangian equation of the problem (5.43) is expressed as

$$\begin{aligned}&\mathcal{L}\left(\mathbf{z}_m,\mathbf{p},\omega,\theta\right)\\&=\sum_{m=1}^{M}\gamma_m^{cp}c_m\tilde{R}_m^{cp}-\sum_{m=1}^{M}\theta_m\left(\mathbf{z}_m^H\mathbf{I}\mathbf{z}_m-1\right)\\&-\sum_{m=1}^{M}\omega_m\left(\frac{l_mP_m}{E_m^{\max}-(1-c_m)E_{l,m}}-c_m\tilde{R}_m^{cp}\right),\end{aligned}\tag{5.44}$$

where $\theta=\{\theta_m\}_{m\in\mathcal{M}}\succeq 0$, $\omega=\{\omega_m\}_{m\in\mathcal{M}}\succeq 0$ are Lagrangian multipliers associated with constraints C4, and $\breve{C}5$, respectively.

Thus, the dual function is expressed as

$$\Gamma\left(\omega,\theta\right)=\max_{\mathbf{z}_m,\mathbf{p}}\mathcal{L}\left(\mathbf{z}_m,\mathbf{p},\omega,\theta\right),\tag{5.45}$$

and the dual problem is given by

$$\min_{\omega,\theta}\ \Gamma\left(\omega,\theta\right)\tag{5.46}$$

$$s.t\ \omega_m\geq 0,\theta_m\geq 0.\tag{5.46a}$$

The objective function in (5.46) is differentiable, and the dual problem exhibits convexity with respect to the dual variables. Consequently, we can employ either the sub-gradient projection method or Newton's method to solve it. We can obtain the optimal solution by setting $\partial\mathcal{L}/\partial\mathbf{z}_m=0$, which can be expressed as

$$\hat{\mathbf{z}}_m=\frac{\mathbf{g}_m\sqrt{P_u}A}{\left(A\Delta+\theta_m\mathbf{I}_{Nr}\right)},\tag{5.47}$$

where A and Δ is expressed as

$$A=\frac{B}{\ln 2}\left(\gamma_m^{cp}p_m+\omega_mp_m\right)c_m,\tag{5.48}$$

$$\Delta=\sum_{m\in\mathcal{M}}\mathbf{g}_m\mathbf{g}_m^HP_u+\mathbf{H}^r\left(\sum_{k=1}^{K}\mathbf{W}_k+\mathbf{S}\right)\left(\mathbf{H}^r\right)^H+\sigma_b^2\mathbf{I}_{Nr}.\tag{5.49}$$

Proof According to the expression of $\mathcal{L}\left(\mathbf{z}_m,\mathbf{p},\omega,\theta\right)$, the first-order derivative of $\mathcal{L}$ w.r.t $\mathbf{z}_m$ can be given, the derivative process can be formulated as

$$\frac{\partial\mathcal{L}}{\partial z_m}=\gamma_m^{cp}c_m\frac{\partial\tilde{R}_m^{cp}}{\partial z_m}-2\theta_m\mathbf{z}_m+\omega_mc_m\frac{\partial\tilde{R}_m^{cp}}{\partial z_m}\tag{5.50}$$

$$= -\frac{B}{\ln 2}\gamma_m^{cp} c_m p_m \frac{\partial e_m}{\partial z_m} - 2\theta_m \mathbf{z}_m - \frac{B}{\ln 2}\omega_m c_m p_m \frac{\partial e_m}{\partial z_m}$$

$$= -\frac{B}{\ln 2}\left(\gamma_m^{cp} c_m + \omega_m c_m\right) p_m \left(2 \sum_{m \in \mathcal{M}} P_u \mathbf{g}_m \mathbf{g}_m^H \mathbf{z}_m\right.$$

$$\left. - 2\mathbf{g}_m \sqrt{P_u} + 2\mathbf{H}^r \left(\sum_{k=1}^{K} \mathbf{W}_k + \mathbf{S}\right) \left(\mathbf{H}^r\right)^H \mathbf{z}_m + \sigma_b^2 \mathbf{z}_m\right) - 2\theta_m \mathbf{z}_m$$

$$= -A\left(2\Delta \mathbf{z}_m - 2\mathbf{g}_m \sqrt{P_u}\right) - 2\theta_m \mathbf{z}_m$$

Then, we have $-A\left(2\Delta \mathbf{z}_m - 2\mathbf{g}_m \sqrt{P_u}\right) - 2\theta_m \mathbf{z}_m = 0$. By solving the equation, the optimal can be expressed as Eqs. (5.47). □

Similarly, we can obtain the optimal solution of auxiliary variables $p(m)$ as

$$\hat{p}_m = e_m^{-1}, \forall m \in \mathcal{M}. \tag{5.51}$$

Considering the convex nature of the dual problem, we can update the Lagrangian multipliers by using the sub-gradient method. The iterative update process proceeds as follows

$$\theta_m(r+1) = \left[\theta_m(r) - t_r^{(\theta_m)}\left(\mathbf{z}_m^H \mathbf{I} \mathbf{z}_m - 1\right)\right]^+, \tag{5.52}$$

$$\omega_m(r+1) = \left[\omega_m(r) - t_r^{(\omega_m)}\left(\frac{l_m P_m}{E_m^{\max} - (1 - c_m) E_{l,m}} - c_m \tilde{R}_m^{cp}\right)\right]^+, \tag{5.53}$$

where r represents the iteration index, $t_r^{(\cdot)}$ is the step size of the dual variable obtained at the r-th iteration, and $[k]^+ = \max\{0, k\}$. By iteratively optimizing $\mathbf{z}_m$ and $\mathbf{p}$ in (5.47), and (5.51), and updating $\theta = \{\theta_m\}_{m \in \mathcal{M}}$, $\omega = \{\omega_m\}_{m \in \mathcal{M}}$ according to (5.52), (5.53), using the dual gradient method with zero dual gap, the optimal solution of problem (5.40) can be obtained. The overall algorithm to solve $\mathcal{P}^1$-4 is summarized in Algorithm 20.

5.2.2.3 Fix ($\mathbf{w}_k$, $\mathbf{S}$, $\mathbf{u}$, $\mathbf{z}_m$, $\mathbf{f}_b$, $\mathbf{c}$) and Solve $\mathbf{f}_l$

For given $\mathbf{w}_k$, $\mathbf{S}$, $\mathbf{u}$, $\mathbf{z}_m$, $\mathbf{f}_b$, $\mathbf{c}$, $\mathcal{P}^0$ can be reformulated as

$$\mathcal{P}^3\text{-}1 : \max_{\mathbf{f}_l} \sum_{m=1}^{M} \gamma_m^{cp} (1 - c_m) \frac{f_{l,m}}{\varepsilon_{l,m}} \tag{5.54}$$

$$s.t.\ 0 \le f_{l,m} \le f_{l,m}^{\max}, \tag{5.54a}$$

where $f_{l,m}^{\max}$ is derived from constraint C5, expressed as

$$f_{l,m}^{\max} = (1 - c_m)\sqrt{\frac{E_m^{\max}}{\sigma l_m \varepsilon_{l,m}}}, \tag{5.55}$$

It is evident that $\mathcal{P}^3$-1 for the variable $\mathbf{f}_l$ is convex. Since the objective function of problem (5.54) increases monotonically with $f_{l,m}$, $m \in \mathcal{M}$, in order to decouple the objective function and constraints, the problem $\mathcal{P}^3$-1 can be decomposed into M subproblems. We can be concluded that the optimal $f_{l,m}$ takes its upper bound, and the optimal value is

$$\hat{f}_{l,m} = f_{l,m}^{\max}. \tag{5.56}$$

Algorithm 21 Proposed joint alternative optimization algorithm

1: **Initialization:**
Given the feasible solution of $\mathbf{w}_k^{(0)}, \mathbf{S}^{(0)}, \mathbf{u}^{(0)}, \mathbf{z}_m^{(0)}, \mathbf{f}_b^{(0)}, \mathbf{f}_l^{(0)}, \mathbf{c}^{(0)}$.
Set maximum number of iterations: T_{max} and t=0.
2: **Repeat**
3: Set $t = t + 1$.
4: **For** $m \in \mathcal{M}$
5: Update $c^t(m)$ by Eq. (5.57).
6: Compute $\Lambda\left(c^t(m)\right)$ by Algorithm 19, Algorithm 20 and Eq. (5.56).
7: **EndFor**
8: Let $(m^t)^* = \arg\max_{m\in\mathcal{M}} \Lambda\left(c^t(m)\right)$.
9: Let $c^t = c^t((m^t)^*)$.
10: **Until:** $t = T_{max}$ or the objective function of problem (5.21) converges.
11: **Return:** $\hat{\mathbf{w}}_k, \hat{\mathbf{S}}, \hat{\mathbf{u}}, \hat{\mathbf{z}}_m, \hat{\mathbf{f}}_b, \hat{\mathbf{f}}_l, \hat{\mathbf{c}}$ and $\hat{\Lambda}$.

5.2.2.4 Fix ($\mathbf{w}_k, \mathbf{S}, \mathbf{u}, \mathbf{z}_m, \mathbf{f}_b, \mathbf{f}_l$) and Solve c

Here, using the obtained information beamforming, sensing covariance matrix, sensing echo receiving beamforming, offloading signal receiving beamforming, local computing resources, and edge computing resources, we apply the CD method to continuously optimize **c** to obtain a local optimal solution [10]. Specifically, given an initial c^0, we denote c^t as the computation mode selection at the t-th iteration. In addition, $c^t(m)$ denotes the computation mode selection after the m-th CP-UE swaps its current mode,i,e.,

$$c^t(m) = \left[c_1^t, c_2^t, \cdots, c_m^t \oplus 1, \cdots, c_M^t\right], m \in \mathcal{M}, \tag{5.57}$$

where $\oplus$ is the modulo-2 summation operation.

Let $\Lambda\left(c^t\right)$ denote the optimal WSR of $\mathcal{P}^1$ with given c^t, and the computation mode selection at the t-th iteration c^t is determined by the CP-UE that achieves the highest WSR after exchanging computing modes, i.e., $c^t = c^t((m^t)^*)$, where $(m^t)^* = \arg\max_{m\in\mathcal{M}}\Lambda\left(c^t\left(m\right)\right)$.

5.2.2.5 Algorithm Convergence and Optimality

The overall scheme for solving $\mathcal{P}^0$ is summarized in Algorithm 21, which is based on the CD method and iteratively optimizes information beamforming, sensing covariance matrix, sensing echo receiving beamforming, offloading signal receiving beamforming, local computing resources and edge computing resources until convergence.

Since Algorithm 21 is solved based on CD, i.e., its outer loop is the CD method, and its convergence can be guaranteed [11]. Therefore we only focus on the convergence of methods for optimizing $\{\mathbf{w}_k, \mathbf{S}, \mathbf{u}, \mathbf{f}_b\}$, $\{\mathbf{z}_m\}$ and $\{\mathbf{f}_l\}$.

Theorem 5.1 *The convergence of Algorithm 21 can be guaranteed.*

Proof In order to prove the convergence of Algorithm 21, we need to prove that after each loop iteration, when the optimization variables $(\mathbf{w}_k, \mathbf{S}, \mathbf{u}, \mathbf{z}_m, \mathbf{f}_b, \mathbf{f}_l, \mathbf{c})$ are updated, the value of the objective function of problem $\mathcal{P}^0$ does not decrease. According to Algorithm 21, we have

$$
\begin{aligned}
&V_{obj}^{(r-1)} = \\
&V\left(\mathbf{w}_k^{(r-1)}, \mathbf{S}^{(r-1)}, \mathbf{u}^{(r-1)}, \mathbf{f}_b^{(r-1)}, \mathbf{z}_m^{(r-1)}, \mathbf{f}_l^{(r-1)}, \mathbf{c}^{(r-1)}\right)\\
&\overset{(I)}{\leq} V\left(\mathbf{c}^{(r)}, \mathbf{w}_k^{(r-1)}, \mathbf{S}^{(r-1)}, \mathbf{u}^{(r-1)}, \mathbf{f}_b^{(r-1)}, \mathbf{z}_m^{(r-1)}, \mathbf{f}_l^{(r-1)}\right)\\
&\overset{(II)}{\leq} V\left(\mathbf{c}^{(r)}, \mathbf{w}_k^{(r)}, \mathbf{S}^{(r)}, \mathbf{u}^{(r)}, \mathbf{f}_b^{(r)}, \mathbf{z}_m^{(r-1)}, \mathbf{f}_l^{(r-1)}\right)\\
&\overset{(III)}{\leq} V\left(\mathbf{c}^{(r)}, \mathbf{w}_k^{(r)}, \mathbf{S}^{(r)}, \mathbf{u}^{(r)}, \mathbf{f}_b^{(r)}, \mathbf{z}_m^{(r)}, \mathbf{f}_l^{(r-1)}\right)\\
&\overset{(IV)}{\leq} V\left(\mathbf{c}^{(r)}, \mathbf{w}_k^{(r)}, \mathbf{S}^{(r)}, \mathbf{u}^{(r)}, \mathbf{f}_b^{(r)}, \mathbf{z}_m^{(r)}, \mathbf{f}_l^{(r)}\right)\\
&\overset{(V)}{=} V_{obj}^{(r)}.
\end{aligned}
\tag{5.58}
$$

Inequality (I) holds since $\mathbf{c}^{(r)}$ is the optimal computation strategy based on CD method, using fixed $\mathbf{w}_k^{(r)}$, $\mathbf{S}^{(r)}$, $\mathbf{u}^{(r)}$, $\mathbf{f}_b^{(r)}$, $\mathbf{z}_m^{(r)}$, $\mathbf{f}_l^{(r)}$. Inequality (II) is derived from the fact that $\mathbf{w}_k^{(r)}$, $\mathbf{S}^{(r)}$, $\mathbf{u}^{(r)}$, $\mathbf{f}_b^{(r)}$ is the optimal information beamforming, sensing covariance matrix, sensing echo receiving beamforming and edge computing resources allocation for Algorithm 19, with $\mathbf{z}_m^{(r-1)}$, $\mathbf{f}_l^{(r-1)}$, $\mathbf{c}^{(r)}$ fixed. Inequality

(III) holds since $\mathbf{z}_m^{(r)}$ is the optimal offloading signal receiving beamforming of Algorithm 20, with $\mathbf{w}_k^{(r)}, \mathbf{S}^{(r)}, \mathbf{u}^{(r)}, \mathbf{f}_b^{(r)}, \mathbf{f}_l^{(r-1)}, \mathbf{c}^{(r)}$ being fixed. Inequality (IV) holds since $\mathbf{f}_l^{(r)}$ is the optimal local computing resource allocation of problem (56), using fixed $\mathbf{w}_k^{(r)}$, $\mathbf{S}^{(r)}$, $\mathbf{u}^{(r)}$, $\mathbf{f}_b^{(r)}$, $\mathbf{z}_m^{(r)}$, $\mathbf{c}^{(r)}$. Finally, according to equation (V), we know that the objective function value of problem (21) does not decrease after optimizing variables in each iteration, thus proves the convergence of Algorithm 21. □

Note that each sub-problem in the proposed Algorithm 19 is convex and guarantees a KKT solution, so the maximum WSR of Algorithm 19 increases monotonically. Due to the limited power of the BS, WSR will converge to a locally optimal solution. For Algorithm 20, since its objective value is the upper-bound by the maximum transmission energy, and each variable is updated in a closed-form for iteration without decreasing, it is guaranteed that WSR converges to a locally optimal solution. The outer loop of Algorithm 21 is based on CD algorithm, and a locally optimal solution can also be obtained [10]. Therefore, it can be guaranteed that the final solution obtained is the locally optimal at least.

5.2.3 Performance Evaluation

In this section, we present numerical results to evaluate the performance of the proposed scheme. We consider a mmWave multiple-input multiple-output (MIMO) channel model as follows [12]:

$$\mathbf{H}_k = \sqrt{\frac{N_r N_s}{L_k}} \sum_{l=1}^{L_k} \alpha_k^{(l)} \mathbf{a}_r\left(\vartheta_k^{(l)}\right) \mathbf{a}_s^H\left(\varphi_k^{(l)}\right), \tag{5.59}$$

where L_k represents the number of paths for the k-th user, and $\alpha_k^{(l)}$ represents the complex gain of the l-th path, $\vartheta_k^{(l)}, \varphi_k^{(l)}$ respectively represent the angle of arrival (AOA) and angle of departure (AOD) of the l-th path. $\mathbf{a}_r\left(\vartheta_k^{(l)}\right)$ and $\mathbf{a}_s\left(\varphi_k^{(l)}\right)$ represent the N_r-dimensional receive steering vector of the l-th path and the N_s-dimensional transmit steering vector of the l-th path respectively. For the ULA with N elements, the steering vector can be expressed as $\mathbf{a}_{ULA}(\vartheta) = \sqrt{\frac{1}{N}} \exp\left(0, \cdots, j2\pi (N-1) \frac{d}{\lambda} \sin(\vartheta)\right)^T$, where d represent the antenna spacing, and λ represents the signal wavelength. Since all users are equipped with a single antenna, for CM-UEs, the channel can be expressed as $\mathbf{h}_k = \sqrt{\frac{N_s}{L_k}} \sum_{l=1}^{L_k} \alpha_k^{(l)} \mathbf{a}_s\left(\varphi_k^{(l)}\right)$, and for CP-UEs, the channel can be expressed as $\mathbf{g}_m = \sqrt{\frac{N_r}{L_m}} \sum_{l=1}^{L_m} \alpha_m^{(l)} \mathbf{a}_r\left(\vartheta_m^{(l)}\right)$.

For all users, we assume $L = 3$, which includes one line-of-sight (LOS) component and two non-line-of-sight (NLoS) components. For all l, we assume

Table 5.1 System parameters

Variable	Description	Value
N_s	Number of transmit antennas at BS	4
N_r	Number of receive antennas at BS	4
K	Number of CM-UEs	4
M	Number of CP-UEs	4
σ_b^2	Noise variance	−80 dBm
σ_u^2	Noise variance	−80 dBm
B	Bandwidth	10 MHz
P_b	Maximum transmit power of BS	30 dBm
P_u	Transmit power of CP-UEs	15 dBm
ε_b	Complexity of computation tasks of BS	500 cycles/bit
$\varepsilon_{l,m}$	Complexity of computation tasks of CP-UE	350 cycles/bit
f_b	CPU frequency of BS	8 GHz
$E_m^{\max}$	The maximum energy budget for CP-UE m	0.04 J
σ	Constants related to hardware architecture	10^{-26}
κ	Calculate power factor	10^{-26}

the complex gains $\alpha_k^{(1)}$ and $\alpha_m^{(1)}$ follow the complex Gaussian distribution with zero mean. For $2 \le l \le L$, $\varphi_k^{(l)}$ and $\vartheta_m^{(l)}$ obey the uniform distribution $\mathcal{U}\left(-\frac{\pi}{2}, \frac{\pi}{2}\right)$.

The main simulation parameters are summarized in Table 5.1. In addition, we assume that the BS is equipped with a ULA and half-wavelength spacing, the sensing target is set to be 50 m away from the BS, the CM-UEs are at an equal distance of 60 m from the BS, and the CP-UEs are randomly distributed in an area with (0, 0) m as the center and radius 5–65 m. The path loss model for all channels is $PL\,(\text{dB}) = 30 + 30\log_{10}(d)$, where d represents the distance from the transmitter to the receiver.

The following scenarios are considered as baselines:

- Locally only: Each CP-UE executes its task only by its on-chip processor.
- Fully offloading: Each CP-UE offloads all its tasks to the edge server for computing.

Figure 5.2 shows the convergence of the proposed algorithm under different number of transmit antennas at the BS. One can observe that the WSR first increases, then quickly stablizes and reaches a maximum value after three iterations, which shows the effectiveness of the proposed algorithm. In addition, increasing the number of transmit antennas at the BS can effectively enhance the WSR, which is intuitively understandable.

Figure 5.3 depicts the relationship between WSR and the maximum transmit power budget (Pb) of the BS, it can be observed that the WSR of all schemes increase with Pb, because there are more resources available for computation at the BS, and the BS can provide stronger beamforming for downlink communication

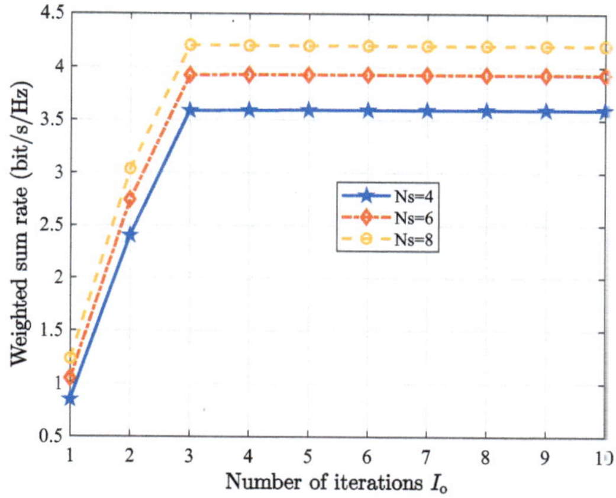

Fig. 5.2 Weighted sum rate versus the number of iterations

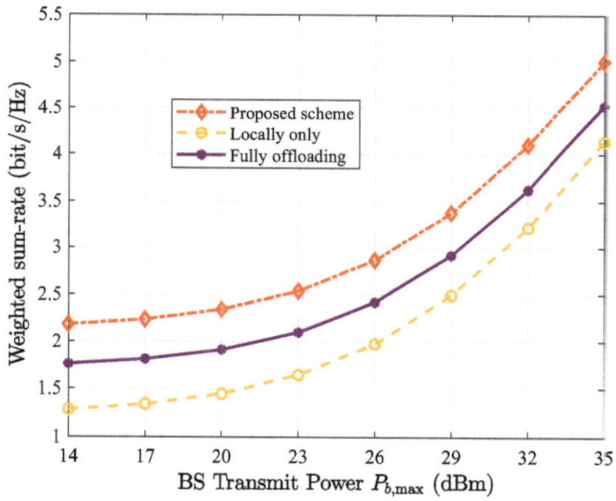

Fig. 5.3 Weighted sum rate versus the BS transmit power P_b

and target sensing. Meanwhile, it can be found that the performance obtained by the proposed scheme is always better than the others.

Figure 5.4 shows the relationship between WSR and the CP-UE's maximum power budget. One can see from the figure that as the maximum power budget increases, both the proposed scheme and full offloading scheme can obtain a higher WSR. When the maximum power budget is relatively small, the proposed scheme obtains the same performance as the locally only scheme, and when the maximum power budget gradually increases, the performance of the proposed scheme gradually converges to that of the fully offloading scheme. This can be explained by the fact that the increase of the CP-UE's maximum power budget can improve the offloading rate. In addition, it can be found that the WSR of the locally only scheme is not affected by the maximum power budget and remains stable.

Figure 5.5 shows the relationship between WSR and the number of CP-UE. We can find that the WSR obtained by all schemes increases as the number of CP-UE increases. When the number of CP-UE is small, the proposed scheme obtains the same performance as the fully offloading scheme. When the number of CP-UEs

Fig. 5.4 Weighted sum rate versus the CP-UE transmit power P_m

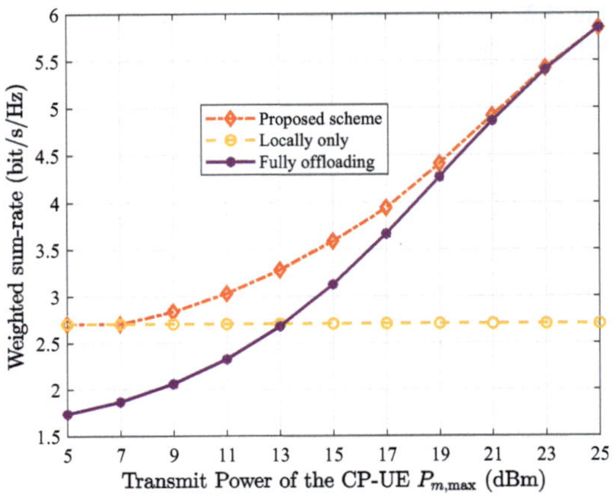

Fig. 5.5 Weighted sum rate versus the number of CP-UE

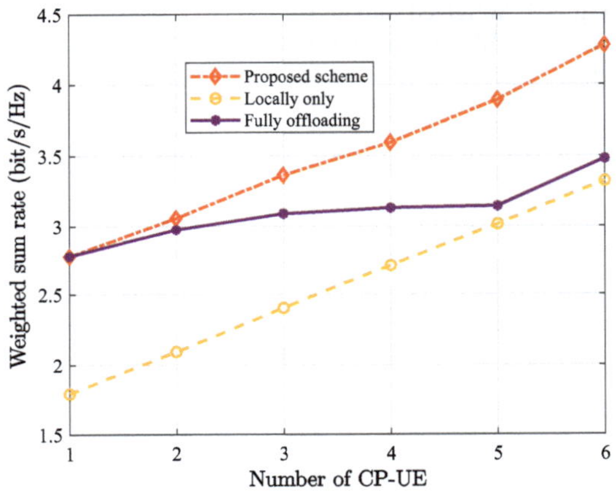

increases, the WSR obtained by the proposed scheme becomes higher than other schemes.

Figure 5.6 depicts the impact of different numbers of receive antennas on WSR. It can be seen that as the number of receive antennas increases, the WSR of all schemes also increases. When the number of receive antennas is relatively small, the WSR obtained by the proposed scheme is higher than that of other schemes. When there are more receive antennas, the WSR performance gap between the proposed scheme and the locally only scheme increases. This can be explained by the fact that increasing the number of receive antennas improves the quality of the received signal and spatial multiplexing gain.

Figure 5.7 depicts the impact of different numbers of transmit antennas on WSR. It can be seen that the WSR obtained by the proposed scheme is always higher than other schemes, and as the number of transmit antennas increases, the WSR of all schemes also increases. The reason is that the increase in the number of transmit antennas helps to improve the signal quality.

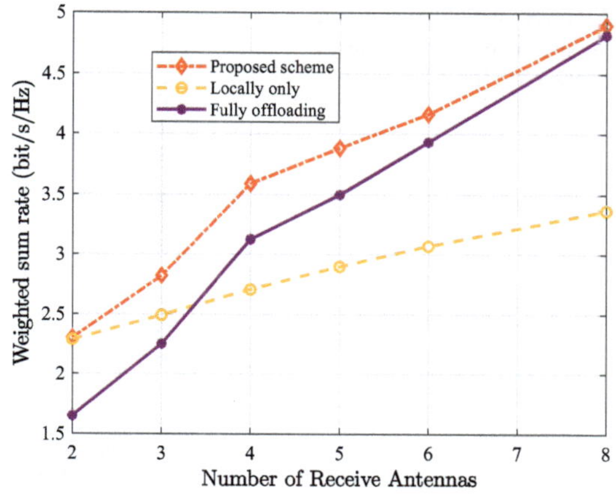

Fig. 5.6 Weighted sum rate versus the number of receive antennas

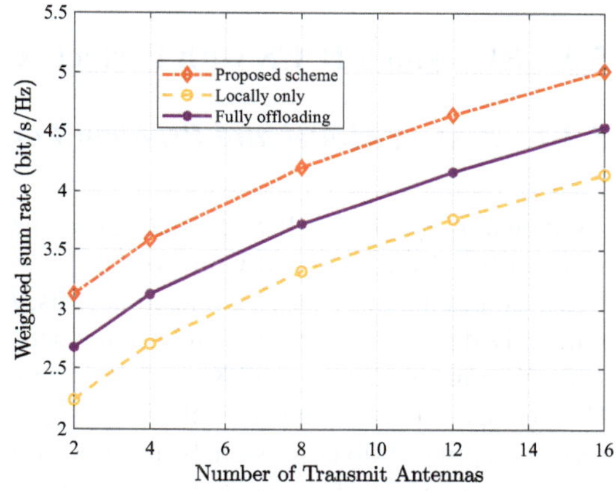

Fig. 5.7 Weighted sum rate versus the number of transmit antennas

Figure 5.8 shows the relationship between WSR and the CP-UE maximum energy consumption budget. As can be seen from the figure, when the CP-UE maximum energy budget is small, the WSR obtained by the proposed scheme is higher than the others, and as the maximum energy consumption budget of the CP-UE increases, the WSR obtained by the proposed scheme gradually approaches that obtained by the locally only scheme, i.e., the offloading scheme selects fully local computing. This is because the increase in the maximum energy consumption budget of the CP-UE improves the rate of the local computing. It can be observed that the full offloading scheme is not affected by the maximum energy consumption budget of CP-UE and remains stable.

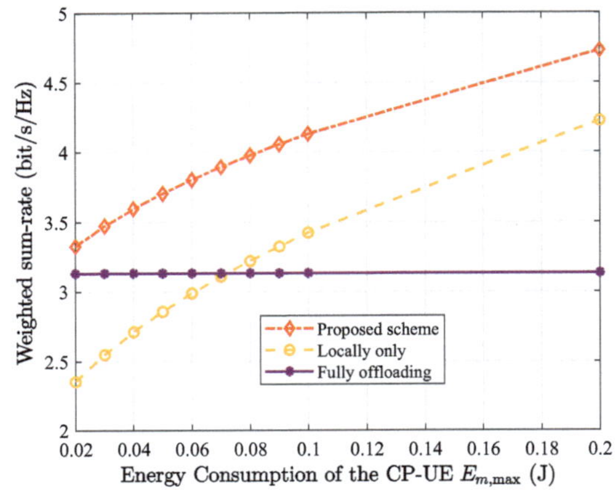

Fig. 5.8 Weighted sum rate versus the maximum energy of the CP-UE

5.3 RIS-Aided ICCS with Perfect ICCS

5.3.1 System Model and Problem Formulation

As shown in Fig. 5.9, an RIS-assisted full-duplex (FD) ICCS system is considered, where a FD BS is equipped with two ULAs, a semi-passive RIS is equipped with ULAs consisting of M passive reflection units, K randomly distributed CM-UEs, L randomly distributed CP-UEs, and a point sensing target. The FD BS is equipped with N_t transmit antennas (TX) and N_r receive antennas (RX), while each CM-UE and CP-UE is equipped with a single antenna. The FD BS simultaneously receives uplink offloading signals and transmits downlink integrated sensing and communication (ISAC) signals for multi-user communication and target sensing

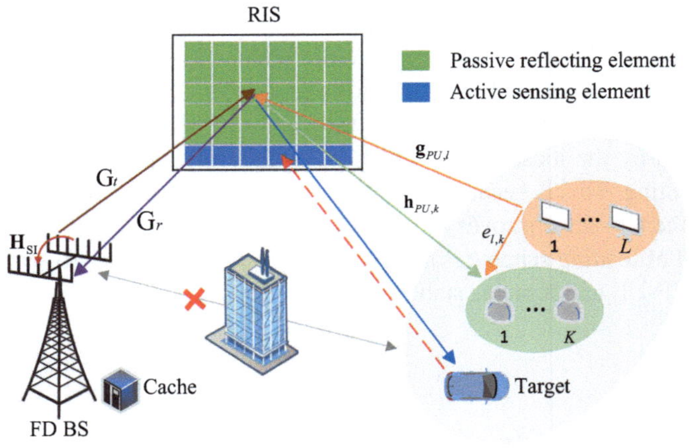

Fig. 5.9 An RIS-assisted FD ICCS system

with the help of RIS. In addition, the FD BS is connected to a local cache with limited storage capacity and connected to the MEC server through a high-capacity backhaul link, which is used for edge computing to perform computing tasks and store user data. For convenience, let $\mathcal{M} = \{1, \ldots, M\}$, $\mathcal{K} = \{1, \ldots, K\}$ and $\mathcal{L} = \{1, \ldots, L\}$ denote the index of RIS elements, CM-UEs, CP-UEs. To address the severe path loss, we assume that in addition to M passive reflecting elements (REs) in the semi-passive RIS, there are M_a active sensing elements (SEs) for receiving the target echo signal. Furthermore, due to the unfavorable environmental propagation, we assume that the direct links between the BS and target as well as users are blocked [13].

5.3.1.1 Signal Model

In this subsection, we first consider the downlink synaesthesia of the system, where a dual-function ISAC signals $\mathbf{x}^{DL} \in \mathbb{C}^{N_t\times 1}$ is used for simultaneous downlink multi-user communications and target sensing via multi-antenna beamforming. Let $s_k^{dl}, k \in \{1, \cdots, K\}$ denote the data symbol of the user k, and $\mathbf{w}_k \in \mathbb{C}^{N_t\times 1}$ denote the corresponding transmit beamforming vector. Similarly, s_0 represents the dedicated sensing signal and $\mathbf{w}_0 \in \mathbb{C}^{N_t\times 1}$ represents the corresponding sensing wave beamforming. Assume that the transmitted information signals s_k^{dl} and s_0 are both independent random variables with unit variance and mean 0, and that the downlink communication and target sensing signals are independent and uncorrelated, i.e., $\mathbb{E}[s_k^{dl} s_0] = 0, \forall k$. According to [14], the signal transmitted by BS can be expressed as

$$\mathbf{x}^{DL} = \sum\nolimits_{k=1}^{K} \mathbf{w}_k s_k^{dl} + \mathbf{w}_0 s_0. \tag{5.60}$$

In addition, we consider the BS total power constraint as $\sum_{k=0}^{K} \|\mathbf{w}_k\|_2^2 \leq P_{BS}$, where P_{BS} represents the maximum transmission power budget at the BS. The FD BS simultaneously receives the target echo and the uplink offloading signal when it performs downlink transmission. The offloading signal transmitted by the l-th CP-UE can be written as

$$x_l^{UL} = \sqrt{p_l} s_l^{ul}, \forall l \in \mathcal{L}, \tag{5.61}$$

where s_l^{ul} and p_l represent the data symbol and transmit power of the l-th CP-UE, respectively. For simplicity, we assume that each s_l^{ul} has unit variance and zero mean, and is uncorrelated with each other.

5.3.1.2 Communication Model

The received signal at CM-UE k can be expressed as

$$y_{com,k} = \underbrace{\mathbf{h}_{PU,k}^{H}\mathbf{\Phi}\mathbf{G}_{t}\mathbf{w}_{k}s_{k}^{dl}}_{\text{Desired signal}} + \underbrace{\sum_{k'\neq k}^{K}\mathbf{h}_{PU,k}^{H}\mathbf{\Phi}\mathbf{G}_{t}\mathbf{w}_{k'}s_{k'}^{dl}}_{\text{Multiuser interference}} + \underbrace{\mathbf{h}_{PU,k}^{H}\mathbf{\Phi}\mathbf{G}_{t}\mathbf{w}_{0}s_{0}}_{\text{Sensing signal}} \tag{5.62}$$

$$+ \underbrace{\sum_{l=1}^{L}\left(e_{l,k} + \mathbf{h}_{PU,k}^{H}\mathbf{\Phi}\mathbf{g}_{PU,l}\right)\sqrt{p_{l}}s_{l}^{ul}}_{\text{UL interference and their reflections from RIS}} + n_{k},$$

where $\mathbf{h}_{PU,k} \in \mathbb{C}^{M\times 1}$ and $\mathbf{G}_t \in \mathbb{C}^{M\times N_t}$ represent the channel vectors between the CM-UE k and RIS, and between BS TX and RIS, respectively. $e_{l,k} \in \mathbb{C}$ and $\mathbf{g}_{PU,l} \in \mathbb{C}^{M\times 1}$ represent the channels between the CM-UE k and the CP-UE l, and between the CP-UE l and the RIS, respectively. $n_k \sim \mathcal{CN}\left(0, \sigma_k^2\right)$ represents the AWGN at the user receiver. The diagonal matrix $\mathbf{\Phi} = \text{diag}\left(e^{j\phi_1}, \cdots, e^{j\phi_M}\right)$ represents the phase shift matrix of RIS, where $\phi_m \in [0, 2\pi), \forall m \in \mathcal{M}$ represents the phase shift of the m-th reflection element.

Therefore, the SINR of the CM-UE k can be written as

$$r_k^{com} = \frac{|\mathbf{h}_k\mathbf{w}_k|^2}{\sum\limits_{k'=0,k'\neq k}^{K}|\mathbf{h}_k\mathbf{w}_{k'}|^2 + \sum\limits_{l=1}^{L}p_l\left|\bar{e}_{l,k}\right|^2 + \sigma_k^2}, \tag{5.63}$$

where $\mathbf{h}_k \triangleq \mathbf{h}_{PU,k}^{H}\mathbf{\Phi}\mathbf{G}_t$ and $\bar{e}_{l,k} \triangleq e_{l,k} + \mathbf{h}_{PU,k}^{H}\mathbf{\Phi}\mathbf{g}_{PU,l}$. The achievable rate from BS to CM-UE k is given as

$$R_k^{com} = B\log\left(1 + r_k^{com}\right), \forall k \in \mathcal{K}, \tag{5.64}$$

where B represents the transmission bandwidth.

5.3.1.3 Sensing Model

Next, we model the target echo signal, assuming that the radar signal composes of a NLoS, and the receive ULA at the RIS and the transmit ULA at the BS are both half-wavelength antenna spacing. The signal received on the RIS SE is expressed as

$$\mathbf{y}_{RIS} = \underbrace{\eta_{RT}\mathbf{a}_a(\theta)\,\mathbf{a}_p^H(\theta)\,\mathbf{\Phi}\mathbf{G}_t\mathbf{x}^{DL}}_{\text{Desired echo signal}} + \underbrace{\sum_{l=1}^{L}\sqrt{p_l}\mathbf{g}_{AU,l}s_l^{ul}}_{\text{UL interference signals}} + \mathbf{n}_s, \tag{5.65}$$

where $\eta_{RT} \in \mathbb{C}$ represents the reflection coefficient of the target, which is mainly determined by the radar cross section and path loss [3]. θ represents the position of the sensing target with respect to the RIS. And $\mathbf{n}_s \sim \mathcal{CN}\left(0, \sigma_s^2 \mathbf{I}_{Ma}\right)$ represents the AWGN at the RIS. $\mathbf{a}_a(\theta) = \left[1, e^{-j2\pi \frac{d}{\lambda} \sin\theta}, \cdots, e^{-j2\pi \frac{d}{\lambda}(M_a - 1)\sin\theta}\right]^T$ and $\mathbf{a}_p(\theta) = \left[1, e^{-j2\pi \frac{d}{\lambda} \sin\theta}, \cdots, e^{-j2\pi \frac{d}{\lambda}(M - 1)\sin\theta}\right]^T$ represent the receive steering vector of RIS SE and the transmit steering vector of RIS RE respectively. As described in [15], we assume that θ and η_{RT} are known or previously estimated in order to design the most appropriate emission signal to detect this specific target.

The performance of radar is largely related to its corresponding SINR. Specifically, the detection probability of a point target usually increases with the increase of the output SINR in a MIMO radar system [16]. Therefore, we use radar SINR directly to characterize the sensing performance. According to (5.65), the radar SINR can be written as

$$r^{tar} = \frac{\left\| \eta_{RT} \mathbf{a}_a(\theta) \mathbf{a}_p^H(\theta) \mathbf{\Phi} \mathbf{G}_t \mathbf{x}^{DL} \right\|_2^2}{\sum_{l=1}^{L} p_l \left\| \mathbf{g}_{AU,l} \right\|_2^2 + \sigma_s^2}. \tag{5.66}$$

5.3.1.4 Computation Model

1. Offloading Computing

The offloading signal received by the FD BS can be expressed as

$$\mathbf{y}_{BS} = \underbrace{\sum_{l=1}^{L} \sqrt{p_l} \mathbf{G}_r^H \mathbf{\Phi} \mathbf{g}_{PU,l} s_l^{ul}}_{\text{Offloading signal}} + \underbrace{\mathbf{H}_{SI} \mathbf{x}^{DL}}_{\text{SI}} + \mathbf{n}_b, \tag{5.67}$$

where $\mathbf{G}_r \in \mathbb{C}^{M \times N_r}$ represents the channel vector between BS RX and RIS. $\mathbf{n}_b \sim \mathcal{CN}\left(0, \sigma_b^2 \mathbf{I}_{N_r}\right)$ represents the AWGN at the BS receiver. SI power can be greatly reduced by utilizing SI cancellation techniques. Without loss of generality, we represent the residual SI signal as $\mathbf{H}_{SI}\mathbf{x}^{DL}$ [1], where $\mathbf{H}_{SI} \in \mathbb{C}^{N_r \times N_t}$ represents the residual SI channel at the FD BS. Due to the severe attenuation of the channel between BS and RIS, we ignore the SI introduced by the RIS reflected synaesthesia signal and the reflected echo interference [17].

Technically, we apply a receive beamforming $\mathbf{u}_l^H \in \mathbb{C}^{N_r \times 1}$ at the BS to recover the offloading signal, and we obtain the corresponding receive SINR for the CP-UE l as

$$r_l^{off} = \frac{p_l \left| \mathbf{u}_l^H \mathbf{g}_l \right|^2}{\sum\limits_{l' \neq l}^{L} p_{l'} \left| \mathbf{u}_l^H \mathbf{g}_{l'} \right|^2 + \left| \mathbf{u}_l^H \mathbf{H}_{SI} \mathbf{x} \right|^2 + \left\| \mathbf{u}_l^H \right\|_2^2 \sigma_b^2}, \tag{5.68}$$

where $\mathbf{g}_l = \mathbf{G}_r^H \mathbf{\Phi} \mathbf{g}_{PU,l}$.

Therefore, the achievable offloading rate of the CP-UE l at the BS is given as

$$R_l^{off} = B \log\left(1 + r_l^{off}\right), \forall l \in \mathcal{L}. \tag{5.69}$$

2. *Local Computing*
We assume that ε_l represents the CPU cycle required for each CP-UE to process a bit of raw data, f_l represents the local CPU computing frequency of the m-th CP-UE, and ζ represents the constant related to the hardware architecture. According to [18, 19], the computation rate and energy consumption at each CP-UE can be expressed as $R_l^{loc} = f_l/\varepsilon_l$ and $E_l^{loc} = T\zeta f_l^3$, respectively.

5.3.1.5 Cache Model

Next, we model the caching strategy at the BS. The file collection V is denoted by $\mathcal{V} = \{1, \cdots, V\}$, and use vector $\mathbf{q} = [q_1, \cdots q_V]$ to represent the length of these files. We assume that in the content database V, all files can be ranked according to their popularity. Furthermore, we utilize a probabilistic caching strategy to randomly cache content with deterministic probability. The caching strategy can be defined as $\mathbf{e} = [e_1, \cdots e_V]^T$, where $e_v \in [0, 1], \forall v \in [1, V]$ represents the content placement indicator. In addition, since the BS cache is limited by the cache capacity F, there is a local cache constraint $\sum\limits_{v=1}^{V} q_v e_v \leq F$. Furthermore, the probability of the v-th file requested by the user is denoted as $\tilde{c}_v, \forall v \in [1, V]$. For simplicity, we assume that the request probability of the v-th file is consistent among different users without loss of generality, e.g., $\tilde{c}_{v,1} =, \cdots, \tilde{c}_{v,L} \triangleq \tilde{c}_v$. It is assumed that users request content files based on their popularity, and the request probability can be modeled as a Zipf distribution, i.e., $\tilde{c}_v = \frac{v^{-\epsilon}}{\sum_{i=1}^{V} i^{-\epsilon}}$, where ϵ is the skewness factor, which represents the deviation of the file popularity.

In content delivery, if the content v is already cached in the local storage of the BS, users can directly access this content by requesting. Otherwise, we need to obtain the content from the BS via a backhaul link. We define the performance metric for acquiring content as the backhaul data rate, e.g., $R_{0,l}$. Therefore, within a channel coherence time T, the total backhaul cost can be modeled as $\mathcal{D}_{total} = T \sum\limits_{v=1}^{V} \rho_v \sum\limits_{l=1}^{L} (1 - e_v)\, \tilde{c}_v R_{0,l}$, where ρ_v represents the pricing of the backhaul cost for the v-th content delivery.

5.3.1.6 Problem Formulation

To evaluate the overall performance, we consider a system utility maximization problem, expressed as the gap between the sum of the communication throughput, the total computation bits (offloading bits and local computation bits) and the total backhaul cost for content delivery. Mathematically, the optimization problem can be expressed as follows

$$\mathcal{P}^0: \max_{\mathbf{w},\mathbf{u},\boldsymbol{\phi},\mathbf{f},\mathbf{p},\mathbf{e}} \sum_{k=1}^{K} T R_k^{com} + \sum_{l=1}^{L} T\left(R_l^{off} + R_l^{loc}\right) - \mathcal{D}_{total} \tag{5.70}$$

$$s.t.\ C1: \sum\nolimits_{k=0}^{K} \|\mathbf{w}_k\|_2^2 \leq P_{BS}, \tag{5.70a}$$

$$C2: r^{tar} \geq \Gamma^{tar}, \tag{5.70b}$$

$$C3: |\phi_m| = 1, \forall m \in \mathcal{M}, \tag{5.70c}$$

$$C4: T p_l + T\zeta f_l^3 \leq E_l^{\max}, f_l \geq 0, p_l \geq 0, \tag{5.70d}$$

$$C5: \sum\nolimits_{v=1}^{V} q_v e_v \leq F, e_v \in [0, 1], \tag{5.70e}$$

where Γ^{tar} represents the target sensing SINR requirement, $E_l^{\max}$ represents the maximum energy budget of the l-th CP-UE. $\mathbf{w} = \{\mathbf{w}_k\}_{k=0}^{K}$ and $\mathbf{u} = \{\mathbf{u}_l\}_{l=1}^{L}$ represents the set of transmit beamforming and receive beamforming at the BS, respectively. $\mathbf{f} = [f_1, \cdots, f_L]^T$ represents the local computing resource vector. $\boldsymbol{\phi} = [\phi_1, \cdots, \phi_M]^T$ represents the phase shift vector of the reflection elements. $\mathbf{p} = [p_1, \cdots, p_L]^T$ represents the CP-UEs power vector.

It is obvious that the formulated problem is a highly non-convex optimization one and is difficult to solve due to the logarithmic nature of the objective function, the coupling of the optimization variables, the radar SNR constraint $C2$, and the unit modulus constraint $C3$. To address these difficulties, we propose to transform the problem into several tractable sub-problems using block coordinate ascent (BCA), weighted minimum mean square error (WMMSE), majorization-minimization (MM), alternative direction method of multipliers (ADMM) and semidefinite programming (SDP) methods and solve them iteratively.

5.3.2 Proposed BCA-Based Algorithm

In this section, we first optimize the cache strategy and then propose the WMMSE method to solve the problem of maximizing the sum of computation bits and communication throughput. Next, we apply the BCA method to divide the coupled variables into several blocks for alternate optimization. The details are as follows.

Algorithm 22 Proposed Algorithm for Solving $\mathcal{P}^0$

Input: $\mathbf{G}_t$, $\mathbf{G}_r$, $\mathbf{G}_s$, $\mathbf{H}_{SI}$, $\mathbf{h}_{PU,k}$, $\mathbf{g}_{PU,l}$, P_{BS}, Γ^{tar}, $E_{\max}$ and $\left\{R_{0,l}\right\}$.

Output: $\hat{\mathbf{w}}$, $\hat{\mathbf{u}}$, $\hat{\boldsymbol{\phi}}$, $\hat{\mathbf{f}}$, $\hat{\mathbf{p}}$, $\hat{\mathbf{e}}$.

Set maximum number of iterations: N_{max} and n=0.
Find $\mathbf{e}$ by solving problem $\mathcal{P}^1$.
Initialize $\mathbf{w}$, $\boldsymbol{\phi}$, $\mathbf{f}$ and $\mathbf{p}$.
Repeat
  Update $\{\alpha_{1,k}\}$, $\{\beta_{1,k}\}$ by (5.76) and (5.77).
  Update $\{\alpha_{2,l}\}$, $\{\beta_{2,l}\}$ by (5.78) and (5.79).
  Update $\boldsymbol{\phi}$ by solving problem $\mathcal{P}^9$.
  Update $\boldsymbol{\psi}$ by (5.92).
  Update λ by (5.93).
  Update $\rho := 0.8\rho$.
  Update $\mathbf{w}$ by solving problem $\mathcal{P}^{13}$.
  Update $\mathbf{u}$ by (5.105).
  Update $\mathbf{f}$ and $\mathbf{p}$ by solving problem $\mathcal{P}^{18}$.
  Set $n = n + 1$.
Until: $n = N_{max}$ or the objective of problem $\mathcal{P}^0$ converges.
Return $\hat{\mathbf{w}} = \mathbf{w}^{(t+1)}$, $\hat{\mathbf{u}} = \mathbf{u}^{(t+1)}$, $\hat{\boldsymbol{\phi}} = \boldsymbol{\phi}^{(t+1)}$, $\hat{\mathbf{f}} = \mathbf{f}^{(t+1)}$, $\hat{\mathbf{p}} = \mathbf{p}^{(t+1)}$ and $\hat{\mathbf{e}}$.

5.3.2.1 Optimal Caching Strategy

To optimize the design of the cache strategy, we rewrite the problem $\mathcal{P}^0$ as follows

$$\mathcal{P}^1 : \min_{\mathbf{e}} \sum\nolimits_{v=1}^{V} (1 - e_v)\, \tilde{c}_v \tag{5.71}$$

$$s.t.\ C5 : \sum\nolimits_{v=1}^{V} q_v e_v \le F,\ e_v \in [0, 1]. \tag{5.71a}$$

Problem $\mathcal{P}^1$ is convex with respect to the optimization variables $\mathbf{e} = [e_1, \cdots e_V]^T$, and it can be solved directly using convex optimization solver [9].

5.3.2.2 Maximize the Sum of Total Computation Bits and Communication Throughput

After optimizing the optimal caching strategy, problem $\mathcal{P}^0$ can be reformulated as maximizing the sum of communication throughput and total computation bits with given the content placement. Hence, we rewrite the problem as

$$\mathcal{P}^2 : \max_{\mathbf{w},\mathbf{u},\boldsymbol{\phi},\mathbf{f},\mathbf{p}} \sum_{k=1}^{K} T R_k^{com} + \sum_{l=1}^{L} T \left(R_l^{off} + R_l^{loc} \right) \tag{5.72}$$

$$s.t.\ C1,\ C2,\ C3,\ C4, \tag{5.72a}$$

In order to make it easier to solve problem $\mathcal{P}^2$, the objective function is first transformed via the WMMSE method [20]. Specifically, by introducing auxiliary variables $\{\alpha_{1,k}\}$, $\{\alpha_{2,l}\}$ and $\{\beta_{1,k}\}$, $\{\beta_{2,l}\}$, we write the original objective function equivalently into two variant forms (5.73) and (5.74).

$$\log\left(1+r_k^{com}\right)= \tag{5.73}$$

$$\underbrace{\max_{\alpha_{1,k}\geq 0}\ \log\left(1+\alpha_{1,k}\right)-\alpha_{1,k}+2\sqrt{1+\alpha_{1,k}}\Re\left\{\beta_{1,k}^{*}\mathbf{h}_k\mathbf{w}_k\right\}-\left|\beta_{1,k}\right|^2\left(\sum_{k'=0}^{K}\left|\mathbf{h}_k\mathbf{w}_{k'}\right|^2+\sum_{l=1}^{L}p_l\left|\bar{e}_{l,k}\right|^2+\sigma_k^2\right)}_{\tilde{R}_k^{com}},$$

$$\log\left(1+r_l^{off}\right)= \tag{5.74}$$

$$\underbrace{\max_{\alpha_{2,l}\geq 0}\ \log\left(1+\alpha_{2,l}\right)-\alpha_{2,l}+2\sqrt{1+\alpha_{2,l}}\Re\left\{\beta_{2,l}^{*}\sqrt{p_l}\mathbf{u}_l^H\mathbf{g}_l\right\}-\left|\beta_{2,l}\right|^2\left(\sum_{l'=1}^{L}p_{l'}\left|\mathbf{u}_l^H\mathbf{g}_{l'}\right|^2+\left|\mathbf{u}_l^H\mathbf{H}_{SI}\mathbf{x}\right|^2+\left\|\mathbf{u}_l^H\right\|_2^2\sigma_b^2\right)}_{\tilde{R}_k^{off}}.$$

Therefore, original problem $\mathcal{P}^2$ can be equivalently expressed as

$$\mathcal{P}^3:\ \max_{\mathbf{w},\mathbf{u},\boldsymbol{\phi},\mathbf{f},\mathbf{p}}\ \sum_{k=1}^{K}\tilde{R}_k^{com}+\sum_{l=1}^{L}\left(\tilde{R}_l^{off}+\frac{R_l^{loc}}{B}\right) \tag{5.75}$$

$$s.t.\ C1,\ C2,\ C3,\ C4, \tag{5.75a}$$

Next, we apply the BCA method to solve problem $\mathcal{P}^3$.

5.3.2.3 Optimizing Auxiliary Variables

Based on the above WMMSE transformation, when other optimization variables are fixed, the optimization of auxiliary variables is an unconstrained convex problem, and the optimal solution of auxiliary variables can be obtained as follows

$$\hat{\alpha}_{1,k}=\frac{\left|\mathbf{h}_k\mathbf{w}_k\right|^2}{\sum\limits_{k'=0,k'\neq k}^{K}\left|\mathbf{h}_k\mathbf{w}_{k'}\right|^2+\sum\limits_{l=1}^{L}p_l\left|\bar{e}_{l,k}\right|^2+\sigma_k^2}, \tag{5.76}$$

$$\hat{\beta}_{1,k}=\frac{\sqrt{1+\alpha_{1,k}}\mathbf{h}_k\mathbf{w}_k}{\sum\limits_{k'=0}^{K}\left|\mathbf{h}_k\mathbf{w}_{k'}\right|^2+\sum\limits_{l=1}^{L}p_l\left|\bar{e}_{l,k}\right|^2+\sigma_k^2}, \tag{5.77}$$

$$\hat{\alpha}_{2,l}=\frac{p_l\left|\mathbf{u}_l^H\mathbf{g}_l\right|^2}{\sum\limits_{l'=1,l'\neq l}^{L}p_{l'}\left|\mathbf{u}_l^H\mathbf{g}_{l'}\right|^2+\left|\mathbf{u}_l^H\mathbf{H}_{SI}\mathbf{x}\right|^2+\left\|\mathbf{u}_l^H\right\|_2^2\sigma_b^2}, \tag{5.78}$$

$$\hat{\beta}_{2,l} = \frac{\sqrt{1+\alpha_{1,l}}\sqrt{p_l}\mathbf{u}_l^H\mathbf{g}_l}{\sum\limits_{l'=1}^{L} p_{l'}\left|\mathbf{u}_l^H\mathbf{g}_{l'}\right|^2 + \left|\mathbf{u}_l^H\mathbf{H}_{SI}\mathbf{x}\right|^2 + \|\mathbf{u}_l^H\|_2^2\sigma_b^2}. \tag{5.79}$$

5.3.2.4 Optimizing Phase Shift $\boldsymbol{\phi}$

Based on other given variables, we study the optimization of the RIS phase shift $\boldsymbol{\phi}$. Problem $\mathcal{P}^3$ is reformulated as

$$\mathcal{P}^4 : \max_{\boldsymbol{\phi}} \sum\nolimits_{k=1}^{K} \tilde{R}_k^{com} + \sum\nolimits_{l=1}^{L} \tilde{R}_l^{off} \tag{5.80}$$

$$s.t.\ C2 : r^{tar} \geq \Gamma^{tar}, \tag{5.80a}$$

$$C3 : \ |\phi_m| = 1, \forall m \in \mathcal{M}. \tag{5.80b}$$

By introducing some new coefficients, the objective function and constraint $C2$ are rewritten as

$$\sum_{k=1}^{K} \tilde{R}_k^{com} + \sum_{l=1}^{L} \tilde{R}_l^{off} = -\boldsymbol{\phi}^H\mathbf{T}_{12}\boldsymbol{\phi} + 2\Re\{\mathbf{t}_{12}^H\boldsymbol{\phi}\} + b_{12}, \tag{5.81}$$

$$\widehat{C2} : b_0 - \boldsymbol{\phi}^H\mathbf{T}_0\boldsymbol{\phi} \leq 0, \tag{5.82}$$

$$\begin{aligned} b_{1,k} &= \log\left(1+\alpha_{1,k}\right) - \alpha_{1,k} - \left|\beta_{1,k}\right|^2\sigma_k^2 \\ &\quad - \left|\beta_{1,k}\right|^2\sum_{l=1}^{L} p_l\left|e_{l,k}\right|^2, \mathbf{E}_{1,k} = \mathrm{diag}\left(\mathbf{G}_t\mathbf{w}_k\right), \end{aligned} \tag{5.83}$$

$$\mathbf{a}_{1,k,l} = \mathbf{h}_{PU,k}^H\mathrm{diag}\left(\mathbf{g}_{PU,l}\right), \mathbf{t}_{1,1,k} = 2\sqrt{1+\alpha_{1,k}}\beta_{1,k}\mathbf{E}_{1,k}^H\mathbf{h}_{PU,k}, \mathbf{t}_{1,2,k}$$

$$= 2\left|\beta_{1,k}\right|^2\sum_{l=1}^{L} p_l e_{l,k}\mathbf{a}_{1,k,l}^H,$$

$$\mathbf{t}_{1,k} = \mathbf{t}_{1,1,k} - \mathbf{t}_{1,2,k}, \mathbf{T}_{1,1,k} = \left|\beta_{1,k}\right|^2\sum_{l=1}^{L} p_l\mathbf{a}_{1,k,l}^H\mathbf{a}_{1,k,l}, \mathbf{T}_{1,2,k}$$

$$= \left|\beta_{1,k}\right|^2\left(\sum_{k'=0}^{K}\mathbf{E}_{1,k'}^H\mathbf{h}_{PU,k}\mathbf{h}_{PU,k}^H\mathbf{E}_{1,k'}\right),$$

$$\mathbf{T}_{1,k} = \mathbf{T}_{1,1,k} + \mathbf{T}_{1,2,k}, b_1 = \sum_{k=1}^{K} b_{1,k}, \mathbf{t}_1 = \sum_{k=1}^{K}\mathbf{t}_{1,k}, \mathbf{T}_1$$

$$
\begin{aligned}
&= \sum_{k=1}^{K} \mathbf{T}_{1,k}, \mathbf{a}_{2,l} = \mathbf{G}_r^H \operatorname{diag}\left(\mathbf{g}_{PU,l}\right), \\
&b_{2,l} = \log\left(1+\alpha_{2,l}\right) - \alpha_{2,l} - \left|\beta_{2,l}\right|^2 \left(\left|\mathbf{u}_l^H \mathbf{H}_{SI}\mathbf{x}\right|^2 + \left\|\mathbf{u}_l^H\right\|_2^2 \sigma_b^2\right), \\
&\mathbf{t}_{2,l} = 2\sqrt{1+\alpha_{2,l}}\beta_{2,l}\sqrt{p_l}\mathbf{a}_{2,l}^H \mathbf{u}_l, \\
&\mathbf{T}_{2,l} = c_{2,l} \sum_{l'=1}^{L} p_{l'} \mathbf{a}_{2,l'}^H \mathbf{u}_l \mathbf{u}_l^H \mathbf{a}_{2,l'}, b_2 = \sum_{l=1}^{L} b_{2,l}, \mathbf{t}_2 = \sum_{l=1}^{L} \mathbf{t}_{2,l}, \mathbf{T}_2 \\
&= \sum_{l=1}^{L} \mathbf{T}_{2,l}, \mathbf{T}_{12} = \mathbf{T}_1 + \mathbf{T}_2, \\
&\mathbf{t}_{12} = \mathbf{t}_1 + \mathbf{t}_2, b_{12} = b_1 + b_2, b_0 = \Gamma^{tar}\left(\sum_{l=1}^{L} p_l \left\|\mathbf{g}_{AU,l}\right\|_2^2 + \sigma_s^2\right), \\
&\mathbf{G}_s = \eta_{RT} \mathbf{a}_a(\theta) \mathbf{a}_p^H(\theta), \\
&\quad \mathbf{t}_0 = \mathbf{G}_t \mathbf{x}, \mathbf{T}_{0,1} = \mathbf{G}_s \operatorname{diag}(\mathbf{t}_0), \mathbf{T}_0 = \mathbf{T}_{0,1}^H \mathbf{T}_{0,1}.
\end{aligned}
$$

where some of these coefficients are defined in (5.83) as shown at the top of the next page.

According to (5.81) and (5.82), we rewrite the reflection phase shift optimization problem as

$$
\mathcal{P}^5: \min_{\boldsymbol{\phi}} \ \boldsymbol{\phi}^H \mathbf{T}_{12} \boldsymbol{\phi} - 2\Re\{\mathbf{t}_{12}^H \boldsymbol{\phi}\} - b_{12} \tag{5.84}
$$

$$
s.t. \ \widehat{C}2: b_0 - \boldsymbol{\phi}^H \mathbf{T}_0 \boldsymbol{\phi} \leq 0, \tag{5.84a}
$$

$$
C3: \ |\phi_m| = 1, \forall m \in \mathcal{M}. \tag{5.84b}
$$

We apply ADMM to solve problem $\mathcal{P}^5$. Since $C3$ is a non-convex constant amplitude constraint, a copy $\boldsymbol{\psi}$ of $\boldsymbol{\phi}$ is introduced to align and decouple. Problem $\mathcal{P}^5$ can be equivalently expressed as

$$
\mathcal{P}^6: \min_{\boldsymbol{\phi}, \boldsymbol{\psi}} \ \boldsymbol{\phi}^H \mathbf{T}_{12} \boldsymbol{\phi} - 2\Re\{\mathbf{t}_{12}^H \boldsymbol{\phi}\} - b_{12} \tag{5.85}
$$

$$
s.t. \ \widehat{C}2: b_0 - \boldsymbol{\phi}^H \mathbf{T}_0 \boldsymbol{\phi} \leq 0, \tag{5.85a}
$$

$$
C6: \boldsymbol{\phi} = \boldsymbol{\psi}, \tag{5.85b}
$$

$$
C7: \ |\psi_m| = 1, \forall m \in \mathcal{M}. \tag{5.85c}
$$

In order to solve problem $\mathcal{P}^6$, based on ADMM [21], we optimize its augmented lagrangian (AL) problem and rewrite the problem as

$$\mathcal{P}^7: \min_{\boldsymbol{\phi},\boldsymbol{\psi},\boldsymbol{\lambda}} \ \phi^H \mathbf{T}_{12}\phi - 2\Re\{\mathbf{t}_{12}^H \boldsymbol{\phi}\} - b_{12} + \frac{1}{2\rho}\|\boldsymbol{\phi} - \boldsymbol{\psi} + \rho\boldsymbol{\lambda}\|_2^2 \tag{5.86}$$

$$s.t.\ \widehat{C}2: b_0 - \boldsymbol{\phi}^H \mathbf{T}_0 \boldsymbol{\phi} \le 0, \tag{5.86a}$$

$$C7: |\psi_m| = 1, \forall m \in \mathcal{M}, \tag{5.86b}$$

where λ represents the dual variable and $\rho > 0$ represents the penalty coefficient. We solve problem $\mathcal{P}^7$ by updating each variable alternately.

1. Update $\boldsymbol{\phi}$

With given $\boldsymbol{\psi}$ and λ, the problem can be simplified as

$$\mathcal{P}^8: \min_{\boldsymbol{\phi}} \ \boldsymbol{\phi}^H \mathbf{T}_{12}\boldsymbol{\phi} - 2\Re\{\mathbf{t}_{12}^H \boldsymbol{\phi}\} - b_{12} + \frac{1}{2\rho}\|\boldsymbol{\phi} - \boldsymbol{\psi} + \rho\boldsymbol{\lambda}\|_2^2 \tag{5.87}$$

$$s.t.\ \widehat{C}2: b_0 - \boldsymbol{\phi}^H \mathbf{T}_0 \boldsymbol{\phi} \le 0. \tag{5.87a}$$

Due to the constraints $\widehat{C}2$, problem $\mathcal{P}^8$ is non-convex. We adopt the MM framework to convexify $\widehat{C}2$ by linearizing the convex term at point $\boldsymbol{\phi}_0$ [22], which is given as

$$\boldsymbol{\phi}^H \mathbf{T}_0 \boldsymbol{\phi} \ge 2\Re\left\{{\boldsymbol{\phi}_0}^H \mathbf{T}_0 \left(\boldsymbol{\phi} - \boldsymbol{\phi}_0\right)\right\} + {\boldsymbol{\phi}_0}^H \mathbf{T}_0 \boldsymbol{\phi}_0. \tag{5.88}$$

Next, we replace $\boldsymbol{\phi}^H \mathbf{T}_0 \boldsymbol{\phi}$ in constraint $\widehat{C}2$ and problem $\mathcal{P}^8$ can be rewritten as

$$\mathcal{P}^9: \min_{\boldsymbol{\phi}} \ \boldsymbol{\phi}^H \mathbf{T}_{12}\boldsymbol{\phi} - 2\Re\{\mathbf{t}_{12}^H \boldsymbol{\phi}\} - b_{12} + \frac{1}{2\rho}\|\boldsymbol{\phi} - \boldsymbol{\psi} + \rho\boldsymbol{\lambda}\|_2^2 \tag{5.89}$$

$$s.t.\ \breve{C}2: -2\Re\left\{{\boldsymbol{\phi}_0}^H \mathbf{T}_0 \boldsymbol{\phi}\right\} + \left({\boldsymbol{\phi}_0}^H \mathbf{T}_0 \boldsymbol{\phi}_0\right)^* + b_0 \le 0. \tag{5.89a}$$

Problem $\mathcal{P}^9$ is a typical second-order cone program (SOCP) and can be solved directly by existing convex optimization solvers, such as CVX [9].

2. Update $\boldsymbol{\psi}$

With fixed $\boldsymbol{\phi}$ and λ, the problem can be simplified as

$$\mathcal{P}^{10}: \min_{\boldsymbol{\psi}} \ \frac{1}{2\rho}\|\boldsymbol{\phi} - \boldsymbol{\psi} + \rho\boldsymbol{\lambda}\|_2^2 \tag{5.90}$$

$$s.t.\ C7: |\psi_m| = 1, \forall m \in \mathcal{M}. \tag{5.90a}$$

Since $\boldsymbol{\psi}$ owns a unit modulus term, the quadratic term in the objective function in terms of $\boldsymbol{\phi}$ is a constant, i.e., $\|\boldsymbol{\psi}\|_2^2/(2\rho) = M/(2\rho)$. Therefore problem $\mathcal{P}^{10}$ can be simplified to

$$\mathcal{P}^{11}: \max_{|\boldsymbol{\psi}|=1_M} \Re\left\{(\boldsymbol{\phi}+\rho\boldsymbol{\lambda})^H\boldsymbol{\psi}\right\} \tag{5.91}$$

It can be seen that when all elements of $\boldsymbol{\psi}$ are aligned with the elements of the $\left(\rho^{-1}\boldsymbol{\phi}+\boldsymbol{\lambda}\right)$, problem $\mathcal{P}^{11}$ can be maximized. Therefore its optimal solution is expressed as:

$$\hat{\boldsymbol{\psi}} = e^{j\cdot\angle(\boldsymbol{\phi}+\rho\boldsymbol{\lambda})}. \tag{5.92}$$

3. Update $\boldsymbol{\lambda}$

After obtaining $\boldsymbol{\phi}$ and $\boldsymbol{\psi}$, the dual variable $\boldsymbol{\lambda}$ is updated via gradient ascent, as follows

$$\boldsymbol{\lambda} := \boldsymbol{\lambda} + \rho^{-1}(\boldsymbol{\phi}-\boldsymbol{\psi}). \tag{5.93}$$

5.3.2.5 Optimizing BS Beamforming $\mathbf{w}_k$

Next, we study the optimization of the BS beamforming $\mathbf{w}_k$ when other variables are fixed. We reformulate the problem as

$$\mathcal{P}^{12}: \max_{\mathbf{W}} \sum_{k=1}^{K} \tilde{R}_k^{com} + \sum_{l=1}^{L} \tilde{R}_l^{off} \tag{5.94}$$

$$s.t.\ C1: \sum_{k=0}^{K} \|\mathbf{w}_k\|_2^2 \le P_{BS}, \tag{5.94a}$$

$$C2: r^{tar} \ge \Gamma^{tar}. \tag{5.94b}$$

The objective function and constraint $C2$ are rewritten by introducing several new coefficients as

$$\tilde{R}_k^{com} = b_{3,k} + \sqrt{1+\alpha_{1,k}}\mathrm{Tr}\left(\Omega_k\tilde{\mathbf{W}}_k\right) - |\beta_{1,k}|^2\sum_{k'=0}^{K}\mathrm{Tr}\left(\mathbf{h}_k^H\mathbf{h}_k\mathbf{W}_{k'}\right), \tag{5.95}$$

$$\tilde{R}_l^{off} = b_{4,l} - |\beta_{2,l}|^2\mathrm{Tr}\left(\mathbf{Z}_l\sum_{k=0}^{K}\mathbf{W}_k\right), \tag{5.96}$$

$$\bar{C}2: \mathrm{Tr}\left(\Omega_0\sum_{k=0}^{K}\mathbf{W}_k\right) \ge b_0, \tag{5.97}$$

where some of these coefficients are defined as follows

$$
\begin{aligned}
b_{3,k} &= \log\left(1+\alpha_{1,k}\right)-\alpha_{1,k}+1 \\
&- \left|\beta_{1,k}\right|^2\left(\sum\nolimits_{l=1}^{L} p_l\left|e_{l,k}+\mathbf{h}_{PU,k}^H\boldsymbol{\Phi}\mathbf{g}_{PU,l}\right|^2+\sigma_k^2\right), \\
b_{4,l} &= \log\left(1+\alpha_{2,l}\right)-\alpha_{2,l} \\
&+ 2\sqrt{1+a_{2,l}}\,\Re\left\{\beta_{2,l}^*\sqrt{p_l}\mathbf{u}_l^H\mathbf{G}_r^H\boldsymbol{\Phi}\mathbf{g}_{PU,l}\right\} \\
&- \left|\beta_{1,l}\right|^2\left(\sum\nolimits_{l'=1}^{L} p_l\left|\mathbf{u}_l^H\mathbf{G}_r^H\boldsymbol{\Phi}\mathbf{g}_{PU,l'}\right|^2+\left\|\mathbf{u}_l^H\right\|_2^2\sigma_b^2\right), \\
\mathbf{W}_k &= \mathbf{w}_k\mathbf{w}_k^H,\ \tilde{\mathbf{w}}_k=\begin{bmatrix}\mathbf{w}_k\\1\end{bmatrix},\ \tilde{\mathbf{W}}_k=\tilde{\mathbf{w}}_k\tilde{\mathbf{w}}_k^H, \\
\Omega_k &= \begin{bmatrix}0 & \left(\beta_{1,k}^*\mathbf{h}_k\right)^H\\ \beta_{1,k}^*\mathbf{h}_k & 0\end{bmatrix},\ \Omega_0=\left(\mathbf{G}_s\boldsymbol{\Phi}\mathbf{G}_t\right)^H\mathbf{G}_s\boldsymbol{\Phi}\mathbf{G}_t, \\
\mathbf{H}_k &= \mathbf{h}_k^H\mathbf{h}_k,\ \mathbf{Z}_l=\mathbf{H}_{SI}^H\mathbf{u}_l\mathbf{u}_l^H\mathbf{H}_{SI}.
\end{aligned}
\tag{5.98}
$$

According to the above transformation, problem $\mathcal{P}^{12}$ can be reformulated as:

$$
\begin{aligned}
\mathcal{P}^{13}:\max_{\tilde{\mathbf{W}}_k}\ &\sum_{k=1}^{K}\left(\sqrt{1+\alpha_{1,k}}\operatorname{Tr}\left(\Omega_k\tilde{\mathbf{W}}_k\right)\right. \\
&\left.-\left|\beta_{1,k}\right|^2\sum_{k'=0}^{K}\operatorname{Tr}\left(\mathbf{H}_k\mathbf{W}_{k'}\right)\right) \\
&-\sum_{l=1}^{L}\left(\left|\beta_{1,l}\right|^2\operatorname{Tr}\left(\mathbf{Z}_L\sum_{k=0}^{K}\mathbf{W}_k\right)\right)
\end{aligned}
\tag{5.99}
$$

$$
s.t.\ C1:\operatorname{Tr}\left(\sum_{k=0}^{K}\mathbf{W}_k\right)\le P_{BS}, \tag{5.99a}
$$

$$
\bar{C}2:\operatorname{Tr}\left(\Omega_0\sum_{k=0}^{K}\mathbf{W}_k\right)\ge b_0, \tag{5.99b}
$$

$$
C8:\left[\tilde{\mathbf{W}}_k\right]_{N_t+1,N_t+1}=1,\ \tilde{\mathbf{W}}_k\succeq 0,\ k\in\{0,\mathcal{K}\}, \tag{5.99c}
$$

$$
C9:\operatorname{rank}\left(\tilde{\mathbf{W}}_k\right)=1. \tag{5.99d}
$$

Due to the rank-one constraint of C9, $\mathcal{P}^{13}$ is still non-convex, so we choose to use SDP technology to obtain the optimal solution of the problem by relaxing constraint C9. Finally, we directly solve it through a convex optimization solver and use the Gaussian randomization method to recover the corresponding rank-one solution [23].

5.3.2.6 Optimization of Offloading Signal Receive Beamforming $\mathbf{u}_l$

Next, we study the optimization of the offloading signal receive beamforming $\mathbf{u}_l$ when other variables are fixed. We reformulate the problem as

$$\mathcal{P}^{14} : \max_{\mathbf{u}} \sum\nolimits_{l=1}^{L} \tilde{R}_l^{off} \tag{5.100}$$

We rewrite the objective function as:

$$\tilde{R}_l^{off} = b_{5,l} + 2\Re\left\{\mathbf{u}_l^H \mathbf{t}_{5,l}\right\} - \mathbf{u}_l^H \mathbf{T}_{5,l} \mathbf{u}_l, \tag{5.101}$$

where several coefficients are defined as follows

$$\begin{aligned} & b_{5,l} = \log\left(1+\alpha_{2,l}\right) - \alpha_{2,l}, \mathbf{t}_{5,l} = \sqrt{1+a_{2,l}}\sqrt{p_l}\mathbf{g}_l, \\ & \mathbf{T}_{5,l} = \left|\beta_{2,l}\right|^2 \left(\sum_{l'=1}^{L} p_{l'}\mathbf{g}_{l'}\mathbf{g}_{l'}^H + \mathbf{H}_{SI}\mathbf{x}(\mathbf{H}_{SI}\mathbf{x})^H + \mathbf{I}_{N_r}\sigma_b^2\right). \end{aligned} \tag{5.102}$$

Based on the above transformation, the problem is reformulated as

$$\mathcal{P}^{15} : \min_{\mathbf{u}} \sum_{l=1}^{L} \left(\mathbf{u}_l^H \mathbf{T}_{5,l}\mathbf{u}_l - 2\Re\left\{\mathbf{u}_l^H \mathbf{t}_{5,l}\right\} - b_{5,l}\right) \tag{5.103}$$

Problem $\mathcal{P}^{15}$ can be decomposed into L independent sub-problems, each of which can be expressed as

$$\mathcal{P}_l^{16} : \min_{\mathbf{u}_l} \mathbf{u}_l^H \mathbf{T}_{5,l}\mathbf{u}_l - 2\Re\left\{\mathbf{t}_{5,l}\mathbf{u}_l\right\} \tag{5.104}$$

Notice that Problem $\mathcal{P}^{16}$ is a unconstrained convex problem. By setting its derivative to zero, the optimal solution can be obtained as follows

$$\hat{\mathbf{u}}_l = \left(\mathbf{T}_{5,l}\right)^{-1}\mathbf{t}_{5,l}, \forall l \in \mathcal{L}. \tag{5.105}$$

5.3.2.7 Optimize User Power and Local Computing Resources

This section considers optimizing the transmission power and local computing resources of all CP-UEs when other variables are given, which is reformulated as

$$\mathcal{P}^{17} : \max_{\mathbf{f},\mathbf{p}} \sum_{k=1}^{K} \tilde{R}_k^{com} + \sum_{l=1}^{L} \left(\tilde{R}_l^{off} + \frac{R_l^{loc}}{B} \right) \tag{5.106}$$

$$s.t.\ C2 : r^{tar} \geq \Gamma^{tar}, \tag{5.106a}$$

$$C4 : T p_l + T\zeta f_l^3 \leq E_l^{\max},\ f_l \geq 0,\ p_l \geq 0. \tag{5.106b}$$

Next, we rewrite the objective function and C2 as

$$\tilde{R}_k^{com} = b_{10,k} - c_{1,k} \sum_{l=1}^{L} p_l b_{11,k,l}, \tag{5.107}$$

$$\tilde{R}_l^{off} = b_{2,l} + \sqrt{p_l} b_{6,l} - p_l b_{7,l}, \tag{5.108}$$

$$\hat{C}2 : \sum_{l=1}^{L} p_l b_{9,l} \leq c_8, \tag{5.109}$$

where several coefficients are defined as follows

$$b_{10,k} = \log\left(1+\alpha_{1,k}\right) - \alpha_{1,k} + 2\sqrt{1+\alpha_{1,k}} \Re\left\{\beta_{1,k}^* \mathbf{h}_k \mathbf{w}_k\right\} - \left|\beta_{1,k}\right|^2 \left(\sum_{k'=0}^{K} |\mathbf{h}_k \mathbf{w}_{k'}|^2 + \sigma_k^2 \right), \tag{5.110}$$

$$b_{11,k,l} = \left| e_{l,k} + \mathbf{h}_{PU,k}^H \mathbf{\Phi} \mathbf{g}_{PU,l} \right|^2,$$

$$b_{2,l} = \log\left(1+\alpha_{2,l}\right) - \alpha_{2,l} - \left|\beta_{2,l}\right|^2 \left(\left|\mathbf{u}_l^H \mathbf{H}_{SI} \mathbf{x}\right|^2 + \left\|\mathbf{u}_l^H\right\|_2^2 \sigma_b^2 \right),$$

$$b_{6,l} = 2\Re\left\{\sqrt{1+\alpha_{2,l}} \mathbf{u}_l^H \mathbf{g}_l\right\},\ b_{7,l} = \sum_{l'=1}^{L} \left|\beta_{2,l'}\right|^2 \left|\mathbf{u}_{l'}^H \mathbf{g}_l\right|^2,$$

$$c_8 = \|\mathbf{G}_s \mathbf{\Phi} \mathbf{G}_t \mathbf{x}\|_2^2 - \sigma_s^2 \Gamma^{tar},\ b_{9,l} = \Gamma^{tar} \left\|\mathbf{g}_{AU,l}\right\|_2^2.$$

Problem $\mathcal{P}^{17}$ can be formulated as

$$\mathcal{P}^{18} : \max_{\mathbf{f},\mathbf{p}} \sum_{l=1}^{L} \left(b_{6,l}\sqrt{p_l} - p_l (b_{7,l} + \sum_{k=1}^{K} c_{1,k} b_{11,k,l}) + \frac{f_l}{\varepsilon_l B} \right) \tag{5.111}$$

$$s.t.\ \bar{C}2: \sum_{l=1}^{L} p_l b_{9,l} \leq c_8, \tag{5.111a}$$

$$C4: T p_l + T\zeta f_l^3 \leq E_l^{\max},\ f_l \geq 0,\ p_l \geq 0. \tag{5.111b}$$

The problem is concave in terms of **f** and **p**, so it is a convex optimization problem and can be directly optimized with existing solvers.

5.3.2.8 Algorithm Convergence and Optimality Analysis

The overall algorithm for solving problem $\mathcal{P}^0$ is summarized in Algorithm 22. After giving appropriate initial values, we iteratively update each subproblem until convergence. Note that the penalty parameter ρ is reduced at each iteration to enforce satisfying the equality constraints. As the penalty parameter is gradually reduced, i.e., $\rho \rightarrow 0$, the solution to problem $\mathcal{P}^7$ eventually guarantees the satisfaction of the unit modulus constraint. And for any given ρ, the objective value achieved by problem $\mathcal{P}^7$ is an upper bound on the objective value achieved by problem $\mathcal{P}^5$. By alternately solving problem $\mathcal{P}^7$, the upper bound can be gradually tightened. Since each subproblem of problem $\mathcal{P}^7$ obtains an optimal solution, the objective function (5.86) is monotonically non-increasing, and the solution obtained by alternative optimization can be guaranteed to converge to the stable point of problem $\mathcal{P}^5$. Furthermore, we can find that problem $\mathcal{P}^2$ is solved by updating ϕ, **w**, **u**, {**f**, **p**} alternately and each subproblem can converge to a stationary points. Note that the objective value (5.72) is non-decreasing over the iterations and that any limit point of any optimization variable is a stationary point of the original optimization problem $\mathcal{P}^2$. In addition, due to the transmit power budget and energy consumption budget, the upper bound of the objective value (5.72) is limited. Therefore, Algorithm 22 can converge to a stable point and a local optimal solution.

5.3.3 Performance Evaluation

In this section, we give the simulation results to verify the performance of the considered systems. First, we model BS TX-RIS RE links, BS RX-RIS RE links, RIS RE-CP UEs links, RIS SE-CP UEs links, and RIS RE-CM UEs links as Rician distribution with a Ricean Rician of 3 dB. The direct link between CP-UEs and CM-UEs is modeled as Rayleigh fading [24]. For all channels, we adopt the typical distance-dependent path loss model [25]. The large-scale fading model is denoted as $PL(d) = \Lambda\left(\frac{d}{d_0}\right)^{-\eta}$, where $\Lambda = -30$ dB represents the path loss at the reference distance $d_0 = 1m$, and d and η represent the propagation distance and path loss exponent, respectively. The path loss exponents between BS-RIS, RIS-UE, RIS-Target, and CP UE-CM UE are $\eta_{BR} = 2.2$, $\eta_{RU} = 2.5$, $\eta_{RT} = 2.2$ and $\eta_{MP} = 3.9$

Table 5.2 System parameters

Variable	Description	Value
N_t	The number of transmit antennas at BS	4
N_r	The number of receive antennas at BS	4
M	The number of passive elements	50
M_a	The number of active elements	10
K	The number of CM-UEs	2
L	The number of CP-UEs	2
B	Bandwidth	1 MHz
P_b	Maximum transmit power of BS	30 dBm
ε_l	Complexity of computation tasks of CP-UE	1000 cycles/bit
$E_m^{\max}$	The maximum energy budget for CP-UE m	0.01 J
ζ	Constants related to hardware architecture	10^{-26}
Γ^{tar}	Predefined target sensing threshold	7 dB
$R_{0,l}=R_0$	The backhaul data rate	100 Mbps
V	The number of file	1000
F	The storage capacity	10^6
q_v	The length of files	10^5
ϵ	Skewness factor	1.4

respectively. For the SI channel, according to [26], each entry of model $\mathbf{H}_{SI} \in \mathbb{C}^{N_r \times N_t}$ is $[\mathbf{H}_{SI}]_{t,r} = \sqrt{\varpi_{t,r}^{SI}} e^{-j2\pi \frac{d_{t,r}}{\lambda}}$, where $d_{t,r} > 0$ represents the distance between the t-th transmit antenna and the r-th receive antenna and $\varpi_{t,r}^{SI} > 0$ represents the residual SI power. For simplicity, we set $\varpi^{SI} = \varpi_{t,r}^{SI} = -110\,\text{dB}$ and let $e^{-j2\pi \frac{d_{t,r}}{\lambda}}$ be a unit modulus variable with random phase for all transceiver antenna pairs (t, r) [27].

Several specific system parameters are shown in Table 5.2. In addition, we assume that BS and RIS are deployed at (−50m, 0) and (0, 6m). All users are randomly distributed in $(d_x\text{m}, d_y\text{m})$, where $d_x \in [10, 40]$ and $d_y \in [0, 1]$. Assume that the radar target is 3m away from the RIS and $\theta = 40°$. The noise power at the BS, each CM-UE, and RIS is set to $\sigma_b^2 = \sigma_k^2 = \sigma_s^2 = -90\,\text{dBm}, \forall k$.

In order to verify the performance of the proposed system, we also include the following solutions for comparison:

- Full offloading: Each CP-UE performs computation offloading only through the RIS.
- Fixed phase shift: We assume that the RIS adopts a fixed phase shift determined by the maximum channel gain.
- Half duplex (HD): Assume that BS uses HD mode, where CM-UEs reception and CP-UEs transmission are implemented in two orthogonal time slots of equal duration. Therefore, the CCI of uplink offloading signals to CM-UEs and SI at the BS do not exist.

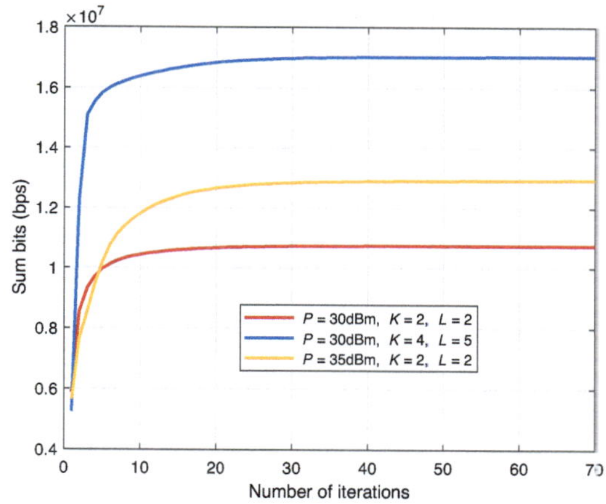

Fig. 5.10 Sum bits versus the number of iterations

- Optimizing caching: In each implementation, the caching strategy is optimized by solving problem $\mathcal{P}^1$.
- Random caching strategy: The probability of BS local random caching depends on the popularity of the cached data, i.e., if the data is more popular, it is more likely to be cached.
- Without caching: Both computation offloading and local computation can be performed without caching.

Figure 5.10 shows the convergence of the proposed algorithm. We present different settings for the relationship between the achievable sum bits and the number of iterations to demonstrate the convergence performances of Algorithm 23. We observe that after 30 iterations, the achievable sum bits trend to stablize, verifying the fast convergence and effectiveness of the proposed algorithm. In addition, it can be seen that as the number of users increases, a higher sum bits can usually be obtained.

Figure 5.11 depicts the relationship between the sum bits of the proposed scheme and the benchmark scheme and the number of RIS reflection elements N. It can be seen that by increasing the number of RIS reflection elements, the sum bits increase under all schemes. This is because that more reflective elements can tailor favorable channels with more degrees of freedom, providing greater passive beamforming gain for all users. Furthermore, our proposed algorithm outperforms both full offloading and fixed phase shift in both FD and HD systems. This highlights the optimality of partial offloading and that by optimizing the phase shift of the RIS, a more favorable propagation environment can be created. In addition, the performance of the FD scheme, i.e., the proposed scheme, is significantly better than that of the traditional HD scheme, this is because in the same time, the FD scheme can fully utilize the degrees of freedom introduced by multiplexing uplink and downlink users on the same spectrum resources, thereby improving system performance.

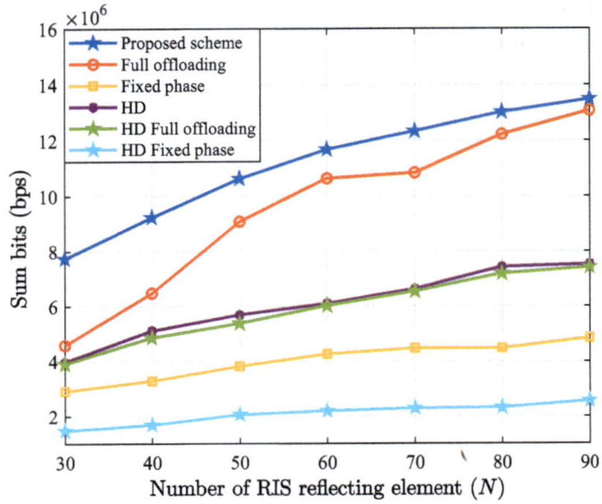

Fig. 5.11 Sum bits versus the number of RIS reflection elements N

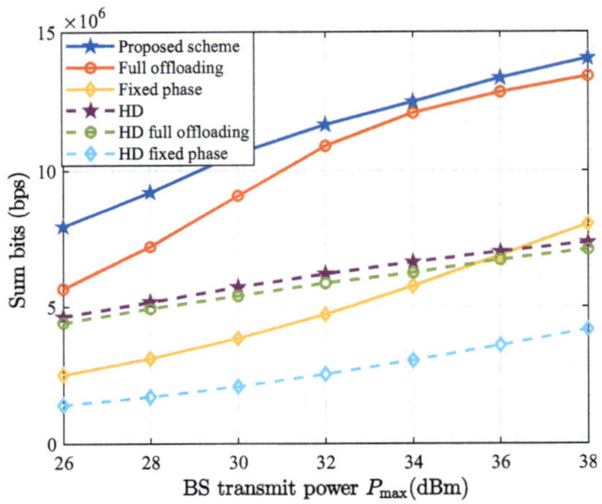

Fig. 5.12 Sum bits versus the BS transmit power P_{BS}

Figure 5.12 depicts the relationship between the sum bits and the maximum transmission power P_{BS} of the BS for the proposed scheme and the benchmark scheme. As expected, the sum bits of all schemes increases monotonically with increasing P_{BS}. A larger P_{BS} provides higher beamforming gain for signal transmission, thereby improving system performance. Furthermore, we observe that the proposed scheme outperforms all other schemes. In fact, compared with other schemes, through the joint optimization of ϕ, $\mathbf{w}$, $\mathbf{u}$, $\mathbf{f}$ and $\mathbf{p}$, this resource allocation scheme can be significantly improved. In contrast, for the full offloading scheme, as increases P_{BS}, both CCI and the remaining SI become more severe, which affects the performance of the system. For the HD scheme, although orthogonal transmission avoids CCI and residual SI, the resulting strictly suboptimal use of uplink and downlink time resources leads to a degradation of system performance.

Figure 5.13 shows the relationship between the sum bits of the proposed scheme and the baseline scheme based on different target sensing requirement Γ^{tar}. We can observe that the sum bits of all solutions decreases as Γ^{tar} increases. This

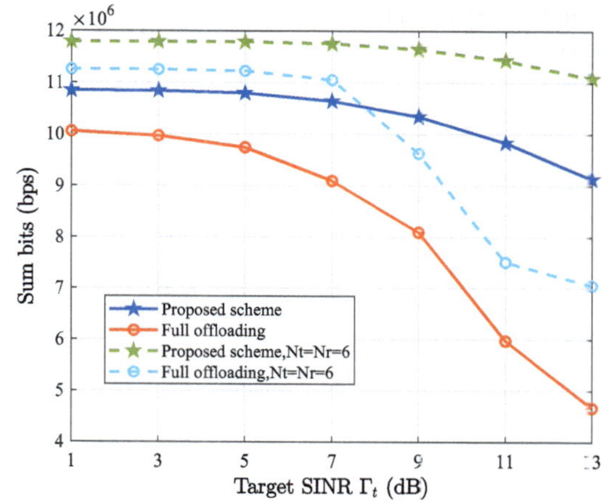

Fig. 5.13 Sum bits versus the target sensing requirement Γ^{tar}

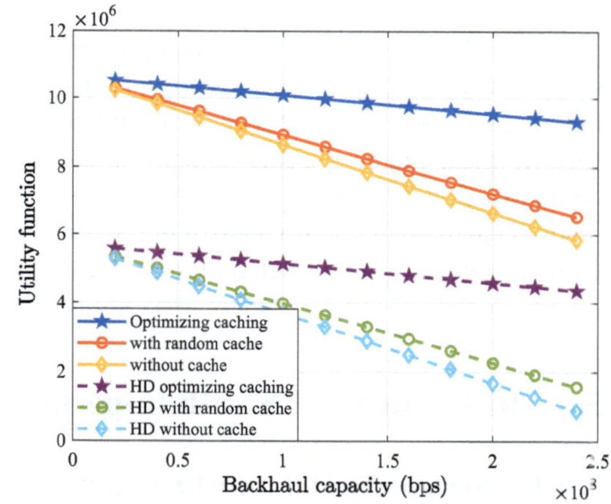

Fig. 5.14 System utility function versus the backhaul data rate R_0

is because when Γ^{tar} increases, the system needs to reduce the communication rate to utilize more transmission power to ensure the sensing demand, which leads to a decrease in system performance. Furthermore, we can see that the system performance improves as the number of BS antennas increases. This is due to the extra degrees of freedom provided by the additional antennas, which provide higher beamforming resolution for both CM-UE reception and CP-UE transmission, leading to higher system performance.

Figure 5.14 shows the relationship between the system utility function and the backhaul data rate R_0. It can be observed that as R_0 increases, the system utility functions of all schemes decrease, which can be explained by the fact that the increase in the backhaul data rate leads to an increase in the total cost of content delivery, thus resulting in a decrease in the system utility function. In addition, the optimal caching scheme outperforms the random caching and without caching schemes in both FD and HD systems.

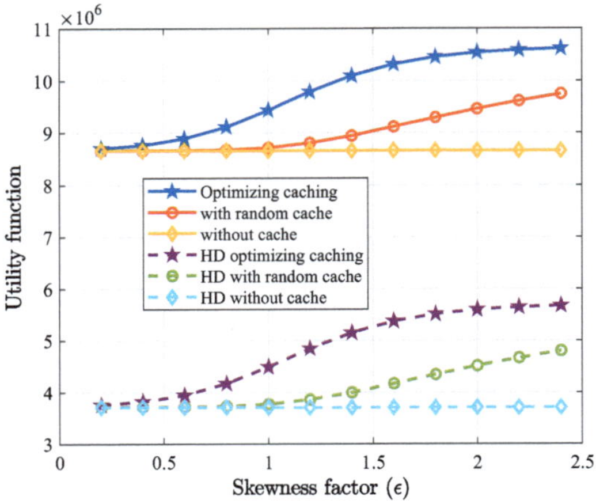

Fig. 5.15 System utility function versus the skewness factor ϵ

Figure 5.15 shows the relationship between the system utility function and the skewness factor ϵ in the Zipf distribution function. As can be observed from the figure, as ϵ increases, the system utility functions of all schemes first gradually show a linear increase trend. When ϵ is larger, the growth of the optimal caching gradually slows down. In addition, the optimal caching scheme outperforms the random caching and without caching schemes in both FD and HD systems. And the without scheme is not affected by ϵ and remains unchanged.

5.4 RIS-Aided ICCS with Imperfect CSI

5.4.1 System Model and Problem Formulation

As shown in Fig. 5.16, we consider an RIS-assisted ICCS system, which includes K downlink CM-UEs and L uplink CP-UEs equipped with a single antenna, and B sensing targets. The FD BS equipped with N_t transmit antennas and N_r receive antennas serves CM-UEs/CP-UEs with the assistance of the RIS and senses B targets directly. For convenience, let $\mathcal{M} \triangleq \{1, \ldots, M\}$, $\mathcal{K} \triangleq \{1, \ldots, K\}$, $\mathcal{L} \triangleq \{1, \ldots, L\}$, $\mathcal{B} \triangleq \{1, \ldots, B\}$ denote the indexes of RIS elements, CM-UEs, CP-UEs, and targets, respectively.

5.4.1.1 Communication Model

Let $\mathbf{w}_{c,k} \in \mathbb{C}^{N_t \times 1}$ and $\mathbf{w}_{r,b} \in \mathbb{C}^{N_t \times 1}$ represent the transmit beamforming vectors for CM-UE k and sensing target b, respectively, $s_{c,k}^{dl}$ and $s_{r,b}$ represent corresponding information symbols, respectively. Assuming that the communication and radar

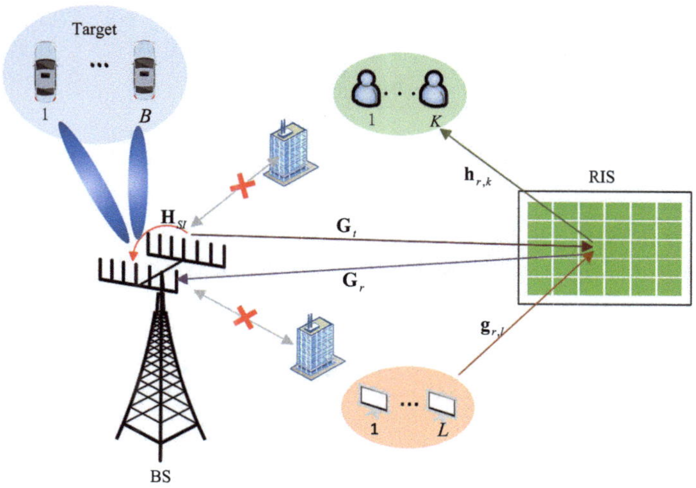

Fig. 5.16 The system model of RIS-assisted ICCS with imperfect CSI

signals are independent and own unit power [14], [22], [23], i.e., $\mathbb{E}\left\{s_{c,k}^{dl}s_{r,b}^{*}\right\} = 0$, $\mathbb{E}\{s_{c,k}^{dl}(s_{c,k}^{dl})^{*}\} = 1$, $\mathbb{E}\left\{s_{r,b}s_{r,b}^{*}\right\} = 1$, $\forall k, b$. Meanwhile, communication signals among different users are unrelated, i.e., $\mathbb{E}\{s_{c,i}^{dl}(s_{c,j}^{dl})^{*}\} = 0, \forall i, j \in \mathcal{K}, \forall i \neq j$. The transmit signal $\mathbf{x}$ at the FD BS can be expressed as

$$\mathbf{x} = \sum_{k=1}^{K} \mathbf{w}_{c,k}s_{c,k}^{dl} + \sum_{b=1}^{B} \mathbf{w}_{r,b}s_{r,b}. \tag{5.112}$$

Let $\mathbf{h}_{r,k} \in \mathbb{C}^{M\times 1}$ represents the channel vector between RIS and CM-UE k, $\mathbf{G}_t \in \mathbb{C}^{M\times N_t}$ represents the channel matrix between RIS and BS. The signal received by the CM-UE k can be expressed as

$$y_k^{com} = \mathbf{h}_{r,k}^{H}\mathbf{\Phi}\mathbf{G}_t\mathbf{x} + n_k, \forall k, \tag{5.113}$$

where $n_k \sim \mathcal{CN}\left(0, \sigma_k^2\right)$ represents the AGWN. Note that, we ignore the interference from CP-UEs because that CP-UE's power is usually very small. The diagonal matrix $\mathbf{\Phi} = \operatorname{diag}\left(e^{j\phi_1}, \cdots, e^{j\phi_M}\right)$ represents the reflection coefficients of RIS, $\phi_m \in [0, 2\pi), \forall m \in \mathcal{M}$ represents the phase shift of the m-th reflection unit.

The corresponding SINR can be expressed as

$$r_k^{com} = \frac{\left|\mathbf{h}_k \mathbf{w}_{c,k}\right|^2}{\sum\limits_{k' \neq k}^{K} \left|\mathbf{h}_k \mathbf{w}_{c,k'}\right|^2 + \sum\limits_{b=1}^{B} \left|\mathbf{h}_k \mathbf{w}_{r,b}\right|^2 + \sigma_k^2}, \tag{5.114}$$

where $\mathbf{h}_k = \mathbf{h}_{r,k}^H \boldsymbol{\Phi} \mathbf{G}_t$.

Therefore, the sum rate of CM-UEs can be calculated as

$$R_{sum}^{com} = \sum_{k=1}^{K} R_k^{com} = \sum_{k=1}^{K} \log\left(1 + r_k^{com}\right), \tag{5.115}$$

5.4.1.2 Sensing Model

The signal received at the FD BS can be expressed as

$$\mathbf{y}_{BS} = \sum_{b=1}^{B} \varpi \mathbf{a}_{r,b}(\theta)\, \mathbf{a}_{t,b}(\theta)^H \mathbf{x} + \sum_{l=1}^{L} \sqrt{p_l} \mathbf{G}_r^H \boldsymbol{\Phi} \mathbf{g}_{r,l} s_l^{ul} + \mathbf{H}_{SI}\mathbf{x} + \mathbf{n}_B, \tag{5.116}$$

where ϖ represents the target radar cross section and $\mathbb{E}\left\{|\varpi|^2\right\} = \xi^2$. $\mathbf{a}_r(\theta_b) \in \mathbb{C}^{N_r \times 1}$ and $\mathbf{a}_t(\theta_b) \in \mathbb{C}^{N_t \times 1}$ represent the channel vectors between the FD BS receive/transmit antennas and the b-th sensing target, respectively. $\mathbf{G}_r \in \mathbb{C}^{M \times N_r}$ represent the channel matrix between the FD BS and RIS. $\mathbf{g}_{r,l} \in \mathbb{C}^{M \times 1}$ represent the channel vector between RIS and the l-th CP-UE. p_l and s_l^{ul} represent the transmit power and information symbol of the l-th CP-UE, respectively. $\mathbf{H}_{SI} \in \mathbb{C}^{N_r \times N_t}$ represents the self-interference (SI) channel matrix between the FD BS transmit and receive antennas, $\mathbf{n}_B \sim \mathcal{CN}\left(0, \sigma_B^2 \mathbf{I}_{N_r}\right)$ represents the AWGN at the FD BS. We use the radar receive beamforming vector $\mathbf{u}_b \in \mathbb{C}^{N_r \times 1}$ to process signal $\mathbf{y}_{BS}$ [22], and thus we have

$$y_b^{tar} = \mathbf{u}_b^H \mathbf{y}_{BS} = \mathbf{u}_b^H \varpi \mathbf{A}_b \mathbf{x} + \mathbf{u}_b^H \varpi \sum_{b' \neq b}^{B} \mathbf{A}_{b'} \mathbf{x} + \mathbf{u}_b^H \left(\sum_{l=1}^{L} \sqrt{p_l} \mathbf{g}_l s_l^{ul} + \mathbf{H}_{SI}\mathbf{x} + \mathbf{n}_B \right), \tag{5.117}$$

where $\mathbf{A}_b = \mathbf{a}_{r,b}(\theta)\, \mathbf{a}_{t,b}(\theta)^H \in \mathbb{C}^{N_r \times N_t}$.

Therefore, the corresponding SINR can be expressed as

$$r_b^{tar} = \frac{\sigma^2 \left|\mathbf{u}_b^H \mathbf{A}_b \mathbf{x}\right|^2}{\sum\limits_{b' \neq b}^{B} \sigma^2 \left|\mathbf{u}_b^H \mathbf{A}_{b'} \mathbf{x}\right|^2 + \sum\limits_{l=1}^{L} p_l \left|\mathbf{u}_b^H \mathbf{g}_l\right|^2 + \left|\mathbf{u}_b^H \mathbf{H}_{SI} \mathbf{x}\right|^2 + \left|\mathbf{u}_b^H\right|^2 \sigma_B^2}. \tag{5.118}$$

5.4.1.3 Computation Model

1. Offloading Computing

Similar to 5.4.1.2, We use the receive beamforming vector $\mathbf{z}_l \in \mathbb{C}^{N_r \times 1}$ to process signal $\mathbf{y}_{BS}$, and thus the l-th effective offloading signal received at the FD BS can be expressed as

$$y_l^{off} = \mathbf{z}_l^H \mathbf{y}_{BS} = \mathbf{z}_l^H \sum_{l=1}^{L} \sqrt{p_l} \mathbf{g}_l s_l^{ul} + \mathbf{z}_l^H \left(\mathbf{A}\mathbf{x} + \mathbf{H}_{SI}\mathbf{x} + \mathbf{n}_B\right), \tag{5.119}$$

where $\mathbf{g}_l = \mathbf{G}_r^H \mathbf{\Phi} \mathbf{g}_{r,l}$.

Therefore, the corresponding SINR is expressed as

$$r_l^{off} = \frac{\left|\mathbf{z}_l^H \mathbf{g}_l\right|^2 p_l}{\sum\limits_{l' \neq l}^{L} \left|\mathbf{z}_l^H \mathbf{g}_{l'}\right|^2 p_{l'} + \left|\mathbf{z}_l^H \left(\mathbf{A} + \mathbf{H}_{SI}\right) \mathbf{x}\right|^2 + \left|\mathbf{z}_l^H\right|^2 \sigma_B^2}. \tag{5.120}$$

The achievable offloading sum rate for CP-UE l at the BS is written as

$$R_{sum}^{off} = \sum_{l=1}^{L} R_l^{off} = \sum_{l=1}^{L} \log\left(1 + r_l^{off}\right). \tag{5.121}$$

2. Local Computing

Assume that υ represents the CPU cycles required for each CP-UE to process one bit of raw data, f_l represents the local CPU computing frequency of the l-th CP-UE, δ represents a constant related to hardware structure. According to [28], the computation rate and energy consumption at each CP-UE can be expressed as $R_l^{loc} = f_l/\upsilon$ and $E_l^{loc} = T\delta f_l^3$.

5.4.1.4 Channel State Information

In this subsection, we assume that the CSI between the FD BS and RIS can be obtained perfectly due the fixed RIS. However, due to the mobility of CM-UEs/CP-UEs, it is difficult to obtain perfect CSI from RIS to these users [24], [25], thus we assume that there exist channel estimation errors. Specifically, the channel $\mathbf{h}_{r,k}$ between RIS and CM-UE k, and the channel $\mathbf{g}_{r,l}$ between RIS and CP-UE l are modeled as

$$\mathbf{h}_{r,k} = \tilde{\mathbf{h}}_{r,k} + \Delta\mathbf{h}_{r,k}, \Delta\mathbf{h}_{r,k}\Delta\mathbf{h}_{r,k}^H \le \varepsilon_{r1,k}^2, \tag{5.122}$$

$$\mathbf{g}_{r,l} = \tilde{\mathbf{g}}_{r,l} + \Delta\mathbf{g}_{r,l}, \Delta\mathbf{g}_{r,l}\Delta\mathbf{g}_{r,l}^H \le \varepsilon_{r2,l}^2, \tag{5.123}$$

where $\tilde{\mathbf{h}}_{r,k}$ and $\tilde{\mathbf{g}}_{r,l}$ are the estimated CSI, $\Delta\mathbf{h}_{r,k}$ and $\Delta\mathbf{g}_{r,l}$ represent the corresponding estimation errors.

5.4.1.5 Problem Formulation

In this subsection, we formulate a sum rate maximization problem by jointly designing the FD BS transmit beamforming vector $\mathbf{w}_i, \forall i \in \{\mathcal{K}, \mathcal{B}\}$, the receive beamforming vector $\mathbf{u}_b$ and $\mathbf{z}_l$, the reflection vector $\boldsymbol{\psi} = [\psi_1, \cdots, \psi_M]^T$, the CP-UE transmit power p_l and the local computing resources f_l. Mathematically, the optimization problem can be expressed as

$$\mathcal{P}^0: \max_{\mathbf{w}_i,\mathbf{u}_b,\mathbf{z}_l,\boldsymbol{\psi},\mathbf{f},\mathbf{p}} \sum_{k=1}^{K} R_k^{com} + \sum_{l=1}^{L}\left(R_l^{off} + R_l^{loc}\right), \tag{5.124}$$

$$s.t.\ C1: \sum_{k=1}^{K}\left\|\mathbf{w}_{c,k}\right\|^2 + \sum_{b=1}^{B}\left\|\mathbf{w}_{r,b}\right\|^2 \le P_{BS}, \tag{5.124a}$$

$$C2: r_b^{tar} \ge \Gamma_b, \forall b, \tag{5.124b}$$

$$C3: \left|\boldsymbol{\psi}_m\right| = 1, \forall m, \tag{5.124c}$$

$$C4: T p_l + T\delta f_l^3 \le E_l^{\max}, \forall l, \tag{5.124d}$$

$$C5: \Delta\mathbf{h}_{r,k}\Delta\mathbf{h}_{r,k}^H \le \varepsilon_{r1,k}^2, \Delta\mathbf{g}_{r,l}\Delta\mathbf{g}_{r,l}^H \le \varepsilon_{r2,l}^2, \forall k, l, \tag{5.124e}$$

where $\mathbf{f} = [f_1, \cdots, f_L]^T$ represents the local computing resource vector, $\mathbf{p} = [p_1, \cdots, p_L]^T$ represents the CP-UE power vector. Constraint $C1$ represents the maximum power budget given by the FD BS, $C2$ represents the radar sensing requirement for each target, $C3$ represents the unit modulus constraint of RIS phase shift, and $C4$ represents the maximum energy budget given by the CP-UE. Due to the radar SINR constraint $C2$, the unit modulus constraint $C3$, and the estimation error upper bound constraint $C5$, it is obvious that problem $\mathcal{P}^0$ is a non-convex optimization problem. In the next section, we propose an alternatively iterative optimization algorithm to solve it.

5.4.2 Proposed Solution

In this section, we propose an alternating iterative optimization scheme. Specifically, the optimization problem is divided into four blocks: $\{\mathbf{w}_i, \mathbf{f}, \mathbf{p}\}$, $\{\mathbf{u}_b\}$, $\{\mathbf{z}_l\}$, $\{\boldsymbol{\psi}\}$. First, we transform the original problem into SDP, use SDR technology to solve the transmit beamforming $\mathbf{w}_i$, transmit power $\mathbf{p}$, local computing resources $\mathbf{f}$, receive beamforming $\mathbf{u}_b$ and $\mathbf{z}_l$. Then, use the SVD technology and SDR to solve the reflection phase shift $\boldsymbol{\psi}$. Finally, repeat the above process until convergence.

5.4.2.1 Optimization W, p, f

With other variables fixed, by introducing two auxiliary variables $\{t_k^{com}\}$, $\{t_l^{off}\}$, problem $\mathcal{P}^0$ can be rewritten as

$$\mathcal{P}^1 : \max_{\mathbf{W},\mathbf{f},\mathbf{p}} \sum_{k=1}^{K} \log\left(1 + t_k^{com}\right) + \sum_{l=1}^{L} \left(\log\left(1 + t_l^{off}\right) + R_l^{loc}\right) \tag{5.125}$$

$$s.t.\ \bar{C}1 : \sum_{i=1}^{K+B} \mathrm{Tr}\left(\mathbf{W}_i\right) \leq P_{BS}, \tag{5.125a}$$

$$C2, C4, C5, \tag{5.125b}$$

$$C6 : t_k^{com} \leq \frac{\left|\mathbf{h}_k \mathbf{w}_{c,k}\right|^2}{\sum\limits_{k' \neq k}^{K} \left|\mathbf{h}_k \mathbf{w}_{c,k'}\right|^2 + \sum\limits_{b=1}^{B} \left|\mathbf{h}_k \mathbf{w}_{r,b}\right|^2 + \sigma_k^2}, \tag{5.125c}$$

$$C7 : t_l^{off} \leq \frac{\left|\mathbf{z}_l^H \mathbf{g}_l\right|^2 p_l}{\sum\limits_{l' \neq l}^{L} \left|\mathbf{z}_l^H \mathbf{g}_{l'}\right|^2 p_{l'} + \left|\mathbf{z}_l^H \left(\mathbf{A} + \mathbf{H}_{SI}\right) \mathbf{x}\right|^2 + \left|\mathbf{z}_l^H\right|^2 \sigma_B^2}, \tag{5.125d}$$

where $\mathbf{W} = [\mathbf{W}_1, \cdots \mathbf{W}_K, \mathbf{W}_{K+1}, \cdots \mathbf{W}_{K+B}]$ and $\mathbf{W}_i = \mathbf{w}_i {\mathbf{w}_i}^H, \forall i \in \{\mathcal{K}, \mathcal{B}\}$.

It is obvious that solving the above problem is challenging due to the non-convexity of constraints $C2$, $C5$, $C6$, and $C7$. Next, to deal with constraint $C5$, we introduce Lemma 5.1.

Lemma 5.1 (S-Procedure [17]) *Suppose a function* $f_i(\mathbf{x})$, $i \in \{1, 2\}$ *is defined as*

$$f_i(\mathbf{x}) = \mathbf{x}^H \mathbf{B}_i \mathbf{x} + 2\mathcal{R}\left\{\mathbf{b}_i^H \mathbf{x}\right\} + b_i, \tag{5.126}$$

where $\mathbf{x} \in \mathbb{C}^{N\times 1}$, $\mathbf{B}_i \in \mathbb{C}^{N\times N}$, $\mathbf{b}_i \in \mathbb{C}^{N\times 1}$, $b_i \in \mathbb{R}$. *Then,* $f_1(\mathbf{x}) \le 0 \Rightarrow f_2(\mathbf{x}) \le 0$ *holds if and only if there exists a* $\kappa \ge 0$ *that satisfies*

$$\kappa \begin{bmatrix} \mathbf{B}_1 & \mathbf{b}_1 \\ \mathbf{b}_1^H & b_1 \end{bmatrix} - \kappa \begin{bmatrix} \mathbf{B}_2 & \mathbf{b}_2 \\ \mathbf{b}_2^H & b_2 \end{bmatrix} \succeq 0. \tag{5.127}$$

Next we introduce slack variables β_b and define $\bar{\mathbf{W}} = \sum_{i=1}^{K+B} \mathbf{W}_i$, then rewrite constraint $C2$ as

$$\bar{C}2a : \sum_{b'\neq b}^{B} \mathrm{Tr}\left(\xi^2 \mathbf{A}_{b'}^H \mathbf{U}_b \mathbf{A}_{b'} \bar{\mathbf{W}}\right) - \Gamma_b^{-1} \mathrm{Tr}\left(\xi^2 \mathbf{A}_b^H \mathbf{U}_b \mathbf{A}_b \bar{\mathbf{W}}\right) + \hbar_b + \beta_b \le 0, \tag{5.128}$$

$$C2b : \sum_{l=1}^{L} p_l \left| \tilde{\mathbf{u}}_b \left(\tilde{\mathbf{g}}_{r,l} + \Delta \mathbf{g}_{r,l}\right)\right|^2 \le \beta_b, \tag{5.129}$$

where $\hbar_b = \mathrm{Tr}\left(\mathbf{H}_{SI}^H \mathbf{U}_b \mathbf{H}_{SI} \bar{\mathbf{W}}\right) + \mathrm{Tr}\left(\mathbf{U}_b\right)\sigma_B^2$, $\mathbf{U}_b{=}\mathbf{u}_b\mathbf{u}_b^H$, $\tilde{\mathbf{u}}_b \triangleq \mathbf{u}_b^H \mathbf{G}_r^H \mathbf{\Phi}$.

The constraint $C2$b can be rewrite as

$$C2b : \sum_{l=1}^{L} p_l \left(\Delta \mathbf{g}_{r,l}^H \tilde{\mathbf{u}}_b^H \tilde{\mathbf{u}}_b \Delta \tilde{\mathbf{g}}_{r,l} + 2\mathcal{R}\left\{\tilde{\mathbf{g}}_{r,l}^H \tilde{\mathbf{u}}_b^H \tilde{\mathbf{u}}_b \Delta \tilde{\mathbf{g}}_{r,l}\right\} + \tilde{\mathbf{g}}_{r,l}^H \tilde{\mathbf{u}}_b^H \tilde{\mathbf{u}}_b \tilde{\mathbf{g}}_{r,l}\right) \le \beta_b. \tag{5.130}$$

By applying Lemma 5.1, we introduce an auxiliary variable $\delta_b \ge 0$ and rewrite constraint $C2$b as

$$\bar{C}2b : \begin{bmatrix} \delta_b \sum_{l=1}^{L} \left(\mathbf{I}_M - \bar{\mathbf{U}}_b p_l\right) & \left(\tilde{\mathbf{g}}_{r,l}^H \bar{\mathbf{U}}_b\right)^H \\ \tilde{\mathbf{g}}_{r,l}^H \bar{\mathbf{U}}_b & -\delta_b \sum_{l=1}^{L} \varepsilon_{r2,l}^2 + \beta_b - \sum_{l=1}^{L} p_l \tilde{\mathbf{g}}_{r,l}^H \bar{\mathbf{U}}_b \tilde{\mathbf{g}}_{r,l} \end{bmatrix} \succeq 0. \tag{5.131}$$

Next, we introduce the slack variable $\vartheta_{1,k}$, $\vartheta_{2,k}$, define $\hat{\mathbf{G}}_t \triangleq \mathbf{\Phi}\mathbf{G}_t$, and rewrite constraint $C6$ as

$$C6a : \vartheta_{1,k} \le \left| \left(\tilde{\mathbf{h}}_{r,k} + \Delta \mathbf{h}_{r,k}\right)^H \hat{\mathbf{G}}_t \mathbf{w}_{c,k} \right|^2, \tag{5.132}$$

$$C6b : t_k^{com} \vartheta_{2,k} \le \vartheta_{1,k}, \tag{5.133}$$

$$C6c:\vartheta_{2,k}\geq\sum_{k'\neq k}^{K}\left|\left(\tilde{\mathbf{h}}_{r,k}+\Delta\mathbf{h}_{r,k}\right)^{H}\hat{\mathbf{G}}_{t}\mathbf{w}_{c,k'}\right|^{2}+\sum_{b=1}^{B}\left|\left(\tilde{\mathbf{h}}_{r,k}+\Delta\mathbf{h}_{r,k}\right)^{H}\hat{\mathbf{G}}_{t}\mathbf{w}_{r,b}\right|^{2}$$
$$+\sigma_k^2. \tag{5.134}$$

Based on Lemma 5.1, $C6$a and $C6$c can be transformed into the following convex linear matrix inequality (LMI) constraints

$$\bar{C}6a:\begin{bmatrix}\tau_{1,k}\mathbf{I}_M+\mathbf{G}_{c,k} & \left(\tilde{\mathbf{h}}_{r,k}^{H}\mathbf{G}_{c,k}\right)^{H}\\ \tilde{\mathbf{h}}_{r,k}^{H}\mathbf{G}_{c,k} & -\tau_{1,k}\varepsilon_{r1,k}^{2}-\vartheta_{1,k}+\tilde{\mathbf{h}}_{r,k}^{H}\mathbf{G}_{c,k}\tilde{\mathbf{h}}_{r,k}\end{bmatrix}\succeq 0, \tag{5.135}$$

$$\bar{C}6c:\begin{bmatrix}\tau_{2,k}\mathbf{I}_M-\mathbf{G}_{t,k} & -\left(\tilde{\mathbf{h}}_{r,k}^{H}\mathbf{G}_{t,k}\right)^{H}\\ -\tilde{\mathbf{h}}_{r,k}^{H}\mathbf{G}_{t,k} & -\tau_{2,k}\varepsilon_{r1,k}^{2}+\vartheta_{2,k}-\tilde{\mathbf{h}}_{r,k}^{H}\mathbf{G}_{t,k}\tilde{\mathbf{h}}_{r,k}-\sigma_k^2\end{bmatrix}\succeq 0, \tag{5.136}$$

where $\mathbf{G}_{c,k}=\hat{\mathbf{G}}_t\mathbf{W}_{c,k}\hat{\mathbf{G}}_t^H$, $\mathbf{W}_{c,k}=\mathbf{w}_{c,k}\mathbf{w}_{c,k}^H$, $\mathbf{G}_{t,k}\triangleq\mathbf{G}-\mathbf{G}_{c,k}$, $\mathbf{G}=\hat{\mathbf{G}}_t\bar{\mathbf{W}}\mathbf{\Theta}_t^H$, $\tau_{1,k},\tau_{2,k}\geq 0$.

Meanwhile, the non-convex constraint $C6$b can be reformulated as

$$\bar{C}6b:\frac{t_k^{com,(n)}}{2\vartheta_{2,k}^{(n)}}\vartheta_{2,k}^2+\frac{\vartheta_{2,k}^{(n)}}{2t_k^{com,(n)}}(t_k^{com})^2\leq\vartheta_{1,k}, \tag{5.137}$$

where $t_k^{com,(n)}$ and $\vartheta_{2,k}^{(n)}$ represent the values of t_k^{com} and $\vartheta_{2,k}$ at the t-th iteration, respectively.

Next, we introduce the slack variable $\chi_{1,l}$, $\chi_{2,l}$ and define $\tilde{\mathbf{z}}_l\triangleq\mathbf{z}_l^H\mathbf{G}_r^H\mathbf{\Phi}$. The constraint $C7$ can be expressed equivalently as

$$C7a:\chi_{1,l}\leq\left|\tilde{\mathbf{z}}_l\left(\tilde{\mathbf{g}}_{r,l}+\Delta\mathbf{g}_{r,l}\right)\right|^2p_l, \tag{5.138}$$

$$C7b:t_l^{off}\chi_{2,l}\leq\chi_{1,l}, \tag{5.139}$$

$$C7c:\chi_{2,l}\geq\sum_{l'\neq l}^{L}\left|\tilde{\mathbf{z}}_l\left(\tilde{\mathbf{g}}_{r,l'}+\Delta\mathbf{g}_{r,l'}\right)\right|^2p_{l'}+|\bar{\mathbf{z}}_l\mathbf{x}|^2+\left|\mathbf{z}_l^H\right|^2\sigma_B^2, \tag{5.140}$$

where $\bar{\mathbf{z}}_l=\mathbf{z}_l^H\left(\mathbf{A}+\mathbf{H}_{SI}\right)$.

Similarly, constraints $C7$a and $C7$c can be transformed into the following convex LMI constraints

$$\bar{C}7a:\begin{bmatrix}\kappa_{1,l}\mathbf{I}_M+\tilde{\mathbf{Z}}_lp_l & \left(\tilde{\mathbf{g}}_{r,l}^{H}\tilde{\mathbf{Z}}_lp_l\right)^{H}\\ \tilde{\mathbf{g}}_{r,l}^{H}\tilde{\mathbf{Z}}_lp_l & -\kappa_{1,l}\varepsilon_{r2,l}^{2}-\chi_{1,l}+\tilde{\mathbf{g}}_{r,l}^{H}\tilde{\mathbf{Z}}_l\tilde{\mathbf{g}}_{r,l}p_l\end{bmatrix}\succeq 0, \tag{5.141}$$

$$\bar{C}7c: \begin{bmatrix} \kappa_{2,l}\sum_{l'\neq l}^{L}\left(\mathbf{I}_M - \tilde{\mathbf{Z}}_l p_{l'}\right) & -\sum_{l'\neq l}^{L}\left(\tilde{\mathbf{g}}_{r,l'}^H \tilde{\mathbf{Z}}_l p_{l'}\right)^H \\ -\sum_{l'\neq l}^{L}\left(\tilde{\mathbf{g}}_{r,l'}^H \tilde{\mathbf{Z}}_l p_{l'}\right) & \kappa_{2,l}\sum_{l'\neq l}^{L}\left(-\varepsilon_{r2,l'}^2 - \tilde{\mathbf{g}}_{r,l'}^H \tilde{\mathbf{Z}}_l \tilde{\mathbf{g}}_{r,l'} p_{l'}\right) + \chi_{2,l} - a_l \end{bmatrix} \succeq 0, \tag{5.142}$$

where $\tilde{\mathbf{Z}}_l \triangleq \tilde{\mathbf{z}}_l^H \tilde{\mathbf{z}}_l$, $a_l = \bar{\mathbf{z}}_l \bar{\mathbf{W}} \bar{\mathbf{z}}_l^H - \left|\mathbf{z}_l^H\right|^2 \sigma_B^2$, $\kappa_{1,l}, \kappa_{2,l} \geq 0$.

Additionally, the non-convex constraint $C7$b can be reformulated as

$$\bar{C}7b: \frac{t_l^{off,(n)}}{2\chi_{2,l}^{(n)}}\chi_{2,l}^2 + \frac{\chi_{2,l}^{(n)}}{2t_l^{off,(n)}}\left(t_l^{off}\right)^2 \leq \chi_{1,l}, \tag{5.143}$$

where $t_l^{off,(n)}$ and $\chi_{2,l}^{(n)}$ represent the values of t_l^{off} and $\chi_{2,l}$ at the t-th iteration, respectively.

Finally, problem $\mathcal{P}^1$ is transformed into the following form

$$\mathcal{P}^2: \max_{\substack{\mathbf{W},\mathbf{f},\mathbf{p},t_k^{com},t_l^{off},\beta_b,\delta_b,\vartheta_{1,k},\vartheta_{2,k},\\ \tau_{1,k},\tau_{2,k},\chi_{1,l},\chi_{2,l},\kappa_{1,l},\kappa_{2,l}}} \sum_{k=1}^{K}\log\left(1+t_k^{com}\right) + \sum_{l=1}^{L}\left(\log\left(1+t_l^{off}\right) + R_l^{loc}\right) \tag{5.144}$$

$$s.t.\ \bar{C}1, \bar{C}2a, \bar{C}2b, C4, \bar{C}6a, \bar{C}6b, \bar{C}6c, \bar{C}7a, \bar{C}7b, \bar{C}7c, \tag{5.144a}$$

$$C8: rank\left(\mathbf{W}_i\right) = 1, \mathbf{W}_i \succeq 0, \forall i \in \{\mathcal{K}, \mathcal{B}\}, \tag{5.144b}$$

$$C9: \delta_b, \tau_{1,k}, \tau_{2,k}, \kappa_{1,l}, \kappa_{2,l} \geq 0, \forall b, k, l, \tag{5.144c}$$

It is obvious that problem $\mathcal{P}^2$ is a classic SDP problem, and we can obtain its solutions based on SDR by relaxing the rank-one constraint $rank\left(\mathbf{W}_i\right) = 1$. If the obtained solutions do not satisfy the rank-one condition, we can obtain the approximate solutions by exploiting the Gaussian randomization technique [7].

5.4.2.2 Optimization $\mathbf{u}_b$

For given $\mathbf{W}$, $\mathbf{p}$, $\mathbf{f}$, $\boldsymbol{\psi}$, $\mathbf{z}_l$, $\mathcal{P}^0$ is a typical feasibility check problem [29]. By maximizing the lower bound of the SINR to update the receive beamforming vector $\mathbf{u}_b$, we reformulate the original problem as

$$\mathcal{P}^3: \max_{\mathbf{u}_b} \frac{\xi^2\left|\mathbf{u}_b^H \mathbf{A}_b \mathbf{x}\right|^2}{\sum_{b'\neq b}^{B}\xi^2\left|\mathbf{u}_b^H \mathbf{A}_{b'}\mathbf{x}\right|^2 + \sum_{l=1}^{L} p_l\left|\mathbf{u}_b^H \mathbf{g}_l\right|^2 + \left|\mathbf{u}_b^H \mathbf{H}_{SI}\mathbf{x}\right|^2 + \left|\mathbf{u}_b^H\right|^2\sigma_B^2}. \tag{5.145}$$

Due to channel uncertainty, it is difficult to be solved directly. We introduce auxiliary variables ρ_b to transform problem $\mathcal{P}^3$ into

$$\mathcal{P}^4 : \max_{\mathbf{u}_b, \rho_b} \ \rho_b \tag{5.146}$$

$$s.t.\ C10 : \rho_b \leq \frac{\xi^2 \left|\mathbf{u}_b^H \mathbf{A}_b \mathbf{x}\right|^2}{\sum_{b' \neq b}^{B} \xi^2 \left|\mathbf{u}_b^H \mathbf{A}_{b'} \mathbf{x}\right|^2 + \sum_{l=1}^{L} p_l \left|\mathbf{u}_b^H \mathbf{g}_l\right|^2 + \left|\mathbf{u}_b^H \mathbf{H}_{SI} \mathbf{x}\right|^2 + \left|\mathbf{u}_b^H\right|^2 \sigma_B^2}. \tag{5.146a}$$

Next, we introduce the slack variable $\tilde{\vartheta}_{1,b}$, $\tilde{\vartheta}_{2,b}$, $\tilde{\beta}_b$ and rewrite constraint $C10$ as

$$C10a : \tilde{\vartheta}_{1,b} \leq \xi^2 \left|\mathbf{u}_b^H \mathbf{A}_b \mathbf{x}\right|^2, \tag{5.147}$$

$$C10b : \rho_b \tilde{\vartheta}_{2,b} \leq \tilde{\vartheta}_{1,b}, \tag{5.148}$$

$$C10c : \tilde{\vartheta}_{2,b} \geq \sum_{b' \neq b}^{B} \xi^2 \left|\mathbf{u}_b^H \mathbf{A}_{b'} \mathbf{x}\right|^2 + \tilde{\beta}_b + \left|\mathbf{u}_b^H \mathbf{H}_{SI} \mathbf{x}\right|^2 + \left|\mathbf{u}_b^H\right|^2 \sigma_B^2, \tag{5.149}$$

$$C10d : \tilde{\beta}_b \geq \sum_{l=1}^{L} p_l \left|\mathbf{u}_b^H \mathbf{G}_r^H \boldsymbol{\Phi} \left(\tilde{\mathbf{g}}_{r,l} + \Delta \mathbf{g}_{r,l}\right)\right|^2, \tag{5.150}$$

Next, constraints $C10$a, $C10$b and $C10$c can be transformed as

$$\bar{C}10a : \tilde{\vartheta}_{1,b} \leq Tr\left(\xi^2 \mathbf{A}_b^H \mathbf{U}_b \mathbf{A}_b \bar{\mathbf{W}}\right), \tag{5.151}$$

$$\bar{C}10b : \frac{\rho_b^{(n)}}{2\tilde{\vartheta}_{2,b}^{(n)}} \tilde{\vartheta}_{2,b}^2 + \frac{\tilde{\vartheta}_{2,b}^{(n)}}{2\rho_b^{(n)}} \rho_b^2 \leq \tilde{\vartheta}_{1,b}, \tag{5.152}$$

$$\bar{C}10c : \tilde{\vartheta}_{2,b} \geq Tr\left(\sum_{b' \neq b}^{B} \xi^2 \mathbf{A}_{b'}^H \mathbf{U}_b \mathbf{A}_{b'} \bar{\mathbf{W}} + \mathbf{H}_{SI}^H \mathbf{U}_b \mathbf{H}_{SI} \bar{\mathbf{W}} + \mathbf{U}_b \sigma_B^2\right) + \tilde{\beta}_b, \tag{5.153}$$

where $\rho_b^{(n)}$ and $\tilde{\vartheta}_{2,b}^{(n)}$ represent the values of ρ_b and $\tilde{\vartheta}_{2,b}$ at the t-th iteration, respectively.

The constraint $C10$d can be transformed into the following convex LMI

$$\bar{C}10d:\begin{bmatrix}\tilde{\tau}_{1,b}\sum_{l=1}^{L}\mathbf{I}_M-p_l\tilde{\mathbf{U}}_b & -\sum_{l=1}^{L}\left(p_l\tilde{\mathbf{g}}_{r,l}^H\tilde{\mathbf{U}}_b\right)^H\\ -\sum_{l=1}^{L}p_l\tilde{\mathbf{g}}_{r,l}^H\tilde{\mathbf{U}}_b & -\tilde{\tau}_{1,b}\sum_{l=1}^{L}\varepsilon_{r2,l}^2-p_l\tilde{\mathbf{g}}_{r,l}^H\tilde{\mathbf{U}}_b\tilde{\mathbf{g}}_{r,l}+\tilde{\beta}_b\end{bmatrix}\succeq 0, \tag{5.154}$$

where $\tilde{\mathbf{u}}_b^H=\mathbf{u}_b^H\mathbf{G}_r^H\mathbf{\Phi}$, $\tilde{\mathbf{U}}_b\triangleq\tilde{\mathbf{u}}_b\tilde{\mathbf{u}}_b^H$, $\tilde{\tau}_{1,b}\geq 0$.

Finally, problem $\mathcal{P}^4$ is transformed into the following form

$$\mathcal{P}^5:\max_{\mathbf{U}_b,\rho_b,\tilde{\beta}_b,\tilde{\vartheta}_{1,b},\tilde{\vartheta}_{2,b}}\ \rho_b \tag{5.155}$$

$$s.t.\ \bar{C}10a,\bar{C}10b,\bar{C}10c,\bar{C}10d, \tag{5.155a}$$

$$C11: rank\left(\mathbf{U}_b\right)=1,\mathbf{U}_b\succeq 0,\forall i\in\mathcal{B}, \tag{5.155b}$$

$$C12:\tilde{\tau}_{1,b}\geq 0. \tag{5.155c}$$

It is obvious that problem $\mathcal{P}^5$ can be solved by SDR technique. Similarly, the final solutions do not satisfy the rank-one condition, we can obtain the approximate solution by exploiting the Gaussian randomization technique.

5.4.2.3 Optimization of $\mathbf{z}_l$

For given other variables, problem $\mathcal{P}^0$ can be rewritten as

$$\mathcal{P}^6:\max_{\mathbf{z}_l}\sum_{l=1}^{L}\log\left(1+\frac{\left|\mathbf{z}_l^H\mathbf{g}_l\right|^2p_l}{\sum_{l'\neq l}^{L}\left|\mathbf{z}_l^H\mathbf{g}_{l'}\right|^2p_{l'}+\left|\mathbf{z}_l^H\left(\mathbf{A}+\mathbf{H}_{SI}\right)\mathbf{x}\right|^2+\left|\mathbf{z}_l^H\right|^2\sigma_B^2}\right). \tag{5.156}$$

This is an unconstrained optimization problem, and the objective function is non-convex. The auxiliary variable $\tilde{t}_l^{loc}$ is introduced to transform the problem into

$$\mathcal{P}^7:\max_{\mathbf{z}_l}\log\left(1+\tilde{t}_l^{loc}\right) \tag{5.157}$$

$$s.t.\ C13:\tilde{t}_l^{off}\leq\frac{\left|\mathbf{z}_l^H\mathbf{g}_l\right|^2p_l}{\sum_{l'\neq l}^{L}\left|\mathbf{z}_l^H\mathbf{g}_{l'}\right|^2p_{l'}+\left|\mathbf{z}_l^H\left(\mathbf{A}+\mathbf{H}_{SI}\right)\mathbf{x}\right|^2+\left|\mathbf{z}_l^H\right|^2\sigma_B^2}. \tag{5.157a}$$

Next, we introduce the slack variable $\tilde{\chi}_{1,l}$, $\tilde{\chi}_{2,l}$, $\bar{\beta}_l$ and rewrite constraint $C13$ as

$$C13a : \tilde{\chi}_{1,l} \leq \left|\tilde{\mathbf{z}}_l^H \left(\tilde{\mathbf{g}}_{r,l} + \Delta\mathbf{g}_{r,l}\right)\right|^2 p_l, \tag{5.158}$$

$$C13b : \tilde{t}_l^{off} \tilde{\chi}_{2,l} \leq \tilde{\chi}_{1,l}, \tag{5.159}$$

$$C13c : \tilde{\chi}_{2,l} \geq \sum_{l' \neq l}^{L} \left|\tilde{\mathbf{z}}_l^H \left(\tilde{\mathbf{g}}_{r,l'} + \Delta\mathbf{g}_{r,l'}\right)\right|^2 p_{l'} + \bar{\beta}_l, \tag{5.160}$$

$$C13d : \bar{\beta}_l \geq \left|\mathbf{z}_l^H \left(\mathbf{A} + \mathbf{H}_{SI}\right) \mathbf{x}\right|^2 + \left|\mathbf{z}_l^H\right|^2 \sigma_B^2. \tag{5.161}$$

The constraints $C13$a and $C13$c can be transformed into the following convex LMI constraints

$$\bar{C}13a : \begin{bmatrix} \tilde{\kappa}_{1,l}\mathbf{I}_M + \tilde{\mathbf{Z}}_l p_l & \left(\tilde{\mathbf{g}}_{r,l}^H \tilde{\mathbf{Z}}_l\right)^H p_l \\ \tilde{\mathbf{g}}_{r,l}^H \tilde{\mathbf{Z}}_l p_l & -\tilde{\kappa}_{1,l}\varepsilon_{r2,l}^2 - \tilde{\chi}_{1,l} + \tilde{\mathbf{g}}_{r,l}^H \tilde{\mathbf{Z}}_l \tilde{\mathbf{g}}_{r,l} p_l \end{bmatrix} \succeq 0, \tag{5.162}$$

$$\bar{C}11c : \begin{bmatrix} \tilde{\kappa}_{2,l} \sum_{l' \neq l}^{L} \left(\mathbf{I}_M - \tilde{\mathbf{Z}}_l p_{l'}\right) & -\sum_{l' \neq l}^{L} \left(\tilde{\mathbf{g}}_{r,l'}^H \tilde{\mathbf{Z}}_l p_{l'}\right)^H \\ -\sum_{l' \neq l}^{L} \tilde{\mathbf{g}}_{r,l'}^H \tilde{\mathbf{Z}}_l p_{l'} & -\tilde{\kappa}_{2,l} \sum_{l' \neq l}^{L} \varepsilon_{r2,l'}^2 + \tilde{\chi}_{2,l} - \bar{\beta}_l - \sum_{l' \neq l}^{L} \left(\tilde{\mathbf{g}}_{r,l'}^H \tilde{\mathbf{Z}}_l \tilde{\mathbf{g}}_{r,l'} p_{l'}\right) \end{bmatrix}$$
$$\succeq 0, \tag{5.163}$$

where $\tilde{\kappa}_{1,l}, \tilde{\kappa}_{2,l} \geq 0$.

The constraint $C13$b can be transformed as

$$\bar{C}13b : \frac{\tilde{t}_l^{off,(n)}}{2\tilde{\chi}_{2,l}^{(n)}} \tilde{\chi}_{2,l}^2 + \frac{\tilde{\chi}_{2,l}^{(n)}}{2\tilde{t}_l^{off,(n)}} \left(\tilde{t}_l^{off}\right)^2 \leq \tilde{\chi}_{1,l}, \tag{5.164}$$

where $\tilde{t}_l^{off,(n)}$ and $\tilde{\chi}_{2,l}^{(n)}$ represent the values of $\tilde{t}_l^{off}$ and $\tilde{\chi}_{2,l}$ at the t-th iteration, respectively.

Next, the constraint $C13$d can be transformed as

$$\bar{C}13d : \bar{\beta}_l \geq Tr\left(\mathbf{Z}_l \mathbf{Q}\right), \tag{5.165}$$

where $\mathbf{Z}_l = \mathbf{z}_l \mathbf{z}_l^H$, $\mathbf{Q} = \left(\mathbf{A} + \mathbf{H}_{SI}\right) \mathbf{x}\mathbf{x}^H \left(\mathbf{A} + \mathbf{H}_{SI}\right)^H + \mathbf{I}_{Nr}\sigma_B^2$.

Finally, problem $\mathcal{P}^7$ is transformed into the following form

$$\mathcal{P}^8: \max_{\mathbf{Z}_l,\bar{t}_l^{loc},\bar{\beta}_l,\tilde{\chi}_{1,l},\tilde{\chi}_{2,l},\tilde{\kappa}_{1,l},\tilde{\kappa}_{2,l}} \log\left(1+\bar{t}_l^{loc}\right) \tag{5.166}$$

$$s.t.\ \bar{C}13a, \bar{C}13b, \bar{C}13c, \bar{C}13d, \tag{5.166a}$$

$$C14: rank\left(\mathbf{Z}_l\right)=1, \mathbf{Z}_l\succeq 0, \tag{5.166b}$$

$$C15: \tilde{\kappa}_{1,l}, \tilde{\kappa}_{2,l} \geq 0, \tag{5.166c}$$

Problem $\mathcal{P}^8$ can also be solved by SDR technique, and we use the Gaussian randomization to deal with the rank-one problem.

5.4.2.4 Optimization of ψ

When other variables are fixed, by introducing two auxiliary variables $\bar{t}_k^{com}, \bar{t}_l^{off}$, problem $\mathcal{P}^0$ can be rewritten as

$$\mathcal{P}^9: \max_{\psi} \sum_{k=1}^{K} \log\left(1+\bar{t}_k^{com}\right) + \sum_{l=1}^{L} \log\left(1+\bar{t}_l^{off}\right) \tag{5.167}$$

$$s.t.\ C2, C3, C5, \tag{5.167a}$$

$$C16: \bar{t}_k^{com} \leq \frac{\left|\mathbf{h}_k \mathbf{w}_{c,k}\right|^2}{\sum\limits_{k'\neq k}^{K} \left|\mathbf{h}_k \mathbf{w}_{c,k'}\right|^2 + \sum\limits_{b=1}^{B} \left|\mathbf{h}_k \mathbf{w}_{r,b}\right|^2 + \sigma_k^2}, \forall k, \tag{5.167b}$$

$$C17: \bar{t}_l^{off} \leq \frac{\left|\mathbf{z}_l^H \mathbf{g}_l\right|^2 p_l}{\sum\limits_{l'\neq l}^{L} \left|\mathbf{z}_l^H \mathbf{g}_{l'}\right|^2 p_{l'} + \left|\mathbf{z}_l^H \left(\mathbf{A}+\mathbf{H}_{SI}\right)\mathbf{x}\right|^2 + \left|\mathbf{z}_l^H\right|^2 \sigma_B^2}, \forall l, \tag{5.167c}$$

First, for constraint $C2$, we can rewrite it as

$$C2: \sum_{l=1}^{L} p_l \left(\tilde{\mathbf{g}}_{r,l}+\Delta\mathbf{g}_{r,l}\right)^H \mathbf{\Phi}^H \mathbf{G}_r \mathbf{U}_b \mathbf{G}_r^H \mathbf{\Phi}\left(\tilde{\mathbf{g}}_{r,l}+\Delta\mathbf{g}_{r,l}\right) + a_b \leq 0, \tag{5.168}$$

where $a_b = \sum\limits_{b'\neq b}^{B} \xi^2 \left|\mathbf{u}_b^H \mathbf{A}_{b'}\mathbf{x}\right|^2 + \left|\mathbf{u}_b^H \mathbf{H}_{SI}\mathbf{x}\right|^2 + \left|\mathbf{u}_b^H\right|^2 \sigma_B^2 - \xi^2 \left|\mathbf{u}_b^H \mathbf{A}_b \mathbf{x}\right|^2 / \Gamma_b^{tar}$.

Next, the SVD technique is applied to deal with the coupling of channel estimation error and optimize the phase shift. We redefine the matrix $\mathbf{G}_r \mathbf{U}_b \mathbf{G}_r^H$ as

$\mathbf{G}_r\mathbf{U}_b\mathbf{G}_r^H = \sum_{i=1}^{I} h_{b,i}\mathbf{v}_{b,i}\mathbf{r}_{b,i}^H$, where $h_{b,i}$ represents the singular values of the matrix, $\mathbf{v}_{b,i}$ and $\mathbf{r}_{b,i}$ represent the left and right singular vectors of the matrix, respectively.

Therefore, we rewrite $\mathbf{\Phi}^H\mathbf{G}_r\mathbf{U}_b\mathbf{G}_r^H\mathbf{\Phi}$ in the constraint $C2$ as

$$\begin{aligned}
&\mathbf{\Phi}^H\mathbf{G}_r\mathbf{U}_b\mathbf{G}_r^H\mathbf{\Phi} \\
&= diag(\boldsymbol{\psi})^H\sum_{i=1}^{I} h_{b,i}\mathbf{v}_{b,i}\mathbf{r}_{b,i}^H diag\left(\boldsymbol{\psi}\right) = \sum_{i=1}^{I} h_{b,i} diag(\mathbf{v}_{b,i})\boldsymbol{\psi}^*\boldsymbol{\psi}^T diag\left(\mathbf{r}_{b,i}^H\right) \\
&= \sum_{i=1}^{I} h_{b,i}\mathbf{V}_{b,i}\mathbf{\Omega}^T\mathbf{R}_{b,i},
\end{aligned} \tag{5.169}$$

where $\mathbf{V}_{b,I} = \begin{bmatrix} diag(\mathbf{v}_{b,i}) & 0 \\ 0 & 0 \end{bmatrix}$, $\mathbf{R}_{b,i} = \begin{bmatrix} diag\left(\mathbf{r}_{b,i}^H\right) & 0 \\ 0 & 0 \end{bmatrix}$, $\boldsymbol{\varphi} = (\boldsymbol{\psi};\, 1)$, $\mathbf{\Omega} = \boldsymbol{\varphi}\boldsymbol{\varphi}^H$.

Therefore, constraint $C2$ can be reformulated as

$$\tilde{C}2: \sum_{l=1}^{L} p_l\left[\left(\tilde{\mathbf{g}}_{r,l} + \Delta\mathbf{g}_{r,l}\right)^H, 0\right]\sum_{i=1}^{I} h_{b,i}\mathbf{V}_{b,i}\mathbf{\Omega}^T\mathbf{R}_{b,i}\mathbf{\Phi}\begin{bmatrix} \left(\tilde{\mathbf{g}}_{r,l} + \Delta\mathbf{g}_{r,l}\right) \\ 0 \end{bmatrix} + a_b \le 0. \tag{5.170}$$

We expand the square term in the constraint $\tilde{C}2$ and reformulate it as

$$\tilde{C}2: \sum_{l=1}^{L} p_l\left(\Delta\mathbf{g}_{r1,l}^H\mathbf{\Lambda}_b\Delta\mathbf{g}_{r1,l} + 2\mathcal{R}\left\{\tilde{\mathbf{g}}_{r1,l}^H\mathbf{\Lambda}_b\Delta\mathbf{g}_{r1,l}\right\} + \tilde{\mathbf{g}}_{r1,l}^H\mathbf{\Lambda}_b\tilde{\mathbf{g}}_{r1,l}\right) + a_b \le 0, \tag{5.171}$$

where $\mathbf{\Lambda}_b = \sum_{i=1}^{I} h_{b,i}\mathbf{V}_{b,i}\mathbf{\Omega}^T\mathbf{R}_{b,i}$, $\tilde{\mathbf{g}}_{r1,l} = [\tilde{\mathbf{g}}_{r,l}^T, 0]^T$, $\Delta\mathbf{g}_{r1,l} = [\Delta\mathbf{g}_{r,l}^T, 0]^T$.

Next, we introduce the auxiliary variable $\bar{\delta}_b \ge 0$ and refer to Lemma 5.1 to transform the constraint into the following convex LMI constraint

$$\hat{C}2: \begin{bmatrix} \bar{\delta}_b\sum_{l=1}^{L}\left(\mathbf{I}_M - p_l\mathbf{\Lambda}_b\right) & -\sum_{l=1}^{L}\left(p_l\tilde{\mathbf{g}}_{r1,l}^H\mathbf{\Lambda}_b\right)^H \\ -\sum_{l=1}^{L} p_l\tilde{\mathbf{g}}_{r1,l}^H\mathbf{\Lambda}_b & -\bar{\delta}_b\sum_{l=1}^{L}\varepsilon_{r2,l}^2 - a_b - \sum_{l=1}^{L} p_l\tilde{\mathbf{g}}_{r1,l}^H\Lambda_b\tilde{\mathbf{g}}_{r1,l} \end{bmatrix} \succeq 0. \tag{5.172}$$

For constraint $C16$, we rewrite it as

$$C16 : \bar{t}_k^{com} \le \frac{\left(\tilde{\mathbf{h}}_{r,k} + \Delta\mathbf{h}_{r,k}\right)^H \mathbf{\Phi}\mathbf{G}_t\mathbf{W}_{c,k}\mathbf{G}_t^H\mathbf{\Phi}^H \left(\tilde{\mathbf{h}}_{r,k} + \Delta\mathbf{h}_{r,k}\right)}{\left(\tilde{\mathbf{h}}_{r,k} + \Delta\mathbf{h}_{r,k}\right)^H \mathbf{\Phi}\mathbf{G}_t\mathbf{W}_{rc,k}\mathbf{G}_t^H\mathbf{\Phi}\left(\tilde{\mathbf{h}}_{r,k} + \Delta\mathbf{h}_{r,k}\right) + \sigma_k^2}, \tag{5.173}$$

where $\mathbf{W}_{rc,k} = \bar{\mathbf{W}} - \mathbf{W}_{c,k}$. Similar to the processing method of constraint $C2$, we use the SVD to re-express $\mathbf{\Phi}\mathbf{G}_t\mathbf{W}_{c,k}\mathbf{G}_t^H\mathbf{\Phi}^H$ and $\mathbf{\Phi}\mathbf{G}_t\mathbf{W}_{rc,k}\mathbf{G}_t^H\mathbf{\Phi}^H$ as

$$\begin{aligned}\mathbf{\Phi}\mathbf{G}_t\mathbf{W}_{c,k}\mathbf{G}_t^H\mathbf{\Phi}^H &= diag\left(\boldsymbol{\psi}\right)\sum_{i=1}^{I}\widehat{h}_{k,i}\widehat{\mathbf{v}}_{k,i}\widehat{\mathbf{r}}_{k,i}^H diag(\boldsymbol{\psi})^H\\ &= \sum_{i=1}^{I}\widehat{h}_{k,i} diag(\widehat{\mathbf{v}}_{k,i})\boldsymbol{\psi}\boldsymbol{\psi}^H diag\left(\widehat{\mathbf{r}}_{k,i}^H\right)\\ &= \sum_{i=1}^{I}\widehat{h}_{k,i}\widehat{\mathbf{V}}_{k,i}\mathbf{\Omega}^T\widehat{\mathbf{R}}_{k,i},\end{aligned} \tag{5.174}$$

$$\begin{aligned}\mathbf{\Phi}\mathbf{G}_t\mathbf{W}_{rc,k}\mathbf{G}_t^H\mathbf{\Phi}^H &= diag\left(\boldsymbol{\psi}\right)\sum_{i=1}^{I}\breve{h}_{k,i}\breve{\mathbf{v}}_{k,i}\breve{\mathbf{r}}_{k,i}^H diag(\boldsymbol{\psi})^H\\ &= \sum_{i=1}^{I}\breve{h}_{k,i} diag(\breve{\mathbf{v}}_{k,i})\boldsymbol{\psi}\boldsymbol{\psi}^H diag\left(\breve{\mathbf{r}}_{k,i}^H\right)\\ &= \sum_{i=1}^{I}\breve{h}_{k,i}\breve{\mathbf{V}}_{k,i}\mathbf{\Omega}^T\breve{\mathbf{R}}_{k,i}\end{aligned} \tag{5.175}$$

where $\widehat{\mathbf{V}}_{k,i} = \begin{bmatrix} diag(\widehat{\mathbf{v}}_{k,i}) & 0\\ 0 & 0\end{bmatrix}$, $\widehat{\mathbf{R}}_{k,i} = \begin{bmatrix} diag\left(\widehat{\mathbf{r}}_{k,i}^H\right) & 0\\ 0 & 0\end{bmatrix}$, $\breve{\mathbf{V}}_{k,i} = \begin{bmatrix} diag(\breve{\mathbf{v}}_{k,i}) & 0\\ 0 & 0\end{bmatrix}$, $\breve{\mathbf{R}}_{k,i} = \begin{bmatrix} diag\left(\breve{\mathbf{r}}_{k,i}^H\right) & 0\\ 0 & 0\end{bmatrix}$. $\widehat{h}_{k,i}$, $\widehat{\mathbf{v}}_{k,i}$, $\widehat{\mathbf{r}}_{k,i}$ and $\breve{h}_{k,i}$, $\breve{\mathbf{v}}_{k,i}$, $\breve{\mathbf{r}}_{k,i}$ denote the corresponding singular values and left and right singular vectors, respectively.

Therefore, we introduce the slack variables $\mu_{1,k}$, $\mu_{2,k}$ and reformulate constraint $C16$ as

$$\tilde{C}16a : \mu_{1,k} \le \left[\left(\tilde{\mathbf{h}}_{r,k} + \Delta\mathbf{h}_{r,k}\right)^H, 0\right]\widehat{\mathbf{\Lambda}}_k\begin{bmatrix}\left(\tilde{\mathbf{h}}_{r,k} + \Delta\mathbf{h}_{r,k}\right)\\ 0\end{bmatrix}, \tag{5.176}$$

$$\tilde{C}16b : \bar{t}_k^{com}\mu_{2,k} \le \mu_{1,k}, \tag{5.177}$$

$$\tilde{C}16c : \mu_{2,k} \geq \left[\left(\tilde{\mathbf{h}}_{r,k} + \Delta\mathbf{h}_{r,k}\right)^H, 0\right] \breve{\mathbf{\Lambda}}_k \begin{bmatrix} \left(\tilde{\mathbf{h}}_{r,k} + \Delta\mathbf{h}_{r,k}\right) \\ 0 \end{bmatrix} + \sigma_k^2, \tag{5.178}$$

where $\widehat{\mathbf{\Lambda}}_k = \sum_{i=1}^{I} \widehat{h}_{k,i} \widehat{\mathbf{V}}_{k,i} \mathbf{\Omega}^T \widehat{\mathbf{R}}_{k,i}$, $\breve{\mathbf{\Lambda}}_k = \sum_{i=1}^{I} \breve{h}_{k,i} \breve{\mathbf{V}}_{k,i} \mathbf{\Omega}^T \breve{\mathbf{R}}_{k,i}$. We define $\tilde{\mathbf{h}}_{r1,k} = [\tilde{\mathbf{h}}_{r,k}^T, 0]^T$, and introduce an auxiliary variables $\varphi_{1,k}, \varphi_{2,k} \geq 0$. $\tilde{C}16a$ and $\tilde{C}16c$ can be expressed as the following convex constraints

$$\bar{C}16a : \begin{bmatrix} \varphi_{1,k}\mathbf{I}_M + \widehat{\mathbf{\Lambda}}_k & \left(\tilde{\mathbf{h}}_{r1,k}^H \widehat{\mathbf{\Lambda}}\right)^H \\ \tilde{\mathbf{h}}_{r1,k}^H \widehat{\mathbf{\Lambda}} & -\varphi_{1,k}\varepsilon_{r1,k}^2 - \mu_{1,k} + \tilde{\mathbf{h}}_{r1,k}^H \Lambda_k \tilde{\mathbf{h}}_{r1,k} \end{bmatrix} \succeq 0, \tag{5.179}$$

$$\bar{C}16c : \begin{bmatrix} \varphi_{2,k}\mathbf{I}_M - \breve{\mathbf{\Lambda}}_k & -\left(\tilde{\mathbf{h}}_{r1,k}^H \breve{\mathbf{\Lambda}}_k\right)^H \\ -\tilde{\mathbf{h}}_{r1,k}^H \breve{\mathbf{\Lambda}}_k & -\varphi_{2,k}\varepsilon_{r1,k}^2 + \mu_{2,k} - \tilde{\mathbf{h}}_{r1,k}^H \breve{\mathbf{\Lambda}}_k \tilde{\mathbf{h}}_{r,k} - \sigma_k^2 \end{bmatrix} \succeq 0, \tag{5.180}$$

The constraint $\tilde{C}16b$ is transformed into

$$\bar{C}16b : \frac{\bar{t}_k^{com,(n)}}{2\mu_{2,k}^{(n)}} \mu_{2,k}^2 + \frac{\mu_{2,k}^{(n)}}{2\bar{t}_k^{com,(n)}} (t_k^{com})^2 \leq \mu_{1,k}, \tag{5.181}$$

where $\bar{t}_k^{com,(n)}$ and $\mu_{2,k}^{(n)}$ represent the values of $\bar{t}_k^{com}$ and $\mu_{2,k}$ at the t-th iteration, respectively.

For constraint $C17$, we rewrite it as

$$C17 : \bar{t}_l^{off} \leq \frac{\left(\tilde{\mathbf{g}}_{r,l} + \Delta\mathbf{g}_{r,l}\right)^H \mathbf{\Phi}^H \mathbf{G}_r \mathbf{Z}_l \mathbf{G}_r^H \mathbf{\Phi} \left(\tilde{\mathbf{g}}_{r,l} + \Delta\mathbf{g}_{r,l}\right) p_l}{\sum_{l' \neq l}^{L} \left(\tilde{\mathbf{g}}_{r,l'} + \Delta\mathbf{g}_{r,l'}\right)^H \mathbf{\Phi}^H \mathbf{G}_r \mathbf{Z}_l \mathbf{G}_r^H \mathbf{\Phi} \left(\tilde{\mathbf{g}}_{r,l'} + \Delta\mathbf{g}_{r,l'}\right) p_{l'} + \bar{a}}, \tag{5.182}$$

where $\bar{a} = \left|\mathbf{z}_l^H \left(\mathbf{A} + \mathbf{H}_{SI}\right)\mathbf{x}\right|^2 + \left|\mathbf{z}_l^H\right|^2 \sigma_B^2$. Similar to the above scheme, we use the SVD to re-express $\mathbf{\Phi}^H \mathbf{G}_r \mathbf{Z}_l \mathbf{G}_r^H \mathbf{\Phi}$ as

$$\begin{aligned} &\mathbf{\Phi}^H \mathbf{G}_r \mathbf{Z}_l \mathbf{G}_r^H \mathbf{\Phi} \\ &= diag\left(\boldsymbol{\psi}\right) \sum_{i=1}^{I} \tilde{h}_{l,i} \tilde{\mathbf{v}}_{l,i} \tilde{\mathbf{r}}_{l,i}^H diag(\boldsymbol{\psi})^H = \sum_{i=1}^{I} \tilde{h}_{l,i} diag(\tilde{\mathbf{v}}_{l,i}) \boldsymbol{\psi}^* \boldsymbol{\psi}^T diag\left(\tilde{\mathbf{r}}_{l,i}^H\right) \\ &= \sum_{i=1}^{I} \tilde{h}_{l,i} \tilde{\mathbf{V}}_{l,i} \mathbf{\Omega}^T \tilde{\mathbf{R}}_{l,i}, \end{aligned} \tag{5.183}$$

where $\tilde{\mathbf{V}}_{l,i} = \begin{bmatrix} diag(\tilde{\mathbf{v}}_{l,i}) & 0 \\ 0 & 0 \end{bmatrix}$, $\tilde{\mathbf{R}}_{l,i} = \begin{bmatrix} diag\left(\tilde{\mathbf{r}}_{l,i}^{H}\right) & 0 \\ 0 & 0 \end{bmatrix}$, $\widehat{h}_{k,i}$, $\widehat{\mathbf{v}}_{k,i}$, $\widehat{\mathbf{r}}_{k,i}$ denote the corresponding singular values and left and right singular vectors, respectively. We introduce the slack variables $\mu_{3,l}, \mu_{4,l}$ and reformulate constraint $C17$ as

$$C17a : \mu_{3,l} \leq \left[\left(\tilde{\mathbf{g}}_{r,l} + \Delta\mathbf{g}_{r,l}\right)^{H}, 0\right] \tilde{\mathbf{\Lambda}}_{l} \begin{bmatrix} \left(\tilde{\mathbf{g}}_{r,l} + \Delta\mathbf{g}_{r,l}\right) \\ 0 \end{bmatrix} p_{l}, \tag{5.184}$$

$$C17b : \bar{t}_{l}^{off} \mu_{4,l} \leq \mu_{3,l}, \tag{5.185}$$

$$C17c : \mu_{4,l} \geq \sum_{l' \neq l}^{L} \left[\left(\tilde{\mathbf{g}}_{r,l'} + \Delta\mathbf{g}_{r,l'}\right)^{H}, 0\right] \tilde{\mathbf{\Lambda}}_{l} \begin{bmatrix} \left(\tilde{\mathbf{g}}_{r,l'} + \Delta\mathbf{g}_{r,l'}\right) \\ 0 \end{bmatrix} p_{l'} + \bar{a}, \tag{5.186}$$

where $\tilde{\mathbf{\Lambda}}_{l} = \sum_{i=1}^{I} \tilde{h}_{l,i} \tilde{\mathbf{V}}_{l,i} \mathbf{\Omega}^{T} \tilde{\mathbf{R}}_{l,i}$. Introducing auxiliary variables $\varphi_{3,l}, \varphi_{4,l} \geq 0$, the constraints are rewritten using the S-P procedure as the following convex constraint

$$\bar{C}17a : \begin{bmatrix} \varphi_{3,l}\mathbf{I}_{M} + \tilde{\mathbf{\Lambda}}_{l} p_{l} & \left(\tilde{\mathbf{g}}_{r1,l}^{H} \tilde{\mathbf{\Lambda}}_{l}\right)^{H} p_{l} \\ \tilde{\mathbf{g}}_{r1,l}^{H} \tilde{\mathbf{\Lambda}}_{l} p_{l} & -\varphi_{3,l}\varepsilon_{r2,l}^{2} - \mu_{3,l} + \tilde{\mathbf{g}}_{r1,l}^{H} \tilde{\mathbf{\Lambda}}_{l} \tilde{\mathbf{g}}_{r1,l} p_{l} \end{bmatrix} \succeq 0, \tag{5.187}$$

$$\bar{C}17b : \frac{\bar{t}_{l}^{off,(n)}}{2\mu_{4,l}^{(n)}} \mu_{4,l}^{2} + \frac{\mu_{4,l}^{(n)}}{2\bar{t}_{l}^{off,(n)}} \left(t_{l}^{off}\right)^{2} \leq \mu_{3,l}, \tag{5.188}$$

$$\bar{C}17c : \begin{bmatrix} \varphi_{4,l} \sum_{l' \neq l}^{L} \left(\mathbf{I}_{M} - \tilde{\mathbf{\Lambda}}_{l} p_{l}\right) & -\sum_{l' \neq l}^{L} \left(\tilde{\mathbf{g}}_{r1,l'}^{H} \tilde{\mathbf{\Lambda}}_{l} p_{l'}\right)^{H} \\ -\sum_{l' \neq l}^{L} \tilde{\mathbf{g}}_{r1,l'}^{H} \tilde{\mathbf{\Lambda}}_{l} p_{l'} & \varphi_{4,l} \sum_{l' \neq l}^{L} \left(-\varepsilon_{r2,l'}^{2} - \tilde{\mathbf{g}}_{r1,l'}^{H} \tilde{\mathbf{\Lambda}}_{l} \tilde{\mathbf{g}}_{r1,l'} p_{l'}\right) + \mu_{4,l} - \bar{a} \end{bmatrix} \succeq 0, \tag{5.189}$$

where $\bar{t}_{l}^{off,(n)}$ and $\mu_{4,l}^{(n)}$ represent the values of $\bar{t}_{l}^{off}$ and $\mu_{4,l}$ at the t-th iteration, respectively.

Finally, problem $\mathcal{P}^{9}$ is transformed into the following form

$$\mathcal{P}^{10} : \max_{\substack{\Omega, \bar{t}_{k}^{com}, \bar{t}_{l}^{off}, \delta_{l}, \mu_{1,k}, \mu_{2,k}, \\ \mu_{3,l}, \mu_{4,l}, \varphi_{1,k}, \varphi_{2,k}, \varphi_{3,l}, \varphi_{4,l}}} \sum_{k=1}^{K} \log\left(1 + \bar{t}_{k}^{com}\right) + \sum_{l=1}^{L} \log\left(1 + \bar{t}_{l}^{off}\right) \tag{5.190}$$

$$s.t. \ \hat{C}2, \bar{C}16a, \bar{C}16b, \bar{C}16c, \bar{C}17a, \bar{C}17b, \bar{C}17c, \ , \tag{5.189a}$$

$$C18 : \Omega\left(m, m\right) = 1, \Omega \succeq 0, \tag{5.189b}$$

Algorithm 23 Proposed Joint Optimization Algorithm

Initialization:
Given the feasible solutions of $\mathbf{w}_i^{(0)}$, $\mathbf{u}_b^{(0)}$, $\mathbf{z}_l^{(0)}$, $\boldsymbol{\psi}^0$, $\mathbf{f}^{(0)}$, $\mathbf{p}^{(0)}$.
Set maximum number of iterations: T_{max} and t=0.
Repeat
Set $t = t + 1$.
Initialize variables $t_k^{com,(0)}$, $t_l^{off,(0)}$, $\vartheta_{2,k}^{(0)}$, $\chi_{2,l}^{(0)}$, maximum iteration number I_{max} and iteration number $i = 1$.
Repeat
Obtain $\mathbf{W}^*$, $\mathbf{f}^*$, $\mathbf{p}^*$ by solving (5.144).
Update variables $t_k^{com,(i)}$, $t_l^{off,(i)}$, $\vartheta_{2,k}^{(i)}$, $\chi_{2,l}^{(i)}$.
Update $i = i + 1$.
Until $i = I_{max}$ or Convergence.
Initialize variables $\rho_b^{(0)}$, $\tilde{\vartheta}_{2,b}^{(0)}$, maximum iteration number N_{max} and iteration number $n = 1$.
Repeat
Obtain $\mathbf{u}_b^*$ by solving (5.155).
Update variables $\rho_b^{(n)}$, $\tilde{\vartheta}_{2,b}^{(n)}$.
Update $n = n + 1$.
Until $n = N_{max}$ or Convergence.
Initialize variables $\tilde{t}_l^{loc,(0)}$, $\tilde{\chi}_{2,l}^{(0)}$, maximum iteration number P_{max} and iteration number $p = 1$.
Repeat
Obtain $\mathbf{z}_l^*$ by solving (5.166).
Update variables $\tilde{t}_l^{loc,(p)}$, $\tilde{\chi}_{2,l}^{(p)}$.
Update $p = p + 1$.
Until $p = P_{max}$ or Convergence.
Initialize variables $t_k^{com,(0)}$, $t_l^{off,(0)}$, $\mu_{2,k}^{(0)}$, $\mu_{4,l}^{(0)}$, maximum iteration number R_{max} and iteration number $r = 1$.
Repeat
Obtain $\boldsymbol{\psi}^*$ by solving (5.189).
Update variables $t_k^{com,(r)}$, $t_l^{off,(r)}$, $\mu_{2,k}^{(r)}$, $\mu_{4,l}^{(r)}$.
Update $r = r + 1$.
Until $r = R_{max}$ or Convergence.
Until: $t = T_{max}$ or the objective function of problem (5.124) converges.

$$C19 : \varphi_{1,k}, \varphi_{2,k}, \varphi_{3,l}, \varphi_{4,l} \geq 0, \tag{5.189c}$$

Similar to the above, problem $\mathcal{P}^{10}$ is a typical SDR problem. We solve it using the standard CVX toolbox and recover the rank-one solutions using Gaussian randomization technique. Finally, we summarize the overall algorithm for solving $\mathcal{P}^0$ in Algorithm 23.

5.4.2.5 Algorithm Convergence and Optimality Analysis

For Algorithm 23, we need to solve $\mathcal{P}^2$, $\mathcal{P}^5$, $\mathcal{P}^8$ and $\mathcal{P}^{10}$ alternately until convergence. Since the rank-one constraints are ignored, they are all convex optimization problems, and the KKT solutions can be guaranteed. In addition, the transmit power of BS and CP-UEs are limited, problem $\mathcal{P}^0$ has an upper bound. Therefore, Algorithm 23 can converge to a stable and local optimal solution at least.

5.4.3 Performance Evaluation

In this section, we provide systematic simulation results to evaluate the performance of the proposed scheme. We assume that the FD BS is located at (0 m, 0 m), the RIS is located at (20 m, 0 m), and all CM-UEs, CP-UEs, and radar targets are randomly distributed on circles centered at (10 m, 10 m), (10m, −10 m), and (0 m, 0 m), with a radius of 5 m. The noise power at the BS and at CM-UEs is set to $\sigma_B^2 = \sigma_k^2 = -90\,\text{dBm}, \forall k$. Unless otherwise specified, we assume $N = N_t = N_r = 4$, $M = 10$, $K = 2$, $L = 2$, $B = 2$. We define the maximum normalized CSI estimation error as $\varepsilon_{r1,k}^2 = \tilde{\varpi}_{r1,k}^2 \left\|\mathbf{h}_{r,k}\right\|^2$, $\varepsilon_{r2,l}^2 = \tilde{\varpi}_{r2,l}^2 \left\|\mathbf{g}_{r,l}\right\|^2$, where $\tilde{\varpi}_{r1,k}^2 = \tilde{\varpi}_{r2,l}^2 = \tilde{\varpi}^2, \forall k \in \mathcal{K}, l \in \mathcal{L}$. For all channels, we use the typical distance-dependent Rician channel model

$$\mathbf{G} = PL\left(d\right)\left(\sqrt{\frac{\tilde{\kappa}}{\tilde{\kappa}+1}}\mathbf{G}_{Los} + \sqrt{\frac{1}{\tilde{\kappa}+1}}\mathbf{G}_{NLos}\right), \tag{5.191}$$

where $\tilde{\kappa}$, $\mathbf{G}_{Los}$, $\mathbf{G}_{NLos}$ represent the Rice factor, Los path, and NLos path, respectively. The large-scale fading model is represented by $PL\left(d\right) = \Lambda\left(\frac{d}{d_0}\right)^{-\tilde{\eta}}$, $\tilde{\eta} \in \{\eta_{BR}, \eta_{RU}, \eta_{BT}\}$, where $\Lambda = -30\,\text{dB}$ represents the path loss at reference distance $d_0 = 1m$, d and $\tilde{\eta}$ represent the propagation distance and path loss index, respectively. The path loss exponents between BS-RIS, RIS-UE, and BS-Target are η_{BR}=1.8, η_{RU}=1.8, and η_{BT}=2.2, respectively. For the residual SI channel at the BS, we follow [30] and model each entry of $\mathbf{H}_{SI} \in \mathbb{C}^{N_r \times N_t}$ as $[\mathbf{H}_{SI}]_{t,r} = \sqrt{\upsilon_{t,r}^{SI}} e^{-j2\pi\frac{d_{t,r}}{\lambda}}$, where $\upsilon_{t,r}^{SI} > 0$ represents the residual SI power, and $d_{t,r} > 0$ represents the distance between the t-th transmit antenna and the r-th receive antenna. For simplicity, we set $\upsilon^{SI} = \upsilon_{t,r}^{SI} = -110\,\text{dB}$ and let $e^{-j2\pi\frac{d_{t,r}}{\lambda}}$ be unit modulo variables with random phases for all transceiver antenna pairs (t, r) [31]. The specific parameters setting are listed in Table 5.3.

To verify the performance of the proposed scheme, we give the following schemes for comparison:

- Full offloading: Each CP-UE performs computation offloading only through the RIS.
- Random phase shift: We assume that the RIS adopts a fixed phase shift randomly.
- HD: We assume that the BS uses HD mode, where CM-UEs reception and CP-UEs transmission are implemented in two orthogonal time slots of equal duration.

Table 5.3 System parameters

Variable	Description	Value
N_t	The number of transmit antennas at BS	4
N_r	The number of receive antennas at BS	4
M	The number of RIS elements	10
K	The number of CM-UEs	2
L	The number of CP-UEs	2
B	The number of targets	2
P_b	Maximum transmit power of BS	20 dBm
ε_l	Complexity of computation tasks of CP-UE	1000 cycles/bit
$E_m^{\max}$	The maximum energy budget for CP-UE m	0.02 J
ζ	Constants related to hardware architecture	10^{-28}
Γ^{tar}	Predefined target sensing threshold	−5 dB
ξ^2	The target radar cross section	1
$\tilde{\kappa}$	Rician factor	1

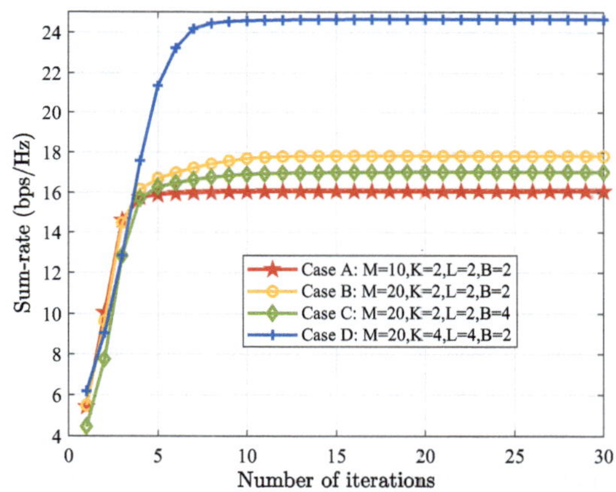

Fig. 5.17 Sum rate versus the number of iterations

Therefore, co-interference between the uplink offloading signal and the target echo signal and SI at the BS do not exist.

Figure 5.17 shows the convergence of the proposed algorithm for different numbers of RIS elements, CM-UEs, CP-UEs, and radar targets. We consider the following four cases: Case A with $M = 10, K = 2, L = 2, B = 2$, case B with $M = 20, K = 2, L = 2, B = 2$, case C with $M = 20, K = 2, L = 2, B = 4$, and case D with $M = 20, K = 4, L = 4, B = 2$. It can be observed that they can all obtain convergence after 10 iterations. For case B and case D, as the number of RIS elements/users increases, the number of iterations increases. In addition, for case C, as the number of radar targets increases, more resources are required from the BS to meet the sensing SINR, thereby reducing the sum rate.

Figure 5.18 depicts the relationship between the sum rate and the BS maximum transmit power budget P_{BS}. It can be observed that the sum rate of all schemes

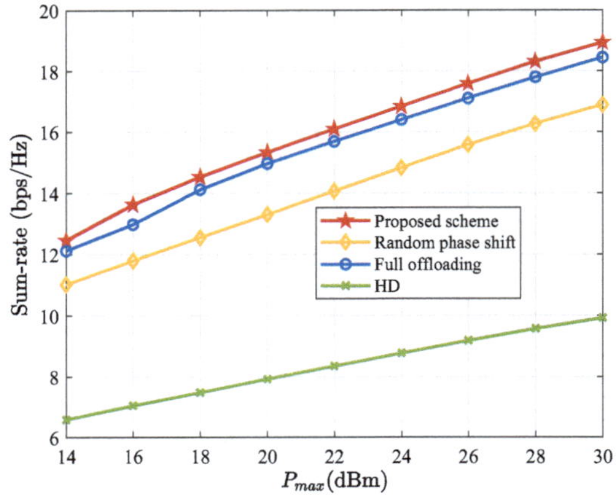

Fig. 5.18 Sum rate versus the BS transmit power P_{BS}

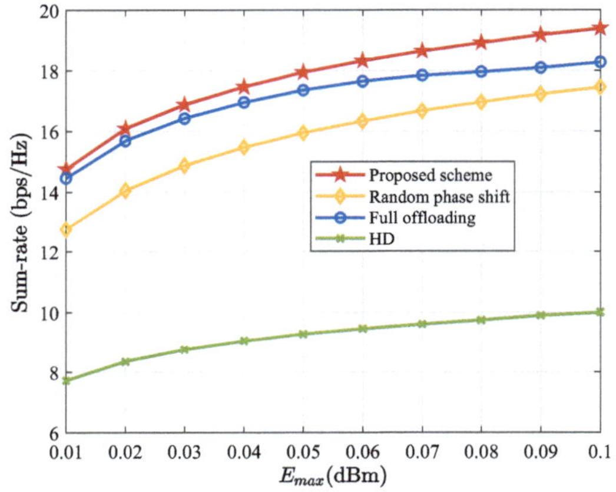

Fig. 5.19 Sum rate versus the user's maximum energy E_{max}

increases with the increase of P_{BS}. This is because that the increase of P_{BS} can provide a higher beamforming gain, thereby improving the system performance. In addition, the sum rate of the random phase shift scheme is lower than that of the proposed scheme based optimizing phase shift of RIS, and this is easy to understand. For the full offloading scheme, the interference from the echo signal to the offloading signal becomes more serious, which decrease the quality of service of the CM-UEs and thus degrades the performance of the system. For the HD scheme, although orthogonal transmission avoids the SI and interference between the echo signal and offloading signal, the uplink and downlink time become half of FD scheme, which degradates the system performance.

Figure 5.19 describes the relationship between the sum rate and the maximum energy budget E_{max}. It can be observed that the sum rate of all schemes increases monotonically with the increase of E_{max}. This is because that the increase of E_{max} provides more resources for the transmission of uplink offloading signals and local computation, thereby improving the system performance. In addition, it is obvious that the sum rate of the proposed scheme outperforms that of all other schemes.

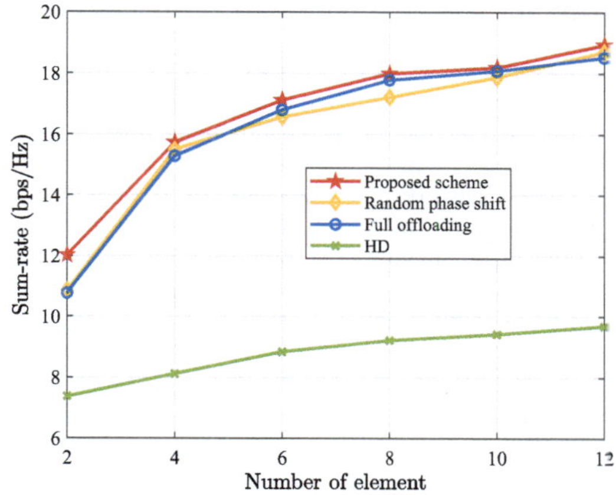

Fig. 5.20 Sum rate versus the number of BS antennas

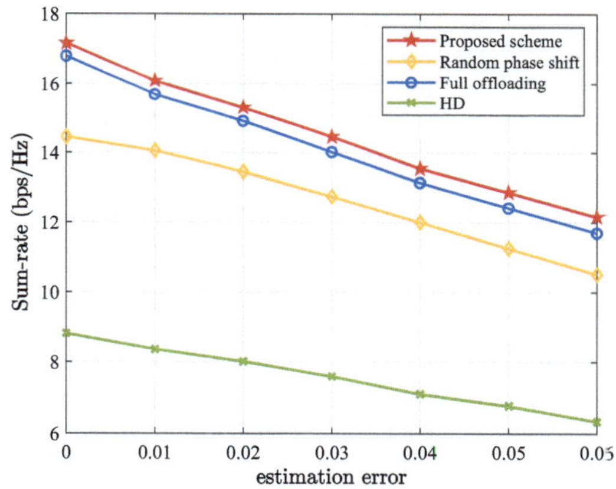

Fig. 5.21 Sum rate versus channel estimation error

Figure 5.20 describes the relationship between the sum rate and the number of BS antennas N. It can be observed that as the number of antennas increases, the sum rate of all schemes also increase. The more number of antennas can improve the quality of the received signal and increase the spatial multiplexing gain, and thus improving the system performance. Figure 5.21 depicts the relationship between the sum rate and the maximum normalized channel estimation error. As expected, the sum rate of all schemes decreases with the increase of channel estimation error. This is because that the signal transmitted by the reflection link cannot be accurately focused on the RIS/CM-UEs. Therefore, as the channel estimation error increases, the power loss and energy consumption will also increase, resulting in a degradation of system performance.

References

1. A. Sabharwal, P. Schniter, D. Guo, D.W. Bliss, S. Rangarajan, R. Wichman, In-band full-duplex wireless: challenges and opportunities. IEEE J. Sel. Areas Commun. **32**(9), 1637–1652 (2014)
2. G. Sun et al., Resource management for integrated communications, computing, and sensing (ICCS) networks. IEEE Trans. Veh. Technol. **73**(12), 18719–18731 (2024)
3. Z. Wang, X. Mu, Y. Liu, X. Xu, P. Zhang, NOMA-aided joint communication, sensing, and multi-tier computing systems. IEEE J. Sel. Areas Commun. **41**(3), 574–588 (2023)
4. N. Huang, T. Wang, Y. Wu, Q. Wu, T.Q.S. Quek, Integrated sensing and communication assisted mobile edge computing: an energy-efficient design via intelligent reflecting surface. IEEE Wirel. Commun. Lett. **11**(10), 2085–2089 (2022)
5. K. Shen, W. Yu, Fractional programming for communication systems—part I: power control and beamforming. IEEE Trans. Signal Process. **66**(10), 2616–2630 (2018)
6. Z. Zhu, Z. Li, Z. Chu et al., Intelligent reflecting surface-assisted wireless powered heterogeneous networks. IEEE Trans. Wirel. Commun. **22**(12), 9881–9892 (2023)
7. N. Li, W. Hao, F. Zhou et al., Min-max latency optimization for IRS-aided cell-free mobile edge computing systems. IEEE Internet Things J. **11**(5), 8757–8770 (2023)
8. C. Pan et al., An overview of signal processing techniques for RIS/IRS-aided wireless systems. IEEE J. Sel. Top. Signal Process. **16**(5), 883–917 (2022)
9. S.P. Boyd, L. Vandenberghe, *Convex Optimization* (Cambridge University Press, Cambridge, 2014)
10. S.S. Rao, *Engineering Optimization: Theory and Practice*, 4th edn. (Wiley, Hoboken, 2009)
11. S. Bi, Y.J. Zhang, Computation rate maximization for wireless powered mobile-edge computing with binary computation offloading. IEEE Trans. Wirel. Commun. **17**(6), 4177–4190 (2018)
12. X. Gao, L. Dai, S. Han, Energy-efficient hybrid analog and digital precoding for mmWave MIMO systems with large antenna arrays. IEEE J. Sel. Areas Commun. **34**(4), 998–1009 (2016)
13. W. Hao, X. Wu, X. Li et al., Resource management for IRS-assisted full-duplex integrated sensing, communication and computing systems. Preprint (2024). arXiv:2409.00364
14. H. Hua, J. Xu, T.X. Han, Optimal transmit beamforming for integrated sensing and communication. IEEE Trans. Veh. Technol. **72**(8), 10588–10603 (2023)
15. L. Chen, Z. Wang, Y. Du, Y. Chen, F.R. Yu, Generalized transceiver beamforming for DFRC with MIMO radar and MU-MIMO communication. IEEE J. Sel. Areas Commun. **40**(6), 1795–1808 (2022)
16. G. Cui, H. Li, M. Rangaswamy, MIMO radar waveform design with constant modulus and similarity constraints. IEEE Trans. Signal Process. **62**(2), 343–353 (2014)
17. D. Xu, X. Yu, Y. Sun, D.W.K. Ng, R. Schober, Resource allocation for IRS-assisted full-duplex cognitive radio systems. IEEE Trans. Commun. **68**(12), 7376–7394 (2020)
18. J. Du et al., Resource pricing and allocation in MEC enabled blockchain systems: an A3C deep reinforcement learning approach. IEEE Trans. Network Sci. Eng. **9**(1), 33–44 (2022)
19. J.A. Zhang et al., Enabling joint communication and radar sensing in mobile networks—a survey. IEEE Commun. Surveys Tuts. **24**(1), 306–345 (2022)
20. Q. Shi, M. Razaviyayn, Z.-Q. Luo, C. He, An iteratively weighted MMSE approach to distributed sum-utility maximization for a MIMO interfering broadcast channel. IEEE Trans. Signal Process. **59**(9), 4331–4340 (2011)
21. R. Liu, M. Li, Q. Liu, A.L. Swindlehurst, SNR/CRB-constrained joint beamforming and reflection designs for RIS-ISAC systems. IEEE Trans. Wirel. Commun. **23**(7), 7456–7470 (2023)
22. Y. Sun, P. Babu, D.P. Palomar, Majorization-minimization algorithms in signal processing, communications, and machine learning. IEEE Trans. Signal Process. **65**(3), 794–816 (2017)
23. W. Hao et al., Robust security energy efficiency optimization for RIS-aided cell-free networks with multiple eavesdroppers. IEEE Trans. Commun. (2024, to appear)

24. M.A. Saeidi, M.J. Emadi, H. Masoumi, M.R. Mili, D.W.K. Ng, I. Krikidis, Weighted sum-rate maximization for multi-IRS-assisted full-duplex systems with hardware impairments. IEEE Trans. Cognit. Commun. Netw. **7**(2), 466–481 (2021)
25. Y. Guo, Y. Liu, Q. Wu, X. Li, Q. Shi, Joint beamforming and power allocation for RIS aided full-duplex integrated sensing and uplink communication system. IEEE Trans. Wirel. Commun. **23**(5), 4627–4642 (2024)
26. X. Chen, S. Zhang, Q. Li, A review of mutual coupling in MIMO systems. IEEE Access **6**, 24706–24719 (2018)
27. Z. He, W. Xu, H. Shen, D.W.K. Ng, Y.C. Eldar, X. You, Full-duplex communication for ISAC: joint beamforming and power optimization. IEEE J. Sel. Areas Commun. **41**(9), 2920–2936 (2023)
28. Z.-Q. Luo, W.-K. Ma, A. M.-C. So, Y. Ye, S. Zhang, Semidefinite relaxation of quadratic optimization problems. IEEE Signal Process. Mag. **27**(3), 20–34 (2010)
29. Q. Zhu, M. Li, R. Liu, Q. Liu, Joint transceiver beamforming and reflecting design for active RIS-aided ISAC systems. IEEE Trans. Veh. Technol. **72**(7), 9636–9640 (2023)
30. S. Zhang et al., Joint beamforming optimization for active STAR-RIS-assisted ISAC systems. IEEE Trans. Wirel. Commun. **23**(11), 15888–15902 (2024)
31. R.S.P. Sankar, S.P. Chepuri, Beamforming in hybrid RIS assisted integrated sensing and communication systems, in *2022 30th European Signal Processing Conference (EUSIPCO)* (2022), pp. 1082–1086

Chapter 6
Conclusions and Future Perspectives

6.1 Conclusions

The main works of this book are summarized into three parts as follows.

6.1.1 Reconfigurable Intelligent Surface MEC

First, we introduce the fundamentals of intelligent MEC and sensing, and then studies the resource optimization problem for different scenarios. We consider the RIS-assisted MEC, including: (1) RIS-assisted cell-free MEC system: Considering WD fairness, a system with multiple BSs and RISs is constructed to jointly optimize computing and communication resources under limited edge computing capacity, aiming to minimize the maximum WD delay. The problem is decoupled into two sub-problems by introducing an auxiliary variable t and using the BCD method. The first is to optimize the amount of offloading data and edge computing resources, and the second is to optimize the MUD matrix and RIS beamforming. Simulation results demonstrate RIS can significantly reduce latency and enhance system performance, particularly under multi-BS collaboration, reasonable computing power configuration and appropriate transmission power. (2) Multi-RIS assisted WP-MEC system: Based on the actual RIS reflection model, RIS receives radio frequency (RF) signals from HAPs to assist WD energy harvesting and task offloading, while multiple HAPs and RISs serve multiple users. Jointly optimize multiple resources under energy causality constraints to maximize the amount of computing data. The problem is divided into two major sub-problems: optimizing resource allocation in the charging phase and in the computing phase. The simulation results show that RIS can improve the computing rate of the WP-MEC system and emphasize the impact of hardware defects on performance under non-ideal reflection models. (3) RIS-assisted wide bandwidth MEC system: Based on the actual RIS reflection

W. Hao et al., *Intelligent Mobile Edge Computing and Sensing*, Wireless Networks,
https://doi.org/10.1007/978-981-96-9400-6_6

model and edge computing capacity constraints, the resource allocation problem in the broadband MEC system is studied. By decoupling the computing resource and communication resource optimization sub-problems, a solution method based on BCD technology is proposed. Simulation results indicate that low-resolution RIS is more cost-effective, increasing edge computing capacity can effectively enhance system performance, and the design based on the actual reflection model is better than the ideal reflection model in large-scale RIS systems.

Then, for the Cooperative Cloud and MEC, this section investigates offloading strategies and resource allocation in cloud-edge collaborative systems, addressing challenges such as latency-energy trade-offs, subtask dependencies, and multivariable coupling. The following three computation offloading scenarios are primarily discussed: (1) Single-user task-dependent computing offloading: The QLOF algorithm is proposed to jointly optimize the offloading transmission power, edge cloud computing frequency, and offloading decisions. By constructing the AETC minimization problem, the bisection method is used to solve the transmission power, and the polynomial analysis method is used to optimize the edge cloud computing frequency. The offloading process is modeled as a MDP, and learning is performed based on the QLOF algorithm to optimize the offloading decisions to improve system performance. Simulation experiments verify the advantages of the algorithm under different parameters. (2) Multi-user multi-edge cloud computing offloading based on bilateral matching: GS-MEMA, GS-MOA and GS-SOA algorithms are proposed to jointly optimize the offloading transmission power, edge cloud computing frequency, matching strategy and offloading decisions. The SETC minimization problem is constructed, and the quasi-convex optimization and polynomial analysis methods are used to optimize the transmission power and computing frequency respectively. Based on the Gale-Shapley matching algorithm to model the matching problem between edge cloud and users, GS-MEMA is proposed to optimize the offloading decisions. GS-MOA and GS-SOA algorithms are proposed through heuristic search to iteratively optimize the offloading decisions, frequency and matching strategy. Experimental results show that the proposed algorithm is superior to other algorithms in performance. (3) Multi-user multi-edge cloud computing offloading based on task dependency scheduling: MLSO, SSO and GTS algorithms are proposed to jointly optimize offloading transmission power, edge cloud computing frequency, offloading decisions and subtask scheduling. The Lagrange multiplier method and the bisection method are used to optimize the edge cloud computing frequency and offloading transmission power respectively. The MLSO and SSO algorithms are proposed based on heuristic search, and the frequency and offloading decisions are optimized through iteration. The GTS algorithm further optimizes the order of edge cloud subtasks and reduces SETC. Experiments verify the superiority of these algorithms under different parameters.

Finally, for the ICSS,this section studies the resource allocation and optimization issues of integrated communication, computing and sensing, mainly discussing the following three scenarios: (1) ICCS system resource optimization: For the ICCS system with multifunctional BS serving multiple users and a sensing target, a weighted sum rate maximization problem is constructed to jointly optimize multiple key elements such as information beamforming and sensing covariance matrix. Some optimization variables are processed by fractional programming based on quadratic transformation and SDR methods, and the offloading signal receive beamforming is optimized using Lagrangian duality and MMSE schemes. A closed-form solution for local computing resource allocation is derived based on energy constraints, and a CD method is proposed to optimize the computing task offloading strategy. An alternating iterative optimization algorithm is used to solve complex non-convex problems. Numerical results are presented to show the efficiency of the proposed algorithm in comparison to the existing benchmark schemes. (2) RIS-assisted ICCS: An RIS is integrated into the FD ISCC system to study resource allocation, with the goal of maximizing system utility, and jointly optimizing variables such as receive beamforming and transmit beamforming. In view of the BS SI and co-channel interference problems in the FD system, the optimization variables are highly non-convexly coupled. First, optimize the cache strategy, reformulate the problem, introduce auxiliary variables using the WMMSE method, and then decompose it into sub-problems. Use ADMM, MM and SDR techniques to transform the sub-problems into convex problems, and finally use the BCA method to alternately solve the optimization variables. Simulation results are provided to verify the effectiveness of the proposed algorithm and demonstrate the advantages of the proposed scheme compared with the baseline scheme. (3) RIS-assisted ICCS with imperfect CSI: Aiming at the multi-target multi-user scenario and channel estimation error problem of the RIS-assisted FD ICCS system, a system model including communication, computing and sensing models is constructed, and the system sum rate maximization optimization problem is formulated, considering multiple constraints. This problem is highly non-convex due to the strong coupling of communication and computing resources and estimation error constraints. An alternating iterative optimization algorithm is proposed to decompose the original problem into four sub-problems. For each sub-problem, auxiliary variables are introduced, and the S-Procedure, SVD decomposition and other technologies are used to transform it into a classic SDP problem, which is solved by relaxing the rank-one constraint or Gaussian randomization technology, in order to effectively handle each optimization variable and enhance the performance of the system in complex scenarios.

6.2 Future Perspectives

This book conducts the following three studies on intelligent MEC and sensing: (1) RIS-assisted MEC, (2) cloud-coordinated MEC, and (3) integrated communication, computing and sensing. However, the systematic research on the integration of intelligent MEC and sensing and the application in actual scenarios needs to be further explored. In future work, the following research directions will be explored.

1. Collaborative optimization of simultaneous wireless information and power transfer (SWIPT) and ICCS: SWIPT is a technology that simultaneously transmits energy and information through radio frequency signals. It can power low-power IoT devices and support data transmission, solving the problem of traditional networks' dependence on fixed power sources. In the ICCS system, the sensing, communication and computing functions of terminal devices need to operate stably for a long time, and SWIPT can provide them with continuous energy supply and data interaction channels. Therefore, it is necessary to further study how to optimize the joint scheduling mechanism of energy and information, such as designing a dynamic resource allocation algorithm to balance energy transmission efficiency and communication rate; and exploring energy capture enhancement technology under collaborative sensing of telepathy, and use environmental sensing data to optimize energy beamforming and improve system energy efficiency. In addition, it is necessary to solve the interference problem of energy competition among multiple devices in high-density scenarios to achieve cross-domain energy sharing and intelligent management.
2. Deep integration of security enhancement and ICCS: Security is the core challenge of the ICCS system. Its multimodel sensing data, distributed computing nodes and open wireless environment are vulnerable to eavesdropping, data tampering and malicious attacks. Especially in the scenario of edge computing and cloud collaboration, the risk of privacy leakage increases significantly. To ensure system security, security mechanisms need to be deeply embedded in the entire process of telecomputing: at the sensing layer, physical layer security technologies (such as channel fingerprint encryption) are used to resist energy theft in wireless energy transmission; at the communication layer, blockchain and lightweight zero-knowledge proof are combined to achieve data traceability and cross-domain identity authentication; at the computing layer, the privacy of distributed computing is ensured through federated learning and trusted execution environment.
3. Terahertz communication enables high-speed and low-latency transmission of ICCS: Terahertz communication utilizes the ultra-large bandwidth of the 0.1–10 THz frequency band to support Tbps-level ultra-high rates and sub-millimeter positioning accuracy. The ICCS system demand for high-sensing environmental perception and real-time computing is highly consistent with the characteristics of terahertz communication: on the one hand, the narrow beam characteristics of the terahertz beam can be combined with the RIS of the computing system to dynamically adjust the beam direction by sensing the environment and improve signal coverage. One the other hand, its ultra-large bandwidth can support the real-time return of massive perception data and the rapid offloading of edge computing tasks. Therefore, in the future, breakthroughs in the integrated hardware design of terahertz tele-sensing and computing are needed, such as the development of RF chips that support joint waveform modulation; at the

same time, research on intelligent allocation algorithms for spectrum sensing and communication resources, and realize dynamic slicing of communication-sensing-computing resources in dense multi-user scenarios, so as to promote the implementation of immersive XR, digital twins and other applications in the 6G era.

MIX
Papier aus verantwortungsvollen Quellen
Paper from responsible sources
FSC® C105338
FSC
www.fsc.org

If you have any concerns about our products,
you can contact us on
ProductSafety@springernature.com

In case Publisher is established outside the EU,
the EU authorized representative is:
Springer Nature Customer Service Center GmbH
Europaplatz 3, 69115 Heidelberg, Germany

Printed by Libri Plureos GmbH
in Hamburg, Germany